The Affect Theory Reader

THE AFFECT THEORY READER

Edited by Melissa Gregg and Gregory J. Seigworth

DUKE UNIVERSITY PRESS   *Durham & London 2010*

© 2010 Duke University Press
All rights reserved
Printed in the United States of America on acid-free paper ∞
Designed by Jennifer Hill. Typeset in Minion Pro by Keystone Typesetting, Inc. Library of
Congress Cataloging-in-Publication Data appear on the last printed page of this book.

Brian Massumi's "The Future Birth of the Affective Fact: The Political Ontology of Threat"
was originally published in *Indexicality and Virtuality*, edited by Griselda Pollock (I. B. Taurus,
2010).

An earlier version of Elspeth Probyn's "Writing Shame" appeared in *Blush: Faces of
Shame* (Minnesota, 2005).

An earlier version of Lauren Berlant's "Cruel Optimism" appeared in *differences*
17(3) (2006): 20–36.

An earlier version of Nigel Thrift's "Understanding the Material Practices of Glamour"
appeared in *Journal of Cultural Economy* 1(1) (2008): 9–23.

An earlier version of Patricia Clough's "The Affective Turn: Political Economy,
Biomedia, and Bodies" appeared in *Theory, Culture, and Society*, 25(1) (2008): 1–22.

In memory of Eve Kosofsky Sedgwick 1950–2009

CONTENTS

Partway through the introduction to this collection, it will become clear why it was significant that I read Greg's final draft while I was cramped on the floor of a late train during a long and crowded commute. I write these words from a new home, having embarked on an experiment to disrupt some old habits and hopefully allow more time to register "the stretching."

By sheer coincidence, during the final stages of this project both Greg and I moved house on opposite sides of the world in the very same week. This is just one of the sweet synergies and sympathies we have shared over the years that I hope will continue long after this publication. It is Greg's venerable alacrity as a reader that makes me so delighted that *a book* now stands as an archive of the hope and sustenance I have gained from a defining intellectual friendship. Greg's brilliant mind, graceful words, and contagious hospitality have made this a far greater achievement than I could have imagined.

Our contributors have been more than generous in offering words, affirmation, and patience during the long gestation of this collection. We thank them for believing in us and persisting through the many stages—and hope they enjoy the result.

Two reviewers of the manuscript provided extensive and engaged feedback that helped us immensely. We thank them for their time and encouragement, knowing that the collection is stronger for their suggestions. That we have a manuscript at all is due to the brilliant editorial work of Bryan Behrenshausen, who has been a complete pleasure to work with. We also thank Ken Wissoker for his enthusiasm and advice from the very beginning, and Mandy Earley for guidance in the later stages.

This book took shape while I was living in Brisbane, Australia, working at the Centre for Critical and Cultural Studies at the University of Queensland. For their help, collegiality, and energy I would like to thank Andrea Mitchell, Rebecca Ralph, Angela Mason, Maureen McGrath, John and Lisa Gunders, Kitty van Vuuren, Adrian Mabbott Athique, Melissa Bellanta, Anita Harris, Jinna Tay, Anna Pertierra, Mark Andrejevic, and Zala Volcic. For supporting this idea and so many others, I give sincere thanks to Graeme Turner. And for making Brisbane home, especially given that it wasn't ours to begin with, my thanks go to Rachel O'Reilly, Zala Volcic, Nadia Mizner, Michelle Dicinoski, and Heather Stewart.

Elspeth Probyn is the main reason I became interested in affect, and it is her remarkable ability to *enthuse* that allowed me to write these words and many more for a living. I am forever grateful. For showing me how to think and write bravely, I also thank Eve Sedgwick, Katie Stewart, Lauren Berlant, Ros Gill, Sara Ahmed, Genevieve Bell, Meaghan Morris, and Catherine Driscoll.

Finally, my deepest thanks go to Jason Wilson, who has taught me the most important lesson about affect: follow your heart.

Melissa Gregg

A register of speeds and slownesses, relations of motion and rest: this is what Deleuze said of Spinoza's philosophy with its special attention to a body's affects. A book is also, as it turns out, very much all about motion and rest, speed and slowness. From start to finish, Melissa has truly been a force of nature, a great gust of wind, and never once flagged through the duration of this project. I have just tried to keep up with her pace, her eminently practical and affective voice, her generosity of spirit. Across longitudes and latitudes, we found a rhythm (several actually) and a mutual capacity for the modes of composition that go into making a book, a book of affect and affects. Or that remains our hope.

And "hope" is in the air as I write these words. While Melissa composed her acknowledgments in the cramped space of a late-night train from Sydney, I write mine within another kind of cramped space, another kind of long, dark train—it is the end of eight years of the Bush-Cheney administration here in the United States. At this very moment, we are on the eve (literally, tomorrow) of the inauguration of Barack Obama. It is difficult to register this change as a shuttling of mere incremental affective intensities. After eight years that have only felt more and more closed, the potential for a world, *this* world, to be otherwise—to open elsewhere, anywhere—is palpable. So much, too much. Promise. We do not yet know. But there is a collective hope, and that's a start—an affective/affectionate start.

This book, for me, began over twenty-five years ago in Clarion, Pennsylvania, when Stan Denski mailed to me an essay by Lawrence Grossberg. In the years since, I have been fortunate to be able to count Stan and Larry as among my dearest friends. It would be impossible for me to sum up what Larry Grossberg's ongoing work has meant to me (I can only keep on writing as small recompense). Likewise, I am tremendously indebted to the inspired work of, as well as my correspondences with, Meaghan Morris, Brian Massumi, Karen Ocana, Gil Rodman, Greg Wise, Ben Anderson, Michael Gardiner, Ben Highmore, Charley Stivale, and Nigel Thrift. Thanks also go to my home institution of Millersville University, where I have been supported while being left free to follow wherever, whatever I desire: in my research and in the classroom. A special shout-out goes to my Lancaster-York best pal Mike Jarrett, both a remarkable sounding board for theories of every stripe and my constant supplier of sounds.

Last, and never least, I thank Jackie and Kendall. Jackie has been around for all of it, affect through and through.

Gregory J. Seigworth

AN INVENTORY OF SHIMMERS

Gregory J. Seigworth & Melissa Gregg

How to begin when, after all, there is no pure or somehow originary state for affect? Affect arises in the midst of *in-between-ness*: in the capacities to act and be acted upon. Affect is an impingement or extrusion of a momentary or sometimes more sustained state of relation *as well as* the passage (and the duration of passage) of forces or intensities. That is, affect is found in those intensities that pass body to body (human, nonhuman, part-body, and otherwise), in those resonances that circulate about, between, and sometimes stick to bodies and worlds, *and* in the very passages or variations between these intensities and resonances themselves. Affect, at its most anthropomorphic, is the name we give to those forces—visceral forces beneath, alongside, or generally *other than* conscious knowing, vital forces insisting beyond emotion—that can serve to drive us toward movement, toward thought and extension, that can likewise suspend us (as if in neutral) across a barely registering accretion of force-relations, or that can even leave us overwhelmed by the world's apparent intractability. Indeed, affect is persistent proof of a body's never less than ongoing immersion in and among the world's obstinacies and rhythms, its refusals as much as its invitations.

Affect is in many ways synonymous with *force* or *forces of encounter*. The term "force," however, can be a bit of a misnomer since affect need not be especially forceful (although sometimes, as in the psychoanalytic study of trauma, it is). In fact, it is quite likely that affect more often transpires within and across the subtlest of shuttling intensities: all the minuscule or molecular events of the unnoticed. The ordinary and its extra-. Affect is born in *in-between-ness* and resides as accumulative *beside-ness*. Affect can be understood then as a gradient of bodily capacity—a supple incrementalism of ever-modulating force-relations—that rises and falls not only along various rhythms and modalities of encounter but also through the troughs and sieves of sensation and sensibility, an incrementalism that coincides with belonging to comportments of matter of virtually any and every sort. Hence, affect's always immanent capacity for extending further still: both into and out of the interstices of the inorganic and non-living, the intracellular divulgences of sinew, tissue, and gut economies, and the vaporous evanescences of the incorporeal (events, atmospheres, feeling-tones). At once intimate and impersonal, affect *accumulates* across both relatedness and interruptions in relatedness, becoming a palimpsest of force-encounters traversing the ebbs and swells of intensities that pass between "bodies" (bodies defined not by an outer skin-envelope or other surface boundary but by their potential to reciprocate or co-participate in the passages of affect). Bindings and unbindings, becomings and un-becomings, jarring disorientations and rhythmic attunements. Affect marks a body's *belonging* to a world of encounters or; a world's belonging to a body of encounters but also, in *non-belonging*, through all those far sadder (de)compositions of mutual in-compossibilities. Always there are ambiguous or "mixed" encounters that impinge and extrude for worse and for better, but (most usually) in-between.

In this ever-gathering accretion of force-relations (or, conversely, in the peeling or wearing away of such sedimentations) lie the real powers of affect, affect as potential: a body's *capacity* to affect and to be affected. How does a body, marked in its duration by these various encounters with mixed forces, come to shift its affections (its being-affected) into action (capacity to affect)? Sigmund Freud once claimed, in his very earliest project, that affect does not so much reflect or think; affect acts (1966: 357–59). However, Freud also believed that these passages of affect persist in immediate adjacency to the movements of thought: close enough that sensate tendrils constantly extend between unconscious (or, better, non-conscious) affect and conscious thought. In practice, then, affect and cognition are never fully separable—if for no other reason than that thought is itself a body, embodied. Cast forward by its open-ended in-between-ness, affect is integral to a body's perpetual *becoming* (always becoming otherwise, however subtly, than what it already is), pulled beyond its seeming surface-boundedness by way of its relation to, indeed its composition through, the forces of encounter. With affect, a body is as much outside itself as in itself—webbed in its relations— until ultimately such firm distinctions cease to matter.

In what undoubtedly has become one of the most oft-cited quotations concerning affect, Baruch Spinoza maintained, "No one has yet determined what the body can do" (1959: 87). Two key aspects are immediately worth emphasizing, or re-emphasizing, here: first, the capacity of a body is never defined by a body alone but is always aided and abetted by, and dovetails with, the field or context of its force-relations; and second, the "not yet" of "knowing the body" is still very much with us more than 330 years after Spinoza composed his *Ethics*. But, as Spinoza recognized, this issue is never the generic figuring of "the body" (any body) but, much more singularly, endeavoring to configure *a* body and its affects/affectedness, its ongoing affectual composition of *a* world, the *this-ness* of a world and a body.

The essays of this collection are, each in their own way, an attempt to address this "yet-ness" of a body's affectual doings and undoings. Each essay presents its own account of encounters with forces and passages of intensity that bear out, while occasionally leaving bare, the singularly and intimately impersonal—even sub-personal and pre-personal—folds of belonging (or non-belonging) to a world. That is the unceasing challenge presented by Spinoza's "not yet," conveying a sense of urgency that transforms the matter and matterings of affect into an ethical, aesthetic, and political task all at once. But then, of course, Spinoza must have also understood that affect's "not yet" was never really supposed to find any ultimate resolution. No one will ever finally exclaim: "So, there it is: now, we know all that a body can do! Let's call it a day." It is this Spinozist imperative, ever renewed by the "not yet" knowing of affective doing, that drives affect—as well as those theories that attempt to negotiate the formative powers of affect—forward toward the next encounter of forces, and the next, and the next, and the next . . .

It would be, though, a rather serious misrepresentation of contemporary theories of affect if we were to understand each of these "not yets" and their "nexts" as moving forward in some kind of integrated lockstep. There is no single, generalizable theory of affect: not yet, and (thankfully) there never will be. If anything, it is more tempting to imagine that there can only ever

be infinitely multiple iterations of affect and theories of affect: theories as
diverse and singularly delineated as their own highly particular encounters
with bodies, affects, worlds. (Isn't theory—any theory with or without a
capital T—supposed to work this way? Operating with a certain modest
methodological vitality rather than impressing itself upon a wiggling world
like a snap-on grid of shape-setting interpretability?)[1] But such a state of
affairs might also go some distance toward explaining why first encounters
with theories of affect might feel like a momentary (sometimes more permanent) methodological and conceptual free fall. Almost all of the tried-and-
true handholds and footholds for so much critical-cultural-philosophical
inquiry and for theory—subject/object, representation and meaning, rationality, consciousness, time and space, inside/outside, human/nonhuman,
identity, structure, background/foreground, and so forth—become decidedly less sure and more nonsequential (any notion of strict "determination"
or directly linear cause and effect goes out the window too). Because affect
emerges out of muddy, unmediated relatedness and not in some dialectical
reconciliation of cleanly oppositional elements or primary units, it makes
easy compartmentalisms give way to thresholds and tensions, blends and
blurs. As Brian Massumi (2002) has emphasized, approaches to affect would
feel a great deal less like a free fall if our most familiar modes of inquiry had
begun with movement rather than stasis, with process always underway
rather than position taken.

It is no wonder too that when theories have dared to provide even a
tentative account of affect, they have sometimes been viewed as naïvely or
romantically wandering too far out into the groundlessness of a world's or a
body's myriad inter-implications, letting themselves get lost in an over-
abundance of swarming, sliding differences: chasing tiny firefly intensities
that flicker faintly in the night, registering those resonances that vibrate,
subtle to seismic, under the flat wash of broad daylight, dramatizing (indeed,
for the unconvinced, *over*-dramatizing) what so often passes beneath mention. But, as our contributors will show, affect's impinging/extruded belonging to worlds, bodies, and their in-betweens—affect in its immanence—
signals the very promise of affect theory too: casting illumination upon the
"not yet" of a body's doing, casting a line along the hopeful (though also
fearful) cusp of an emergent futurity, casting its lot with the infinitely con-
nectable, impersonal, and contagious belongings to *this* world.

Affectual Orientations

So, what can an affect theory do? Unquestionably, there has been an increased interest in various manifestations/conceptualizations of affect—as can be found in a growing number of essays and books (such as this one), as well as conference themes, special journal issues, symposia, and so forth. But it would be impossible to believe that these diverse renderings of affect can somehow be resolved into a tidy picture. There is no single unwavering line that might unfurl toward or around affect and its singularities, let alone its theories: only swerves and knottings, perhaps a few marked and unremarked intersections as well as those unforeseen crosshatchings of articulations yet to be made, refastened, or unmade. Traveling at varying tempos and durations within specific fields of inquiry while also slipping past even the most steadfast of disciplinary boundaries (for example, the affective interface of neurology and architecture, anyone?), the concept of "affect" has gradually accrued a sweeping assortment of philosophical/psychological/physiological underpinnings, critical vocabularies, and ontological pathways, and, thus, can be (and has been) turned toward all manner of political/pragmatic/performative ends. Perhaps one of the surest things that can be said of both affect and its theorization is that they will exceed, always exceed the context of their emergence, as the excess of ongoing process.

Undoubtedly the watershed moment for the most recent resurgence of interest and intrigue regarding affect and theories of affect came in 1995 when two essays—one by Eve Sedgwick and Adam Frank ("Shame in the Cybernetic Fold") and one by Brian Massumi ("The Autonomy of Affect")— were published. Not only has the theoretical content of these particular works proven to be invigorating (combining affect's displacement of the centrality of cognition with affect theory's own displacement of debates over the centrality of structuralism and poststructuralism) but the voice and stylistics of their writings—where affect serves as force and form—have likewise contributed to their wide circulation and considerable influence in the years since. These two essays from 1995, along with subsequent work undertaken by their authors, have given substantial shape to the two dominant vectors of affect study in the humanities: Silvan Tomkins's psychobiology of differential affects (1962) (Sedgwick and Frank) and Gilles Deleuze's Spinozist ethology of bodily capacities (1988a) (Massumi). With Tomkins, affect follows a quasi-Darwinian "innate-ist" bent toward matters of evolutionary hardwiring. But these wires are by no means fully insulated nor do they terminate with the brain or flesh; instead they spark and fray just enough to transduce those influences borne along by the ambient irradiation of social relations. Meanwhile, Deleuze's Spinozan route locates affect in the midst of things and relations (in immanence) and, then, in the complex assemblages that come to compose bodies and worlds simultaneously. There is, then, a certain sense of reverse flow between these lines of inquiry—a certain inside-out/outside-in difference in directionality: affect as the prime "interest" motivator that comes to put the drive in bodily drives (Tomkins); affect as an entire, vital, and modulating field of myriad becomings across human and nonhuman (Deleuze). While there is no pretending that these two vectors of affect theory could ever be easily or fully reconciled, they can be made to interpenetrate at particular points and to resonate (see, in particular, the work of Gibbs, Probyn, and Watkins in this volume).

But there are far more than just two angles onto affect's theorization. For now (and only for now), we can tentatively lay out, as a set of necessarily brief and blurry snapshots, eight of the main orientations that undulate and sometimes overlap in their approaches to affect. Each of these regions of investigation—enumerated for convenience's sake and in no particular order—highlights a slightly different set of concerns, often reflected in their initiating premises, the endpoints of their aims, or both.

1   One approach is found in the sometimes archaic and often occulted practices of human/nonhuman nature as intimately interlaced, including phenomenologies and post-phenomenologies of embodiment as well as investigations into a body's incorporative capacities for scaffolding and extension (Vivian Sobchack, Don Ihde, Michel Henry, Laura Marks, Mark Hansen, and others).

2   Another is located along an intertwined line to the first item: in the more recent but, in some ways, no less occulted (though better-funded) assemblages of the human/machine/inorganic such as cybernetics, the neurosciences (of matter, of distributed agency, of emotion/sensation, and so on), ongoing research in artificial intelligence, robotics, and bio-informatics/bio-engineering (where life technologies work increasingly to smudge the affectional line between the living and the non-living).

3   The third is found in certain nonhumanist, ofttimes subterranean, and generally non-Cartesian traditions in philosophy, usually linking the movements of matter with a processual incorporeality (Spinozism): particularly as found in those contemporary approaches that try to move beyond various gendered and other cultural limitations in phi-

losophy, whether in feminist work (Rosi Braidotti, Elizabeth Grosz, Genevieve Lloyd, and Moira Gatens), or in Italian autonomism (Paolo Virno or Maurizio Lazzaratto), or in philosophically inflected cultural studies (Lawrence Grossberg, Meaghan Morris, Brian Massumi), or in political philosophy (Giorgio Agamben and Michael Hardt and Antonio Negri).

4 The fourth occurs in certain lines of psychological and psychoanalytic inquiry where a relatively unabashed biologism remains co-creatively open to ongoing impingements and pressures from intersubjective and interobjective systems of social desiring (early Sigmund Freud, Silvan Tomkins, Daniel Stern, Mikkel Borch-Jacobsen, and so forth). It is similar to the third item above, although generally more prone—by way of disciplinary expectations—to a categorical naming of affects and also quite likely to provide operationally defined contours for a particular range of affects, with ultimate aims that are often more human-centered.

5 The fifth is found in the regularly hidden-in-plain-sight politically engaged work—perhaps most often undertaken by feminists, queer theorists, disability activists, and subaltern peoples living under the thumb of a normativizing power—that attends to the hard and fast materialities, as well as the fleeting and flowing ephemera, of the daily and the workaday, of everyday and every-night life, and of "experience" (understood in ways far more collective and "external" rather than individual and interior), where persistent, repetitious practices of power can simultaneously provide a body (or, better, collectivized bodies) with predicaments and potentials for realizing a world that subsists within and exceeds the horizons and boundaries of the norm.

6 The sixth can be seen in various (often humanities-related) attempts to turn away from the much-heralded "linguistic turn" in the latter half of the twentieth century—from cultural anthropology to geography to communication and cultural studies to performance-based art practices to literary theory—and often toward work increasingly influenced by the quantum, neuro-, and cognitive sciences, especially far-from-equilibrium physics (see the second item above); but also by returning to and reactivating work that had been taking place well before and alongside the linguistic turn and its attendant social constructionisms. Here we could note examples such as Raymond Williams's "structure of feeling," Frantz Fanon's "third person consciousness," Walter Benjamin's non-sensual mimesis, Susanne Langer's "open ambient," and

John Dewey's pragmatic idealities. This turn to affect theory is sometimes focused on understanding how the "outside" realms of the pre-/extra-/para-linguistic intersect with the "lower" or proximal senses (such as touch, taste, smell, rhythm and motion-sense, or, alternately/ultimately, the autonomic nervous system) while also arguing for a much wider definition for the social or cultural. Frequently this work focuses on those ethico-aesthetic spaces that are opened up (or shut down) by a widely disparate assortment of affective encounters with, for example, new technological lures, infants, music, dance, and other more non-discursive arts (particularly architecture), animals (companion or not), and so on.

7 The seventh appears in critical discourses of the emotions (and histories of the emotions) that have progressively left behind the interiorized self or subjectivity (thus, following from the third item, how to think or feel in an era "post"-cogito?) to unfold regimes of expressivity that are tied much more to resonant worldings and diffusions of feeling/passions—often including atmospheres of sociality, crowd behaviors, contagions of feeling, matters of belonging (for example, the recent resurgence of interest in Gabriel Tarde) and a range of postcolonial, hybridized, and migrant voices that forcefully question the privilege and stability of individualized actants possessing self-derived agency and solely private emotions within a scene or environment. How might emotion—taking on then decidedly affectual qualities—be reconsidered without requiring place-positions for subject and object as the first condition (see, for example, Terada 2001)?

8 The eighth approach is located in practices of science and science studies themselves, particularly work that embraces pluralist approaches to materialism (quite often threaded through the revivification of Alfred North Whitehead's writings); hence, scientific practices that never act to eliminate the element of wonder or the sheer mangle of ontological relatedness but, in Isabelle Stengers's words, "make present, vivid and mattering, the imbroglio, perplexity and messiness of a worldly world, a world where we, our ideas and power relations, are not alone, were never alone, will never be alone" (2007, 9). Here affect is the hinge where mutable matter and wonder (ofttimes densely intermingled with world-weary dread too) perpetually tumble into each other.

Again, this is by no means a fully comprehensive or neatly contoured accounting of the many actual and yet to be realized or imagined convergences and divergences undertaken by contemporary theories of affect. There will always be more; undoubtedly there *are* more—as other means of inquiry are invented to account for the relational capacities that belong to the doings of bodies or are conjured by the world-belongingness that gives rise to a body's doing. Already moving across and beneath nearly all of these strands, one need only consider, for example, the intellectually and politically fertile work (maybe not always explicitly invoking affect or theories of affect but drawing from them nonetheless) of Donna Haraway, Erin Manning, William Connolly, J. K. Gibson-Graham, Lisa Blackman, John Protevi, Sianne Ngai, Ghassan Hage, Jane Bennett, Paul Gilroy, Karen Barad, Steven Shaviro, Elizabeth Wilson, Alphonso Lingis, and Michael Taussig. For now anyway, these eight affectual orientations offer a useful enough sketch of a framework so that we can tease out some of the key resonances among our contributors' concerns in the book that follows.

Bloom-Spaces: Promise and Threat

If the individual essays of this volume are momentarily united, it is in their collectively singular attempts to address what transpires in the affective bloom-space of an ever-processual materiality. What Raymond Williams defined as the necessary critical task of always "moving beyond one after another 'materialism'" (1980, 122) chimes with Isabelle Stengers's words above. The affective qualities of this adjacent but incorporeal bloom-space are figured in a variety of ways by our contributors: as excess, as autonomous, as impersonal, as the ineffable, as the ongoingness of process, as pedagogico-aesthetic, as virtual, as shareable (mimetic), as sticky, as collective, as contingency, as threshold or conversion point, as immanence of potential (futurity), as the open, as a vibrant incoherence that circulates about zones of cliché and convention, as a gathering place of accumulative dispositions. Each of these figurations, in its own way, names that Spinozist "not yet" of affect as its "promise"—stated most forthrightly by Sara Ahmed, Ben Anderson, and Lauren Berlant (for her, a "cluster of promises") but implicit among other of our contributors too. (For one very complementary angle, see "hope" [as promise] in Zournazi 2002.)

At the same time, this promise of affect and its generative relay into affect theory must also acknowledge, in the not yet of never-quite-knowing, that there are no ultimate or final guarantees—political, ethical, aesthetic, pedagogic, and otherwise—that capacities to affect and to be affected will yield an actualized next or new that is somehow better than "now." Such seeming moments of promise can just as readily come to deliver something worse. This state of affairs is emphasized by Lawrence Grossberg when he discusses "received" modernity and alternate, co-existing modernities, by Brian Massumi addressing "threat" in the affective birth of the future, and by Patricia Clough in her analysis of capital's entanglements with matter's affective capacities. Thus, in the affective bloom of a processual materialism, one of the most pressing questions faced by affect theory becomes "Is that a promise or a threat?" No surprise: any answer quite often encompasses both at the same time (hence Berlant's "cruel optimism").

As much as we sometimes might want to believe that affect is highly *invested* in us and with somehow magically providing for a better tomorrow, as if affect were always already sutured into a progressive or liberatory politics or at least the marrow of our best angels, as if affect were somehow producing always better states of being and belonging—affect instead bears an intense and thoroughly immanent neutrality. Maybe this is one reason why, in his penultimate lectures collected as *The Neutral*, Roland Barthes calls for "a hyperconsciousness of the affective minimum, of the microscopic fragment of emotion . . . which implies an extreme changeability of affective moments, a rapid modification, into shimmer" (2005, 101). The neutral, for Barthes, is not synonymous in the least with ready acquiescence, political neutrality, a lapse into grayness; in short, it does not imply a well-nurtured indifference to the present, to existing conditions. Instead, the neutral works to "outplay the paradigm" of oppositions and negations by referring to "intense, strong, unprecedented states" that elude easy polarities and contradictions while also guarding against the accidental consolidation of the very meaning that the Neutral (as "ardent, burning activity") seeks to dissolve (7). Likewise, the neutral is not bound to the formed/formal matters of space or time nor has it anything to do with the linearizing axes and abrupt angles of structuralism, but "only intervals, only the relation between two moments, two spaces or objects" (146–47). In these in-betweens or blooming intervals, intensities are continually divulged in the supple relations between a world's or a body's interleavings and their vectors of gradience—where gradient is "progressive accentuation, spatial or temporal, in the intensive dimensions [concentration, speed] of a stimulus [gradient of odor, gradient of luminosity] or of a comportment [gradient of goal]" (196). Analyses would no longer proceed, Barthes proposed, by way of the binaries of structuralism ("yes/no"), their slippages, inversions, convolutions, but instead must begin—as with "plus/minus"—to "register a form that is rarely taken into account: the stretching"

(196–97). It becomes then a matter of accounting for the progressive accentuation (plus/minus) of intensities, their incremental shimmer: the stretching of process underway, not position taken.

From the midst of such stretching, the neutral served as Barthes's attempt to forge an ethics or "discourse of the 'lateral choice' " or, as he went on to say, this approach afforded him "a free manner—to be looking for my own style of being-present to the struggles of my time" (8). What should follow as critical practice, Barthes argued, is a neutrally inflected, immanent *pathos* or "patho-logy" that would be an "inventory of shimmers, of nuances, of states, of changes (*pathè*)" as they gather into "affectivity, sensibility, sentiment," and come to serve as "the passion for difference" (77). Here affect theory is, at one level, an "inventory of shimmers" while, upon another register, it is a matter of affectual composition (in a couple of senses of the word "composition"—as an ontology always coming to formation but also, more prosaically, as creative/writerly task). This is a passion for differences as continuous, shimmering gradations of intensities. Making an inventory (of singularities). And in the interval, is the stretching: unfolding a patho-logy (of "not yets").[2]

Bruno Latour also discovered what he too calls "a patho-logical definition of [a] body"—although without any reference to Roland Barthes—when, at a conference, he asked everyone to write down the antonym of the word "body." Of all the antonyms (apart from the "predictable and amusing ones like 'antibody' or 'nobody' "), the ones that Latour found most intriguing were "unaffected" and "death" (2004, 205). He surmises: "If the opposite of being a body is dead [and] there is no life apart from the body . . . [then] to have a body is to learn to be affected, meaning 'effectuated,' moved, put into motion by other entities, humans or nonhumans. If you are not engaged in this learning, you become insensitive, dumb, you drop dead" (205). The body becomes less about its nature as bounded substance or eternal essence and more about the body "as an interface that becomes more and more describable when it learns to be affected by many more elements" (205). Ironically, while Barthes spoke of the slope of affective intensities as "progressive accentuation," then alluding briefly to how one might recognize these near-inconspicuous affects in everyday encounters with such things as gradients of odors or of luminosity, Latour takes the former, quite literally, for his own example of a body's becoming effectuated. In an extended elaboration, Latour considers specifically how one becomes "a nose" (how noses are trained for work in the perfume industry).

As one might imagine, what Latour goes on to outline is the absolute co-extension and interpenetration of olfactory science, perfume industry, subject-nose, chemical components of smell molecules, odor names, and training sessions. Through it all, there is no clear delineation of subject/ object, no easily sustained interior/exterior world in such a processual engagement of becoming a nose. In the accumulation of gradient tweakings, one finds the simultaneous delivery of a bodily capacity and a world of sometimes near-infinitesimal difference: nurturing differences through affective relay into perpetually finer-grained (and concurrently enlarged) postures or comportments until there are only articulations of a world in its expressiveness: expressions that are only ever the interval between sensings or *the stretching* of this sensuous interval that comes to progressively produce (when successful) a passion for difference, where the patho-logy of a body meets the pedagogy of an affective world. In fact, as much as anything, perhaps that is what such a "neutral" bloom-space offers: the patho-logy of a body intersecting with the pedagogy of an affective world. As Ben Highmore suggests, at the end of his essay on taste in this collection, this is "the transformation of ethos through experiments in living. Here politics is a form of experiential pedagogy, of constantly submitting your sensorium to new sensual worlds that sit uncomfortably within your ethos. There is hope here. . . ."

We would maintain that affect theories, whatever their multiple trajectories, must persistently work to invent or invite such a "patho-logy" into their own singular instantiations—not only as inventory (though, heaven knows, sometimes that can be work enough) but also as a generative, pedagogic nudge aimed toward a body's becoming an ever more worldly sensitive interface, toward a style of being present to the struggles of our time. Or, as Lauren Berlant phrases it in her essay, considering those moments when one briefly slips free of the cruelty of normative optimism: how "the substitution of habituated indifference with a spreading pleasure might open up a wedge into an alternative ethics of living, or not." Maybe that's the "for-now" promise of affect theory's "not yet," its habitually rhythmic (or near rhythmic) undertaking: endeavoring to locate that propitious moment when the stretching of (or tiniest tear in) bloom-space could precipitate something more than incremental. If only. Affect as promise: increases in capacities to act (expansions in affectability: both to affect and to be affected), the start of "being-capable" (Uexküll, quoted in Agamben 2004, 51), resonant affinities of body and world, being open to more life or more to life (Massumi 2002). Or again not. As Lauren Berlant indicates in her essay in this volume, there is also the lingering, numbing downside that, even though a propitious moment "*could* become otherwise, . . . shifts in affective atmosphere are not equal to changing the world" (emphasis added).

Conversely then, affect can also serve as a leading visceral indicator of potent threat. Brian Massumi's essay in this volume states: "Understand the political ontology of threat requires returning thought to [the] affective twilight zone . . . that bustling zone of indistinction." Zone of indistinction equals the neutral in its state of most brute and potentializing indifference. Under the conditions of a political ontology of threat, a pedagogic world and patho-logical body find themselves at an impasse and perhaps begin to contract or retract their powers of affectivity/affectability. Suspend, wither, maybe die.[3] But this split—promise or threat—is *rarely* so stark. Take, for instance, Patricia Clough's argument—the most unflinching essay of this collection—which provides more than sufficient concern for the ways that the word "rarely" is quickly becoming "more frequently"—in the real subsumption of "life itself" by biomedia and in "the sovereign right to kill in the context of biopolitics." Despite this, Clough finds a wedge, a small "and yet." Maybe the neutral can always be colored more hopefully. It has to be (after all, affect speaks in the voice of an imperative). And so Clough ends, albeit in what feels like a gasp for a tiny crack of airspace, by writing that "there is always a chance for something else, unexpected, new." Who doesn't want to believe that we live in a world ceaselessly recomposing itself in the unforeseen passages through the best of all possible impasses?

Within these mixed capacities of the in-between, as undulations in expansions and contractions of affectability arrive almost simultaneously or in close-enough alternation, something emerges, overspills, exceeds: *a form of relation* as a rhythm, a fold, a timing, a habit, a contour, or a shape comes to mark the passages of intensities (whether dimming or accentuating) in body-to-body/world-body mutual imbrication.[4] It is this relationality— often working, as Anna Gibbs clearly shows in her contribution, by mimetic means—that persists, in adjacency and duration, alongside the affects and bodies that gather up in motley, always more-than-human collectivity. This is the topography most widely shared by theories of affect, threaded through their myriad ways of constructing an inventory (consider here, for example, Megan Watkins's essay on debates over pedagogic theories and the role played by the accumulation of affect as "dispositional tendency") as well as in their own diffuse patho-logies. It is through these durational indices of shapes, timings, rhythms, folds, and contours that the contributors to this volume begin to give name (a variety of different names actually) to the singular affectual bloom-spaces of a processually oriented materialism.

No wonder then that, in theory, the "what" of affect often gives way to matters of "how" in the rhythm or angle of approach: thus, why a great many theories of affect do not sweat the construction of any elaborate step-by-step methodology much at all, but rather come to fret the presentation or the style of presentation, the style of being present, more than anything else. If Sara Ahmed's essay leads off our collection, it is because her attention to the "hap" (the contingency or potential in what she calls the "messiness of the experiential") of happiness is precisely the entry into the neutral bloom-space that affect theory is forever shifting into and out of, incrementally and intensely. She writes that "we may walk into the room and 'feel the atmosphere,' but what we may feel depends on the angle of our arrival. Or we might say that the atmosphere is already angled; it is always felt from a specific point. The pedagogic encounter is full of angles." This is the kind of aesthetically inflected moment that underlies almost any theoretical orientation toward affect. Not aesthetics in its "dominant mode" where, as Ben Highmore argues in his essay, it both moralizes and takes "satisfaction in the end form of a process"; rather this decidedly affect-driven aesthetics is interested "in the messy *informe* of the ongoing-ness of process." How to enter *that* room, suddenly feeling the angles already inhabiting *this* bloom-space. And then to look for a means to articulate, to compose a singularizing aesthetic that captures both the stretchy-processual and the inherently sticky pragmatics of right now, right here. How also to register the intensity of difference in writing, and yet to relay this difference in ways that can be felt, shared? Referencing the Tomkins-inspired work of Sedgwick and Frank, Elspeth Probyn in her essay points to how a "general gesture to Affect won't do the trick. If we want to invigorate our concepts, we need to follow through on what different affects do, at different levels. The point needs to be stressed: different affects make us feel, write, think, and act in different ways." This engagement of affect and aesthetics is more a matter of "manner" than of essence: "not *what* something is, but how it is—or, more precisely, *how* it affects, and how it is affected by, other things" (Shaviro 2007, 8). Thus, this "how" of an aesthetics of affect becomes one way to bridge from "not yet" to the "next." For now. But without advance guarantees.

The political dimensions of affect generally proceed through or persist immediately alongside its aesthetics, an ethico-aesthetics of a body's capacity for becoming sensitive to the "manner" of a world: finding (or not) the coordinating rhythms that precipitate newness or change while also holding close to the often shimmering (twinkling/fading, vibrant/dull) continuities that pass in the slim interval between "*how* to affect" and "*how* to be affected." In their analysis of the political stakes raised by Australia's "red ship" refugee event, Lone Bertelsen and Andrew Murphie neatly illustrate the ethico-aesthetic paradigm and its consequences for affect theory in precisely the ways that we have been outlining here. It is at once a twin maneuver of inventory ("the infinity of little affective events that make up our everyday lives") and of durational patho-logy (the development of new "regimes of sensation"). Drawing primarily on Félix Guattari's writings, Bertlesen and Murphie set forth their particular experiential pedagogy: "to develop a creative responsibility for modes of living *as they come into being*." Such is the open-ended ethos of their invocation of "the refrain" and its politically inflected gathering together of modes of living in an impurely humane (all too human and always more than human) sense of collectivity or belonging: the vital "more" to life, simultaneously right now and "not yet."

This same sense of the affectively, impurely human—the point where concerns of the all too human meet the always more than human—guides Steven Brown's and Ian Tucker's approach to the management of psychiatric relations and regularly prescribed psychoactive medications. What they find, by means of affect theory, is a way of articulating the experience of a patient and the complexities of the healthcare system (as "dispositif" or apparatus) without collapsing back into humanism. Brown and Tucker describe affect as providing them with "a continuous gestalt switch, where foreground and background, experience and dispositif alternate. . . . An attention to affect allows us to propose that persons differ from other creatures and things only quantitatively, by the number and complexity of the planes of experience that intersect, and intensively, through the particular connections and engagements that the human body is capable of supporting." Their notion of "a continuous gestalt switch" is a rather nice alternative phrasing for what transpires when the patho-logy of a body intersects with the pedagogy of an affective world (as they mutually constitute a rhythm, contour, shape, timing).

For her part, Anna Gibbs in her essay will invoke this gestalt switch as a "duplicity that necessitates an oscillation between two perspectives . . . [between] a certain strategic humanism viewed through the optic of representation that focuses on the culturally plastic and historically changing forms of subjectivity . . . [and] the world of 'nonlocal,' asubjective becomings in which these forms appear simply as momentary traces of other movements."

In finding the durational index by which foreground and background oscillate in sympathetic or mimetic rhythm, a motley more-than-human collectivity (as dispositif) shimmers into view alongside the multiple planes of
experience (as embodied subjectivity). Thus, when Brown and Tucker later
turn to their notion of "intermediary concepts," it is in order to steady and
sustain this view long enough to peer into the affective dimensions of the
ineffable and extract a prudent singularity, one fitted to the narrowly inhab-
itable margin (although as full of angles as any patient-body-world monad
would be) that barely separates "how to affect" from "how to be affected."
Affect's contribution to the empirical unfolds as an aesthetic or art of dos-
ages: experiment and experience. Feel the angles and rhythms at the interface of bodies and worlds.

Whereas Brown and Tucker focus on closely and modestly tailoring the
"how" of affect to the oscillatory co-production of psychiatric patient and
disciplinary apparatus, Nigel Thrift in his essay extrudes the "how" of affect directly out of the other, decidedly more immodest side of this formulation. Describing the near endless proliferation of worlds-within-worlds and
worlds-upon-worlds as well as the growing extimacies (public intimacies) of
subjectivity, Thrift enthuses over the potential countertendencies and mo-
mentums unleashed through "the establishment of human-nonhuman fields
of captivation." Not so accidentally, these aesthetic qualities of everyday life in
early twenty-first-century capitalism sound eerily reminiscent of Clough's
excavation of the contemporary intertwinings of biomedia and biopolitics—
where "the boundaries between alive and not alive and material and immaterial have become increasingly blurred, so that what is considered as alive
can become thing-like and what was considered as dead is able to show signs
of life" (Thrift). Except what Clough finds by following the fates of affect
down to those biopolitical and bioscientific substrates operating so very
deeply within the pulsings of "life itself," Thrift locates everywhere already on
eager surface-display in capitalism's "worldings." In this infectious generating of new environments for experience (simultaneously real and ideal),
there is a constantly re-amplifying set of refractions, according to Thrift,
"[where] every surface communicates," which, in the process, works to produce "new kinds of cultural nerve, if you like, which build extra facets of
'you.'" Eschewing the critical, near knee-jerk impulse that immediately cries
out against capitalist totalitarianism and life-world domination, Thrift wonders instead about the ways that these "series of overlapping affective fields"
might serve as the site for counterpractices of aesthetic and political modula-

tion. It is, he knows, a rhythmic matter (and manner) of tipping a worlding's affective bloom-space into the more lateral stretch of the neutral, toward the patho-logical promise (and threat) of right now and not yet: the promise that the next set of encounters and the "manner" in which we undertake them could always guarantee more.

This might be the one guarantee that affect theory offers with some certainty: what Ben Anderson maintains is affect's "perpetually deferred promise on the horizon of cultural theory," a horizon that is not "stable ground or excessive outside" but offers the neutral lateralization of one after another materialism of the processual in-between of bodies/bodyings and world(ing)s. This inextricability of affect's promise and peril is, as we have tried to highlight, what is pried apart and/or relayed through the patho-logy of a body's doings in the pedagogic encounter with a world's shimmerings.

Encounters

It is no coincidence that we begin the last essay of this book, an interview with Lawrence Grossberg, by asking him to reflect upon his first encounters with affect. Grossberg's reply is, as one might expect from someone who has thought and written a great deal about affect for more than a quarter century, a guided tour through many of the major figures and attendant conceptual formations that have contributed tremendously to our present-day understandings of affect. Grossberg is especially good of course at highlighting affect's often tenuous and turbulent theoretical intersections with practices of cultural studies, always mapping out where affect has been and where it has yet to go. We the editors of this book first discovered affect—and its place in cultural studies in particular—through Grossberg's work, and then through those who influenced him (such as Spinoza, Freud, Williams, Deleuze, and so on) and those who followed later (particularly Probyn, Massumi, Sedgwick, and many among our contributors). When we met for the first time at a Michel de Certeau symposium organized by Ben Highmore in September 2002, it didn't take long to realize we shared an ongoing interest and investment in theories of affect. Now fragments of discussion and shimmers of inspiration caught over years of email contact have accumulated to produce something concrete.

Yet since our initial encounter, and the enthusiasms subsequently shared, the fate of affect as a fashionable theory has played on our minds as it also played out in public (or at least our main public: academia). From the moment the idea for this collection began, we have experienced everything from the exacerbation of colleagues who "never want to hear the word affect again" through to the opposite reaction of delight from those who anticipate this collection with a sigh of relief. For this latter group, given this somewhat ephemeral and ubiquitous thing called affect theory, perhaps a "reader" promises to offer an authoritative overview that could fill a pesky void in conceptual accumulation. Both of these reactions make us quite conscious of cultural theory's own temporality when, most of all, we would prefer that this collection took on a life that might be more untimely: unfurling, in unexpected ways, beyond its presumed moment, provoking some readers to delve even more deeply into the variegated histories and entangled orienta-tions that continue to feed into the ever-emergent discourse of affect, per-petuating the "not yet" of affect's doing.

While we acknowledge the difficulty of avoiding trends in academic curi-osity, the idea that desirable paradigms simply appear, ostensibly from no-where, traveling and propagating across continents in accordance with num-bers of international conference delegates, is as naïve as the belief that any single book will help someone resolve a perceived deficit in their cultural theory capital. Still, throughout the writing and editing of this collection we have wondered and worried whether we too are guilty of exploiting an all too common scenario in the powerful transnational economy of global theory (see Morris 2006). At a time when various utilitarian agendas appear para-mount in academic publishing, we will be pleased if the book intensifies appreciation for the delight and desirability of thought and feeling (and investigations of the relationship between both) as endpoints for intellectual practice in themselves. Leaving aside the theoreticist drive to master yet an-other canon of work (and the internecine battles that do sometimes emerge between different standpoints presented by the affect theorists here), we hope this collection manages to convey—more than once—the contagiousness of one or other of Tomkins's two positive affects: whether enjoyment-joy at the prospect of an undiscovered set of connections, or interest-excitement in the unveiling of an entirely fresh perspective. Without these moments of revela-tion and reflection—without breaks in the consumption and reproduction of established ideas to really imagine—theory itself begins to feel intractable, a stifling orthodoxy that has more in common with another Tomkinsesque pairing: fear or shame of not reproducing a norm.

In this introduction we have tried to give some sense of the wide range of theoretical possibilities and subtleties that an awareness of affect enables, letting the reader decide which threads ultimately prove the most productive. In this same manner, we think it fitting to conclude by offering two brief vignettes, each relaying our initiating encounters with affect and theories of affect while also giving some sense of the contours that have followed. With their slightly different trajectories, these anecdotes reveal for us the generative nature that circulates about the concept of affect, but also the "hap" or contingencies that color our unique perspectives. As Morris has shown (2006, 21–22), anecdotes need not be true in order to function in a communicative exchange; still, what we write below are truthful *enough* representations of our recollections of encountering affect. They are offered in the spirit of materializing and capturing the path that affect theory has taken within and around our own scholarly development: the angle of arrival, the feel of an atmosphere. It is also to show that no one "moment" or key "theorist" inaugurated "a" "turn" "to" affect; like others, we have been caught and enamored of affect *in turns*, in conjunction with new quotidian realities.

Greg

I first met affect, as a concept, when a manila envelope arrived at my apartment's doorstep in rural northwestern Pennsylvania sometime in 1984. At the time, I was working as a sound engineer in a music recording studio. The envelope was mailed to me by a college friend, a bit older than me, who had gone off to graduate school. It contained an essay (I still remember it, quite vividly, as badly photocopied and then unevenly chopped by a paper cutter) entitled "Another Boring Day in Paradise: Rock and Roll and the Empowerment of Everyday Life," by Lawrence Grossberg (1984). The piece was written in a vibrant but rather unwieldy theoretical language that detailed this passionate thing called "affect" in ways that I could not always quite follow, although fortunately the musical references were immediately recognizable and that helped me to roughly intuit the theory. While I puzzled over Grossberg's rendering of particular musical artists and genres, something about the theory must have leaped up from those pages and struck me, stuck with me . . . because by the fall of 1985 I had quit my day job as an engineer and my evening/weekend job as a clerk at an independent record store. I too was off to graduate school.

But it was a second essay by Grossberg, "Is There Rock after Punk?"

published in the journal *Critical Studies in Communication* (1986), that truly caused me to take seriously the whole matter of affect and cultural studies. Grossberg's multilayered approach to popular music and fandom enlarged the ways that I had previously understood my own relationship to music (connecting it with broader movements afoot in culture) and, again, the concept of "affect" was crucial, even if I still couldn't quite fully comprehend all of its ins and outs. But the lure that really cinched everything for me was dangled by the American music writer Greil Marcus in a critical response that immediately followed Grossberg's piece (1986). There is one paragraph from Marcus in particular that has never left me and has remained a major touchstone for my subsequent work.

Marcus's response revolves, in part, around an anecdote concerning Henri Lefebvre (a social theorist and philosopher of everyday life) in France of the 1920s. In Marcus's retelling, Lefebvre is hounded on the streets of Paris by a playfully incensed Tristan Tzara, who is angry because Lefebvre, in his review of Tzara's *7 Manifestes Dada*, dared to write that "Dada has smashed the world, but the pieces are fine." Apparently for days after, Tzara would stop Lefebvre on the street to taunt him: "So! You're picking up the pieces! Are you going to put them back together?" Finally, Lefebvre replied: "No, I'm going to finish smashing them." There is a vibrancy to this short anecdote (and a mini-lesson about the role of critique) but, even more, I appreciated how Marcus uses it to bridge the writerly contents of his critical reflections. Marcus describes how Lefebvre

> argued that social theorists had to examine not just institutions but moments—moments of love, poetry, justice, resignation, hate, desire— and he insisted that within the mysterious but actual realm of everyday life (not one's job, but in one's life as a commuter to one's job, or in one's life as daydreamer during the commute) these moments were at once all-powerful and powerless. If recognized, they could form the basis for entirely new demands on the social order, because the thoughts one thought as one commuted to one's job were satisfied neither by systems of transportation nor by systems of compensation. The rub was that no one knew how to talk about such moments. (79)

These are sentences that I have never been able to let go, or allow them to let me go. Through Lefebvre, Marcus lays down what I took to be a challenge for affect theory and, in many ways, I have always understood it as cultural studies' challenge as well.

A few years later in the early 1990s, when I attended the University of Illinois to work on my Ph.D. and study with Lawrence Grossberg, I began to finally find my way toward addressing such affective moments. I discovered the ways that Grossberg sought to locate the movements of affect within what he called "mattering maps" and, thus, the ways that affect must always be articulated and contextualized. But I also came to notice how affect always points to a future that is not quite in view from the present, a future that scrambles any map in advance of its arrival, if indeed the moment (as a demand on the social) ever fully arrives. Or, perhaps it is that even if "the moment" never fully arrives, it nonetheless remains, as Grossberg details in our interview, *virtually* present in duration. Whatever the futures of affect theory might portend, it always and already calls for a critical practice—what Lefebvre called "a theory of moments"—that must seek to imaginatively/ generatively nudge these moments along (or sometimes smash them) because they quite often reside along the "cusp of semantic availability" (as Raymond Williams would say of his concept of "structure of feeling" [1977, 134]), frequently revealing themselves in the clumsiness of bodily adjustments and in worldly accommodations barely underway. That is, these affective moments—at once all-powerful and powerless—do not arise in order to be deciphered or decoded or delineated but, rather, must be nurtured (often smuggled in or, at other times, through the direct application of pressure) into lived practices of the everyday as perpetually finer-grained postures for collective inhabitation. These matters—the shimmering relays between the everyday and affect and how these come to constitute ever new and enlarged potentials for belonging—remain my prime focus. Indeed, I have never really tried to imagine cultural studies as being about anything else.

Melissa

Punk rock was also key in my decision to go to grad school, but for me it was less a case of wanting to theorize music's place in everyday life than to escape a string of heartbreaks at the hands of a succession of bass players and drummers in a very small scene in Hobart, Tasmania. When I moved from an isolated island capital to the home of the millennial Olympics and gay pride, my intellectual coming of age was fostered by the inspiring work of local feminist scholars including Elspeth Probyn, Linnell Secomb, Gail Mason, Catherine Driscoll, Anna Gibbs, Katrina Schlunke, Ien Ang, Ruth Barcan, Kath Albury, Natalya Lusty, Catharine Lumby, Elizabeth Wilson,

Melissa Hardie, Laleen Jayamanne, and Zoe Sofoulis, among others. As I was soaking up the history of British cultural studies in the beginning stages of my thesis, Elspeth and Anna were sharing the ideas of Silvan Tomkins, intrigued like so many others by Eve Sedgwick's and Adam Frank's influential essay of 1995, "Shame in the Cybernetic Fold." As their respective projects developed, these discoveries were passed on to students and colleagues in a range of courses and seminars over the years; my challenge was to bring these seemingly unrelated bodies of theory together.

At the time, I hardly grasped the problems Sedgwick in particular was responding to: the consequences for thought posed by cherished theoretical mantras, especially in the competitive and privileged environment of Ivy League American graduate schools. She seemed to suggest that theoretical proficiency was useful for students seeking a tenure-track position or a stimulating dinner party conversation but less so for understanding the disturbing realities of the wider culture. As she wrote in *Touching Feeling*,

> I daily encounter graduate students who are dab hands at unveiling the hidden historical violences that underlie a secular, universalist liberal humanism. Yet these students' sentient years, unlike the formative years of their teachers, have been spent entirely in a xenophobic Reagan-Bush-Clinton-Bush America where "liberal" is, if anything, a taboo category and where "secular humanism" is routinely treated as a marginal religious sect, while a vast majority of the population claims to engage in direct intercourse with multiple invisible entities such as angels, Satan, and God. (2003, 139–40)

Sedgwick questioned the prolonged deployment of outdated hermeneutics, and even if I hadn't yet mastered them myself, her readings of Tomkins (along with the work of Tomkins himself) were incredibly enabling for a graduate student suspicious of the political nihilism that seemed inherent to successful scholarly practice and the defeatism accompanying the corporatization of higher education in her country. Unlike Sedgwick's students', my sentient years coincided with twelve years of conservative government under one leader—John Howard—and yet as Bertelsen's and Murphie's essay elucidates, it was a similar capacity to fan xenophobia that had secured his initial election at the start of my university life.

These experiences were central to the final form taken by my Ph.D. dissertation and subsequent book, *Cultural Studies' Affective Voices* (2006). In their unflagging optimism, each iteration sought to challenge the pessimism of available visions of leftist politics in cultural studies in a consciously performative way, taking inspiration from those (like Raymond Williams, Stuart Hall, Meaghan Morris, Lawrence Grossberg, and Andrew Ross) who had previously done so. Yet since this time, a growing awareness of the singularity of my critical formation makes me conscious that affect theory has now perhaps also joined the privileged circuits of graduate education and indoctrination that were key to Sedgwick's earlier critique.

In any case, my move to Queensland for postdoctoral study and the chance to meet Sedgwick herself while writing my book in 2004 led my interest in affect in new directions. It wasn't just the impact of watching Sedgwick teach in the classroom, guiding and inviting thoughts from her own graduate students, in a voice so delightfully modest I could hardly believe it had the same origin as the biting polemics I'd treasured in her written arguments. It had as much to do with her cancellation of a second lunch date for an important doctor's appointment that hastened my change in perspective. A sudden confrontation with the fragility of the body that contained that powerful mind put matters of theoretical nuance, disciplinary politics, and career advice beyond any realm of relevance.

Maybe this was a gap in age and experience that was always going to be corrected: a fresh-faced researcher eagerly navigating the streets of Manhattan to find a hero only too accustomed to the inflated and unrelenting expectations of acolytes. Indeed, upon her reading my work prior to our meeting, it was all of the negative and indifferent aspects of scholarly life—of writing and the living that intruded upon it—that Sedgwick had found missing, whether the fear of writer's block, the ferocity of colleagues, the vicissitudes of motivation, or the paralysis that might be overcome if confidence returned. I should have realized that Sedgwick's work has been just as significant for demonstrating affect's place in *disabling* as much as accompanying intellectual practice, whether in her explorations of Melanie Klein (2007), her public battle with illness (as witnessed in the haunting "A Dialogue on Love" [1998]), or her commitment to friends whose experience of a cruel disease robbed them of further encounters in this life.[5] In her generous way, Sedgwick showed that my desire to make a positive to fit a preestablished political objective had left my vision blinkered, even though this was a condition I had regularly diagnosed in others.

In the years since our conversation I've become more sensitive to the range of factors effectively limiting the likelihood of *positive* "scholarly affect." This includes a higher education environment in which senior colleagues are constantly outraged at the neoliberal accounting procedures that have infiltrated teaching and research, yet so convinced of the futility of any efforts to resist that the sense of mourning and loss is pervasive. Meanwhile, for the younger generation moving through, the corporate university culture consecrates a kind of compulsory conviviality in the workplace (discussed in my essay)—from the smiley faces of office email to the team-building exercises of after work drinks—which defines the landscape of affective labor in the information economy. This incitement to friendship papers over the grim competitiveness of the job market, blurring the line between "friend," "colleague," and "contact." Such instances of gung-ho positivity and careerist collegiality are perhaps most explicit in the proliferating genre of Internet-based social networking sites that so many of us (and our students) use. Today's white collar workers while away hours logged on to the network, craving the benefits of these various demonstrations of presence, community, and connection. "Mood indicators" and "status updates" kindly invite us to describe how we *feel*; and yet the software itself remains dubiously positioned to change any of the broader conditions leading to the more chronic forms of expression, which swing violently from "rolling on the floor laughing" to illusions of murdering a co-worker in the adjoining cubicle for the most trivial of habits. On these sites, entrepreneurial selves busily amass a security blanket of online contacts to alleviate the pressures of an aestheticized work culture consisting of long hours and an unknown employment future. It is this new frontier for affective labor that Alan Liu (2004) terms the "eternal, inescapable friendship" of knowledge work. And it is a world that cultural theory is better equipped to navigate than most.

For if it is clear that this networked world without enemies cannot really ease the loneliness of the office cubicle or writer's garret, affect theory may help us fight the limited range of subjective states available in the contemporary workplace, and in doing so, help us identify and denounce the distribution of winners and losers in contemporary society. Then again, as many of the essays in this collection prompt us to wonder, there may be little benefit in simply developing a vocabulary to explain exploitation *better*. How does our own attraction to affect theory allow us to feel more or less hopeful, powerful, or vindicated than others?

This is the point at which we would want to mark a limit for theory's usefulness, and offer these essays as incitements to *more than* discourse. We want them to touch, to move, to mobilize readers. Rather than offering mere words, we want them to show what affect can *do*. Subsequent pages offer just a sample of how some of our leading writers register these possibilities, at this moment. For now, we hope they carry intensities and resonances that impinge well beyond the printed page, and this passing conjuncture.

Notes

1   John Law's *After Method: Mess in Social Science Research* is a more than worthy and messy methodological text for what we have in mind here (2004).

2   Sianne Ngai's discussion, in the introduction to her *Ugly Feelings*, of Paolo Virno's "neutral kernel" of affective attitudes and dispositions (2005, 4–5) is immediately applicable here, as is her slightly later discussion of stalled or suspended "moments of conspicuous activity [that] remain affectively charged" (14).

3   We are thinking here especially of the middle chapters in Agamben's *The Open* (2004, 39–70) on Jakob von Uexküll, Martin Heidegger, and the Rostock tick.

4   We are following here Lauren Berlant's essay "Love, a Queer Feeling" (2001). She argues that we might think "about love's form not only as norm and institution, but also as an index of duration." Berlant writes, "I think of it as a kind of tattoo, a rhythm, a shape, timing. An environment of touch or sound that you make so that there is something to which you turn and return. Thinking about these qualities of love can tell us something else more general, more neutral or impersonal, about intimacy . . ." (439). See also Seigworth on indices of duration such as activation contours and affective attunements (2003, 75–105).

5   The writing of Sedgwick and Lauren Berlant has done much to teach me about the many queer world-making efforts cut short by the AIDS crisis in the United States, especially under the Reagan administration. I can only endorse Ann Cvetkovich's (2007, 461) claim that the archive of queer AIDS activism is "a repository of grief and optimism" that should be cherished and promoted, particularly for subsequent generations. For a U.S.-Australian perspective on the AIDS crisis, see Michaels 1997.

PART ONE   IMPINGEMENTS

Sara Ahmed

I might say, "You make me happy." Or I might be moved by something, in such a way that when I think of happiness I think of that thing. Even if happiness is imagined as a feeling state, or a form of consciousness that evaluates a life situation achieved over time (Veenhoven 1984, 22–3), happiness also turns us toward objects. We turn toward objects at the very point of "making." To be made happy by this or that is to recognize that happiness starts from somewhere other than the subject who may use the word to describe a situation.

In this essay, I want to consider happiness as a happening, as involving affect (to be happy is to be affected by something), intentionality (to be happy is to be happy about something), and evaluation or judgment (to be happy about something makes something good). In particular, I will explore how happiness functions as a promise that directs us toward certain objects, which then circulate as social goods. Such objects accumulate positive affective value as they are passed around. My essay will offer an approach to thinking through affect as "sticky." Affect is what sticks, or what sustains or preserves the connection between ideas, values, and objects.

My essay contributes to what has been described by Patricia Clough (2007) as "the affective turn" by turning to the question of how we can theorize positive affect and the politics of good feeling. If it is true to say that much recent work in cultural studies has investigated bad feelings (shame, disgust, hate, fear, and so on), it might be useful to take good feeling as our starting point, without presuming that the distinction between good and bad will always hold. Of course, we cannot conflate happiness with good feeling. As Darrin McMahon (2006) has argued in his monumental history of happiness, the association of happiness with feeling is a modern one, in circulation from the eighteenth century onward. If happiness now evokes good feeling, then we can consider how feelings participate in making things good. To explore happiness using the language of affect is to consider the slide between affective and moral economies. In particular, the essay will explore how the family sustains its place as a "happy object" by identifying those who do not reproduce its line as the cause of unhappiness. I call such others "affect aliens": feminist kill-joys, unhappy queers, and melancholic migrants.

Affect and Intentionality

I do not assume there is something called affect that stands apart or has autonomy, as if it corresponds to an object in the world, or even that there is something called affect that can be shared as an object of study. Instead, I would begin with the messiness of the experiential, the unfolding of bodies into worlds, and the drama of contingency, how we are touched by what we are near. It is useful to note that the etymology of "happiness" relates precisely to the question of contingency: it is from the Middle English "hap," suggesting chance. The original meaning of happiness preserves the potential of this "hap" to be good or bad. The hap of happiness then gets translated into something good. Happiness relates to the idea of being lucky, or favored by fortune, or being fortunate. Happiness remains about the contingency of what happens, but this "what" becomes something good. Even this meaning may now seem archaic: we may be more used to thinking of happiness as an effect of what you do, as a reward for hard work, rather than as being "simply" what happens to you. Indeed, Mihály Csíkszentmihályi argues that "happiness is not something that happens. It is not the result of good fortune or random choice, it is not something that money can buy or power command. It does not depend on outside events, but, rather on how we interpret them. Happiness, in fact is a condition that must be prepared for, cultivated and defended privately by each person" (1992, 2). Such a way of understanding happiness could be read as a defense against its contingency. I want to return to the original meaning of happiness as it refocuses our attention on the "worldly" question of happenings.

What is the relation between the "what" in "what happens" and the "what" that makes us happy? Empiricism provides us with a useful way of addressing this question, given its concern with "what's what." Take the work of the seventeenth-century empiricist philosopher John Locke. He argues that what is good is what is "*apt to cause or increase pleasure, or diminish pain in us*" (Locke 1997, 216). We judge something to be good or bad according to how it affects us, whether it gives us pleasure or pain. Locke uses the example of the man who loves grapes. He argues that "when a man declares in autumn, when he is eating them, or in spring, when there are none, that he loves grapes, it is no more, but that the taste of grapes delights him" (215). For Locke happiness (as the highest pleasure) is idiosyncratic: we are made happy by different things, we find different things delightful.

Happiness thus puts us into intimate contact with things. We can be happily affected in the present of an encounter; you are affected positively by something, even if that something does not present itself as an object of consciousness. To be affected in a good way can survive the coming and going of objects. Locke is after all describing the "seasonal" nature of enjoyment. When grapes are out of season, you might recall that you find them delightful, you might look forward to when they will be in season, which means that grapes would sustain their place as a happy object in the event of their absence. However, this does not mean that the objects one recalls as being happy always stay in place. As Locke argues, "Let an alteration of health or constitution destroy the delight of their taste, and he can be said no longer to *love* grapes" (216–17). Bodily transformations might also transform what is experienced as delightful. If our bodies change over time, then the world around us will create different impressions.

To be affected by something is to evaluate that thing. Evaluations are expressed in how bodies turn toward things. To give value to things is to shape what is near us. As Edmund Husserl describes in the second volume of *Ideas*, "Within the joy we are 'intentionally' (with feeling intensions) turned toward the joy-Object as such in the mode of affective 'interest' " (1989, 14). Some things you might say capture our attention. Objects we do things with generate what Husserl might call "our near sphere" or "core sphere" (2002,

149–50), as a sphere of practical action. This sphere is "a sphere of things that I can reach with my kinestheses and which I can experience in an optimal form through seeing, touching etc." (149).

Happiness might play a crucial role in shaping our near sphere, the world that takes shape around us, as a world of familiar things. Objects that give us pleasure take up residence within our bodily horizon. We come to have our likes, which might even establish *what we are like*. The bodily horizon could be redescribed as a horizon of likes. To have our likes means certain things are gathered around us. Of course, we do encounter new things. To be more and less open to new things is to be more or less open to the incorporation of things into our near sphere. Incorporation maybe conditional on liking what we encounter. Those things we do not like we move away from. Away-ness might help establish the edges of our horizon; in rejecting the proximity of certain objects, we define the places that we know we do not wish to go, the things we do not wish to have, touch, taste, hear, feel, see, those things we do not want to keep within reach.

To be affected "in a good way" involves an orientation toward something as being good. Orientations register the proximity of objects, as well as shape what is proximate to the body. Happiness can thus be described as *intentional* in the phenomenological sense (directed toward objects), as well as being *affective* (contact with objects). To bring these arguments together we might say that happiness is an orientation toward the objects we come into contact with. We move toward and away from objects through how we are affected by them. After all, note the doubling of positive affect in Locke's example: we *love* the grapes if they taste *delightful*. To say we love what tastes delightful is not to say that delight causes our love, but that the experience of delight involves a loving orientation toward the object, just as the experience of love registers what is delightful.

To describe happiness as intentional does not mean there is always any simple correspondence between objects and feelings. I suspect that Robin Barrow is right to argue that happiness does not "have an object" the way that other emotions do (1980, 89). Let's stay with Locke's example of the man who loves grapes. Grapes acquire meaning for us, as something we can consume, grapes can be tasted and "have" a taste, even though we cannot know whether my grape taste is the same as yours. The pleasure evoked by the grapes is the pleasure of eating the grapes. But pleasures are not only directed toward objects that can be tasted, that come into a sensuous prox-imity with the flesh of the body, as a meeting of flesh. We can just recall pleasure to experience pleasure, even if these pleasures do not involve exactly the same sensation, even if the impressions of memory are not quite as lively.[1] Pleasure creates an object, even when the object of pleasure appears before us.

We are moved by things. And in being moved, we make things. An object can be affective by virtue of its own location (the object might be *here*, which is *where* I experience this or that affect) and the timing of its appearance (the object might be *now*, which is *when* I experience this or that affect). To experience an object as being affective or sensational is to be directed not only toward an object, but to "whatever" is around that object, which includes what is behind the object, the conditions of its arrival. What is around an object can become happy: for instance, if you receive something delightful in a certain place, then the place itself is invested with happiness, as being "what" good feeling is directed toward. Or if you are given something by somebody whom you love, then the object itself acquires more affective value: just seeing something can make you think of another who gave you that something. If something is close to a happy object then it can become happy by association.

Happiness can generate objects through proximity. Happiness is not then simply about objects, or directed toward objects that are given to consciousness. We have probably all experienced what I would call "unattributed happiness"; you feel happy, not quite knowing why, and the feeling can be catchy, as a kind of brimming over that exceeds what you encounter. It is not that the feeling floats freely; in feeling happy, you direct the feeling to what is close by, smiling for instance, at a person who passes you by. The feeling can also lift or elevate a proximate object, making it happy, which is not to say that the feeling will survive an encounter with anything. It has always interested me that when we become conscious of feeling happy (when the feeling becomes an object of thought), happiness can often recede or become anxious. Happiness can arrive in a moment and be lost by virtue of its recognition. Happiness as a feeling appears very precarious, easily displaced not only by other feelings, but even by happiness itself, by the how of its arrival.

I would suggest that happiness involves a specific kind of intentionality, which I would describe as "end orientated." It is not just that we can be happy *about* something, as a feeling in the present, but some things become happy *for us*, if we imagine they will bring happiness *to us*. Happiness is often described as "what" we aim for, as an endpoint, or even an end in itself. Classically, happiness has been considered as an end rather than as a means.

In *Nicomachean Ethics*, Aristotle describes happiness as the Chief Good, as "that which all things aim at" (1998, 1). Happiness is what we "choose always for its own sake" (8). Anthony Kenny describes how, for Aristotle, happiness "is not just an end, but a perfect end" (1993, 16). The perfect end is the end of all ends, the good that is good always for its own sake.

We don't have to agree with the argument that happiness is the perfect end to understand the implications of what it means for happiness to be thought in these terms. If happiness is the end of all ends, then *all other things become means to happiness.*[2] As Aristotle describes, we choose other things "with a view to happiness, conceiving that through their instrumentality we shall be happy" (1998, 8). Aristotle is not talking here about material or physical objects, but is differentiating between different kinds of goods, between instrumental goods and independent goods. So honor or intellect we choose "with a view to happiness," as being instrumental to happiness, and the realization of the possibility of living a good or virtuous life.

If we think of instrumental goods as objects of happiness then important consequences follow. Things become good, or acquire their value as goods, insofar as they point toward happiness. Objects become "happiness means." Or we could say they become happiness pointers, as if to follow their point would be to find happiness. If objects provide a means for making us happy, then in directing ourselves toward this or that object we are aiming somewhere else: toward a happiness that is presumed to follow. The temporality of this following does matter. Happiness is what would come after. Given this, happiness is directed toward certain objects, which point toward that which is not yet present. When we follow things, we aim for happiness, as if happiness is what we get if we reach certain points.

Sociable Happiness

Certain objects become imbued with positive affect as good objects. After all, objects not only embody good feeling, but are perceived as necessary for a good life. How does the good life get imagined through the proximity of objects? As we know, Locke evokes good feeling through the sensation of taste: "For as pleasant tastes depend not on the things themselves, but their agreeability to this or that palate, wherever there is great variety; so the greatest happiness consists in having those things which produce the greatest pleasure" (1997, 247). Locke locates difference in the mouth. We have different tastes insofar as we have different palates.

We can see here that the apparent chanciness of happiness—the hap of whatever happens—can be qualified. It is not that we just find happy objects anywhere. After all, taste is not simply a matter of chance (whether you or I might happen to like this or that), but is acquired over time. As Pierre Bourdieu showed in his monumental *Distinction*, taste is a very specific bodily orientation that is shaped by "what" is already decided to be good or a higher good. Taste or "manifested preferences" are "the practical affirmation of an inevitable difference" (1984, 56). When people say, "How can you like that?!" they make their judgment against another by refusing to like what another likes, by suggesting that the object in which another invests his or her happiness is unworthy. This affective differentiation is the basis of an essentially moral economy in which moral distinctions of worth are also social distinctions of value, as Beverley Skeggs (2004) has shown us. What "tastes good" can function as a marker of having "good taste."

We can note here the role that habit plays in arguments about happiness. Returning to Aristotle, his model of happiness relies on habituation, "the result of the repeated doing of acts which have a similar or common quality" (1998, vii). The good man will not only have the right habits, but his feelings will also be directed in the right way: "a man is not a good man at all who feels no pleasure in noble actions; just as no one would call that man just who does not feel pleasure in acting justly" (11). Good habits involve work: we have to work on the body such that the body's immediate reactions, how we are impressed upon by the world, will take us in the "right" direction. It is not only that we acquire good taste through habits; rather, the association between objects and affects is preserved through habit. When history becomes second nature (Bourdieu 1977), the affect becomes literal: we assume we experience delight because "it" is delightful.

The circulation of objects is thus the circulation of goods. Objects are sticky because they are already attributed as being good or bad, as being the cause of happiness or unhappiness. This is why the social bond is always rather sensational. Groups cohere around a shared orientation toward some things as being good, treating some things and not others as the cause of delight. If the same objects make us happy—or if we invest in the same objects as being what should make us happy—then we would be orientated or directed in the same way. Consider that the word "promise" comes from the Latin *promissum* "to send forth." The promise of happiness is what sends happiness forth; it is what allows happiness to be out and about. Happy objects are passed around, accumulating positive affective value as social goods.

Is happiness what passes? If we were to say that happiness was passed around, we could be suggesting that happiness is contagious. David Hume's approach to moral emotions in the eighteenth century rested precisely on a contagious model of happiness. He suggests that "others enter into the same humour, and catch the sentiment, by a contagion or natural sympathy" and that cheerfulness is the most communicative of emotions: "the flame spreads through the whole circle; and the most sullenly and remorse are often caught by it" (1975, 250–51; see also Blackman 2008).[3] A number of scholars have recently taken up the idea of affects as contagious, drawing on the work of the psychologist of affect, Silvan Tomkins, among others (Gibbs 2001, Sedgwick 2003, Brennan 2004, Probyn 2005). As Anna Gibbs describes it, "Bodies can catch feelings as easily as catch fire: affect leaps from one body to another, evoking tenderness, inciting shame, igniting rage, exciting fear—in short, communicable affect can inflame nerves and muscles in a conflagration of every conceivable kind of passion" (2001, 1). Thinking of affects as contagious does help us to challenge an "inside out" model of affect by showing how affects pass between bodies, affecting bodily surfaces or even how bodies surface. However, I think the concept of affective contagion tends to underestimate the extent to which affects are contingent (involving the hap of a happening): to be affected by another does not mean that an affect simply passes or "leaps" from one body to another. The affect becomes an object only given the contingency of how we are affected, or only as an effect of how objects are given.

Consider the opening sentence of Teresa Brennan's book, *The Transmission of Affect*: "Is there anyone who has not, at least once, walked into a room and 'felt the atmosphere'?" (2004, 1). Brennan writes very beautifully about the atmosphere "getting into the individual," using what I have called an "outside in" model, which is also very much part of the intellectual history of crowd psychology and the sociology of emotion (Ahmed 2004a, 9). However, later in the introduction she makes an observation that involves a quite different model. Brennan suggests here, "If I feel anxiety when I enter the room, then that will influence what I perceive or receive by way of an 'impression'" (Brennan 2004, 6). I agree. Anxiety is sticky: rather like Velcro, it tends to pick up whatever comes near. Or we could say that anxiety gives us a certain kind of angle on what comes near. Anxiety is, of course, one feeling state among others. If bodies do not arrive in neutral, if we are always in some way or another moody, then what we will receive as an impression will depend on our affective situation. This second argument challenges for me Brennan's first argument about the atmosphere being what is "out there" getting "in": it suggests that how we arrive, how we enter this room or that room, will affect what impressions we receive. After all, to receive is to act. To receive an impression is to make an impression.

So we may walk into the room and "feel the atmosphere," but what we may feel depends on the angle of our arrival. Or we might say that the atmosphere is already angled; it is always felt from a specific point. The pedagogic encounter is full of angles. Many times have I read students as interested or bored, such that the atmosphere seemed one of interest or boredom (and even felt myself to be interesting or boring) only to find students recall the event quite differently. Having read the atmosphere, one can become tense, which in turn affects what happens, how things move along. The moods we arrive with do affect what happens: which is not to say we always keep our moods. Sometimes I arrive heavy with anxiety, and everything that happens makes me feel more anxious, while at other times, things happen that ease the anxiety, making the space itself seem light and energetic. We do not know in advance what will happen given this contingency, given the hap of what happens; we do not know "exactly" what makes things happen in this way and that. Situations are affective given the gap between the impressions we have of others, and the impressions we make on others, all of which are lively.

Think too of experiences of alienation. I have suggested that happiness is attributed to certain objects that circulate as social goods. When we feel pleasure from such objects, we are aligned; we are facing the right way. We become alienated—out of line with an affective community—when we do not experience pleasure from proximity to objects that are already attributed as being good. The gap between the affective value of an object and how we experience an object can involve a range of affects, which are directed by the modes of explanation we offer to fill this gap. If we are disappointed by something that we expected would make us happy, then we generate explanations of why that thing is disappointing. Such explanations can involve an anxious narrative of self-doubt (why am I not made happy by this, what is wrong with me?) or a narrative of rage, where the object that is "supposed" to make us happy is attributed as the cause of disappointment, which can lead to a rage directed toward those that promised us happiness through the elevation of this or that object as being good. We become strangers, or affect aliens, in such moments.

So when happy objects are passed around, it is not necessarily the feeling that passes. To share such objects (or have a share in such objects) would simply mean you would *share an orientation toward those objects as being good*. Take for instance the happy family. The family would be happy not because it causes happiness, and not even because it affects us in a good way, but because we share an orientation toward the family as being good, as being what promises happiness in return for loyalty. Such an orientation shapes what we do; you have to "make" and "keep" the family, which directs how you spend your time, energy, and resources.

To be orientated toward the family does not mean inhabiting the same place. After all, as we know from Locke, pleasures can be idiosyncratic. Families may give one a sense of having "a place at the table" through the conversion of idiosyncratic difference into a happy object: loving "happily" means knowing the peculiarity of a loved other's likes and dislikes. Love becomes an intimacy with what the other likes and is given on condition that such likes do not take us outside a shared horizon. The family provides a shared horizon in which objects circulate, accumulating positive affective value.

What passes through the passing around of happy objects remains an open question. After all, the word "passing" can mean not only "to send over" or "to transmit," but also to transform objects by "a sleight of hand." Like the game Telephone, what passes between proximate bodies might be affective precisely because it deviates and even perverts what was "sent out." Affects involve perversion, and what we can describe as conversion points.

One of my key questions is how such conversions happen, and "who" or "what" gets seen as converting bad feeling into good feeling and good into bad. When I hear people say "the bad feeling is coming from 'this person' or 'that person'" I am never convinced. I am sure a lot of my skepticism is shaped by childhood experiences of being the feminist daughter in a conventional family home. Say your childhood experiences were like mine. Say you are seated at the dinner table with your family, having polite conversations, where only certain things can be brought up. Someone says something you consider offensive. You respond, carefully, perhaps. You say why you think what that person has said is problematic. You might be speaking quietly, but you are beginning to feel "wound up," recognizing with frustration that you are being wound up by someone who is winding you up. However you speak in this situation, you, as the person who speaks up or out as a feminist, will be read as *causing the argument*, as if you just have a point to pick.

Let us take seriously the figure of the feminist kill-joy. Does the feminist kill other people's joy by pointing out moments of sexism? Or does she expose the bad feelings that get hidden, displaced, or negated under public signs of joy? The feminist is an affect alien: she might even kill joy because she refuses to share an orientation toward certain things as being good because she does not find the objects that promise happiness to be quite so promising.

We can place the figure of the feminist kill-joy alongside the figure of the angry black woman, explored so well by black feminist writers such as Audre Lorde (1984) and bell hooks (2000). The angry black woman can be described as a kill-joy; she may even kill feminist joy, for example, by pointing out forms of racism within feminist politics. As Audre Lorde describes: "When women of Color speak out of the anger that laces so many of our contacts with white women, we are often told that we are 'creating a mood of helplessness,' 'preventing white women from getting past guilt,' or 'standing in the way of trusting communication and action'" (1984, 131). The exposure of violence becomes the origin of violence. The black woman must let go of her anger for the white woman to move on.

Some bodies are presumed to be the origin of bad feeling insofar as they disturb the promise of happiness, which I would re-describe as the social pressure to maintain the signs of "getting along." Some bodies become blockage points, points where smooth communication stops. Consider Ama Ata Aidoo's wonderful prose poem, *Our Sister Killjoy*, where the narrator, Sissie, as a black woman, has to work to sustain the comfort of others. On a plane, a white hostess invites her to sit at the back with "her friends," two black people she does not know. She is about to say that she does not know them, and hesitates. "But to have refused to join them would have created an awkward situation, wouldn't it? Considering too that apart from the air hostess's obviously civilized upbringing, she had been trained to see the comfort of all her passengers" (1977, 10).

Power speaks here in this moment of hesitation. Do you go along with it? What does it mean not to go along with it? To create awkwardness is to be read as being awkward. Maintaining public comfort requires that certain bodies "go along with it," to agree to where you are placed. To refuse to be placed would mean to be seen as trouble, as causing discomfort for others. There is a political struggle about how we attribute good and bad feelings, which hesitates around the apparently simple question of who introduces what feelings to whom. Feelings can get stuck to certain bodies in the very way we describe spaces, situations, dramas. And bodies can get stuck depending on what feelings they get associated with.

Promising Directions

I have suggested that when we share happy objects, we are directed in the right way. But how do we find such objects? Returning to Locke, we might describe his story of happiness as quite casual. We happen upon the grapes, and they happen to taste delightful. If others happen upon them in the same way, then we would share an object of delight. But if happiness involves an end-orientated intentionality, then happiness is already associated with some things more than others. We arrive at some things *because* they point us toward happiness.

To explain how objects can be affective before they are encountered, we need to consider the question of affect and causality. In *The Will to Power*, Nietzsche argues that the attribution of causality is retrospective (1968, 294–95). We might assume that the experience of pain is caused by the nail near our foot. But we only notice the nail when we experience an affect. We search for the object: or as Nietzsche describes, "a reason is sought in persons, experiences, etc. for why one feels this way or that" (354). The very tendency to attribute an affect to an object depends upon "closeness of association," where such forms of closeness are already given. We apprehend an object as the cause of an affect (the nail becomes known as a pain-cause, which is not the only way we might apprehend the nail). The proximity of an encounter can survive an encounter. In other words, the proximity between an affect and object is preserved through habit.

Nietzsche helps us to loosen the bond between the object and the affect by recognizing the form of their bond. The object is not what simply causes the feeling, even if we attribute the object as its cause. The object is understood retrospectively as the cause of the feeling. I can just apprehend the nail and I will experience a pain affect, given that the association between the object and the affect is already given. The object becomes a feeling-cause. Once an object is a feeling-cause, it can cause feeling, so that when we feel the feeling we expect to feel we are affirmed. The retrospective causality of affect that Nietzsche describes quickly converts into what we could call an *anticipatory causality*. We can even anticipate an affect without being retrospective insofar as objects might acquire the value of proximities that are not derived from our own experience. For example, with fear-causes, a child might be told not to go near an object in advance of its arrival. Some things more than others are encountered as "to be feared" in the event of proximity, which is exactly how we can understood the anticipatory logic of the discourse of stranger danger (see Ahmed 2000).

So rather than say that what is good is what is apt to cause pleasure, we could say that what is apt to cause pleasure is already judged to be good. This argument is different from Locke's account of loving grapes because they taste delightful: I am suggesting that the judgment about certain objects as being "happy" is already made. Certain objects are attributed as the cause of happiness, which means they already circulate as social goods before we "happen" upon them, which is why we might happen upon them in the first place.

In other words, we anticipate that happiness will follow proximity to this or that object. Anticipations of what an object gives us are also expectations of what we should be given. How is it that we come to expect so much? After all, expectations can make things seem disappointing. If we arrive at objects with an expectation of how we will be affected by them, then this affects how they affect us, even in the moment they fail to live up to our expectations. Happiness is an expectation of what follows, where the expectation differentiates between things, whether or not they exist as objects in the present. For example, a child might be asked to imagine happiness by imagining certain events in the future, such as his or her wedding day, "the happiest day of your life." This is why happiness provides the emotional setting for disappointment even if happiness is not given: we just have to expect happiness from "this or that" for "this and that" to be experienceable as objects of disappointment.

The apparent chanciness of happiness can be qualified: we do not just find happy objects anywhere. As I argued in *Queer Phenomenology* (2006), for a life to count as a good life, it must return the debt of its life by taking on the direction promised as a social good, which means imagining one's futurity in terms of reaching certain points along a life course. The promise of happiness thus directs life in some ways rather than others.

Our expectations come from somewhere. To think the genealogy of expectation is to think about promises and how they point us somewhere, which is "the where" from which we expect so much. We could say that happiness is promised through proximity to certain objects. Objects would not refer only to physical or material things, but also to anything that we imagine might lead us to happiness, including objects in the sense of values, practice, and styles, as well as aspirations. Doing x as well as having x might be what promises us happiness. The promise of happiness takes this form: that if you have this or have that or do this or do that, then happiness is what follows.

Happiness is not only promised by certain objects, it is also what we promise to give to others as an expression of love. I am especially interested in the speech act, "I just want you to be happy." What does it mean to want "just" happiness? What does it mean for a parent to say this to a child? In a way, the desire for the child's happiness seems to offer a certain kind of freedom, as if to say: "I don't want you to be this, or to do that; I just want you to be or to do 'whatever' makes you happy." You could say that the "whatever" seems to release us from the obligation of the "what." The desire for the child's happiness seems to offer the freedom of a certain indifference to the content of a future decision.

Take the psychic drama of the queer child. You could say that the queer child is an unhappy object for many parents. In some parental responses to the child coming out, this unhappiness is not so much expressed as being unhappy about the child being queer, but about *being unhappy about the child being unhappy*. Queer fiction is full of such moments, as in the following exchange that takes place in the lesbian novel *Annie on My Mind* (1982) by Nancy Garden:

> "Lisa," my father said, "I told you I'd support you and I will . . . But honey . . . well, maybe it's just that I love your mother so much that I have to say to you I've never thought gay people can be very happy—no children for one thing, no real family life. Honey, you are probably going to be a very good architect—but I want you to be happy in other ways, too, as your mother is, to have a husband and children. I know you can do both. . . ." I am happy, I tried to tell him with my eyes. I'm happy with Annie; she and my work are all I'll ever need; she's happy too—we both were until this happened. (1982, 191)

The father makes an act of identification with an imagined future of necessary and inevitable unhappiness. Such an identification through grief about what the child will lose reminds us that the queer life is already constructed as unhappy, as a life without those "things" that would make you happy (husband, children). The desire for the child's happiness is far from indifferent. The speech act "I just want you to be happy" can be directive at the very point of its imagined indifference.

For the daughter, it is only the eyes that can speak; and they try to tell an alternative story about happiness and unhappiness. In her response, she claims happiness, for sure. She is happy "*with* Annie," which is to say that she is happy with *this* relationship and *this* life that it will commit her to. She says we were happy "until" this happened, where the "until" marks the moment when the father speaks his disapproval. The unhappy queer is here the queer who is judged to be unhappy. The father's speech act creates the very affective state of unhappiness that is imagined to be the inevitable consequence of the daughter's decision. When "this" happens, unhappiness does follow.

The social struggle within families involves contradictory attributions of "what" makes people unhappy. So in situations where feelings are shared or are in common (we might all be unhappy), antagonism is produced through the very explanation of that unhappiness, which attributes the causes of bad feeling differently (which is the point of conversion), which in turn locates responsibility for the situation in different places. The father is unhappy as he thinks the daughter will be unhappy if she is queer. The daughter is unhappy as the father is unhappy with her being queer. The father witnesses the daughter's unhappiness as a sign of the truth of his position: that she will be unhappy because she is queer. The happy queer becomes unhappy at this point. In other words, the unhappy queer is made unhappy by the world that reads queers as unhappy. And clearly the family can only be maintained as a happy object, as being what is anticipated to cause happiness, by making the unhappiness of the queer child the point.

We can turn to another novel, *Babyji* by Abha Dawesar (2005). Set in India, this novel is written from the point of view of Anamika Sharma, a fun, smart, spirited, and sexy teenager who seduces three women: an older divorcee she names India, a servant girl called Rani, and her school friend Sheela. In this book, we do not notice happiness being used as the reason why Anamika should give up her desire. Instead, the first use of happiness as a speech act is of a rather queer nature: " 'I want to make you happy,' I said as I was leaving. 'You do make me happy,' India said. 'No, I don't mean that way. I mean in bed' " (31). Anamika separates her own desire to make her lover happy from "that way," from the ordinary way, perhaps, that people desire to make others happy by wanting to give them a good life. Instead she wants to make India happy "in bed," to be the cause of her pleasure. Anamika refuses to give happiness the power to secure a specific image of what would count as a good life.

Babyji is certainly about the perverse potential of pleasure. This is not to say that Anamika does not have to rebel or does not get into trouble. The trouble centers on the relationship between the father and the queer daughter and again turns to the question of happiness. Anamika says to her father: "You like tea, I like coffee. I want to be a physicist, and Vidur wants to join the army. I don't want to get married, and mom did. How can the same formula make us all happy?," to which he replies, "What do you mean you don't want to get married?" (177). Anamika recognizes what I have called the idiosyncratic nature of happy object choices; different people are made happy by different things, we have a diversity of likes and dislikes, including marriage as one happy object choice among others. The inclusion of marriage as something that one might or might not like is picked up by the father, turning queer desire into a question that interrupts the flow of the conversation.

The exchange shows us how object choices are not equivalent, how some choices such as marrying or not marrying are not simply presentable as idiosyncratic likes or dislikes, as they take us beyond the horizon of intimacy, in which those likes can gather as a shared form. Although the novel might seem to articulate a queer liberalism, whereby the queer subject is free to be happy in her own way, it evokes the limits of that liberalism by showing how the conflation of marriage with the good life is maintained as the response to queer deviation. While the queer might happily go beyond marriage, or refuse to place her hope for happiness in the reproduction of the family, it does not follow that the queer will be promised happiness in return. Although we can live without the promise of happiness, and can do so "happily," we live with the consequences of being a cause of unhappiness for others.

Happiness, Freedom, Injury

The speech act, "I just want you to be happy" protects the happy family by locating the causes of unhappiness in the failure to reproduce its line. This is not to say that happy families only locate happiness in reproduction. I want to explore how the family can sustain its place as a happy object by creating the very illusion that we are free to deviate from its line. Let's take the film *Bend It Like Beckham* (2002), a happy "feel good" film about a migrant family. One of the most striking aspects is how the conflict or obstacle of the film is resolved through this speech act, addressed from father to daughter, that takes the approximate form: "I just want you to be happy." How does this speech act direct the narrative?

To answer this question, we need to describe the conflict of the film, or the obstacle to the happy ending. The film depicts generational conflict within a migrant Indian Sikh family living in Hounslow, London. Jess, one of the daughters, is good at football. Her idea of happiness would be to bend it like Beckham, which requires that she bend the rules about what Indian girls can do. Her parents want her to be a good Indian girl, especially as their other daughter, Pinkie, is about to get married. The happy occasion of marriage requires the family to be imagined in a certain way, as reproducing its inheritance. The generational conflict between parents and daughter is also represented as a conflict between the demands of cultures: as Jess says, "Anyone can cook Alo Gobi but who can bend the ball like Beckham?" This contrast sets up "cooking Alo Gobi" as commonplace and customary, against an alternative world of celebrity, individualism, and talent.

It is possible to read the film by putting this question of cultural difference to one side. We could read the story as being about the rebellion of the daughter, and an attempt to give validation to her re-scripting of what it means to have a good life. We might cheer for Jess as she "scores" and finds happiness somewhere other than where she is expected to find it. We would be happy about her freedom and her refusal of the demand to be a happy housewife. We might applaud this film as showing the happiness that can follow when you leave your parents' expectations behind and follow less well-trodden paths. Yet, of course, such a reading would fall short. It would not offer a reading of "where" the happiness of this image of freedom takes us.

The climactic moment of the film is when the final of the football tournament coincides with Pinkie's wedding. The coincidence matters: Jess cannot be at both events at once. Unhappiness is used to show how Jess is "out of place" in the wedding. She is unhappy as she is not where she wants to be; she wants to be at the football match. We want her to be there too and are encouraged to identify with the injustice of being held back. At this point, the point of Jess's depression, her friend Tony intervenes and says she should go. Jess replies, "I can't. Look how happy they are, Tony. I don't want to ruin it for them." In this moment, Jess accepts her own unhappiness by identifying with the happiness of her parents: she puts her own desire for happiness to one side. But her father overhears her, and says, "Pinkie is so happy and you look like you have come to your father's funeral . . . if this is the only way I am going to see you smiling on your sister's wedding day then go now. But when you come back, I want to see you happy on the video." Jess's father lets her go because he wants to see her happy, which also means he wants to see others witness the family as being happy, as being what causes happiness.

Jess's father cannot be indifferent to his daughter's unhappiness: later he says to his wife, "Maybe you could handle her long face, I could not." At one level, this desire for the daughter's happiness involves a form of indifference

Jess and Joe at a "conversion point" (video still from *Bend It Like Beckham*).

to the "where" that she goes. However, from the point of view of the film, the desire for happiness is far from indifferent: indeed, the film works partly by "directing" the apparent indifference of this gift of freedom. After all, this moment is when the father "switches" from a desire that is out of line with the happy object of the film (not wanting Jess to play) to being in line (letting her go), which in turn is what allows the film's happy ending. Importantly, the happy ending is about the coincidence of happy objects. The daughters are happy (they are living the lives they wish to lead), the parents are happy (as their daughters are happy), and we are happy (as they are happy). Good feeling involves these "points" of alignment. We could say positive affect is what sutures the film, resolving the generational and cultural split: as soon as Jess is allowed to join the football game, the two worlds "come together" in a shared moment of enjoyment. While the happy objects are different from the point of view of the daughters (football, marriage) they allow us to arrive at the same point.

And yet, the film does not give equal value to the objects in which good feelings come to reside. Jess's happiness is contrasted to that of her sister, Pinkie, who is ridiculed throughout the film as not only wanting less, but as being less in the direction of her want. Pinkie asks Jess why she does not want "this." Jess does not say that she wants something different; she says it is because she wants something "more." That word "more" lingers, and frames the ending of the film, which gives us "flashes" of an imagined future (pregnancy for Pinkie, photos of Jess on her sports team, her love for her football coach, Joe, her friendship with Jules). During the sequence of shots as Jess gets ready to join the football final, the camera pans up to show an airplane. Airplanes are everywhere in this film, as they often are in diasporic films. In *Bend It Like Beckham*, they matter as technologies of flight, signifying what goes up and away. Happiness in the film is promised by what goes "up and away." The desire to play football, to join the national game, is read as leaving a certain world behind. Through the juxtaposition of the daughter's happy objects, the film suggests that this desire gives a better return.

In reading the "directed" nature of narratives of freedom, we need in part to consider how the film relates to wider discourses of the public good. The film locates the "pressure point" in the migrant family that pressures Jess to live a life she does not want to live. And yet, many migrant individuals and families are under pressure to integrate, where integration is a key term for what they now call in the United Kingdom "good race relations." Although integration is not defined as "leaving your culture behind" (at least not officially), it is unevenly distributed, as a demand that new or would-be citizens embrace a common culture that is already given. In this context, the immigrant daughter who identifies with the national game is a national ideal; the "happy" daughter who deviates from family convention becomes a sign of the promise of integration. *The unconventional daughter of the migrant family may even provide a conventional form of social hope.*

It is the father who is represented as the cause of unhappiness. By identifying with the daughter's happiness, we also identify the cause of unhappiness as his unhappiness. The point of the film is thus to convert the father. What are the conversion points in the film? We can focus here on two speeches made by Jess's father: the first takes place early on in the film, and the second at the end:

When I was a teenager in Nairobi, I was the best fast bowler in our school. Our team even won the East African cup. But when I came to this country, nothing. And these bloody gora in the club house made fun of my turban and set me off packing. . . . She will only end up disappointed like me.

When those bloody English cricket players threw me out of their club like a dog, I never complained. On the contrary, I vowed that I would never play again. Who suffered? Me. But I don't want Jess to suffer. I don't want her to make the same mistakes her father made, accepting life, accepting situations. I want her to fight. And I want her to win.

In the first speech, the father says she *should not play* in order not to suffer like him. In the second, he says she *should play* in order not to suffer like him. The desire implicit in both speech acts is the avoidance of the daughter's suffering, which is expressed in terms of the desire not to repeat his own. I would argue that the father is represented in the first speech as melancholic: as refusing to let go of his suffering, as incorporating the very object of his own loss. His refusal to let Jess go is readable as a symptom of melancholia: as a stubborn attachment to his own injury, or as a form of self-harm (as he says, "Who suffered? Me"). I would argue that the second speech suggests that the refusal to play a national game is the "truth" behind the migrant's suffering: the migrant suffers because he or she does not play the game, where not playing is read as a form of self-exclusion. For Jess to be happy he lets her be included, narrated as a form of letting go. By implication, not only is he letting her go, he is also letting go of his own suffering, the unhappiness caused by accepting racism, as the "point" of his exclusion.

The figure of the melancholic migrant is a familiar one in contemporary race politics. The melancholic migrant holds onto the unhappy objects of differences, such as the turban, or at least the memory of being teased about the turban, which ties it to a history of racism. Such differences become sore points or blockage points, where the smooth passage of communication stops. The melancholic migrant is the one who is not only stubbornly attached to difference, but who insists on speaking about racism, where such speech is heard as laboring over sore points. The duty of the migrant is to let go of the pain of racism by letting go of racism as a way of understanding that pain. The melancholic migrant's fixation with injury is read not only as an obstacle to his or her own happiness, but also to the happiness of the generation to come, and to national happiness. This figure may even quickly convert in the national imaginary to what I have called the "could-be-terrorist" (Ahmed 2004a). His anger, pain, and misery (all understood as forms of bad faith insofar as they won't let go of something that is presumed to be already gone) become "our terror."

To avoid such a terrifying endpoint, the duty of the migrant is to attach to a different, happier object, one that can bring good fortune, such as the national game. The film ends with the fortune of this reattachment. Jess goes to America to take up her dream of becoming a professional football player, to a land that makes the pursuit of happiness an originary goal. This reattachment is narrated as moving beyond the unhappy scripts of racism. We should note here that the father's experience of being excluded from the national game is repeated in Jess's own encounter with racism on the football pitch (she is called a "Paki"), which leads to the injustice of her being sent off. In this case, however, Jess's anger and hurt do not stick. She lets go of her suffering. How does she let go? When she says to Joe, "You don't know what it feels like," he replies, "Of course I know how it feels like, I'm Irish." It is this act of identification with suffering that brings Jess back into the national game (as if to say, "we all suffer, it is not just you"). The film suggests that whether racism hurts depends upon individual choice and capacity: we can let go of racism as "something" that happens, a capacity that is attributed to skill (if you are good enough, you will get by), as well as the proximate gift of empathy, where the hurt of racism is reimagined as a common ground.

The love story between Jess and Joe offers another point of reattachment. The acceptance of interracial heterosexual love is a conventional narrative of reconciliation, as if love can overcome past antagonism and create what I would call "hybrid familiality": *white with color, white with another.* Such fantasies of proximity are premised on the following belief: *if only we could be closer, we would be as one.* Proximity becomes a promise: the happiness of the film is the promise of "the one," as if giving love to the white man would allow us to have a share in this promise.

In the film, we end with the happy family: a hybrid family, where difference is reconciled. The family of the film could be understood as the multicultural nation, reimagined as a space of peace and love, where "fellow feeling" is translated into a feeling of fellowship. Given this, the father in the film originally occupies the place of the bad child, the one who must be taught to overcome bad feeling, by reproducing the family line. Just take the final scene of the film, which is a cricket scene. As we know, cricket is an unhappy object in the film, associated with the suffering of racism. Jess's father is batting. Joe, in the foreground, is bowling. He smiles as he approaches us. He turns around, bowls, and gets the father out. In a playful scene, Joe then celebrates and his body mimics that of a plane, in a classic football gesture. As I have suggested, planes are happy objects in the film, associated with flight, with moving up and away. By mimicking the plane, Joe becomes the agent that converts bad feeling (unhappy racism) into good feeling (multicultural happiness). It is the white man who enables the father to let go of his injury about racism and to play cricket again. It is the white man who brings the suffering migrant back into the national fold. *His body is our conversion point.*

Beyond the Affirmative Gesture

We need to question what is appealing in the appeal to happiness and good feeling. And yet, some critics suggest that we have paid too much attention to melancholia, suffering, and injury and that we need to be more affirmative. Rosi Braidotti, for example, suggests that the focus on negativity has become a problem within feminism, calling for a more affirmative feminism. She offers a bleak reading of bleakness: "I actively yearn for a more joyful and empowering concept of desire and for a political economy that foregrounds positivity, not gloom" (2002, 57).

What concerns me is how much this affirmative turn actually depends on the very distinction between good and bad feelings that presumes that bad feelings are backward and conservative and good feelings are forward and progressive. Bad feelings are seen as orientated toward the past, as a kind of stubbornness that "stops" the subject from embracing the future. Good feelings are associated here with moving up and getting out. I would argue that it is the very assumption that good feelings are open and bad feelings are closed that allows historical forms of injustice to disappear. The demand that we be affirmative makes those histories disappear by reading them as a form of melancholia (as if you hold onto something that is already gone). These histories have not gone: we would be letting go of that which persists in the present. To let go would be to keep those histories present.

I am not saying that feminist, anti-racist, and queer politics do not have anything to say about happiness other than to point to its unhappy effects. I think it is the very exposure of these unhappy effects that is affirmative, that gives us an alternative set of imaginings of what might count as a good or better life. If injustice does have unhappy effects, then the story does not end there. Unhappiness is not our endpoint. If anything, the experience of being alienated from the affective promise of happy objects gets us somewhere. Affect aliens can do things, for sure, by refusing to put bad feelings to one side in the hope that we can "just get along." A concern with histories that hurt is not then a backward orientation: to move on, you must make this return. If anything we might want to reread melancholic subjects, the ones who refuse to let go of suffering, who are even prepared to kill some forms of joy, as an alternative model of the social good.

Notes

1   See David Hume's discussion of the relationship between ideas and impressions in *A Treatise of Human Nature* (1985, 49–55). Memory and imagination are described as the two faculties in which we "repeat our impressions" (56), involving the connection or association between ideas in the form of contiguity and resemblance. Hume offers a rich reflection on what we might call empirical psychology and the habits of sense making. See Deleuze's (1991) excellent analysis of Hume's contribution. Also note how much the Freudian concern with displacement and condensation and the Lacanian concern with metaphor and metonymy are consistent with Hume's associationism. English empiricism and psychoanalysis could be described as potentially productive bedfellows.

2   The way in which a teleological model of happiness makes "all other things" "happiness means" is explicit in John Stuart Mill's utilitarianism. As he puts it, "The utilitarian doctrine is that happiness is desirable and the only thing desirable, as an end; *all other things being only desirable as means to that end*" (1906, 52, emphasis added).

3   David Hume's model of affective contagion contrasts in interesting ways with Adam Smith's *The Theory of Moral Sentiments* (2000). Both stress the importance of sympathy or compassion, as what Smith calls "fellow-feeling," where you feel with others and are affected by how others feel. In the case of happiness, to be sympathetic would be to feel happy when another is happy. Sympathy is expressed by *returning feeling with like feeling*. In Smith's model, sympathy is more explicitly conditional: you enter into another's happiness if you agree with it, in the sense that you think his or her happiness is appropriate and is expressed appropriately. As he describes quite dramatically, "it gives us the spleen, on the other hand, to see another too happy, or too much elevated, as we call it, with any little piece of good fortune. We are *disobliged even with his joy*; and, because we cannot go along with it, call it levity and folly" (2000, 13, emphasis added). So for Smith, to be affected sympathetically is dependent on whether emotions "appear to this last, just and proper, and suitable to their objects" (14). I would also argue that sharing emotion involves conditional judgment. But rather than saying that we share happiness if we agree with its object (which makes the agreement secondary), I would say that to share in the happiness of others is how we come to have a direction toward something, which is *already* an agreement that the object is appropriate. To get along, in other words, is to share a direction.

The Political Ontology of Threat

Brian Massumi

Future Superlative

"The next pandemic," screams a 2005 headline in Quebec's re-putedly most sober newspaper, "does not exist yet." Beneath, in a supersize, full-color portrait, deceptively innocent-looking, peers a chicken. "The threat, however, could not be more real" (Soucy 2005).

Observation: We live in times when what has not happened qualifies as front-page news.

Human-adapted avian flu is just one of many nonexistent entities that has come from the future to fill our present with menace. We live in times when what is yet to occur not only climbs to the top of the news but periodically takes blaring precedence over what has actually happened. Yesterday was once the mainstay of the journalist's stock-in-trade. Today it may pale in the glare of tomorrow's news. "I think we agree," prophesied a future president on the cusp of a millennium whose arrival was overshadowed by a nonexistent bug of an-other color, "the past is over."[1]

Question: How could the nonexistence of what has not hap-pened be *more* real than what is now observably over and done with?

Threat is from the future. It is what might come next. Its eventual location and ultimate extent are undefined. Its nature is open-ended. It is not just that it is not: it is not in a way that is never over. We can never be done with it. Even if a clear and present danger materializes in the present, it is still not over. There is always the nagging potential of the next after being even worse, and of a still worse next again after that. The uncertainty of the potential next is never consumed in any given event. There is always a remainder of uncertainty, an unconsummated surplus of danger. The present is shadowed by a remaindered surplus of indeterminate potential for a next event running forward back to the future, self-renewing.

Self-renewing menace potential is the future reality of threat. It could not be more real. Its run of futurity contains so much more, potentially, than anything that has already actually happened. Threat is not real in spite of its nonexistence. It is superlatively real, because of it.

Observation: The future of threat is forever.

Futures Past

Rewind: It is the summer of 2004. George W. Bush is campaigning for a second term as president. He is on the defensive about the war in Iraq, as pressure mounts for him to admit that the reasons his administration set forth to justify the invasion, in particular the allegation that Saddam Hussein possessed an arsenal of weapons of mass destruction, had no basis in fact. For the first time he admits what had been known all along to those who cared to examine the evidence. He goes on to argue that the lack of factual basis for the invasion does not mean that he made the wrong decision. "Although we have not found stockpiles of weapons, I believe we were right to go into Iraq. America is safer today because we did. We removed a declared enemy of America, who had the capacity of producing weapons of mass destruction, and could have passed that capability to terrorists bent on acquiring them" (Schmitt and Stevenson 2004, A9).

The invasion was right because *in the past there was a future threat*. You cannot erase a "fact" like that. Just because the menace potential never became a clear and present danger doesn't mean that it wasn't there, all the more real for being nonexistent. The superlative futurity of unactualized threat feeds forward from the past, in a chicken run to the future past every intervening present. The threat *will have* been real for all eternity.

It will have been real because it was *felt* to be real. Whether the danger was existent or not, the menace was felt in the form of fear. What is not actually real can be felt into being. Threat does have an actual mode of existence: fear, as foreshadowing. Threat has an impending reality in the present. This actual reality is affective.

Fear is the anticipatory reality in the present of a threatening future. It is the felt reality of the nonexistent, loomingly present as the *affective fact* of the matter.

Once a nonexistent reality, always a nonexistent reality. A past anticipation is still an anticipation, and it will remain having been an anticipation for all of time. A threat that does not materialize is not false. It has all the affective reality of a past future, truly felt. The future of the threat is not falsified. It is deferred. The case remains forever open. The futurity doesn't stay in the past where its feeling emerged. It feeds forward through time. It runs an endless loop forward from its point of emergence in the past present, whose future it remains. Threat passes through linear time, but does not belong to it. It belongs to the nonlinear circuit of the always will have been.

Proposition: If we feel a threat, there was a threat. Threat is affectively self-causing.

Corollary: If we feel a threat, such that there was a threat, then there always will have been a threat. Threat is once and for all, in the nonlinear time of its own causing.

Double Conditional

The felt reality of threat legitimates preemptive action, once and for all. Any action taken to preempt a threat from emerging into a clear and present danger is legitimated by the affective fact of fear, actual facts aside.[2] Preemptive action will always have been right. This circularity is not a failure of logic. It is a different logic, operating on the same affective register as threat's self-causing.

The logic of affectively legitimated fact is in the conditional: Bush did what he did because Saddam could have done what he didn't do. Bush's argument doesn't really do justice to the logic of preemption. Saddam didn't actually even have the "capacity," and that poses no problem for preemptive logic, which is based on a *double conditional*. "The Pentagon neocons argued that the CIA overemphasized what Saddam *could do* instead of stressing *what he would do if he could*" (Dorrien 2004, 186).

Bush was being modest in a CIA kind of way. From the prevailing neoconservative perspective, he was understating why he was right. He was right even though Saddam did *not* have the capacity, because Saddam "would have if he could have." The case remains open. At any moment in the future, he could have acquired the means, and as soon as he could, he would. Would have, could have: double conditional.

Present threat is logically recessive, in a step-by-step regress from the certainty of actual fact. The actual fact would have been: Saddam Hussein has WMD. The first step back from that is: he had the capacity to have WMD. The next step is: he didn't have the capacity, but he still would have if he could have. The recessive assertion that he "would have" is based on an assumption about character and intent that cannot be empirically grounded with any certainty. But it is proffered with certainty. It carries a certainty, underivable from actual fact, which it owes to the affective fact of the matter. The felt reality of the threat is so superlatively real that it translates into a felt certainty about the world, even in the absence of other grounding for it in the observable world. The assertion has the felt certainty of a "gut feeling." Gut feeling was proudly and publicly embraced by Bush as his peak decision-making process in the lead-up to the war in Iraq and beyond.[3]

Preemption's logical regress from actual fact makes for a disjointedness between its legitimating discourse and the objective content of the present context, which its affirmations ostensibly reference. Its receding from actual fact produces a logical disjunction between the threat and the observable present. A logical gap opens in the present through which the reality of threat slips to rejoin its deferral to the future. Through the logical hatch of the double conditional, threat makes a runaround through the present back toward its self-causing futurity.

The affect-driven logic of the would-have/could-have is what discursively ensures that the actual facts will always remain an open case, for all pre-emptive intents and purposes. It is what saves threat from having to materialize as a clear and present danger—or even an emergent danger—in order to command action. The object of preemptive power, according to the explicit doctrine, is "not yet fully emergent *threat*." The doctrine doesn't say emergent danger—let alone clear and present danger.[4] And again (and again), when threat strikes it is once and for all.

Problem: How can preemptive politics maintain its political legitimacy given that it grounds itself in the actual ungroundedness of affective fact? Would not pointing out the actual facts be enough to make it crumble?

Observation: Bush won his reelection.

Right Again

Fast forward: It is one year later, the summer of 2005. For the first time in the polls, more than two years after the invasion, a majority of Americans oppose the war in Iraq. The legitimation of preemptive action—or that particular action at any rate—is faltering. The downturn had begun long after the lack of actual facts behind the decision to invade had become common knowledge. It began with the counteraffective strike that came with the release and widespread circulation of shocking images of torture at Abu Ghraib.[5] It was only then that the lack of actual-factual basis for the invasion began to resonate with a voting public rendered less receptive, for the moment, to the logic of preemption by the affective countercoup of torture graphically revealed. Bush makes a valiant attempt to kick-start the logic of preemption again. He delivers a major radio address to the nation explaining his refusal to withdraw. He deploys an argument that he will continue to use for at least the next two years.[6]

"Some may agree," he says, "with my decision to remove Saddam Hussein from power, but all of us can agree that the world's terrorists have now made Iraq a central front in the war on terror" (Bush 2005). The presence of terrorist links between Al Qaeda and Saddam Hussein had been the second major argument, behind wmd, originally used to justify the invasion. The Bush administration had already been obliged to withdraw the assertion long before this speech. The fact that Al Qaeda had *not* been in Iraq at the time of the invasion now becomes the reason it was right to invade. The fact that they are there now just goes to prove that if they could have been there then, they would have.

The could-have/would-have logic works both ways. If the threat does not materialize, it still always would have if it could have. If the threat does materialize, then it just goes to show that the future potential for what happened had really been there in the past. In this case, the preemptive action is retroactively legitimated by future actual facts.

Bush does not point out that the reason Al Qaeda is now in Iraq is *because of* the invasion that was mounted to keep it out of Iraq, that the preemptive action actually *brought about* the result it was meant to fight.

Observation: Preemptive action can produce the object toward which its power is applied, and it can do so without contradicting its own logic, and without necessarily undermining its legitimation.

Proposition: Because it operates on an affective register and inhabits a nonlinear time operating recursively between the present and the future, preemptive logic is not subject to the same rules of noncontradiction as normative logic, which privileges a linear causality from the past to the present and is reluctant to attribute an effective reality to futurity.

Flour Attack

Pause: Around the same time, a state of emergency is called at the Montreal airport. There has been a "toxic substance alert." White powder has been seen leaking from a suitcase. The actual facts of the case are still two weeks in the future after the necessary lab work will have been done. Action, however, cannot wait. It *could be* anthrax. That potential threat must be acted upon. The airport is closed. Highways to the airport are closed. Men in white decontamination suits descend. SWAT teams and police personnel pour in. Terrified passengers are sequestered in the terminal. News helicopters hover overhead. Live coverage takes over the local airwaves. All of the actions that *would be* taken if the powder were anthrax are taken preemptively. The dramatic rapid response of the public security apparatus causes a major disruption of commerce and circulation. The site is quickly decontaminated, and life returns to normal.

Observations: Preemptive power washes back from the battlefield onto the domestic front (even in countries not militarily involved). On the domestic front, its would-have/could-have logic takes a specific form associated with public security procedures involving the signaling of alert. The alert, set off at the slightest *sign* of potential threat, triggers immediate action. The actions set in motion in response to the threat are of the same kind and bring on many of the same effects as would have accompanied an actual danger. The preemptive measures cause the disruption to the economy and everyday life that terrorist attacks are designed to produce beyond their immediate impact.

Proposition: Defensive preemptive action in its own way is as capable as offensive preemptive action of producing what it fights. Together with the increasing speed and vigor of defensive action, this blurs the boundaries between defense and offense, between domestic security and military action.

Two weeks later, the powder is identified. It is flour. News articles following up on the story after the discovery of no toxic substance continue to refer to the incident as a "toxic substance alert."[7] No one refers to the incident as a "flour alert." The incident is left carrying an affective dusting of white-powdered terror. Flour has been implicated. It is tainted with the fear of anthrax, guilty by association for displaying the threatening qualities of whiteness and powderiness. In preemptively logical terms, the incident *was* a toxic substance alert—not because the substance was toxic, but because the *alert* was for a potential toxic substance.

Observations: An alarm may determine the generic identity of a potential threat, without specifically determining the actual identity of the objects involved. This declares what will later prove actually to have been innocent objects (or in other circumstances, persons) as officially threatening for the duration of the alert, based on their displaying material qualities answering to the generic description. Afterward, they remain tainted by their affective involvement in the incident, for they really always will have been associated with the fear produced by the alert, and fear feeds threat forward.

Proposition: The affective reality of threat is contagious.

Proposition: Threat is capable of overlaying its own conditional determination upon an objective situation through the mechanism of alarm. The two determinations, threatening and objective, coexist. However, the threat-determined would-be and could-be takes public precedence due to its operating in the more compelling, future-oriented, and affective register. This gives it superior political presence and potential.[8]

The incident comes to a close with follow-up articles about improvements in government safety procedure as a result of the toxic substance alert. The false alert is presented in the news media as having palpably increased the security of airplane passengers ("ADM" 2005).

Proposition: The security that preemption is explicitly meant to produce is predicated on its tacitly producing what it is meant to avoid: preemptive security is predicated on a production of insecurity to which it itself contributes. Preemption thus positively contributes to producing the conditions for its own exercise. It does this by capturing for its own operation the self-causative power native to the threat-potential that it takes as its object.

Specifically Imprecise

Rewind: New York City, October 2005. Mayor Michael Bloomberg puts the city on alert, citing a chillingly specific threat to bomb the metropolitan subway and bus system simultaneously at "as many as nineteen" different locations. "This is the first time we have had a threat with this level of specificity," he says at a televised news conference (Bajaj 2005). The FBI announces that arrests related to the plot have already been made in Iraq, based on "reliable" information. "Classified operations have already partially disrupted this threat." Although offensive preemptive action has already been taken, there is still felt to be a menacing remainder of threat. Preemptive action is retaken, this time defensively. Transit passengers on the home front are briefed on security procedures and asked to contribute to the city's surveillance by keeping an eye out for suspicious persons and objects. A suspicious bottle, which could have been filled with hazardous material, is sighted at Penn Station. It is isolated and destroyed (if it could have, it would have . . .).

The next day, the Homeland Security Department weighs in to say that "the intelligence community has been able to determine that there are very serious doubts about the credibility of this specific threat." The threat had been "very, very specific. It had specific time, specific object and modality," the city police commissioner assured. "So, you know, we had to do what we did. . . . I believe in the short term we'll have a much better sense of whether or not this has, you know, real substance to it" (Weissenstein 2005).

A threat can have specificity and lead to decisive preemptive actions with a corresponding level of specificity without having "real substance" or objective "credibility." The preemptive actions taken in response to the threat are still logically and politically correct if they were commensurate with the urgency of the threat, if not with the urgency of the actual situation. They will still have been justified even if the information proves objectively imprecise and there was no actual danger.[9]

Proposition: An alert is not a referential statement under obligation to correspond with precision to an objective state of affairs. The measure of its correctness is the immediacy and specificity of the preemptive actions it automatically triggers. The value of the alert is measured by its *performance*. Rather than referential truth-value, it has performative *threat-value*. More than any correspondence between its semantic content and an objective referent, it is the performed commensurability of the threat and the triggered actions that qualifies the alert as correct. Its correctness, felt as a question of collective security, is directly political. The threat-alert, as *sign of* danger, is subject to different criteria of reliability and effectiveness than referential language *about* danger.

Proposition: Threat has no actual referent.

Corollary: Preemption is a mode of power that takes threat, which has no actual referent, as its object. When the politics of preemption captures threat's potential for its own operation, it forgoes having an actual object of power.

"The 9–11 Generation"

Fast forward on rewind: It is now the lead-up to the U.S. presidential elections of 2008. Ex-mayor Rudolph Giuliani of New York is revving up his campaign by looping back to 9–11, toward future preemptive action. He writes an article in *Foreign Affairs* taking a hardline neoconservative position in continuity with Defense Secretary Donald Rumsfeld's first-term Bush administration policies. The article argues that the attacks of 9–11 inaugurated a new world-historical era. The fall of the Twin Towers was an originating moment of what he calls, following Rumsfeld, the "Long War" against terrorism, in much the same way that the building of the Berlin Wall inaugurated the cold war, according to Giuliani. "We are all members of the 9–11 generation," he declares (Giuliani 2007).

September 11 was an actual event that killed thousands and put more thousands of lives in immediate danger. People were agape in shock at the enormity of it. The immediate shock gave way to lingering fear, relaying the danger into a remainder of surplus threat. September 11 was an excess-threat-generating actual event that has perhaps done more than any other threat-o-genic source to legitimate preemptive politics. It was continually cited by the Bush administration to reinvoke potential threat for use in legitimating policy. Candidates of both parties in the race to succeed Bush also invoked it regularly in order to establish their own national security credentials.[10] And yet . . .

Question: Can the threat-potential fueling preemptive politics have an identifiable origin?

There were precursors to 9–11. The "war on terror" was declared by President Richard Nixon in the early 1970s. Between that time and September 2001, there were any number of attacks characterized as terrorist, including the earlier, less successful, bombing of the World Trade Center in 1993. Since 9–11 there have been further attacks. If the historical and geographical parameters are enlarged, attacks that could be qualified as "terrorist" stretch indefinitely.

Observation: 9–11 belongs to an *iterative series* of allied events whose boundaries are indefinite.

An event where threat materializes as a clear and present danger extrudes a surplus-remainder of threat-potential that can contaminate new objects, persons, and contexts through the joint mechanisms of the double conditional and the objective imprecision of the specificity of threat. Threat's self-causing proliferates. Threat alerts, performatively signed threat-events, are quick to form their own iterative series. These series tend to proliferate robustly thanks to the suppleness and compellingness of the affective logic generating them. As an indication, according to the Homeland Security Department, in the United States alone in 2003 there were 118 airport evacuations. In 2004, there were 276. None was linked to a terrorist attempt, let alone an actual bombing.[11]

As the series proliferate, the distinction between the series of actual attacks and the series of threat-events blurs. At the same time, the range of generic identities under which the threat and its corresponding performance may fall also expands. The terrorist series includes torpedoing buildings with airplanes, air missile attacks, subway bombs, suicide car attacks, roadside bombings, liquid explosives disguised as toiletries, tennis-shoe bombs, "dirty" bombs (never actually observed), anthrax in the mail, other unnamed bioterrorist weapons, booby-trapped mailboxes, Coke cans rigged to explode, bottles in public places . . . The list is long and ever-extending. The mass affective production of felt threat-potential engulfs the (f)actuality of the comparatively small number of incidents where danger materialized. They blend together in a shared atmosphere of fear.

In that atmosphere, the terrorist threat series blends into series featuring other generic identities. There is the generic viral series, including threats, real and nonexistent, as heterogeneous as human-adapted avian flu, SARS, West Nile virus, and the Millennium Bug, just to mention a few from the first years of this century. There is no apparent limit to the generic diversification of threat, which can cross normative logical boundaries with impunity, like that between biological and computer viruses. Or consider food and pathogens: "Comparing junk food to a possible avian flu epidemic, provincial Health Minister Philippe Couillard said yesterday that the province is preparing a crackdown to get sugar-laden soft drinks and junk food out of schools" (Dougherty 2007). The series combine and intertwine, and together they tend to the infinite, preemptive action in tow.

The atmosphere of fear includes this tendential infinity of threat series on the same performative basis as an actually occurring terrorist attack. The generic identity of threat overall stretches to the limit to accommodate the endless proliferation of specific variations. The object of threat tends toward an ultimate limit at which it becomes purely indeterminate, while retaining a certain quality—menace—and the capacity to make that quality felt. The portrait of a chicken can embody this quality and make it felt as reliably as a terrorist's mug shot.

At the limit, threat is a *felt quality*, independent of any particular instance of itself, in much the way the color red is a quality independent of any particular tint of red, as well as of any actually occurring patch of any particular tint of red. It becomes an abstract quality. When threat self-causes, its abstract quality is affectively presented, in startle, shock, and fear. As presented affectively, its quality suffuses the atmosphere. Threat is ultimately *ambient*. Its logic is purely *qualitative*.

Proposition: Threat's ultimately ambient nature makes preemptive power an *environmental* power.[12] Rather than empirically manipulate an object (of which actually it has none), it *modulates* felt qualities infusing a life-environment.

Question: If 9–11 is not an origin, what is it? How does it figure in the tendentially infinite series to which it belongs? Is it possible to periodize preemptive power?

Rather than assigning it as an origin, 9–11 may be thought of as marking a threshold. It can be considered a turning point at which the threat-environment took on an ambient thickness, achieved a consistency, which gave the preemptive power mechanisms dedicated to its modulation an advantage over other regimes of power.

Proposition: To understand the political power of threat and the preemptive politics availing itself of threat-potential, it is necessary to situate preemptive power in a field of interaction with other regimes of power, and to analyze their modes of coexistence as well as their evolutionary divergences and convergences.[13] In a word, it is necessary to adopt an *ecological* approach to threat's environmental power.

Corollary: Each regime of power in the ecology of powers will have its own *operative logic* implicating unique modes of causality and having a singular time-signature. The causal and temporal processes involved will endow the objects of each regime of power with an ontological status different from those of any other regime. Correlative to its ontology, each regime will have a dedicated epistemology guiding the constitution of its political "facts" and guaranteeing their legitimation. The political analysis of regimes of power must extend to these metaphysical dimensions.

Stop

Question: What is an operative logic?

Call an operative logic one that combines an ontology with an epistemology in such a way as to endow itself with powers of self-causation. An operative logic is a productive *process* that inhabits a shared environment, or field of exteriority, with other processes and logics. It figures in that field as a formative movement: a *tendency* toward the iterative production of its own variety of constituted fact. The forms of determination it brings into being as fact have an inborn tendency toward proliferation by virtue of the self-causative powers of their formative process. An operative logic is a process of becoming formative of its own species of being.

Question: What does an operative logic want?

Itself. Its own continuance. It is autopoietic. An operative logic's self-causative powers drive it automatically to extend itself. Its autopoietic mode of operation is one with a drive to universalize itself. Depending on the logic, that drive will take fundamentally heterogeneous forms (from the ecumenical to the imperialist, from the pastoral to the warlike).

Proposition: An operative logic is a *will-to-power*.

This will-to-power is impersonal because it necessarily operates in a field of exteriority in perpetual interaction with other operative logics, with which it is always in a dynamic state of reciprocal presupposition. It is a field phenomenon. The interaction actualizes in a diversity of regimes of power cohabiting the same field in reciprocal exteriority and potential interlinkage. An operative logic's actualization may be, to varying degrees, in more than one regime. An operative logic not fully actualized in any regime of power interacts with the others virtually (anticipatorily, as a present force of futurity, or, as "negatively prehended").[14]

Question: In the case of threat as an operative logic, how can an effective analysis of it be carried out, given that the kind of fact it constitutes is affective and largely independent of actual fact, not to mention that its object is superlatively, futurely nonexistent?

There is a common category of entities, known to all, that specializes in making what is not actually present really present nonetheless, in and as its own effect: *signs*. The sign is the vehicle for making presently felt the *potential force* of the objectively absent.

Proposition: To understand preemptive power as an operative logic it is necessary to be able to express its productive process of becoming as a *semiosis*. Since preemption's production of being in becoming pivots on affect as felt quality, the pertinent theory of signs would have to be grounded first and foremost in a metaphysics of *feeling*.

Smoke of Future Fires

Imagine a dreamer who suddenly hears a loud and prolonged fire alarm.

"At the instant it begins he is startled. He instinctively tries to get away; his hands go to his ears. It is not so much that it is unpleasing, but it forces itself so upon him. The instinctive resistance is a necessary part of it. . . . This sense of acting and being acted upon, which is the sense of the reality of things—both of outward things and ourselves—may be called the sense of Reaction. It does not reside in any one Feeling; it comes upon the breaking of one feeling by another feeling" (Peirce 1998d, 4–5).

A fire alarm is the kind of sign C. S. Peirce calls *indications* or indexes. Indexes "act on the nerves of the person and force his attention." They are nervously compelling because they "show something about things, on account of their being physically connected to them" (1998d, 5) in the way smoke is connected to fire. Yet they "*assert nothing.*" Rather, they are in the mood of the "imperative, or exclamatory, as 'See there!' or 'Look out!' " (1998c, 16). The instant they "show" we are startled: they are immediately performative.

A performative always strikes as a self-executing command. The indexical sign effecting the command may assert nothing, but it still conveys a form. "The form conveyed is always a determination of a dynamical object of the *command*. The dynamical object . . . means something forced upon the mind in perception, but including more than perception reveals. It is an object of actual *Experience*" (Peirce 1998b, 478).

Now what happens when there is no fire and the alarm sounds nonetheless? The sign of alarm has asserted more nothing. It is still just as imperative, still as automatically executing a command. It still startles us awake to a sense of a reality of things, outwardly and selfward at once. It still forces attention, breaking into the feeling before with a transition to a next. Something still happens. A sign-event has transpired. This is an actual *Experience,* including all the more more-than-perception reveals.

It is not just that the putative object of experience, the fire, is nonexistent. It is that it is absent from perception essentially, not just circumstantially. There is no fire. The alarm was in error. How can a falsity have a superlatively real hold on experience?

How could it not? For Peirce, the "dynamical object" is not the fire. The dynamical object is the innervated flesh to which the sign performatively correlates "fire," existent or nonexistent. It is the nervous body astartle that is "the object of the command" to alertness. That performance takes place wholly between the sign and the "instinctively" activated body whose feeling is "broken" by the sign's command to transition to a new feeling. At that instant, nothing but this transitional break exists. *Its* feeling, the sudden bustle, fills the still dreamily reawakening world of experience.

The form "conveyed," the dynamical object exclaimed by the sign of alarm, is nothing other than the dynamic form of the body at this instant of reawakening to its world on alert, imperatively altering. It is nothing else than the activation event launching the body into a transition to a next experience in which its waking world will have undergone a change. Everything takes place between the activated body and the sign of its *becoming*. Fire or no fire, transition to and through alert is made.

What happens when the fire is not falsely nonexistent, but nonexistent in a future tense? What happens if the smoke is that of fires yet to come? What happens if the sign-event is triggered by a future cause?

That is the semiotic question of threat.

Semiosis is sign-induced becoming. It is the question of how a sign as such *dynamically* determines a body to become, in actual experience. It is the question of how an *abstract force* can be *materially* determining. The question is the same for a nonexistent present fire signed in error, and for the futurity of a fire yet to come. There is one difference, however. For the future-causal fire, there can be no error. It will always have been preemptively right.

That one difference makes all the difference. The question becomes, what are the experiential political implications of the a priori rightness of smokes of future fires? What are the existential effects of the body having to assume, at the level of its activated flesh, one with its becoming, the rightness of alert never having to be in error? Of the body in a perpetual innervated reawakening to a world where signs of danger forever loom? Of a world where once a threat, always a threat? A world of infinitely seriating menace-potential made actual experience, with a surplus of becoming, all in the instant?

Imagine a waker hearing a sudden and loud alarm and therewith falling forward back into a world where the present is a foreshadow cast retrospectively by the future, where the present's becoming is the backcast dream of a future's will have been.

A Bustle of It All

Peirce insists that the sign's forcing itself upon the body, and the "resistance" the body instinctively feels "in reaction," cannot be "distinguished as agent and patient" (1998a, 171). The bodily activation event occurs at a threshold of reawakening where there is as yet no distinction between activity and passivity. This means that the body cannot distinguish its own "instincts" from the reawakening force conveyed by the sign's formative performance.

The zone of indistinction between the body reactivating and the action of the sign extends to the shared environment that encompasses and ensures their correlation. Is not the waking distinction between the body and its environment one of activity in a surrounding passivity, or of activity coming from the surrounding to passively impress itself on the body? Prior to the distinction between agent and patient, in the bustle of the reawakening, there is no boundary yet between the body and its environment, or between the two of them and the correlated sign. Or between the dream and the event. These distinctions will reemerge from the bustle, after a transition, in the settling into a next determinate feeling. The form conveyed is a felt dynamic form of unbounded activation germinal of determinate feeling—pure affect, in a redawning universe. This is what the sign "shows."

Understanding the political ontology of threat requires returning thought to this affective twilight zone of indexical experience. In that bustling zone of indistinction, the world becomingly includes so much more than perception reveals. For that reason, thought's approach cannot be phenomenological. It must be unabashedly metaphysical. It must extend to that which conditions what is appearing *next,* itself never appearing: what Whitehead terms the reality *of* appearance (1933).

The reality of appearance is the ontogenetic effectiveness of the nonexistent. It is the surplus of reality of what has not happened, paradoxically as an event, and in the event happens to be productive of a startling transition toward more determinate being.

Look out!

"The occasion has gathered the creativity of the Universe into its own completeness, abstracted from the real objective content which is the source of its own derivation" (Whitehead 1933, 212). This "results from the fusion of the ideal with the actual" (211) in a mutual immanence of contemporary occasions "allied to the immanence of the future in the present" (217).

See there!

"The light that was never was, on sea or land" (Whitehead 1933, 211).

Last question: Does it shine beyond preemption?

Notes

1   George W. Bush, *Dallas Morning News*, May 10, 2000, cited in Miller 2002, 251.
2   By "actual fact," I mean the situation as defined (by rule, convention, or consensus) by a normative system for the establishment of publicly recognized fact under whose jurisdiction the question normally falls, when that system's operation is not preempted (for example, a judicial system, an administrative review process, a peer-review process, and so forth).

3   On Bush and gut feeling as decision-making principle, see Woodward 2002, 16, 136–37, 145, 168.

4   The classical doctrine of war allows preemptive action in cases where there is a "clear and present danger" of attack. Preemption is only allowed defensively, in the face of actual danger. The contemporary neoconservative doctrine of preemption justifies offensive action against threats that are not fully emergent, or, more radically, that have not even begun to emerge. President Bush spelled this out in the address to the nation in which he formally enunciated the new doctrine for the first time in the lead-up to the war in Iraq: "If we wait for threats to fully materialize, we will have waited too long. We must take the battle to the enemy, disrupt his plans and confront the worst threats before they emerge" (Bush 2007).

5   The images from Abu Ghraib first came to light in April 2004. For a compendium of the Bush administration's documents justifying the use of torture, see Greenberg and Dratel 2005.

6   See, for example, Knowlton 2007.

7   See, for example, "ADM" 2005 (in particular the photo and caption).

8   The affective tainting of objects or bodies implicated in a threat-event can go so far as to functionally substitute the affective fact of the matter for what is accepted as actual fact (as defined above in note 2). The actual fact is neither directly contested nor forgotten, yet is disabled. It slips behind the affective fact, which comes to the fore to take over as the operative reality. To cite an example of this affective-factual eclipse, in August 2007 President Bush retracted earlier statements expressing an intent to close the extraterritorial prison camp at Guantánamo Bay. Guantánamo Bay had become a political liability after the torture scandal at Abu Ghraib, revelations of shady "black site" prisons into which "enemy combatants" disappeared without a trace, and criticism of CIA kidnapping of suspects on foreign soil for delivery to third nations known systematically to use torture (known euphemistically as "rendition"). What placed Guantánamo Bay in the same category as these other extraterritorial practices is that they all aim to preempt regulated governmental treatment of suspects according to standard juridical procedures. The strategy is to surge in, in order to rush the production of the *results* of normal juridical procedures before they have had a chance to operate. Imprisonment and punishment come suddenly, before any actual crime is proven. The grabbed bodies are treated, a priori, as guilty. This is done purely on the basis of *signs of threat* that happened to actualize in their vicinity. Some of the inhabitants of Guantánamo who were subsequently released after years of imprisonment were swooped up in Afghanistan during the U.S. invasion and turned out simply to have been in the wrong place at the wrong time. The treatment of the detainees as a priori guilty attaches this quality to them for life, regardless of their actual actions and the actual danger they posed. They are stained, *as if* they had been guilty all along. The felt quality of guilt has its own affective ambience, which can transmute into a number of specific emotions: hatred, resentment, disgust, distrust. The detainee becomes an affective pariah. According to the Bush administration, certain prisoners scheduled for release will not be taken in by any country, even their own countries of origin. These are detainees whom the U.S. military has not been able to bring to trial,

meaning that their cases are not strong enough to transfer into the domestic crimi-
nal system—or even bring before the newly established military commissions where
the bar of the burden of proof is set extravagantly low and the possibilities of defense
for those accused are sorely limited. Bush explained, without displaying a hint of
irony or in any way acknowledging the paradox, that it is because of cases such as
these that Guantánamo Bay must be kept open. The prison doors must remain
locked in order to detain those who are technically innocent. "This is not as easy a
subject as some may think on the surface," the explanation went. "A lot of people
don't want killers in their midst, and a lot of these people are killers." "These people"
should be released because they are innocent, but they can't be released because they
are "killers." Bush's reasoning is not as illogical as it might be supposed as judged by
the standards of normative logic. The apparent inconsistency corresponds to a
change in factual level occurring between the recognition of innocence and the
assertion of guilt. A shift has occurred mid-logic from actual to affective fact. The
affective fact is that these innocents are as good as killers. Nothing will change the
fact that those preemptively treated as guilty are now, as a result of affective tainting,
permanently guilty *in effect*. They are *effectively* guilty (presumably, they would have
if they could have). Indefinite internment is now the hard, life-wasting affective fact
of their situation. Affective facts stand only on their own preemptive occurrence. Yet
they may come effectively to stand in for actual facts. See "President Bush Holds a
News Conference" 2007.

9   After this incident, there was no questioning in the press about who had been
preemptively attacked based on the now incredible information, or what their present circumstances might be. Had they been killed? Had they been "renditioned" to a
third country? Disappeared into a "black site" prison? Sent to Guantánamo for
indefinite detention? Would their cases ever be heard? The question, it seemed,
occurred to no one. The event was not taking place at that actual-factual level,
but rather on the affective level where threat plays itself out through fear. See note 8
above.

10   The invocation of 9–11 makes good populist political sense given that, according to a
Zogby International Poll, a full six years after the event 81 percent of Americans
listed it as the most important historical event of their lives. The percentage rises to
90 percent on the East Coast. See "Attacks Were Most Important Historical Events in
Our Lives" 2007, A17.

11   "Plus de panique!" 2005 (report on comments by then Homeland Security "Czar"
Tom Ridge). The French headline captures the ambivalence of preemption: taken in
isolation it can be read either as "more panic" or "no more panic" (the latter
interpretation being the one suggested in the body of the article).

12   Michel Foucault characterized American neoliberalism, the economic politics that
created the conditions for the neoconservative move toward preemption and away
from normative governmental logic, as a governmentality becoming "*environmentality.*" Environmentality, he writes, represents a "massive pull-back as regards the
normative-disciplinary system ... [which had] as its correlate a technology of human
behavior, an individualizing 'governmentality' comprising: disciplinary gridding
(*quadrillage*), ongoing regulation, subordination-classification, the norm." Neo-

liberalism and neoconservatism remain closely imbricated operative logics, with many positive feedbacks coupling them. They overlap in their mutual embrace of "environmentality." They ply the same far-from-equilibrium global threat environment, in different but strongly reciprocally presupposing ways. Foucault 2008, 260.

13 Gilles Deleuze and Félix Guattari (1987) analyze the relations between modes of power in terms of "a threshold or degree" beyond which what is already active as a tendency "takes on consistency."

14 What is being called operative logics here corresponds to what Deleuze's and Guattari (1987) call "machinic processes" or "abstract machines." "We define social formations by *machinic processes* and not by modes of production (these on the contrary depend on the processes). . . . Precisely because these processes are variables of coexistence that are the object of a social topology, the various corresponding formations are coexistent" (435). "There is not only an external coexistence of formations but also an intrinsic coexistence of machinic processes. Each process can also function at a 'power' other than its own; it can be taken up by a power corresponding to another process" (437). "Everything coexists, in perpetual interaction" (430). Machinic processes operate according to "reverse causalities that are *without finality* but testify nonetheless to an action of the future on the present," which implies "an inversion of time. . . . These reverse causalities shatter evolution. . . . It is necessary to demonstrate that what does not yet exist is already in action, in a different form than that of its existence" (431). The machinic processes of most concern to Deleuze and Guattari in this chapter form "apparatuses of capture." "As a general rule, there is a primitive accumulation whenever an apparatus of capture is mounted, with that very particular kind of violence that creates or contributes to the creation of that which it is directed against, and thus presupposes itself" (447). Violence creative of that which it is directed against employs "anticipation-prevention mechanisms" (439)—in other words, it acts productively by acting preemptively. "Anticipation-prevention mechanisms have a high *power of transference*" or of contagion between processes and their corresponding formations (437). In Deleuze's and Guattari's terms, the preemptive power analyzed here is an emergent species of highly virulent apparatus of capture effecting a "primitive accumulation" of threat-value and spreading its operative logic through affective contagion.

One of the modes in which there is effective interaction between operative logics "in a different form than that of their existence" is termed negative prehension by Alfred North Whitehead (1979). "A negative prehension is the definite exclusion of [an] item from positive contribution to the subject's [the process's] real internal constitution. . . . The negative prehension expresses a bond. . . . Each negative prehension has its own subjective form, however trivial and faint . . . it adds to the emotional complex [the affective atmosphere], if not to the objective data. . . . [Negative prehensions] are required to express *how* any one item is felt . . . the negative prehension of an entity [a process] is a positive fact with its emotional subjective form [it is an affective fact]; there is a mutual sensitivity of the subjective forms of prehensions [there is an ecology of reciprocal presupposition effectively extending to what is negatively prehended]" (41–42).

In Deleuze's and Guattari's vocabulary, the "bond" constituted by a negative prehension is an example of the "non-localizable liaisons" characteristic of capture (1987, 446). Threat, at the limit where it is "trivially and faintly" felt only as an atmospheric quality independent of any actual instance of itself, constitutes such a non-localized bond, even when it is not specifically expressed in a sign of alarm. It still contributes in a real but abstract way to the "how" of the mutual sensitivity of subjective forms, even when it is not positively felt. It still adds to the shared "emotional complex" that is the affective environment conditioning *how* forms feelingly pursue their individuation. This is particularly the case once the "primitive accumulation" of threat-value has reached a certain level and extension throughout the environment due to the "high transference power" of its processual mechanisms. Threat operating in this way, at the limit where it is not actually signed but still negatively prehended, felt vaguely and purely qualitatively, constitutes what in earlier work I described as "low-level" background fear capable of insinuating itself into the constitution of subjectivities. It is affective fact at its most abstract. See Massumi 1993, 3–38.

Elspeth Probyn

I first began to have sympathy for Charles Darwin when I read about the terrible toll his research and writing seem to have taken on his body. Apparently he went through long bouts of illness during which he continually threw up, had diarrhea, and was forced to take to his bed. He believed in what we now call alternative therapies, especially hydrotherapy, which sometimes worked for him.

I thought about Darwin when, between waking and thinking, I felt the presence of something dreadfully pressing. Ah yes, the book. And then I retched. This kept happening as I pondered my case. There was no great stress in my life. I was on research leave far away from the pressures of my job, and all I had to do was to write, rewrite, and rewrite a book. I tried to ignore this little routine my body had set up. That didn't work; my body insisted I pay attention. I reviewed what was happening. I would go to bed and sleep soundly in a seemingly dreamless state. On waking I would notice that my hands and feet hurt. It became clear that during the night my body contorted itself: my fists tightened, my feet tensed, and I ground my teeth.

I lectured my body sternly, but it wouldn't listen to reason. To my mind, it was just the pressure of a deadline that was making me ill. All I had to do was get the manuscript done before it finished me. A friend, worried about my deteriorating state of health, was unconvinced by my expedient logic. She has been researching violence, shame, and honor among young men.[1] She quickly pointed out what I should have known: shame is a painful thing to write about. It gets into your body. It gets to you.

Of course shame is a painful thing to write about: an exposure of the intimacies of selves in public. But it wasn't quite the shame of exposure I was feeling. Something else was agitating me. It's possible that reading too much about affect leads to hypochondria. It certainly makes you more aware of the operation of different affects in the body. I decided from the outward signs that it wasn't exactly shame my body was exhibiting. What my doctor had termed fight or flight was closer to what Silvan Tomkins would call fear-terror (Sedgwick and Frank 1995b, 35). Yes, that was what I felt: the clenching of fists and jaw, the twisting and tensing of feet. It dawned on me that I was experiencing the terror of not being equal to the interest of my subject. The idea that I would not interest readers triggered what seemed to be a mixture of fear and shame.

There is a shame in being highly interested in something and unable to convey it to others, to evoke the same degree of interest in them and to convince them that it is warranted. The risk of writing is always that you will fail to interest or engage readers. Disappointment in yourself looms large when you can't quite get the words right or get the argument across. Simply put, it's the challenge of making the writing equal to the subject being written about. The gulf between the two may bring on the feeling of being a sham or, as I'll argue here, a deeper shame. Lynn Barber, a journalist who has interviewed some of the great writers of our time, describes the former. Reflecting on her interview with the prolific essayist Christopher Hitchens, Barber finds an undertow: "Perhaps his sense of imposture is the one all writers have—that they care more about writing than they do about their subject" (2002, 10).

By calling it imposture, Barber paints the problem in terms that threaten to slip from the fairly minor to the major. *Imposture* implies making it up, hiding behind a mask of competence. Etymologically *shame* comes from the Goth word *Scham*, which refers to covering the face. The crucial element that turns sham into shame is the level of interest and desire involved. There is no shame in being a sham if you don't care what others think or if you don't care what you think. But if you do, shame threatens. To care intensely about what you are writing places the body within the ambit of the shameful: sheer disappointment in the self amplifies to a painful level.

My argument here is about writing shame, a phrase I use to capture both the affective, bodily feeling of betraying interest, and also about how we might envision writing shame as part of an ethical practice. Shame forces us to reflect continually on the implications of our writing. The insights provided by different kinds of writers will show that writing shame is a visceral reminder to be true to interest, to be honest about why or how certain things are of interest. The writers I focus on are from quite different realms. They are a novelist, a witness and victim of atrocities, and a philosopher. There is, of course, a difference between the objectives of a fiction writer and those of an academic one. Crudely put, if you make things up, does it matter that you care more about your writing than your subject matter? Conversely, if you are an academic writer, why should you even care about writing rather than "ideas"? The insights of writers as different as Stephen King, Primo Levi, and Gilles Deleuze make these distinctions disappear. Exemplary in writing about shame, they discuss the need for modesty, what we can learn about writing from the body in shame, and above all they provide lessons about writing without affectation. None of them escapes the toll writing takes on the body. In the most extreme case, Levi speaks of having to write the story of Auschwitz as a "violent impulse to the point of competing with . . . elementary needs" (cited in Ginzburg 1992, 96). If the inclusion of Levi in the company of a popular American writer and a French philosopher is shocking, it needs to be remembered and celebrated that Levi's great passion was writing, a love he turned to as something separate from testifying. Levi was an example to all who aspire to write.

Academic Anxieties

Sometimes it seems that academics do not aspire to be writers. In fact the aspiration may be ridiculed in a society with a prevailing belief that academics cannot write. Even within the humanities, the notion of the researcher as writer is still, or is once again, considered dubious. Of course, whole disciplines have had their "literary turns," and "poetics" is appended to everything from ethnography to history. But the question of writing per se has tended to be brushed aside in the guise of "writing up research." While the pretense of academic writing as purely objective might be fading, there's little thought about what will replace the dominant mode of "writing up." The gulf between research and writing is becoming especially fraught with the increase in academic studies about emotions and affects.[2] As Sedgwick and Frank point out, current treatises on affect tend to lack feeling. "Affect is treated as a unitary category, with a unitary history and unitary politics. There is no theoretical room for any difference between, say, being amused, being disgusted, being ashamed, and being enraged. . . . Genres are differentiated not in relation to the kind of affect they may evoke or generate but, far more simply, by the presence or absence of some rarified substance called Affect" (1995a, 17).

An abstract way of approaching affect and emotion places the writing itself in an uninterested relation to affect. This is a contradiction in terms— affects are inherently interested. For Sedgwick and Frank, a distanced and general use of affect represents "a theoretical decision: as if what is presented could not finally *be* 'theory' if it made any definitional room at all for qualitative differences among affects" (1995a, 17). How can you represent a sense of emotional and affective intensity if the feeling in question is generalized in the amorphous category of Affect?

An epistemological point hovers in the background: a precise emotion demands precise description. In other words, affects have specific effects; it makes no sense to talk about them outside this understanding. Precise descriptions of the affective—in my case, shame—can also affect other concepts: ideas such as the body and its relation to writing or rethinking an ethics of writing. A general gesture to Affect won't do the trick. If we want to invigorate our concepts, we need to follow through on what different affects do, at different levels. The point needs to be stressed: different affects make us feel, write, think, and act in different ways. Shame, for example, works over the body in certain ways. It does this experientially—the body feels very different in shame than in enjoyment—but it also reworks how we understand the body and its relation to other bodies or, for want of a better word, to the social. This matters at the level of theory. It matters in terms of what we want writing to do.

Words and Things

Like many, I became an academic mainly because the relation between words and things fascinates me. Words and things: many will recall *Les mots et les choses*, the French title for Michel Foucault's book *The Order of Things* (1973).

It traces how "things," produced in relationship to different orders of knowledge, have been arranged over the centuries. It is also charged with an insistence that things don't have to be the way they are. Working as a waitress in Montreal, I read Foucault's book in a bar between shifts. To say that it opened new vistas is not overly dramatic. As I read I would look up, listen, and observe people's interactions. Sometimes you can catch a whole worldview from a snippet of bar talk. The relation between words and things is not just cerebral; it is, I think, at the very heart of what makes humans interesting.

It's a strange segue from Foucault, one of the great philosophers of the twentieth century, to Stephen King, one of the most popular novelists. But they are both entranced by the relationship between words and things. King is, of course, most noted for his horror stories. He is prolific, with some thirty-nine novels to date, many of which have been made into films. Something like three million people have read each of his novels. His wide appeal may be why King's writing is disdained by many. It's that old bugbear of commercial success: how could someone that popular be any good? King's meditation *On Writing* (2000) responds to this prejudice. In the genre of memoir but also marked with the precision of an instruction manual, it's a set of instructions for writing with a gripping narrative.

King's depiction of writing and shame is instructive. In King's memory, it was a high school teacher who first made him aware that there might be something shameful about his writing. The teacher asked him why he wrote such junk: "I had no answer to give. I was ashamed. I have spent a good many years since—too many, I think—being ashamed about what I write" (46).

King finally got over the shame she induced. But he remains very clear about writing he sees as shameful: writing that lacks honesty. Honesty for him includes the precise relationship between words and things; he is also concerned with the structural aspects of writing such as grammar and dialogue. His rant about words makes poststructuralism seem pragmatic: "The word is only a representation of meaning; even at its best, writing almost always falls short of full meaning. Given that, why in God's name would you want to make things worse by choosing a word which is only cousin to the one you really wanted to use?" (130).

If King is not above shaming his readers into being good writers—"it's *writing*, damn it, not washing the car or putting on eyeliner" (117)—it is because he is passionate about honest writing. Being honest about writing also means becoming an honest reader. King is scathing about "people who read very little (or not at all in some cases) [and then] presume to write and expect people to like what they have written" (167). While academics read a lot, I sometimes wonder whether we read only for ideas, with a focus on what we're trying to write rather than on the writing that we're reading. King is very good at describing the effects of being read: waiting as his Ideal Reader (his wife) reads a draft, he says, "I try to watch her when she gets to a particular scene, hoping for at least a smile or—jackpot, baby!—that big, belly laugh with the hands up, waving in the air" (262).

This framing of his nervous expectation explains what King means by honesty. Has he interested the reader in what he cares about so passionately? King is also up-front about the toll such interest takes: "You can approach the act of writing with nervousness, excitement, hopefulness, or even despair." He concludes, "Come to it any way but lightly." He repeats in italics: "*You must not come lightly to the blank page*" (118).

King's lessons have stayed with me. His arguments are challenging. For King, the goal of writing is a telepathic connection between reader and writer, whereby the reader "catches" the writer's interest. It's what you're trying to say to the reader, not how good you sound to yourself. It's about recognizing what you're trying to *do* to the reader (although, strangely enough, King doesn't talk about the effects of horror on the reader) and what writing does to the writer. Simply put, writing affects bodies. Writing takes its toll on the body that writes and the bodies that read or listen.

Body-Affects

Writing is a corporeal activity. We work ideas through our bodies; we write through our bodies, hoping to get into the bodies of our readers. We study and write about society not as an abstraction but as composed of actual bodies in proximity to other bodies. This point is elaborated by Gilles Deleuze. His ideas about bodies shake up assumptions about their boundedness —what we take to be our own and how one body relates to others. Influenced by Spinoza, he argues that the body is not a unified entity but is composed of many moving elements. As Moira Gatens has argued, affect leads us to "question commonsense notions of the privacy or 'integrity' of bodies through exposing the breaches in the borders between self and other evidenced by the contagiousness of 'collective' affects" (2004, 115). Affect in this model does not impinge on the body from the outside, nor does it erupt from the inside. Deleuze's model makes such distinctions incomprehensible. Gatens sums it up as the body is "always already wholly implicated in its milieu" (2004, 115).

In this model, the body is defined by kinetic and dynamic relations. It helps to picture the body as composed of thousands of bits all whizzing around. At the level of kinesis, "it is the relations of motion and rest, of speeds and slownesses between particles that define a body, the individuality of a body" (Deleuze 1992, 625). This recalls Brian Massumi's point about the ways in which feelings are in motion with other feelings. Massumi finds evidence of this in scientific ideas about proprioception—the sensors that register the body's movements in relation to its own movement: "*It moves as it feels and it finds itself moving*" (2002, 1, emphasis added).

Interest in the body's feelings and movements goes back to William James's theory of emotions (1884), which also emphasizes the different feelings of different emotions.[3] James's theory of how we feel goes like this: (a) I perceive a lion; (b) my body trembles; (c) I am afraid. In other words, the body perceives itself perceiving the trigger of emotion, which sets off movement (trembling), and then gets named as a cognitive state (fear). Or there is Deleuze's description of this sequence: (a) the perception of a situation; (b) the modification of the body; (c) the emotion of consciousness or the mind (1997, 123).

The other way Deleuze defines the movement of bodies is through their dynamic interactions with other bodies: "A body affects other bodies, or is affected by other bodies; it is this capacity for affecting and being affected that also defines a body in its individuality" (1992, 625). Thinking, writing, and reading are integral to our capacities to affect and to be affected. In Deleuze's terms this "is a complex relation of speed and slowness, in the body but also in thought, and it is a capacity for affecting and being affected, pertaining to the body or thought" (1992, 626). In everyday life we experience this abstract thought in practice. William Connolly describes the relationship between thinking, bodies, and sensibilities as "everyday techniques, both gross and subtle, by which thinking is altered in its direction, speed, intensity, or sensibility" (2002, 100). He asks us to ponder how, say, listening to Mozart or "going dancing to music that inspires and energizes" will change "the relays that connect word, gesture, memory, sound, rhythm, mobility, image, and thinking" (100–102).

Shame and Glory

Deleuze's ideas about the capacity of bodies to affect and to be affected are forcefully conveyed in his discussion of T. E. Lawrence's depictions of shame and glory. Lawrence of Arabia was the heroic Englishman in the desert. He was also the writer of the *Seven Pillars of Wisdom* (1926) and *The Mint* (1955), which recounted in part his misadventures and traumas, which included being raped. The man and his writing were steeped in shame and honor.

Deleuze is particularly interested in what he calls "the subjective disposition" of Lawrence's writing. We could more simply say that Lawrence's writing was heavily autobiographical and psychological, but Deleuze shifts the meanings of those terms. He starts with an appreciation of Lawrence's skill as a portraitist, citing these descriptions: " 'Though usually merry, he had a quick vein of suffering in him'; 'his mind, like a pastoral landscape, had four corners to its view: cared-for, friendly, limited, displayed'; 'upon his coarse eyelashes the eyelids sagged down in tired folds, through which, from the overhead sun, a red light glittered into his eye sockets and made them look like fiery pits in which the man was slowly burning' " (1997, 116).

The deftness with which Lawrence paints characters is remarkable. As Deleuze puts it, "The finest writers have singular conditions of perception that allow them to draw on or shape aesthetic percepts like veritable visions" (116). Deleuze elaborates this claim through the notion of a subjective character or disposition. This is something quite beyond a personal identity. If we remember that for Deleuze there is no unified person as such, then the idea of an autobiographical or personal style of writing becomes impossible. Rather, the subjective for Deleuze is the affective assemblage of bodies of different orders and elements. "Lawrence's writing, his style, makes use of this . . . the subjective disposition, that is to say, the force through which the images are projected is inseparably political, erotic, and artistic" (118).

In an echo of King's admonition about honesty, Deleuze also notes how true Lawrence's images are. "The images Lawrence projects into the real are not inflated images that would sin by false extension, but are valid solely through the pure intensity, whether dramatic or comic, that the writer is able to give to the event" (119). Lawrence doesn't portray just people in this way; he applies the same intensity to abstractions and ideas—what Deleuze calls "entities." As part and parcel of Lawrence's subjective disposition, and indeed perhaps of his honesty as a writer, he has "a gift for making entities live passionately in the desert, alongside people and things, in the jerking rhythm of a camel's gait" (119).

This gift becomes pronounced in Lawrence's depiction of shame. In Deleuze's words: "Never before has shame been sung like this, in so proud and haughty a manner" (120). It's here that the writer, the writing, an idea, and bodies all meld. Lawrence's shame is not the result of a simple psychological quality that is to be explained by some aspect of his person, such as his putative homosexuality. Deleuze makes such characterizations of Lawrence's shame beside the point. Shame is a product of the machine of subjective disposition, which produces shame as both idea and affect. The subjective, in Lawrence's case, is deeply connected to the context in which he lives and writes. Deleuze describes some of the prompts to Lawrence's shame. He was an Englishman in the desert masquerading as an Arab. "Shame is first of all the shame of betraying the Arabs, since Lawrence never stops guaranteeing English promises that he knows perfectly well will not be kept" (120).

In *T. E. Lawrence: An Arab View* (1966), Suleiman Mousa gives a historical account of Lawrence's shame. Mousa quickly sketches early conditions that may have produced Lawrence as prone to shame. Lawrence's father had four daughters with his first wife before eloping with the governess, Lawrence's mother. He not only left behind his first family, he also cut any links by changing his name from Chapman to Lawrence. T. E. Lawrence therefore grew up with the stigma that his mother was from another class, his father masqueraded under another name, and their offspring were illegitimate. Lawrence obtained a scholarship to Oxford by reason of his Welshness, another shameful little detail. He was born in Wales, where the family stayed only briefly, because his father needed somewhere cheap to live after he had run away with his mistress.

After Lawrence attended the university, his interest in archaeology took him in 1910 to the Middle East, where he learned Arabic. Mousa's sources say he didn't speak Arabic terribly well, although he portrays himself as capable of passing as an Arab. Soon after his arrival he began to dress in Arab clothing. Mousa writes of that period: "One of the secrets of his later success was his ability to penetrate the inner self of the Arab individual" (1966, 5). When the First World War broke out, Lawrence found himself unhappily employed in the British Intelligence Service. When his request to transfer to the Arab Bureau was turned down, Lawrence resorted to intriguing tactics. Mousa reports that he approached his goal by "capitalizing on his superiors' mistakes, exposing their ignorance and inefficiency and even revealing their grammatical errors and ridiculing the style of their reports" (28). This grammatical humiliation worked, and Lawrence was to be involved in the Arab Revolt, which was, of course, his stepping stone to fame.

Mousa's summation of Lawrence's character was that he had two natures. "His "first" nature led him to brave the elements and to take troubles and difficulties in his stride, without fully satisfying his excessive ambition"

(278). This nature led to "his supplementary bragging, falsification and fabrication. . . . At the same time, his 'second' nature aroused the conscience of the educated man in him, who would act as auditor and judge" (278). As Mousa puts it, this combination makes for an uncomfortable feeling: "Deep within himself, Lawrence knew that the greater part of his fame was based on fraud." He was driven "in the hope of atoning for earlier mistakes, which haunted him in secret" (278). In this we hear clearly the passage from sham to shame.

While Deleuze's account of Lawrence's character concurs with much of what Mousa wrote some thirty years earlier, his interests led him to consider what Lawrence's shame means for a philosophy of the body. Lawrence, writes Deleuze, "has shame because he thinks the mind, though distinct, is inseparable from the body." This has a particular meaning and implication. "The body is not even a means or a vehicle for the mind, but rather a 'molecular sludge' that adheres to all the mind's actions" (1997, 123). In this we can't forget how proud Lawrence was of his physical strength, nor can we forget that he was tortured and belatedly admitted to having been raped by the bey in 1917. Deleuze sees in Lawrence's account a particular form of shame: "The mind depends on the body; shame would be nothing without this dependency, this attraction for the abject, this voyeurism of the body. Which means that the mind is ashamed *of* the body in a very special manner; in fact, it is ashamed *for* the body. It is as if it were saying to the body: You make me ashamed, You ought to be ashamed . . . 'A bodily weakness which made my animal self crawl away and hide until the shame was passed' " (123).

This feeling of shame and its relation to the body may not be as unusual as Deleuze seems to think. In many accounts of rape or torture, the splitting off from the body is one way in which victims say they were able to endure the experience. Deleuze goes on to describe what may be happening in this splitting: "The mind begins by coldly and curiously regarding what the body does, it is first of all a witness; then it is affected, it becomes an impassioned witness, that is, it experiences for itself affects that are not simply effects of the body, but veritable critical *entities* that hover over the body and judge it" (124).

It's a lovely description, but what are these ghostly hovering critical entities? Deleuze's argument is that emotions and affects are ideas. But they are not solely of the mind. They arise out of a violent collision of mind and body. As such they are not, properly speaking, of either; they are a particular combination of thought and body in which a distinction between the two is no longer important. In regard to writing, this is of crucial importance: the affects "are not only the eyes of the mind, but its Powers and its Words." In Deleuze's reading, Lawrence's depiction of shame is expressed at the limit of the body and of language, and it makes language work differently. It is a shame that, as Deleuze says, is "consubstantial with being" and reveals "an insolent beauty that shows . . . at what point 'the coming out of shame was easy,' at least for a moment" (125).

This is an immensely powerful description of the challenge of writing shame: shame is produced out of the clashing of mind and body, resulting in new acts of subjectivity consubstantial with the words in which they are expressed. Deleuze's idea of the subjective disposition allows us to understand something of the relationship between the writer, experience, expression, affect, and its effects. Shame cannot be conceived of as an external object that could be dispassionately described, nor is it a purely personal feeling. Shame is subjective in the strong sense of bringing into being an entity or an idea through the specific explosion of mind, body, place, and history.

Shame is the product of many forces. It is "a singular composition, an idiosyncrasy . . . marking the unique chance that *these* entities had been retained and willed, that *this* combination had been thrown and not another" (Deleuze 1997, 120). As Deleuze says, one particular combination "is named Lawrence" (121). Lawrence as a subjective disposition that produced such a powerful expression of shame is, in Deleuze's words, a "dice throw." Deleuze remarks that "Lawrence can say with Kafka: 'It was as if the shame of it must outlive him.' Shame enlarges the man" (121). In making the man larger, shame does not necessarily make him easier to understand or more likable. From Mousa's account of Lawrence, the man was complex and probably hard to be around.

If writing shame doesn't necessarily make you a good person, why have I insisted that it may have an ethical implication in how we write? Deleuze sees in Lawrence's writing a shame that reconfigures how we think about it and about the body. In this sense, shame enlarges the man by opening up possibilities of how we conceive of the relationship between ideas and affects, or between thinking and feeling. It also provides an argument against considering expressions of shame as merely a personal affliction. While many have argued that shame is about self-evaluation or, more precisely, the evaluation of the self by the self, Deleuze's argument breaks with a tendency to conceptualize shame in banal psychological terms as an interior quality. Shame in

Deleuze's description comes from a complex disposition: it combines the inherent and the lived experience of social structures—the biology and biography of a person. However, Deleuze goes further in radically depersonalizing shame. Shame is an affect that crosses many different orders of bodies. In this way, Lawrence is not a mere cipher for the shame of what the English were doing to the Arabs, nor is he a personification of a shameful history. Rather, Deleuze seems to be arguing that a new idea of shame was produced out of the dice throw that is Lawrence. It is a shame that is intimately connected with the character of empire at the time: haughty and proud, and deeply filled with shame.

Shame, Proximity, and Distance

Recall the phrase from Kafka that Deleuze uses to describe Lawrence: "It was as if the shame of it must outlive him." Deleuze concludes: "Shame enlarges the man" (1997, 121). As we've seen, shame arises from a collision of bodies, ideas, history, and place. But Lawrence as a writer is more than just a vehicle for a shameful moment in history: his writing of shame reworks its meaning and remakes the experience of shame into "an insolent beauty" (125).

I now want to turn to Primo Levi, the writer who ensured that the shame of the Holocaust would outlive him. Kafka appears in one of Levi's remarks about writing contained in a recent collection of Levi's interviews. Having translated *The Trial*, Levi describes Kafka as possessing "an almost animalesque sensitivity, like snakes that know when earthquakes are coming" (2001, 159). This description captures how the affects of writing can penetrate the body of the writer and the reader. Levi's perspicacity is not surprising: he is the writer most associated with making us *feel* that shame is intrinsic to both humanity and inhumanity.

Levi the writer, like Lawrence before him, was a dice throw of history. An Italian Jew from Piedmont, he was arrested in 1943 for being involved in a partisan faction against the Fascists. He told the police that he was Jewish because he feared he would otherwise be executed as a partisan. His admission led to his deportation in 1944 to Auschwitz-Monowitz. He managed to survive the *Lager* because of what he describes as a combination of chance circumstances. Having graduated in chemistry before the war, he happened to end up in the Buna plant, which was part of Auschwitz and owned by the large chemical company I. G. Farben. "And this was one of my great strokes of luck," he said later, "because I said I was a chemist, without knowing that we were labourers in a chemical factory" (Levi 2001, 212). Levi also attributes his survival to having learned some German while reading chemistry. One of the major themes that emerges in interviews with Levi is the necessity of being able to communicate. Most of the Italians who were deported with Levi died soon after their arrival at Auschwitz because they could not understand the German or Polish orders.

Levi comes to us, in his own words, as a chemist who was made into a writer by Auschwitz. Levi is often read as a witness or as a documentalist, which, of course, correctly describes his two first books, *If This Is a Man* (1958) and *The Truce* (1963). But he was also an extremely skilled writer who was proud of his craft and talked of it in precise ways. I want to consider first how his writing and testifying use shame to give us a map of humanity and inhumanity. Then I'll discuss his insights about writing, which constitute, I think, an undervalued resource.

In the spring of 1982, Primo Levi returned to Auschwitz as a tourist (his own term). His presence among a group of Italian students and professors as well as other camp survivors must have made it a remarkable tour. As Levi later recounts, an Italian interviewer points out the incongruity of the signs of normality in the town of Auschwitz. He says to Levi, "It seems today we'll eat in a restaurant at Auschwitz." Levi responds in that unique mixture of common sense and exquisite clarity that marks his writing: "Yes, this is almost comical that there would be a restaurant at Auschwitz. I don't know what I'll eat. It seems to me almost profane, something absurd. On the other hand we must remember that Auschwitz was, is, a city where there are restaurants, theatres, even a nightclub probably. They have some in Poland too. There are children, schools, back then as now, alongside Auschwitz—a concept by now; Auschwitz is the *Lager*—this other Auschwitz of the living exists" (*Sorgente di vita* 2001).[4]

The mind expands before the enormity of the scene. Levi, the man who wrote so carefully of his experiences in the camp, is back in its grip. But there, surrounded by a past that his writing makes part of our present, he calmly remarks that Auschwitz is a place where people live, and they must have restaurants, nightclubs, schools. The mundane fact of Auschwitz as a place where people live, eat, shop, and dance is still hard to countenance. Levi's Auschwitz, the place of horror, has grown into "our" Auschwitz, the source of shame that haunts our consciousness.

Levi's writing challenges any departmentalization or ownership of shame. It is not a personal capacity that is possessed by only some individuals. We must clearly acknowledge that the trauma of the camps and of the Holocaust belongs more closely to some: to the survivors and their relations, to Jewish people in general, to Gypsies, homosexuals, Communists, and intellectuals. How close we can get to Auschwitz is dependent on writers like Levi, but we do not all have equal rights to that proximity. Levi's writing makes one viscerally aware of distinctions in proximity—and getting too close can be a source of shame. Satoshi Ukai (2001) argues that there is a distinction between the shame of being human and shame as human. The former refers to an abstract idea about the shameful nature of humanity; the latter positions shame as inherent to us as human beings. Levi doesn't seem to subscribe to such hard and fast distinctions. He speaks about the gray zone, or the plurality and shades of shame. Deleuze describes this as "the shame of there being men who became Nazis; the shame of being unable, not seeing how to stop it; the shame of having compromised with it" (cited in Ukai 2001, 23).

Levi's writing continually avoids grandiose ideas. His desire for precision is played out in his descriptions of the everyday activities and aspirations of humankind. The honesty of his writing shames any attempt to make abstract remarks about shame. His modest voice warns against turning shame, the experience of the Holocaust, or any aspect of human behavior into an abstract point of theory. Levi is a figure that cannot be appropriated; at the same time he doesn't license us to stand in awe before him. The pragmatic and practical tone of his comments on writing clearly demonstrates his purpose: to put descriptions of shame—but equally of joy and hope—to work in furthering an appreciation of what humans can do, for bad or for good.

The first memoir of Levi's experiences in Auschwitz, *If This Is a Man*, was written soon after he returned to Turin after the war and was originally published in 1958; the second, *The Truce*, was published in 1963. At the end of *The Truce* Levi recalls a dream that he continued to have following his release. It is a nightmare of the darkest hues, which rips the reader's breath.

It is a dream within a dream, varied in detail, one in substance. I am sitting at a table with my family, or with friends, or at work, or in the green countryside; in short, in a peaceful relaxed environment, apparently without tension or affliction; yet I feel a deep and subtle anguish, the definite sensation of an impending threat. And in fact, as the dream proceeds, slowly or brutally, each time in a different way, everything collapses and disintegrates around me, the scenery, the walls, the people, while the anguish becomes more intense and more precise. Now everything has changed to chaos; I am alone in the centre of a grey and turbid nothing, and now I *know* what this thing means, and I also know that I have always known it; I am in the Lager once more, and nothing is true outside the Lager. All the rest was a brief pause, a deception of the senses, a dream; my family, nature in flower, my home. Now this inner dream, this dream of peace, is over, and in the outer dream, which continues, gelid, a well-known voice resounds: a single word, not imperious, but brief and subdued. It is the dawn command of Auschwitz, a foreign word, feared and expected: get up, "*Wstawach.*" (1979, 380)

The geography of affect that Levi creates in his description moves from out to in, and the freedom of the outside is always enfolded in the terror of the camp. Contrary to Levi's description of the ways in which Auschwitz coexists with reality—it is a place where people ate and drank and worked and continue to do so—here in his dream reality is always pushed away and torn apart by the outer dream, the reality of the *Lager*. The dream of the "present" fails before the dream of the past.

Years later, after Levi's reported suicide in April 1987, debate raged about why, or indeed whether, Levi had killed himself. The question was fueled by the circumstances of his death. He fell from his apartment staircase and to all knowledge did not leave a note. The desire to find Levi's death accidental is understandable. But it may also stem from a need to assuage our collective shame and guilt. Jorge Semprún, a survivor of Buchenwald, attests to the high cost of writing about the experience of the camps, arguing that the writing is not cathartic for the writer but instead reconnects him or her with the horror of the camps (1984).

It's a strange and uncomfortable debate that seems to turn on whether it was the original experiences or the representation of them that resulted, or not, in Levi's suicide. But if writers commit suicide because of their writing, surely we, the bystanders of history, are more fully implicated in their anguish and death. This understanding would charge our reading of their work. The shame in reading about the atrocities committed by humans on humans would be amplified by and combined with guilt and even disgust; readers might have to turn away. Would we turn away from Levi if this were the case? I hope not.

Marco Belpoliti, the editor who collected Levi's interviews, argues that in Levi's writing "there is a distance between the narrator and the listener; the narrator, of course, counsels his interlocutor, but there is always a certain distance between them" (2001, xix). This observation connects with the more theoretical points made by Dominick LaCapra about the necessity of not getting too close to, or overidentifying with, the writings of survivors. Was Levi helping us, his readers, in this exigency? For LaCapra, being too close leads to "acting out," an "unchecked identification," a confusion of self and other, whereby the experience of the other becomes incorporated in the self. Against this he advocates "the goal of a critically controlled dialogic exchange with the past" (2000, 67).

The dialogic exchange is guided by the questions: "What is the other saying or doing? How do I—or we—respond to it?" (LaCapra 2000, 67). These reminders are important even if the metaphor of dialogue can be mindlessly abstract—I may "dialogue" with the past, but how can it "dialogue" with me? Strictly speaking, of course, it can't. Yet shame and other affects can seem to get into our bodies, altering our understanding of our selves and our relation to the past. In Deleuze's description of Lawrence's writing of shame, the body and mind react so as to reorder the subjective. Or in LaCapra's terms, "empathy should be understood in terms of an affective relation, rapport, or bond with the other recognized as other" (212). The unifying point seems to be that strong affect radically disturbs different relations of proximity: to our selves, bodies, pasts.

Listening to Levi Write

Levi himself made a distinction between what he called his autobiographical writings about the camp and his later "real" writing. Of the first, he talked about the absolute necessity to bear witness: "I came back from the camp with a narrative impulse that was pathological" (2001, 129). The rawness and indeed the embodiment of trauma, "the unhealing wound, in life and in memory, is what produces the need for the word, for clear communication" (Levi cited in Belpoliti 2001, xx).

Levi repeats again and again the need for communication and the high price of not being understood. "A book," he says, "has to be a telephone that works" (cited in Belpoliti 2001, xix). This is, as we've seen, a pragmatic consideration painfully learned from his experience in the camp, where not being understood meant a quick death. It also became part of Levi's philosophy of writing as a craft. Writing is a tool or a technology that, like the telephone, has to work. When asked whether he suffered because of "what [he was] writing about or for the writing itself," Levi replies, "No, not for what I'm writing about. I sometimes feel the inadequacy of the medium.

Ineffability, it's called, and it's a beautiful word. Our language is human, born to describe things at a human level" (2001, 173).

Levi continually emphasizes the difference between the type of writing he did as a witness and his writing when, as he put it, he became a writer. But as in his other "paranoiac split" (being a chemist and being a writer), the two sides fed each other. In response to whether he would have become a writer if not for Auschwitz, Levi replies, "Without knowing 'what to say,' without 'the content,' there is no story" (cited in Belpoliti 2001, xxi). Having become a writer rather than remaining a witness, he also speaks of the shame of writing. He calls himself a "counterfeiter" in reference to stories that were not based in his experiences of the camp. But he also defends this choice: "Was I supposed to be a survivor for my entire life? Let's be clear, I am a survivor, but I don't want to write only about Auschwitz" (Levi 2001, 94).

However, the worries remained: of "feeling false," of writing "not to record facts but for pleasure or edification" (133). In another interview he is explicit about "abstaining from embellishment, from extras added in just to make the writing look good." More emphatically, he states, "I don't write for myself, or if I do, I tear it up, destroy what I've written. I think it's wrong to write for oneself" (172). After more questions he returns to say, "There is only one risk, of writing badly," which he qualifies as writing that is useless. Evoking his technical job, he describes how writing is close to manual labor: "You make a plan, at least mentally, an outline, a design, and then you try to make a product as close as possible to the plan" (172).

Whether in writing or in providing testimony, Levi's passion for his métier as a chemist continually informed his experience of being a writer. He was a great believer in biology as a science and also as a force in life. Of his stories and the hope they carried, he says, "I am built that way: I like to tell people stories." Of his optimism: "This attitude of mine comes from my roots and isn't thought out or deliberated: it's a constitutional optimism." Such an attitude is also "a duty": it is a "disservice to the reader or humanity . . . to inject doses of pessimism" (130).

Driven by biology, reworked through biography, and fueled by his love of chemistry, Levi's writing is marked with precision; as he puts it, writing is "a high precision work" (168). Precision manifests itself in the "almost juridical form" of his testimony in the first books, and it is always there in his arguments and his descriptions about the singularity of existence, displayed perhaps most obviously in his novel *The Periodic Table* (1975). Levi's description of his own survival and that of others is anchored in his sense of the singular and extraordinary throw of the dice: "All of us survivors are, by definition, exceptions, because in the *Lager* you were destined to die. If you did not die it was through some miraculous stroke of luck; you were an exception, a singularity not generic, totally specific" (2001, 122).

In Levi's account of surviving the Holocaust, we see that one of the striking aspects is the seeming lack of affect with which he takes us through the experiences of the camp. The scarce mention of affect or emotion suggests that being captured within the closed space of camp did not allow for that degree of reflexivity. Levi shows the suppression of emotion in a realm where people are stripped of their humanity. For instance, no mention of shame is made in his account of being inside. This becomes all the more shocking when at the beginning of *The Truce* and at the moment of their liberation, Levi writes of the shame that filled the survivors when the Russians soldiers entered the camp. "They did not greet us, nor did they smile; they seemed oppressed not only by compassion but by a confused restraint, which sealed their lips and bound their eyes to the funereal scene" (1979, 188).

Levi goes on to describe the awareness in hindsight of the shame the inmates had felt at each turn of the camp's outrages. From the shame these inmates of the *Lager* felt at their own bodies exposed in the gaze of the other, Levi describes the different aspects of shame: what "the just man experiences at another man's crime; the feeling of guilt that such a crime should exist, that it should have been introduced irrevocably into the world of things that exist, and that his will for good should have proved too weak or null, and should not have availed in defense" (188).

Listen again to how Levi describes those eyes that will induce shame in individuals who thought they had nothing left to be ashamed of, men and women who thought they were no longer human. The soldiers bow their heads in shame, sowing the seeds of shame in the inmates. Levi shows how shame is contagious. As he recounts the near farce of his long and constantly backtracked route home to Turin, he comes upon many who are described in shame. The Ukrainian women who, through a mixture of Nazi propaganda and hardship, had nonetheless "assented" of their own "free will" to leave their homeland and work for the Germans: "In Germany they had found bread, barbed wire, hard work, German order, servitude and shame; now under the weight of their shame they were being repatriated, without joy, without hope" (293). For Levi, shame in its shades of gray is plural. The experiences of shame are also what remind him of his humanity.

Levi speaks frequently about how the camps turned him into a writer. He also is clear about how they turned him into a Jew. As he puts it, "Before Hitler I was a middle-class Italian boy" (2001, 262). His experiences of the Holocaust made that identity impossible to maintain. After the war he integrated parts of his identity as Piedmontese with parts of Jewish tradition. One of the aspects of Jewish culture he came to value most was "the Talmudic tradition of impassioned but precise argument" (1979, 262). Of the many aspects of Levi that inspire, his way of combining passion and precision stands as a model of what we might hope for in writing. The passion that animates Levi's writing is like a slow burn. The lack of affect in his examples is also, at times, very precise—a lacuna of feeling that structures the text. He makes us feel the emptiness of that affectless state, how inhuman it is. When he turns to describing the slow return of humanity following the liberation, we see the different emotions that emerge as from a deep freeze. Levi's passion combined with precision powerfully challenges the current practice of writing about affects and emotion in a generalized and abstract way. This tendency uncouples writing from the real effects that affects such as shame produce in the world and for the world. Writing is interested; it is deeply embedded in contexts, politics, and bodies. Of course, the ways in which shame is written need to be carefully handled by the writer and the reader.

So what might a shame-induced ethics of writing entail? The specter of not interesting readers and the constant worry about adequately conveying the interest of our chosen topics should send a shiver down the spines of all writers. The blush of having failed to connect with readers should compel any writer to return to the page with renewed desire to do better—to get better—at this task of communicating that some of us take on. As Levi puts it, writing is like a telephone that works.

In Deleuze's description of writing shame, the stakes are high. The writer is more than a cipher conveying shameful moments. The body of the writer becomes the battleground where ideas and experiences collide, sometimes to produce new visions of life. This somewhat heroic description is tempered by King's prosaic argument about writing honestly. Finding the words to pitch ideas to your reader seems a long way from philosophy. But his insistence that writing is a serious activity that makes ideas and stories matter is not so different from Deleuze's insistence that ideas have to be generative. Ideas and writing about shame seek to generate new ways of thinking about how we are related to history and how we wish to live in the present. This is the legacy that Levi has bequeathed to us: the gift of shame. It is an uneasy task, this writing shame. How could it be otherwise when it involves a body grappling with interests, hoping to engage others?

Notes

1   My thanks go to Jeannie Martin for her encouragement and ideas. Martin has presented fascinating research on how young men, mainly of Lebanese background, negotiate notions of honor and shame in Australia. See Martin 2000. I also want to thank Jane Simon and Clifton Evers for their help in this project.
2   Kathleen Woodward addresses the problems academics face when dealing with the affective: "the stringent rules of emotionless rationality, especially in regards to research and writing" (1996, 760).
3   For an extended discussion of James's theory of emotion, see Redding 1999, and Barbalet 1998.
4   This quotation comes from a television interview conducted by Daniel Toaff and Emanuele Ascarelli, which was carried out on the journey to Auschwitz in 1982 and later broadcast on Italian TV (25 January 2001). A different translation of the same interview is published in Levi's *The Voice of Memory*, under the title "Return to Auschwitz." The only real difference between the two is that in the book Levi is translated as saying, "I don't know if I will eat" (2001, 213), which is rather different from "I don't know what I'll eat."

PART TWO   AESTHETICS AND THE EVERYDAY

4 CRUEL OPTIMISM

Lauren Berlant

When we talk about an object of desire, we are really talking about a cluster of promises we want someone or something to make to us and make possible for us. This cluster of promises could be embedded in a person, a thing, an institution, a text, a norm, a bunch of cells, smells, a good idea—whatever. To phrase "the object of desire" as a cluster of promises is to allow us to encounter what is incoherent or enigmatic in our attachments, not as confirmation of our irrationality but as an explanation for our sense of *our endurance in the object*, insofar as proximity to the object means proximity to the cluster of things that the object promises, some of which may be clear to us while others not so much. In other words, all attachments are optimistic. That does not mean that they all *feel* optimistic: one might dread, for example, returning to a scene of hunger or longing or the slapstick reiteration of a lover's or parent's typical misrecognition. But the surrender to the return to the scene where the object hovers in its potentialities is the operation of optimism as an affective form. In optimism, the subject leans toward promises contained within the present moment of the encounter with their object (Ghent 1990).[1]

"Cruel optimism" names a relation of attachment to compromised conditions of possibility whose realization is discovered either to be *im*possible, sheer fantasy, or *too* possible, and toxic. What's cruel about these attachments, and not merely inconvenient or tragic, is that the subjects who have *x* in their lives might not well endure the loss of their object or scene of desire, even though its presence threatens their well-being; because whatever the *content* of the attachment is, the continuity of the form of it provides something of the continuity of the subject's sense of what it means to keep on living on and to look forward to being in the world. This phrase points to a condition different than that of melancholia, which is enacted in the subject's desire to temporize an experience of the loss of an object or scene with which she has identified her ego continuity. Cruel optimism is the condition of maintaining an attachment to a problematic object *in advance* of its loss. One more thing: the cruelty of an optimistic attachment is, I think, usually something an analyst observes about someone's or some group's attachment to *x*, since usually that attachment exists without being an event, or even better, seems to lighten the load for that individual or group. But if the cruelty of an attachment *is* experienced by someone or some group, even in disavowed fashion, the fear is that the loss of the object or scene of promising itself will defeat the capacity to have any hope about anything. Often this fear of loss of a scene of optimism as such is unstated and only experienced in a sudden incapacity to manage startling situations, as we will see below.

One might point out that all objects or scenes of desire are problematic in that investments in them and projections onto them are less about them than about what cluster of desires and affects we can manage to keep magnetized to them. I have indeed wondered whether all optimism is cruel, because the experience of loss of the conditions of its reproduction can be so breathtakingly bad, just as the threat of the loss of *x* in the scope of one's attachment drives can feel like a threat to living-on itself. But some scenes of optimism are clearly crueler than others: where cruel optimism operates, the very vitalizing or animating potency of an object or scene of desire contributes to the attrition of the very thriving that is supposed to be made possible in the work of attachment in the first place. This might point to something as banal as a scouring love, but it also opens out to obsessive appetites, working for a living, patriotism, all kinds of things. One makes affective bargains about the costliness of one's attachments, usually unconscious ones, most of which keep one in proximity to the scene of desire or attrition.

This means that a poetics of attachment always involves some splitting off of the *story* I can tell about wanting to be near *x* (as though *x* has autonomous qualities) from the *activity* of the emotional habitus I have constructed by having *x* in my life in order to be able to project out my endurance as proximity to the complex of what *x* seems to offer and proffer. To understand cruel optimism, therefore, one must embark on an analysis of rhetorical indirection as a way of thinking about the strange temporalities of projection into an enabling object that is also disabling. I learned how to do this from reading Barbara Johnson's work on apostrophe and free indirect discourse. In her poetics of indirection, each of these rhetorical modes is shaped by the ways a writing subjectivity conjures other ones so that, in a performance of fantasmatic intersubjectivity, the writer gains superhuman observational authority, enabling a performance of being made possible by the proximity of the object. Because this object is something like what I am describing in the optimism of attachment, I will describe a bit of the shape of my transference with her thought.

In "Apostrophe, Animation, and Abortion" (1986), which will be my key referent here, Johnson tracks the political consequences of apostrophe for what has become fetal personhood: a silent, affectively present but physically displaced interlocutor (a lover, a fetus) is animated in speech as distant enough for a conversation but close enough to be imaginable by the speaker in whose head the entire scene is happening. But the condition of projected possibility, of a hearing that cannot take place in the terms of its enunciation ("you" are not here, "you" are eternally belated to the conversation with you that I am imagining), creates a fake present moment of intersubjectivity in which, nonetheless, a performance of address can take place. The present moment is made possible by the fantasy of you, laden with the *x* qualities I can project onto you, given your convenient absence. Apostrophe therefore appears to be a reaching out to a you, a direct movement from place *x* to *y*, but it is actually a turning back, an animating of a receiver on behalf of the desire to make something happen *now* that realizes something *in the speaker*, makes the speaker more or differently possible, because she has admitted, in a sense, the importance of speaking for, as, and to, two: but only under the condition, and illusion, that the two is really (in) one.

Apostrophe is thus an indirect, unstable, physically impossible but phenomenologically vitalizing movement of rhetorical animation that permits subjects to suspend themselves in the optimism of a potential occupation of the same psychic space of others, the objects of desire who make you possible (by having some promising qualities, but also by not being there).[2] Later work, such as on "Muteness Envy" (1998), elaborates Johnson's description of the gendered rhetorical politics of this projection of voluble intersubjectivity. The paradox remains that the conditions of the lush submerging of one consciousness into another require a double negation: of the speaker's boundaries, so she or he can grow bigger in rhetorical proximity to the object of desire; and of the spoken of, who is more or less a powerful mute placeholder providing an opportunity for the speaker's imagination of her, his, or their flourishing.

Of course psychoanalytically speaking all intersubjectivity is impossible. It is a wish, a desire, and a demand for an enduring sense of being with and in *x*, and it is related to that big knot that marks the indeterminate relation between a feeling of recognition and misrecognition—recognition is the misrecognition you can bear, a transaction that affirms you without, again, necessarily feeling good (it might idealize, it might affirm your monstrosity, it might mirror your desire to be nothing enough to live under the radar, it might feel just right, and so on).[3] Johnson's work on projection shows that scenes of impossible identity, rhetorically rendered, open up meaning and knowledge by mining the negative—projective, boundary-dissolving— spaces of attachment to the object of address who must be absent in order for the desiring subject of intersubjectivity to get some traction, to stabilize her proximity to the object or scene of promise. In free indirect discourse, a cognate kind of suspension, the circulation of this kind of merged and submerged observational subjectivity has less pernicious outcomes, at least when Johnson reads Zora Neale Hurston's practice of it. In a narrator's part-merging with a character's consciousness, say, free indirect discourse performs the impossibility of locating an observational intelligence in one or any body, and therefore forces the reader to transact a different, more open relation of unfolding to what she is reading, judging, being, and thinking she understands. In Johnson's work such a transformative transaction through reading or speaking "unfolds" the subject in a good way, despite whatever desires he or she may have not to become significantly different (Johnson 2002, 8). In short, Johnson's work on projection is about the optimism of attachment, and it is often itself optimistic about the negations and extensions of personhood that forms of suspended intersubjectivity demand from the reader.

What follows is not so buoyant: this is an essay politicizing Freud's observation that "people never willingly abandon a libidinal position, not even, indeed, when a substitute is already beckoning to them" (1957, 244). It comes from a longer project about the politics, aesthetics, and projections of political depression. Political depression persists in affective judgments of the world's intractability—evidenced in affectlessness, apathy, coolness, cynicism, and so on—modes of what might be called detachment that are really not detached at all but constitute ongoing relations of sociality.[4] The politically depressed position is manifested in the problem of the difficulty of detaching from life-building modalities that can no longer be said to be doing their work, and which indeed make obstacles to the desires that animate them; my archive tracks practices of self-interruption, self-suspension, and self-abeyance that indicate people's struggles to change, but not traumatically, the terms of value in which their life-making activity has been cast (Sedgwick 2006).

Cruel optimism is, then, like all phrases, a *deictic*, a phrase that points to a proximate location: as an analytic lever it is an incitement to inhabit and to track the affective attachment to what we call "the good life," which is for so many a bad life that wears out the subjects who nonetheless, and at the same time, find their conditions of possibility within it. My assumption is that the conditions of ordinary life in the contemporary world even of relative wealth, as in the United States, are conditions of the attrition or the wearing out of the subject, and that the irony that the labor of reproducing life in the contemporary world is also the activity of being worn out by it has specific implications for thinking about the ordinariness of suffering, the violence of normativity, and the "technologies of patience" or lag that enable a concept of the later to suspend questions of the cruelty of the now (Berlant 1997, 222). Cruel optimism is in this sense a concept pointing toward a mode of lived imminence, one that grows from a perception about the reasons why people are not Melville's Bartleby, why they do not prefer to interfere with varieties of rimmiseration, but instead choose to ride the wave of the system of attachment that they are used to, to syncopate with it, or to be held in a relation of reciprocity, reconciliation, or resignation that does not mean defeat by it. Or perhaps they move to normative form to get numb with the consensual promise and to misrecognize that promise as an achievement. This essay traverses three episodes of suspension—from John Ashbery (2005), Charles Johnson (1994), and Geoff Ryman (1992)—of the reproduction of habituated or normative life. These suspensions open up revelations about the promises that had clustered as people's objects of desire, stage moments of exuberance in the impasse near the normal, and provide tools for suggesting why these exuberant attachments keep ticking not like the time bomb they might be but like a white noise machine that provides assurance that what seems like static really is, after all, a rhythm people can enter into while they're dithering, tottering, bargaining, testing, or otherwise being worn out by the promises that they have attached to in this world.

The Promise of the Object

A recent, untitled poem by John Ashbery stages the most promising version of this scene of promises for us, foregrounding the Doppler effect of knowledge, phrasing as a kind of spatial lag the political economy of disavowal we drag around like a shadow, and yet providing an experience of liveness in the object that is not only livable, but at once simplifying and revolutionary— the bourgeois dream couplet:

> We were warned about spiders, and the
>   occasional famine.
> We drove downtown to see our
>   neighbors. None of them were home.
> We nestled in yards the municipality had
>   created,
> reminisced about other, different places—
> but were they? Hadn't we known it all
>   before?
>
> In vineyards where the bee's hymn
>   drowns the monotony,
> we slept for peace, joining in the great
>   run.
> He came up to me.
> It was all as it had been,
> except for the weight of the present,
> that scuttled the pact we made with
> heaven.
> In truth there was no cause for rejoicing,
> nor need to turn around, either.
> We were lost just by standing,
> listening to the hum of the wires overhead
>
>   (Ashbery 2005)

The opening frame is the scene of the American Dream not realized, but almost—or as Ashbery says in a contiguous poem, "Mirage control has sealed the borders/with light and the endless diffidence light begets" (Ashbery, "Filagrane"). In this poem, home and hymn *almost* rhyme; but nature threatens our sense of plenitude; and then there is what the speaker calls "the weight of the present" that makes our politics, therefore, quietist, involving sleeping for peace, deflating the symbolic into the somatic. How long have people thought about the present as having weight, being a thing disconnected from other things, as an *obstacle* to living? Everything in this poem is very general, and yet we can derive some contexts from within it— imagining, for example, the weight of the default space of the poem as it instantiates something of the American Dream, suburb-style. Is it merely moralistic or politically smug to note that the people who maintain the appearance of manicured space are not present in the poem's "we," that the poem does not image the workers who make possible the reproduction of the lovely life, and where they came from, and the noises of their day, and their leisure? That the sounds of suburban leisure are other people's labor sounds? That the unmarked speaking people are probably white and American and their servants so often not?

These concerns are not foregrounded in the poem's sense of its event or scene of prolific consciousness, but it does not violate the poem's aesthetic autonomy or singularity to think about the conditions of the production of autonomy in it. If anything, the explicit rhetoric of the neighbor shows it to be aware, after all, that the American Dream does not allow a lot of time for curiosity about people it is not convenient or productive to have curiosity about. It is a space where the pleasure that one's neighbors give is in their propinquity, their light contact: in the American Dream we see neighbors when we want to, when we're puttering outside or perhaps in a restaurant, and in any case the pleasure they provide is in their relative distance, their being parallel to, without being inside of, the narrator's "municipally" zoned property, where he hoards, I mean enjoys, his leisured pleasure, as though in a vineyard in the country, and where intrusions by the nosy neighbor, or superego, would interrupt his projections of happiness from the empire of the backyard.[5] The buzz of other people's labor in the vineyards is the condition of the privilege of being bored with life and three-quarters detached, absorbed in a process of circulating, in a vaguely lateral way.

In short, in this untitled poem, "we" have chosen to be deadened citizens, happy to be the color someone has placed inside of the lines: "we" would be tickled if, after all, "we" were those characters in Donald Barthelme's short story "I Bought a Little City" (1976), who live simply in a housing complex that, seen from the sky, reproduces the *Mona Lisa* for anyone with the time and money to inhabit a certain perspective. "We" live our lives as works of formal beauty, if not art: "we" live with a sense of slight excitement, composing ourselves patiently toward fulfilling the promise of living not too intensely the good life of what Slavoj Žižek might call a decaffeinated sublime (2004). There is nothing especially original or profound in Ashbery's send-up of suburban pleasures: the comforting sound and slightly dull rhythm of cliché performs exactly how much life one can bear to have there, and what it means to desire to move freely within the municipality, a manicured zone of what had been a fantasy.

The political economy of perspective in its relation to property, and property in its relation to self-medication, is commented on by Marx in the *Economic and Philosophic Manuscripts*:

> Private property has made us so stupid and one-sided that an object is only *ours* when we have it—when it exists for us as capital, or when it is directly possessed, eaten, drunk, worn, inhabited, etc.,—in short, when it is *used* by us. . . . In the place of all physical and mental senses there has therefore come the sheer estrangement of all these senses, into the sense of *having*. The human being had to be reduced to this absolute poverty in order that he might yield his inner wealth to the outer world. . . . The abolition of private property is therefore the complete *emancipation* of all human senses and qualities, but it is this emancipation precisely because these senses and attributes have become, subjectively and objectively, human. The eye has become a *human* eye, just as its *object* has become a social, human object—an object made by man for man. *The senses* have therefore become directly in their practice theoreticians. They relate themselves to the thing for the sake of the thing, but the thing itself is an *objective human* relation to itself and to man, [in practice I can relate myself to a thing humanly only if the thing relates itself humanly to the human being] and vice versa. Need or enjoyment [has] consequently lost its *egotistical* nature, and nature has lost its mere *utility* by use becoming *human* use. (1974, 162)

The resonances of Marx's analysis of the senses penetrate Ashbery's poem complexly. As Marx would predict, the "we" of this poem begins by owning what it sees and seeing what it owns, feeling nature as an impingement on his autoreferential world: but, then, it is haunted that its knowledge is a repetition of a something it can't quite remember, perhaps because, as subjects of productive and consumer capital, "we" were willing to have our memories rezoned by the constant tinkering required to maintain the machinery and appearance of dependable life. "We" were docile, compliant, good sports. "We" live in proximity to a desire now bound up in this version of the good life and can almost remember being alive in it, flooded by a sense of expectation that "we" knew was only pointed to by property and the dependable life we meant to make for it. Our senses are not yet theoreticians because they are bound up by the rule, the map, the inherited fantasy, and the hum of worker bees who fertilize materially the life we are moving through. Then again, maybe we did not really want our senses to be theoreticians because then we would see ourselves as an effect of an exchange with the world, beholden to it, useful for it, rather than sovereign, at the end of the day. What do we do for a living, after all? "We" seem to be folks of leisure, of the endless weekend, our own exploitation off-screen, where a consumer's happy circulation in familiarity is almost all that matters: "Hadn't we known it all before?"

But despite the presenting face of it, as a poem voiced from within the community of faceless universal subjects of self-referentiality, the action of the poem is not bound up wholly in the vague attachment to an American Dream that is actually lived as a series of missed encounters with disaster and human contact, cut to size in barely experienced episodes. The action of the poem is charted in the small movement between home, hymn, and hum. Most importantly, there is an event that breaks up the undramatic self-hoarding of the collective life, and it is not the vacation in the vineyards that the relief of suburban unproductivity suggests.

Ashbery might be having a Christian thought, in the space between reverie and reverence: the bees seem to echo the famous passage from Sir Thomas Browne's *Religio Medici* that describes how the wisdom of bees is far in advance of what human reason understands about its condition.[6] Relatedly, with all the Miltonic and Eliotic resonance of the poem's tropes he might be revising his relation to religious lyric.[7] We might even think that the point is to contrast the poem's wittily ironic and vaguely sacred meditations with its key present and fleshly event, that scene of gayness in America embodied in the phrase: "He came up to me." It's like "Chloe liked Olivia": the sensorium-shaking transformative event in Ashbery's lyric remembers the efficiency of a similar transformation for Virginia Woolf (1957).[8] He came up to me and broke my contract with heaven not to be gay. Queerness and religious affect open up a space of reverence here: in the end, life is at the best imaginable of impasses. Life has been interrupted or, as Badiou would say, seized by an event that demands fidelity.[9]

This event, however, also has impact *despite* the autobiographical. The poem closes by focusing on what happens when someone allows himself to be changed by an event of being with the object, not in the semi-anonymous projected proximity of apostrophe or the we-did-this and we-did-that sociality of the first stanza and not in terms of a dramatics of an uncloseted sexual identity, indeed not in terms of biography at all. The seismic shift takes place in yielding to the proximity of an intimacy undefined by talking, made by a gesture of approach that holds open a space between two people just standing there linked newly.

This shift in registers, which relocates the speaker of the poem into somewhere suspended, might be understood in a Habermasean way. In *The Structural Transformation of the Public Sphere* (1989) Habermas talks about the public/private zoning of normative being in terms of a split within the man of modernity, who is a man of the house and a man of the market. Habermas suggests that the problem of living capitalist modernity is in managing the relations between these spheres as a bourgeois and a subject of emotions. A bourgeois is someone who instrumentalizes his social relations in terms of the rules of the market, and who is zoned by the people who assign value to property as having value in proximity to his property and his being self-possessed. For the bourgeois there is property, there is home, and the man is a little leader in the home, and everyone recognizes his authority wherever he carries his propriety onto property. At the same time the man cultivates an image of himself as fundamentally shaped in transactions of feeling, not capital. The "*homme*" in the house who sees himself as effective in the world and an authority in all domains of activity is distinguished and made singular by participation in a community of love, among people who choose each other, who, one might say, can come up to each other (30–50). The poem says that "in truth there was no cause for rejoicing": there was no cause for rejoicing in truth, or objectivity. Instead, there is the expectation of intimacy. And lyric poetry.

What live intimacy there is in this poem, though, seems to happen outside of the home and the municipality, in an unzoned locale. The event of the poem is the thing that happens when "he" comes "up to me" and reminds me that I am not the subject of a hymn but of a hum, the thing that resonates around me, which might be heaven or bees or desire or electric wires, but whatever it is it involves getting lost in proximity to someone and in becoming lost there, in a lovely way. He and I together experience a hum not where "we" were but all around, and that hum is a temporizing, a hesitation in time that is not in time with the world of drives and driving;

nor is it in a mapped space, but rather a space that is lost. What intersubjectivity there is has no content but is made in the simultaneity of listening, a
scene of subjective experience that can only be seen and not heard. This
intimacy is visible and radically private, and pretty uncoded. Life amongst *les
hommes* between home and hymn becomes interrupted by an um, an interruption of truth, where the people are now lost but alive and unvanquished
in their displacement.

It might be kind of thrilling to think about this poem as delineating a
means of production of the impasse of the present that hasn't yet been
absorbed in the bourgeois senses, but takes one out to the space of sociality
that listens, is receptive, and calls for theory. Be open to he who comes up to
you. Be changed by an encounter. Become a poet of the episode, the elision,
the ellipsis . . .

At the same time, one might note that it matters who wrote this poem, a
confident person. He finds possibility in a moment of suspension and requires neither the logic of the market to secure his value nor the intimate
recognition of anything municipally normal or domestic to assure that he
has boundaries. He can hold a non-space without being meaningful. This
does not seem to threaten him. Thus this instance of optimism might or
might not be a part of cruel optimism: we don't know. The promise is
everywhere, and the dissolution of the form of being that existed before the
event is not cause for mourning or rejoicing: it is just a fact. Does the
episodic nature of the interruption enable him, after the moment, to return
to the suburbs refreshed? Will they go to a high-end café and buy some
intensified coffee supercharged by sugar and milk? Will they go get otherwise stimulated? Will they become different in a way that they can build a
world on? Is the couple a stand-in for the collective that can now be awake
for peace rather than somnambulant? Does the aesthetic moment of the
different autonomy they get when they exist together in reverie become not a
condition for *detaching* from the market but the condition of living in it, so
that they can think that who they *really are* are people who can be lost in a
moment? Habermas would perhaps note that the fantasy of the lovers' apo-
theosis enables Market Man to drown out the news that he is also the
exploiter of gardeners, an instrumental and instrumentalizing agent. John
Ricco (2002) might argue that the men's outsideness and outsiderness demonstrate the potential resource of all gayness to make a queer antinorma-
tivity that does not look back to domesticity wishfully. It is impossible to say
how deep the break is. By the end, the speaker thinks he *really* lives now, in a

moment of suspension. He *really* is a lover, an intimate, no longer the user of gas and fertilizer and the delegator of hard labor to others. That was in another life, so it seems.

Or, perhaps we can read the scale of the shift in terms of the humming soundtrack. The soundtrack is the genre of ineloquence most conventional to melodrama: it is what tells you that you are really most at home in yourself bathed by emotions you can always recognize and that whatever material harshness you live is not the real, but an accident that you have to clean up after, which will be more pleasant if you whistle while you work. The concept of "the soundtrack of our lives," to cite a cliché that is also the ironic name of a great post-punk neo-psychedelic band and a growing category of niche marketing, is powerful because it accompanies one as a portable hoard that expresses one's true inner taste and high value; it holds a place open for an optimistic rereading of the rhythms of living and confirms everybody as a star. Your soundtrack is one place where you can be in love with yourself and express your fidelity to your own trueness in sublime conventionality, regardless of the particularity of the sounds. We hear the hum of the universe, says Ashbery's optimist, and aspire to be in proximity to it: but the analyst of cruel optimism wants to understand how much an instance of sentimental abstraction or emotional saturation costs, what labor fuels the shift from the concrete real to the soundtrack reel, who is in control of the meaning of the shift, the pacing of the shift, and the consequences of detaching, even for a moment, from the consensual mirage. Moving from home to hymn to hum, the poem by Ashbery makes an interruptive stillness that is ineloquent and eloquent, meaningful and a placeholder for an unformed experience. The soundtrack he hears is like lyric itself, comfortable with displacing realism about the material reproduction of life and the pain of intimacy and numbness to another time and space.

Moving from home to hum, to *homme* to um, an interruption: it sounds like punning, this Thoreauvian method of sounding out the space of a moment to measure its contours, to ask what is being stopped, who gets to do it, and what it would mean to be in this moment and then beyond it. It is always a risk to let someone in, to insist on a pacing different than the productivist pacing, say, of capitalist normativity. Of course "he" is not my object, my cluster of promises: "he" came up to *me*. Even if being the object is more secure than having one and risking disappointment, the poem stops before anyone gets too deep into the projecting and embedding. It is a poem about being open to an encounter that is potentially transformative, without having yet congealed into the couple form, a friendship, a quick sexual interlude, anything. It gestures toward being lost or suspended in a process of knowing nothing about how a scene of collaborative action will open up a space of potential liveness that is not a space on which anything can be built. In the space of lag between he and me something happens and the royal or sovereign we of the poem is no longer preoccupied but gets to catch up to himself in the um of a singular sociality whose political economy we are asking questions of. Its happiness might be cruel, requiring someone else's expenditure; we'll never know: the substitution of habituated indifference with a spreading pleasure might open up a wedge into an alternative ethics of living, or not. What happens next is the unfinished business of the poem: right now, the senses it stages are open to becoming theoreticians.

Whatever it is, sounding the poem for the meaning of the impasse it portrays in an event that displaces and dissolves ordinary life does not confirm that all lyric or episodic interruptions are even potentially a condition of possibility for imagining a radically resensualized post-Fordist subject. But analytically this singular lyric opens up an opportunity to learn to pay attention to, have transference with, those moments of suspension in which the subject can no longer take his continuity in history for granted but feels full of a *something* ineloquently promising, a something that reveals, at the same time, a trenchant *nothing* general about conditions of optimism and cruel optimism. Attending to the heterosonic and heterotemporal spaces within capital in which an event suspends ordinary time, sounds, and senses can change, potentially, how we can understand what being historical means. Because Ashbery's speaker is confident, because he has the ballast of normative recognitions and modes of social belonging in the habit of his flesh, I believe, he can stand detaching from the promise of his habituated life and can thrive in the openness of desire to form, as heady as that might be. If it is to be any more than a story about his singularity, though, the new intersubjective scene of sense would have to be able to extend the moment to activity that would dissolve the legitimacy of the optimism embedded in the now displaced world, with its promising proprietary zones, scenes, scapes, and institutions. Otherwise this is not an event, but an episode in an environment that can well absorb and even sanction a little spontaneous leisure.

The Promise of Exchange Value

Ashbery's speaker is very lucky that he gets to dissolve and thrive in the collaborative unknowing initiated by the gesture, the encounter, and potentially the event that unbottle whatever it is that "he/me" can now rest in hearing. In Charles Johnson's "Exchange Value" (1994) a situation that might also have turned out that way does not, and the story's enumeration of what happens to the people who enter a new atmosphere of new objects, a scene between one habituated life and another yet to be invented, says something about why the phrase "political economy" must run alongside our analysis of cruel and usual optimism. Why do some people have the chops for improvising unknowing while others run out of breath, not humming but hoarding?

As with Ashbery's lyric, this story begins with a meditation on neighbors and neighborhoods. "Exchange Value" takes place during the 1970s on the South Side of Chicago, around 49th Street.[10] The protagonists, eighteen-year-old Cooter and his older brother, Loftis, are poor and African American. They do not drive downtown regularly to see their friends, or frequent other neighborhoods, regularly: they do not have cars. Home and the hood are spaces of localized, personalized practices of encountering, wandering, and scrounging. But here, the intimacy of proximity has nothing to do with anyone's lyric intersubjectivity, even though the story takes place in the meditative rhythms of Cooter's way of parsing a new situation. The subjects of "Exchange Value" are expressive and opaque, but with quite different valences than in our previous example.

The story develops as the two brothers concoct a plan to rob their possibly dead neighbor, Miss Bailey. Who is Miss Bailey? Nobody knows: she is a neighbor, so one does not need to know her; her job is to be around, to be a "character," which is what you call someone who performs a familiar set of actions around you but is not intimate with you. Miss Bailey dresses in cast-off men's clothes; like Cooter and Loftis, she eats free meals that she begs off of a local Creole restaurant; when Cooter gives her pocket change, she doesn't spend it, she eats it. This is what Cooter knows about her, deducing nothing more about her from her actions. The story takes place because she is always around and then she isn't. Cooter and Loftis think that perhaps she has died, and they determine to get the first pickings.

This kind of behavior, this scavenging in other people's stuff, is not characteristic of Cooter, but it doesn't violate his fundamental relation to the world either. Compared to his brother, he has always been branded a loser. "Mama used to say it was Loftis, not me, who'd go places. . . . Loftis, he graduated fifth at DuSable High School, had two gigs and, like Papa, he be always wanting the things white people had out in Hyde Park, where Mama did daywork sometimes." The children's parents are both dead by this point in their lives: Papa from overwork and Mama because she was as "big as a Frigidaire." Having watched this, Cooter refuses to ride the wave of the American Dream: remembering his parents "killing theyselves for chump change—a pitiful li'l bowl of porridge—I get to thinking that even if I ain't had all I wanted, maybe I've had, you know, all I'm ever gonna get" and so organizes his life through the lateral enjoyments of fantasy. "I can't keep no job and sorta stay close to home, watching TV, or reading *World's Finest* comic books, or maybe just laying dead, listening to music, imagining I see faces or foreign places in water stains on the wallpaper" (28–29).

During the 1970s the *World's Finest* series paired Batman and Superman as a crime-fighting team. But Cooter's fantasies aren't mimetic—they are aleatory and passive ways of inhabiting and making an environment in which attachments are not optimistically pointing toward a cluster of transcendent promises, but toward something else, something bearable that holds off not just the imminence of loss but the loss that, inevitably, just happened. For Cooter fantasy isn't a plan. It calibrates nothing about how to live. It is the *action* of living for him, his way of passing time not trying to make something of himself in a system of exploitation and exchange, which in the political economy of his world does not produce rest or waste but slow death, the attrition of subjects by the exchange values of capital, which are to trade the worker's body for a deferred enjoyment that, if they are on the bottom of the class structure, they are not likely to be around to take pleasure in, as his parents' fate demonstrates (Berlant 2007a).

In contrast, Loftis's relation to fantasy is realist. He inherited his parents' optimism toward his life by being ambitious. But his strategies are strictly formal. He takes classes from Black Nationalists at the "Black People's Topographical Library," reads *Esquire* and *The Black Scholar*, and sews upscale labels onto his downscale clothes: to him getting ahead is what counts, whether it is via power, labor, or the "hustle" (29). His opinion of Cooter is quite low because the younger brother is dreamy and has no drive. Nonetheless, they decide to do the job together.

Miss Bailey's apartment is pitch dark and reeks of shit: a newspaper clipping from the *Chicago Defender* among the garbage reveals that her former employer, Henry Conners, had left her his entire estate, and that all of the years of scavenging and weirdness masked her possession of enormous wealth. It all makes sense in the dark. But when the light turns on, Cooter notes, "Shapes come forward in the light and I thought for an instant like I'd slipped in space" (30). In this moment Cooter enters an impasse: his talent at making out foreign shapes becomes applied to his own life, which he can no longer occupy, as hearing the soundtrack in the mode of deadened life is no longer available as a means of passing time.

> Her living room, webbed in dust, be filled to the max with dollars of all denominations, stacks of stock in General Motors, Gulf Oil, and 3M company in old White Owl cigar boxes, battered purses, or bound in pink rubber bands . . . everything, like a world inside the world, you take it from me, so like picturebook scenes of plentifulness you could seal yourself off in here and settle forever. Loftis and me both drew breath suddenly. There be unopened cases of Jack Daniel's, three safes cemented to the floor, hundreds of matchbooks, unworn clothes, a fuel-burning stove, dozens of wedding rings, rubbish, World War II magazines, a carton of a hundred canned sardines, mink stoles, old rags, a birdcage, a bucket of silver dollars, thousands of books, paintings, quarters in tobacco cans, two pianos, glass jars of pennies, a set of bagpipes, an almost complete Model A Ford dappled with rust, and I swear, three sections of a dead tree. (30–31)

How do we understand this collection not only of things but of details? Cooter's verbal response is not to be a historian, but a moralist: "A *tree* ain't normal" (31). But to my eye the story's main event, the scene of potential change, is somatic. Change is an impact lived on the body before anything is understood, and it is simultaneously meaningful and ineloquent, an atmosphere that Cooter and Loftis spend the rest of the story and their lives catching up to. It's like winning the lottery, getting a wash of money you haven't earned: being possessed by coming into possession of possessions, they are shocked into something impassive. This crack in the necessities of history makes Cooter's head get light—"My knees failed; then I did a Hollywood faint" (32); Loftis "pant[s] a little" and "for the first time . . . looked like he didn't know his next move" (31): their bodies become suspended.

But if riches change history, they also make it possible for history to be something other than a zone of barely or badly imagined possibility. Loftis returns to crazy reason and puts the brake on their adrenalin. He forces Cooter to catalogue everything. Eventually,

> that cranky old ninnyhammer's hoard adds up to $879,543 in cash, thirty-two bank books . . . I wasn't sure I was dreaming or what, but I suddenly flashed on this feeling, once we left her flat, that all the fears Loftis and me had about the future be gone, 'cause Miss Bailey's property was the past—

the power of that fellah Henry Conners trapped like a bottle spirit— which we could live off, so it was the future too, pure potential: can *do*. Loftis got to talking on about how that piano we pushed home be equal to a thousand bills, jim, which equals, say, a bad TEAC A-3340 tape deck, or a down payment on a deuce-and-a-quarter. Its value be (Loftis say) that of a universal standard of measure, relational, unreal as number, so that tape deck could turn, magically, into two gold lamé suits, a trip to Tijuana, or twenty-give blow jobs from a ho—we had $879,543 worth of wishes, if you can deal with that. Be like Miss Bailey's stuff is raw energy, and Loftis and me, like wizards, could transform her stuff into anything else at will. All we had to do, it seemed to me, was decide exactly what to exchange it for. (34–35)

Cooter's senses, awakened to the promises clustered around things, have truly become theoreticians. Exchange value is not identical to the price of things, but marks a determination of what else a thing can get exchanged *for*, as though money were not involved, exactly, in the mediations. Your coat for a piano. Your money for your life.

The scene of shocking wealth changes the terms of the meaning of life, of the reproduction of life, and of exchange itself. Loftis gets very quiet. Cooter grabs a bunch of money and goes downtown to spend it. But though downtown Chicago is just a few miles away, it is like a foreign country to Cooter: he does not speak its economic language. Theory aside, in practice Cooter doesn't have a clue what to do with the money and realizes sickeningly, right away, that money can't make you feel like you belong if you are not already privileged to feel that way. He buys ugly, badly made, expensive clothes that shame him right away. He eats meat till he gets sick. He takes cabs everywhere. When he gets home, his brother's gone psychotic. Loftis has built an elaborate trap, a vault to protect the money. He yells at Cooter for spending, because the only power is in hoarding. Loftis says, "As soon as you buy something you *lose* the power to buy something." He cannot protect himself from Miss Bailey's fate: "suffering that special Negro fear of using up what little we get in this life" (37); inheritance "put her through changes, she be spellbound, possessed by the promise of life, panicky about depletion, and locked now in the past because *every* purchase, you know, has to be a poor buy: a loss of life" (37–38).

Notice how frequently Johnson reverts to the word "life": can a person on the bottom survive living "life" stripped of the illusion of indefinite endurance via whatever kinds of fantasmatic practices he has been able to cobble together? How quickly can one dispense with the old bargains between defense and desire, adapting to a regime whose rules provide no felt comfort? Is the story of the break to which the brothers cannot adapt the proof that time is money? "Exchange Value" demonstrates the proximity of two kinds of cruel optimism: with little cultural or economic capital and bearing the history of a racial disinheritance from the norms of white supremacist power, you work yourself to death, or coast to nonexistence; or, with the ballast of capital, you hoard against death, deferring life, until you die. Cooter is the realist; he can see that there is no way out, now, no living as if not in a relation to death, which is figured in all of the potential loss that precedes it.

This story is exquisitely tender toward the surrealism of survival in the context of poverty so extreme that riches can only confirm insecurity. On either side of the capital divide, human creativity, energy, and agency are all bound up in bargaining, strategizing: it only begins with the mother at the sink predicting which of her sons has the sense to ride the rhythms of remuneration in the system; the parents dying before the kids are of age because of having had to scavenge for what Cooter scathingly calls "chump change"; Cooter choosing to live to feed his passivity and capacity for fantasy; and Loftis living amorally among a variety of styles for gaining upward mobility. Before the windfall they all manifest the improvisatory opportunism of people on the bottom who, having little to lose, and living in an economy of pleading, sharing, and hiding, will go for something if the occasion permits (29).

But the inheritance the men engineer produces a sensorial break for them, and whereas the earlier modes of optimism included a community and a meanwhile that meant being somewhere and knowing people no matter what style of living one chose, the later modes almost force privacy, hoarding, becoming pure potential itself. The inheritance becomes the promise of the promise, of a technical optimism; it sutures them both to life lived without risk, in proximity to plenitude without enjoyment. For Loftis it destroys the pleasure of the stress of getting through the day because the scale of potential loss is too huge. Cooter is more passive: he will fold himself into his brother's crypt because that is who he is, a person who navigates available spaces, not makes them. At the same time, the withdrawal of the brothers from even vague participation in a life made from scheming mimes one aspect of the logic of capital in which they have been relocated. The post-inheritance sensibility is crazy in the way that reason is crazy, because the cruel optimism of capital fragments into so many contradictory logics. Hoarding controls the promise of value without enjoyment; consumption promises satisfaction and then denies it because all objects are placeholders for the enjoyment of never being satisfied; spending is not an exchange, but a loss and a letdown more emotional than actuarial. In "Exchange Value" insanity substitutes for the mirage that enables disavowing the knowledge that when owning money mediates sociality, exchange value *is* the fantasy and there was never ever any exchange value.

Optimism, even under the racial mediations of experiencing entrenched capitalist inequalities in the United States, involves thinking that in exchange one can achieve recognition. But, one must always ask, recognition of what? One's self-idealization, one's style of ambivalence, one's tender bits, or one's longing for the event of recognition itself? For Ashbery recognition's exchange value takes him out of personality, that cluster of familiar repetitions: it is pure potentiality in the good sense, and it provides a lovely experience of realizing that the flurry of activity that stood in for making a life was an impasse now passed by and replaced by another, a slower one, where one is experiencing something, hanging around, letting something or someone in the way a sound comes, undefensively, and not feeling yet that the condition of possibility has become misrecognized by becoming embedded in mere objects or scenes. For the men who still feel like boys at the close of "Exchange Value" the affect attached to optimism is either panic or numbness, not humming. While, as defenses, these modes of vibrating near-paralysis are cognate to the modes of getting by that preceded Miss Bailey's death, those earlier styles of floating beneath value while tending toward fantasies of it now seem utopian compared to the crypt of shattered being that pecuniary optimism cruelly engenders.

The Promise of Being Taught

It is striking that these moments of optimism, which mark a possibility that the habits of a history might *not* be reproduced, release an overwhelmingly negative force: one predicts such effects in traumatic scenes, but it is not usual to think about an optimistic event as having the same potential consequences. The conventional fantasy that a revolutionary lifting of being might happen in the new object or scene of promise would predict otherwise than that a person or a group might prefer, after all, to surf from episode to episode while leaning toward a cluster of vaguely phrased prospects. And yet, at a certain degree of abstraction both from trauma and optimism the sensual experience of self-dissolution, radically reshaped consciousness, new sensoria, and narrative rupture can look similar; the subject's grasping toward stabilizing form, too, in the face of dissolution, looks like classic compensation, the production of habits signifying predictability as a defense against losing emotional shape entirely.

I have suggested that the particular ways in which identity and desire are articulated and lived sensually within capitalist culture produce such counterintuitive overlaps. But it would be reductive to read the preceding as a claim that anyone's subjective transaction with the optimistic structure of value in capital *produces* the knotty entailments of cruel optimism as such. People *are* worn out by the activity of life-building, especially the poor and the non-normative. But lives are singular; people make mistakes, are inconstant, cruel, and kind; and accidents happen. This essay's archive focuses on artworks that explicitly remediate singularities into cases of non-universal but general abstraction, providing narrative scenarios of how people learn to identify, manage, and maintain the hazy luminosity of their attachment to being *x* and having *x*, given that their attachments were promises and not possessions after all.

Geoff Ryman's historical novel *Was* (1992) offers yet a different scenario for tracking the enduring charisma of the normative. Weaving highly subjective activities of fantasy-making through agrarian Kansas and the mass culture industry, *Was* uses encounters with *The Wizard of Oz* to narrate the processes by which people hoard themselves against dissolution and yet seek to dissolve their hoard in transformative experiences of attachment whose effects are frightening, exhilarating, the only thing that makes living worthwhile, and yet a threat to existence itself. *Was* provides a kind of limit case of cruel optimism, as its pursuit of the affective continuity of trauma and optimism in self-unfolding excitement is neither comic, tragic, nor melodramatic, but meta-formal: it absorbs all of these into a literary mode that validates fantasy (from absorption in pretty things to crazy delusion) as a life-affirming defense against the attritions of ordinary violent history.

In this novel as in our other examples, the affective feeling of normativity is expressed in the sense that one ought to be dealt with gently by the world, and to live happily with strangers and intimates without being torn and worn out by the labor of disappointment and the disappointment of labor. Here, though, evidence of the possibility of enduring that way in one's object or scene is not embedded in the couple form, the love plot, the family, fame, work, wealth, or property. Those are the sites of cruel optimism, scenes of conventional desire that stand manifestly in the way of the subject's thriving. Instead, the novel offers a two-step of saturation in mass fantasy and history as solutions to the problem of surviving the brutality of trauma *and* optimism in the ordinary world. It sees leaving the singular for the general through a wide range of kinds of stranger intimacy as the best resource for thriving: but at least in one case, even those encounters endanger the subject so worn out by the work of surviving the bad life, as all she has left, in a sense, is her defenses.

Was constructs a post-traumatic drama that is held together, in the end, by the governing consciousness of Bill Davison, a mental health worker, a white heterosexual midwesterner whose only previous personal brush with trauma had been ambivalence toward his fiancée, but whose professional capacity to enter into the impasse with his patients, and to let their impasses into him, makes him the novel's optimistic remainder, a rich witness. The first traumatic story told is about the real Dorothy Gale, spelled Gael, partly, I imagine, to link up the girl who is transported to Oz on a strong breeze to someone in prison, and also to link her to the Gaelic part of Scotland, home of the historical novel, the genre whose affective and political conventions shape explicitly Ryman's meditation on experiences and memories whose traces are in archives, landscapes, and bodies scattered throughout Kansas, Canada, and the United States. Like Cooter, this Dorothy Gael uses whatever fantasy she can scrape together to survive her scene of hopeless historical embeddedness. But her process is not to drift vaguely but intensely, by way of multi-generic invention: dreams, fantasies, private plays, psychotic projection, aggressive quiet, lying, being a loud bully and a frank truth-teller. Dorothy's creativity makes a wall of post-traumatic noise, as she has been abandoned by her parents, raped and shamed by her Uncle Henry Gulch, shunned by children for being big, fat, and ineloquent. Part 2 of *Was* tells the story of Judy Garland as the child Frances Gumm. On the *Wizard of Oz* set she plays Dorothy Gale as a desexualized sweetheart, her breasts tightly bound so that she can remain a child and therefore have *her* childhood stolen from her. It is not stolen through rape but by parents bound up in their own fantasies of living through children in terms of money and fame (Gumm's mother) or sex (Gumm's father, whose object choice was young boys). The third story in *Was* is about a fictional gay man, a minor Hollywood actor named Jonathan, whose fame comes from being the monster in serial killer movies titled *The Child Minder* and who, as the book begins, is offered a part in a touring *Wizard of Oz* company while he is entering AIDS dementia. All of these stories are about the cruelty of optimism revealed to people without control over the material conditions of their lives, or whose relation to fantasy is such that the perverse shuttling between fantasy and realism destroys, according to Ryman, people and the nation. I cannot do justice here to the singularities of what optimism makes possible and impossible in this entire book but want to focus on a scene that makes the whole book possible. In this scene Dorothy Gael encounters a substitute teacher, Frank Baum, in her rural Kansas elementary school.

"The children," writes Ryman, "knew the Substitute was not a real teacher because he was so soft" (168). "Substitute" derives from the word "succeed," and the sense of possibility around the changeover is deeply embedded in the word. A substitute brings optimism if he hasn't yet been defeated—by life or by the students. He enters their lives as a new site for attachment, a dedramatized possibility. He is by definition a placeholder, a space of abeyance, an aleatory event. His coming is not personal—he is not there for anyone in particular. The amount of affect released around him says something about the intensity of the children's available drive to be less dead, numb, neutralized, or crazy with habit; but it says nothing about what it would feel like to be in transit between the stale life and all its others, or whether that feeling would lead to something good.

Of course often students are cruel to substitutes, out of excitement at the unpredictable and out of not having fear or transference to make them docile or even desiring of a recognition that has no time to be built. But this substitute is special to Dorothy: he is an actor, like her parents; he teaches them Turkish; and he tells them about alternative histories lived right now and in the past (171). Dorothy fantasizes about Frank Baum not in a narrative way, but with a mixture of sheer pleasure and defense: "Frank, Frank, as her uncle put his hands on her" (169); then she berates herself for her "own unworthiness" (169) because she knows "how beautiful you are and I know how ugly I am and how you could never have anything to do with me" (174). She says his name, Frank, over and over: it "seemed to sum up everything that was missing from her life" (169). Yet face to face she cannot bear the feeling of relief from her life that the Substitute's being near provides for her. She alternately bristles and melts at his deference, his undemanding kindness. She mocks him and disrupts class to drown out her tenderness, but she obeys him when he asks her to leave the room to just write something, anything.

What she comes back with is a lie, a wish. Her dog, Toto, had been murdered by her aunt and uncle, who hated him and who had no food to spare for him. But the story she hands in to the substitute is a substitute: it is about how happy she and Toto are. It includes sentences about how they play together and how exuberant he is, running around yelping "like he is saying hello to everything" (174). Imaginary Toto sits on her lap, licks her hand, has a cold nose, sleeps on her lap, and eats food that Auntie Em gives her to give him. The essay suggests a successful life, a life where love circulates and extends its sympathies, rather than the life she actually lives, where "it was as if they had all stood back-to-back, shouting 'love' at the tops of their lungs, but in the wrong direction, away from each other" (221). It carries traces of all of the good experience Dorothy has ever had. The essay closes this way: "I did not call him Toto. That is the name my mother gave him when she was alive. It is the same as mine" (175).

Toto, Dodo, Dorothy: the teacher sees that the child has opened up something in herself, let down a defense, and he is moved by the bravery of her admission of identification and attachment. But he makes the mistake of being mimetic in response, acting soft toward her in a way he might imagine that she seeks to be: "I'm very glad," he murmured, "that you have something to love as much as that little animal." Dorothy goes ballistic at this response and insults Baum, but she goes on to blurt out all of the truths of her life, in public, in front of the other students. She talks nonstop about being raped and hungry all the time, about the murder of her dog, and about her ineloquence: "I can't say anything," she closes (176). That phrase means she can't do anything to change anything. From here she regresses to yelping and tries to dig a hole in the ground, to become the size she feels, and also to become, in a sense, an embodiment of the last thing she loved. After that, Dorothy goes crazy, lives in a fantasy world of her own, wandering homeless and free, especially, of the capacity to reflect on loss in the modalities of realism, tragedy, or melodrama. To protect her last iota of optimism she goes crazy.

In *Was* Baum goes on to write *The Wizard of Oz* as a gift of alternativity to the person who can't say or do anything to change her life materially, and who has taken in so much that one moment of relief from herself produces a permanent crack in the available genres of her survival. In "What Is a Minor Literature?" Deleuze and Guattari exhort people to become minor in exactly that way, to de-territorialize from the normal by digging a hole in sense like a dog or a mole (1990). Creating an impasse, a space of internal displacement, in this view, shatters the normal hierarchies, clarities, tyrannies, and confusions of compliance with autonomous individuality. This strategy looks promising in the Ashbery poem. But in "Exchange Value," a moment of relief produces a psychotic defense against the risk of loss in optimism. For Dorothy Gael, in *Was*, the optimism of attachment to another living being is itself the cruelest slap of all.

From this cluster we can understand a bit more of the magnetic attraction to cruel optimism, with its suppression of the risks of attachment. A change of heart, a sensorial shift, intersubjectivity, or transference with a promising object cannot generate on its own the better good life: nor can the collaboration of a couple, brothers, or pedagogy. The vague futurities of normative optimism produce small self-interruptions as the utopias of structural inequality. The texts we have looked at here stage moments when it could become otherwise, but shifts in affective atmosphere are not equal to changing the world. They are, here, only pieces of an argument about the centrality of optimistic fantasy to surviving in zones of compromised ordinariness. And that is one way to measure the impasse of living in the overwhelmingly present moment.

Notes

1   Emmanuel Ghent's contribution to this sentence is the word "surrender," which, he has argued, has an importantly different valence than the word "submission" with great consequences to the ways this essay calibrates the difference between being absorbed in something and being dominated by it. Daniel Stern's phrase "the present moment" (2004) introduces here a conceptualization of "the present" as a duration that is not just always lost and fleeting but which people slow down by projecting or moving it into space.

2   One senses that Johnson conjures, in this scene, the absent presence of the Lacanian *petit objet à*; but in many ways Johnson's work on rhetorical intersubjectivity is closer to Mikkel Borch-Jacobsen's construction of projection in mimetic attachment in *The Freudian Subject* (1988).

3   For further elaboration of enduring in transference with the object, see Jessica Benjamin (1994). In accounting for the analysand's insistence on being found or recognized somewhere, by someone, this wonderful essay also overaligns the formal optimism of attachment as such and the *affects* of self-preserving desire.

4   The phrase "political depression" emerges from discussions in a working group on public feelings: special appreciation goes to Ann Cvetkovich, Katie Stewart, Debbie Gould, Rebecca Zorach, and Mary Patten.

5   The neighbor has been slowly emerging as a figure for adjudicating the complexities of intimacy, recognition, and misrecognition in situations of unequal power: I cite

here Joan Copjec's analysis of the transferential relations among colonial and colonized neighbors in *Read My Desire* (1994, 65–116); Slavoj Žižek's "Neighbor and Other Monsters: A Plea for Ethical Violence" (Žižek, Santner, and Reinhard 2006); and Amy Hempel's story "Beach Town" (2005), in which, in order not to experience the atrophy of her own life, a narrator sits in her backyard listening to her neighbor's conversation with another woman about the neighbor's betrayal and abandonment by her husband.

6   "Indeed what Reason may not go to School to the Wisdom of Bees, Ants, and Spiders? What wise hand teacheth them to do what Reason cannot teach us? Ruder heads stand amazed at those prodigious pieces of Nature, Whales, Elephants, Dromedaries and Camels; these, I confess, are the Colossus and majestick pieces of her hand: but in these narrow Engines there is more curious Mathematicks; and the civility of these little Citizens more neatly sets forth the Wisdom of their Maker" (Browne 2007, section 15).

7   Bradin Cormack has suggested to me that, in breaking with heaven, Ashbery breaks with Milton as well: see the poem "On His Blindness," which closes with "They also serve who only stand and wait." Ashbery is breaking with Milton's account of standing: it is no longer God's watch but that of he who approaches. The waiting here too is now luscious and sensual, open and unhidden, having nothing to do with servitude: but in alignment with Milton, it's not sight that's privileged by Ashbery but the hearing that becomes more intensified when one is not, as it were, constantly searching and driving. As for Eliot, the famous lines from *Ash Wednesday* speak here: "Because I do not hope to turn again/Because I do not hope/Because I do not hope to turn/Desiring this man's gift and that man's scope/I no longer strive to strive towards such things/(Why should the aged eagle stretch its wings?)/Why should I mourn/The vanished power of the usual reign? Because I do not hope to know again. . . ." One might also note the poem's proximity to Theodore Roethke's "I Knew a Woman": "How well her wishes went! She stroked my chin/She taught me Turn, and Counter-turn, and stand;/She taught me Touch, that undulant white skin:/I nibbled meekly from her proffered hand;/She was the sickle; I, poor I, the rake,/Coming behind her for her pretty sake/(But what prodigious mowing did we make.)" All of Ashbery's emendations tend toward a radical revision of what glorious impassivity might mean to someone not as an opposite to action, but as most apposite.

8   The whole phrase is worth reading: " 'Chloe liked Olivia . . .' Do not start. Do not blush. Let us admit in the privacy of our own society that these things sometimes happen. Sometimes women do like women" (Woolf 1957, 82).

9   To be seized by the event is to become a subject organized by fidelity to the unknowns released into the field of possibility by the event's truth processes. Badiou links the truth potentials in the love encounter to less personal seizures of affect, including revolutionary activity (Badiou 2001, 41–43, 118).

10 Cooter notes his brother's "Geoffrey Holder" laugh, which places this story in the mid-1970s, which is when Holder would have been famous for his role in *Live and Let Die* and also as the spokesman for 7-Up, "the uncola."

Affect, Food, and Social Aesthetics

Ben Highmore

Affect gives you away: the telltale heart; my clammy hands; the note of anger in your voice; the sparkle of glee in their eyes. You may protest your innocence, but we both know, don't we, that who you *really* are, or *what* you really are, is going to be found in the pumping of your blood, the quantity and quality of your perspiration, the breathless anticipation in your throat, the way you can't stop yourself from grinning, the glassy sheen of your eyes. Affect is the cuckoo in the nest; the fifth columnists out to undermine you; your personal polygraph machine. When I was growing up "affect trials" were the daily business of the playground. There, in clusters of boys, in a small war zone of incipient masculinity, we goaded, teased, and baited. The open secret was to maintain minimum intensity: keep cool. The job of everyone was to get a "rise out" of someone: a blush would do, but the main prize was getting someone to "lose it"—to go, as we never described it then, "postal." And of course someone (but, I remember, not everyone) always did. For most of us it was clear, we were simply not in control of ourselves.

Sense Affects

Cultural inquiry in the last dozen years or so has increasingly turned its attention toward what might be thought of as a series of awkward materialities. Inaugurating this interest was a renewed enthusiasm for studies that privileged the body (perhaps the most awkward materiality of all) as a problematic locus for meaning, experience, and knowledge.[1] While some of this work heralded new concerns with the physical actuality of culture and a shift away from the perceived obscurities and ultra-abstractions of advanced textualism, it was also (and paradoxically) criticized precisely for its bloodlessness: "the body that eats, that works, that dies, that is afraid—that body just isn't there" (Bynum 1995, 1). *The* body, it seemed, was all too often to be found in the body of the text. Yet a body free of the trappings (and traps) of discourse, of culture, might not be much of a human body at all. The sense of tension between a creaturely body (bones, gristle, mucus, bile, blood, and so on) and the body reflected back through metaphor or other figural elements plays out a dualism that has long cast its shadows over philosophy. Of course, in a less troubled vein, it might be possible to simply say that, yes, these are the kinds of creatures we are: when suffering from toothache, we are likely to make mountains out of molehills.

In the demand for the concrete (a concreteness sophisticated and complex enough to be desirable to minds drilled in the rigors of poststructuralism and the like) cultural inquiry turned toward a materialism where a body would be understood as a nexus of finely interlaced force fields. In this essay I want to draw on this approach, especially on the critical studies of emotions and affects, of perception and the management of attention, and on studies of the senses, the sensorial, and the human sensorium. More particularly I want to build on the intuition that cultural experience is often a densely woven entanglement of all these aspects. Indeed the proposition that drives this essay is that the sticky entanglements of substances and feelings, of matter and affect are central to our contact with the world. Moreover, I want to argue here that these entanglements don't require critical untangling (the scholarly and bureaucratic business of sorting categories and filing phenomena); instead what is required is a critically entangled contact with affective experience. This means getting in among the murky connections between fabrics and feelings, between the glutinous and the guffaw (for example).

Work on the senses showed immediately the difficulty of establishing and studying discrete sensual, experiential, and cognitive modes (a world of touch separable from a world of sight, for instance). The neurological condition of synesthesia (where one cognitive pathway bleeds into and triggers another, resulting in, for instance, sound being perceived as color) offers an extreme case of a more general condition of sensual interconnection. Eating food, for instance, might necessarily privilege taste, yet to concentrate on taste to the exclusion of other senses means to fail to recognize that the experience of eating is also dependent on the haptic sensitivity of tongues and mouths, on our olfactory abilities, and on sight and sound (the cacophony of crunching might actually be part of the "flavor" of potato chips, for example). More pertinent though would be the cross-modal networks that register links between perception, affect, the senses, and emotions. Here the work that emerges out of the various body-oriented fields of cultural inquiry might require an overarching umbrella to fully attend to the more general condition of synesthesia pertaining to human subjects. Here senses and affect bleed into one another. This is where every flavor has an emotional resonance (sweetness, sourness, bitterness). Here the bio-cultural arena of disgust (especially disgust of ingested or nearly ingested foods) simultaneously invokes a form of sensual perception, an affective register of shame and disdain, as well as bodily recoil. When emotions are described by flavors, though, are these simply metaphorical conventions? Or does the emotional condition of bitterness, for instance, release the same gastric response as the ingestion of bitter flavors? How do we make our way from one modality to another?

In common English usage the words designating affective experience sit awkwardly on the borders of the material and the immaterial, the physical and the metaphysical: we are *moved* by a sentiment; our *feelings* are hurt; I am *touched* by your presence. The interlacing of sensual, physical experience (here, the insistent reference to the haptic realm—touch, feel, move) with the passionate intensities of love, say, or bitterness, makes it hard to imagine untangling them, allotting them to discrete categories in terms of their physicality or their ideational existence. The bruising that I experience when I am humiliated in front of a loved one is intractably both literal and metaphorical: I am bruised, I sit slightly slumped, more weary and wary, yet this bruising also reaches inside, I feel internally battered. Could you possibly "feel" that you were in love if you couldn't also feel your beating heart climbing into your throat or your palms sweat? Would I really be moved by a tragedy if I didn't experience rivulets of tears trickling down my cheeks? The cold, acrid sweat that runs down my side, the bundle of bees nesting in my stomach tell me I am anxious. The wind that bites, that gets under my skin and gnaws at my bones with its bitter chill is a memory or a foretaste of a terrible coldness that is the feeling of isolation, homesickness, alienation, despair. The register of hot and cold, of warmth and frost, of passion and dispassion is an emotional and affective register. It is also, as is immediately suggested, a register of sensorial perception, and sensual expression.

Social Aesthetics

The umbrella term that I have in mind for cross-modal investigation is the term "aesthetics," more specifically (and as a way of avoiding a certain amount of confusion) "social aesthetics." The story of aesthetics is not well enough known to avoid having to repeat it (however briefly) again here. Aesthetics emerged as a named arena of philosophy in the mid-eighteenth century in the work of Alexander Baumgarten. For Baumgarten aesthetics was the field of sensate perception—the world perceived through what he called the "lower cognitive faculties" (Baumgarten 2000a, 489). Baumgarten's work recognized that philosophy's traditional preoccupation with logical and conceptual thinking simply remaindered whole territories of life. Terry Eagleton vividly describes this territory as "nothing less than the whole of our sensate life together—the business of affections and aversions, of how the world strikes the body on its sensory surfaces, of that which takes root in the gaze and the guts and all that arises from our most banal, biological insertion into the world" (Eagleton 1990, 13). Aesthetics, in its initial impetus, is primarily concerned with material experiences, with the way the sensual world greets the sensate body, and with the affective forces that are generated in such meetings. Aesthetics covers the terrain of both "the vehement passions" (fear, grief, rapture, and so on) and the minor and major affects and emotions (humiliation, shame, envy, irritation, anxiety, disdain, surprise, and so forth).[2] It is attuned to forms of perception, sensation, and attention (distraction, spectacle, concentration, absorption, for example); to the world of the senses (haptic, aural, gustatory, olfactory, and visual experience); and to the body (as gestalt and in pieces).[3] Most importantly and most suggestively, it would be concerned with the utter entanglements of all of these elements.

Anyone interested in the history of aesthetics must be faced with this odd predicament: how does a form of inquiry that was once aimed at the entire creaturely world end up as a specialized discourse about fine art? How did an ambitious curiosity about the affects, the body, and the senses end up fixated on only one tiny area of sensual life—beauty and the sublime? What happens to fear, anger, disappointment, contentment, smell, touch, boredom, frustration, weariness, hope, itchiness, backache, trepidation, and the mass of hardly articulated feelings and moods that saturate our social, sexual, political, and private lives? And aren't these the elements (rather than beauty and the sublime) that fill most of our lives most of the time? The answer is right there in aesthetic discourse from the start and it takes two forms. First is the a priori assumption that certain experiences are simply better than others (thus beauty will win out over boredom each and every time because beauty is seen as edifying and morally uplifting whereas boredom would simply register as the failure of self-discipline and moral vigilance ["the devil makes work for idle hands"]). Second is the difficulty of speaking and writing about creaturely, experiential life, except through exemplification (an exemplification that is most often provided by art). It is this second characteristic of aesthetic discourse that results in the misdirection of aesthetics, directing it to become simply synonymous with art theory. For Baumgarten the worry is that "impressions received from the senses, fantasies, emotional disturbances, etc. are unworthy of philosophers and beneath the scope of their consideration" (Baumgarten 2000a, 490). Being generally untrustworthy and unedifying, this creaturely life has to be transformed, and in the end (but also in the beginning) this is what aesthetics becomes—a form of moral improvement—where the improvement is aimed at sensation, sentiment, and perception. One way of pursuing such improvement is via exemplary acts of sensual appropriateness: thus poetry becomes an example of the striving toward sensual perfection (Baumgarten 2000b). Here the artwork is a moral lesson, an aesthetic example to be mimicked and developed for the pursuit of the good and the true.

The almost complete suppression of the fullness of human creaturely life within much aesthetic discourse and the concomitant obsessive concentration on the artwork deserve more space than I can give them here.[4] In one sense it is an unexceptional story. Just as social scientists today find themselves having to turn to novels and films when they want to explore the world of emotions, affects, and sensuality, so the study of aesthetics has engaged with the poets and the painters as providers of the most useable materials. There are, of course, many forms of inquiry that use artworks for underpinning their theories. Freudian psychoanalysis with its reliance on classical myth is only the most famous. Yet the situation of aesthetics is singular here: if psychoanalysis had given up on the idea that the unconscious was socially ubiquitous and ordinary and decided instead that it would be most profitably found only in the work of novelists and painters, then psychoanalysis would be approaching the situation of aesthetics. Psychoanalysis, though, lives or dies on its ability to talk to our common existence—even if this existence is often experienced in the lonely grip of individualism.

Aesthetic discourse, certainly in its classic period (in the work of Kant, for instance), perpetually slides between actuality and the artwork. For Kant it is always first and foremost nature and our experience of nature that will furnish the setting for experiences of the sublime and the beautiful. But it is also the artwork that will really concretize this experience into something for aesthetic appreciation. Thus while Kant always starts out with an engagement with nature, it is in the end the artwork that will offer the firmest assurance of the longevity (and value) of such an experience. This sense that the artwork completes sensual experience (resolves it into more satisfying and morally superior forms) is a central tenet within aesthetic discourse, and it immediately suggests that there is something generally incomplete and unsatisfactory about day-to-day experience (which, surely, is often the case). But from this perspective aesthetics can *only* be interested in those forms of experience that are available to be resolved and completed (the meal that achieves gastronomic heights; the portrait that distils the essence of the sitter; the story that resolves the problematic encounter). Aesthetic satisfaction (in its dominant mode) is satisfaction in the end form of a process, rather than in the messy *informe* of the ongoing-ness of process. Much of what constitutes the day-to-day is irresolvable and desperately incomplete, yet, for all that, also most vital. Take a number of affective states like frustration, irritation, restlessness—it is impossible to imagine an artwork that completes these affects into satisfying forms (without abandoning the specificity of the affect), because the character of these affects is dissatisfaction and incompletion (irritation works by de-completion, so to speak). Beauty, as a responsive, creaturely register, is favored by aesthetics because of its moralizing mission (it addresses betterment) and because it is seen to reside in *stabilized* patterns and shapes, proportions or ratios, narrative forms and tonal sequences, and so on.

So if "aesthetics" is going to work as an umbrella term for heuristic inquiry into affect and its interlacing of sense perception and bodily dispensation then it will have to work hard to disconnect itself from the tradition of aesthetic thinking that has remained bound to the moral mission of the artwork and its evaluation. It will mean connecting to a countertradition of aesthetic thinking (from Georg Simmel through to Jacques Rancière) as well as recruiting voices to this countertradition that might otherwise seem to be almost completely situated within the evaluative tradition of aesthetics (John Dewey for one).[5] While certain forms of aesthetic thinking will have to be jettisoned, other aesthetic terms should become newly resonant.

Taste

The term "taste," often center stage in evaluative aesthetic discourse, vividly registers the imbrication of sense and status, of discernment and disdain, of the physical and the ideational. The very mobilization of the word "taste" to describe refined and discerning choice (and the social status that might go with it) should alert us to the way that bodily sensorial life is implied in such judgments from the start. Given the privileging of the "higher" senses (hearing and seeing, but also touch) in the history of Western thought it might seem that the very idea of "taste" to signify discernment is already flirting with distaste by invoking the "lower" senses (smell and taste). One aspect of this distribution of sense (both cognition and sensation) is the way that seeing and hearing are invoked in matters of ideational cognition ("ah, I see," "I hear you"), whereas "taste" is mobilizing sensorial realms that are, in the end, impervious to rationalist dictates.

"Taste" is a perilous business. It is hedged in from all sides by the physical possibility of revulsion, disgust, and disdain. Who can be certain of their taste? As David Hume made clear in the mid-eighteenth century: "We are apt to call *barbarous* whatever departs widely from our own taste and apprehension; but soon find the epithet of reproach retorted on us" (Hume 2008, 134). But if we are socially vulnerable in our discernment, that vulnerability is intensified by an affective pull that makes taste matter in very specific ways. After all distaste is not simply disagreement: even in its mildest form it involves the wrinkling of noses, turning the head away, and so on. At its most extreme, distaste is revolt, physical nausea, vomiting, and retching. In ordinary circumstances distaste is signaled through a register of affects sliding from condescension to disdain to scorn and contempt: how could you possibly have imagined that this disgusting item would be appealing to me? Disdain, then (as the most general mode of showing distaste), is one way of inflicting affective pain, and it is most effective when emotional interest is involved and where approbation is sought. Disdain works to push away and to ruin simultaneously.

Jonathan Franzen's ambitious novel, *The Corrections* (2001), provides, among other things, an emotional vivisection of a white, midwestern, middle-class, elderly couple, and the more sophisticated and metropolitan lives of their children. A sprawling novel that chillingly portrays disintegrating mental states as well as international financial networks, *The Corrections* is constantly weaving links between mentalities and markets. While none of the characters are conventionally sympathetic, one of the least sympathetically drawn characters is the mother, Enid. Taste matters for Enid; and it matters so considerably because she is never quite certain of her taste, or rather, of the status of her taste in the wider world. Within the confines of her home she can wield taste as a weapon in the constant war of her disappointing marriage. Her husband, who has retired and is suffering from Parkinson's disease, has bought his first piece of furniture, a vast blue leather armchair. The chair provokes Enid to the point where she redecorates their sitting room so as to have an excuse for expelling the chair:

> Enid looked at the chair. Her expression was merely pained, no more. "I never liked that chair."
>
> This was probably the most terrible thing she could have said to Alfred. The chair was the only sign he'd ever given of having a personal vision of the future. Enid's words filled him with such sorrow—he felt such pity for the chair, such solidarity with it, such astonished grief at its betrayal—that he pulled off the dropcloth and sank into its arms and fell asleep. (Franzen 2001, 11)

(Franzen's book is, as you might have gathered, something of a black comedy.) Here taste is more than cultural capital, it is cultural power played out on a violently affective plane. This chair sits uncomfortably with other chairs; for me it echoed the chair in the U.S. TV comedy *Frasier*, where a sophisticated Seattle psychiatrist (Frasier) lives with his blue-collar, ex–police officer dad in a swanky, tastefully designed apartment. Martin, the dad, has one piece of furniture, an ill-repaired, sickly green Barcalounger. The chair sits there in a field of intense affect, constantly puncturing Frasier's aesthetic realm (Highmore 2001).

Enid knows how to use taste to wound because she is constantly aware of how it would be possible for certain people (most specifically her daughter— Denise) to completely undo her through taste and distaste: "Enid had, true enough, had fun at Dean and Trish's party, and she'd wished that Denise had been there to see for herself how elegant it was. At the same time, she was afraid that Denise would not have found the party elegant at all, that Denise would have picked apart its specialness until there was nothing left but ordinariness. Her daughter's taste was a dark spot in Enid's vision, a hole in her experience through which her own pleasures were forever threatening to leak and dissipate" (Franzen 2001, 113).

Denise can wield such power in matters of taste, not simply because she has left the Midwest for the seemingly more sophisticated pastures of the Eastern Seaboard, but because she has become the head chef at Philadelphia's coolest restaurant. Haute cuisine, even in the pseudo-rustic casual elegance of its contemporary performance, is tastefulness in a pristine but dogmatic state. The strong relationship between food and taste is not simply based on the metaphoric association of "taste" with discernment. Rather food is the sine qua non of taste's affective function. Not only does food provide so many opportunities for the production of shame and humiliation in the face of social ignorance and squeamishness (not being sufficiently knowledgeable about food) as well as biological uncouthness (not having a sensitive palate), it intensifies such production because food is orchestrated around the body (its surfaces, its interiors, its ingestions). The crumpled shame experienced by the protagonist of Sylvia Plath's *The Bell Jar* is occasioned by the class humiliation she feels when she thinks a bowl of water and petals, provided for cleaning diners' fingers, is a very light soup (Plath 2001). She feels this so strongly because her "mistake" involves her mouth and her alimentary self.

Taste is an orchestration of the sensible, a way of ordering and demeaning, of giving value and taking it away. On the one hand it seems to occupy a thin level of culture (the preoccupation of snobs, gourmands, and the like); on another it will seem as the very basis of culture, not simply its system of values but the way that set of values gets under your skin and into your bones. While it might seem an overstatement to suggest that groups might go to war over taste disputes, it is hard to imagine that what we term culture is not in the end (and endlessly) driven by the peculiar admix of affect, sensual perception, and bio-power that is instanced by taste. From one angle at least, social struggle is struggle through, in, and about taste. But if this statement reeks of "bad taste," of a glib condescension whereby desperate economic survival is reduced to aesthetics, I only need to think of the disdain that greets many forms of popular democracy to think it has some pertinence.

Schismogenesis and Ethos

In late 1935, with one eye probably on the rise of fascism in Europe and the other on the role that anthropology has played as an arm of colonial administration, Gregory Bateson outlined a research project for the study of schismogenesis. Schismogenesis is Bateson's name for forms of acculturation (the cultural processes arising from the meeting of distinct cultural groups or cultural factions) that, often aggressively, result in the intensification of cultural differences or cultural rivalry. While Bateson is clear that cultural interchange can result in "acceptance and adaptation" and in forms of "approximate equilibrium," he is—in 1935—particularly interested in, and aware of, "drastic disturbances which follow contacts between profoundly different communities" (Bateson 1935, 179). For Bateson the study of schismogenesis would be an essential project for a class of expert social scientists whose job it would be to inform political administrators.

Schismogenesis is Bateson puzzling to understand how and why groups don't undergo some sort of cultural osmosis when they come into contact with one another, why cultural mixing doesn't result in "melting pot" cultures, and why distinction and rivalry are often intensified through contact. Of course, he is not naïve enough to forget that cultural contact is nearly always forged under conditions of violent domination, but he is also enough of an anthropologist to have examples of cultures where antagonistic intergroup contact is an essential element of their general life-world. Schismogenesis is Bateson's initial attempt to bring a form of systems theory to bear on social life. For Bateson there are two (often overlapping) forms of schismogenesis: symmetrical schismogenesis and complementary schismogenesis. Acculturation often leads "toward more intense rivalry in the case of symmetrical schismogenesis, or toward increasing differentiation of role in complementary schismogenesis" (Bateson 1958, 285). After the Second World War the spectacular proliferation of nuclear weapons by the protagonists in the cold war offered a vivid example of symmetrical schismogenesis. Generally symmetrical schismogenesis occurred and occurs between two separate units that encounter one another (nation-states, tribal groups, and so forth). Complementary schismogenesis is more ubiquitous: Bateson sees it occurring between genders within communities, and between the old and the young; and we could see it as a form of class distinction, where class differences intensify at moments of close proximity. In contemporary multicultural society complementary schismogenesis is perhaps even more visible.

Distinctions between symmetrical and complementary schismogenesis are hard to maintain for long: it is hard, for instance, to see something like the cold war as not intensifying difference (ideological and cultural) at the same time as rivalry. Similarly the idea that forms of complementary schismogenesis don't also entail forms of rivalry is difficult to sustain. What is more important, though, is the way Bateson understands the conditions necessary for schismogenesis to occur: after all it is perfectly possible for schismogenesis not to occur. For Bateson schismogenesis is dependent on the particular "ethos" of a group. While we are used to thinking of a "group ethos" as a fairly innocuous ethic (fairness, for instance), Bateson means something at once more intricate and more expansive by the term. But even from its ordinary sense you can see how an ethos of superciliousness, for instance, that two groups might share would result in schismogenesis while an ethos of sharing and empathy might not. For Bateson the ethological approach is premised on the idea "that we may abstract from a culture a certain systematic aspect called ethos which we may define as the expression of *a culturally standardised system of organisation of the instincts and emotions of the individuals*" (Bateson 1958, 118, emphasis in original). In a world more alert to difference it might be that we would want to temper the sense of standardization being offered here, but the "organisation of the instincts and emotions" might well fit with the sense of social aesthetics I am keen to suggest.

Bateson goes on to describe "ethos" as a "definite tone of appropriate behaviour," as "a definite set of sentiments towards the rest of the world," as "an emotional background," and so on. This, as Bateson claims, is an abstraction, an abstraction based on the purview of the social scientist, yet within its abstract surface lie real concrete elements, ways of doing (hugs, handshakes, kisses, slaps, and the like), forms of perceiving (social recognition and misrecognition of class, caste, gender, sexuality, and so on), affective intensities (affordances of anger, uses of humiliation, and so forth), and more.[6] Ethos might well best be approached as something like a tonality, or a feeling, but its polyphonic dimension must be continually stressed. Ethos, to borrow a term from Jacques Rancière, could be thought of as the "distribution of the sensible" (*le partage du sensible*): "the system of *a priori* forms determining what presents itself to sense experience. It is a delimitation of spaces and times, of the visible and the invisible, of speech and noise, that simultaneously determines the place and stakes of politics as a form of experience" (Rancière 2004, 13). Ethos, then, would be the orchestration of perception, sensorial culture, affective intensities, and so on: more pertinently it will be the interlacing of these. Forms and techniques of personal hygiene or food preparation, for instance, might differ between two cultures. Such differences might be the site of friction when two cultures meet or need to coexist. From this might come a rudimentary understanding of schismogenesis. Ethos (or social aesthetics) allows you to see why and how a particular style of washing matters; it links the perception of cleanliness and dirt, or purity and impurity, to orchestrations of shame and comfort, to resonances of other sensual worlds, and on to the social ontology of bodies.

Orwell

At the same time as Gregory Bateson was undertaking fieldwork among the Iatmul people in New Guinea, and while he was writing about schismogenesis and ethos back in Cambridge, the journalist and novelist George Orwell was undertaking his own empirical study of schismogenesis. In the late 1920s and early 1930s in London and Paris, and again in 1936 in the industrial towns of Yorkshire and Lancashire, Orwell plunged himself into a world of poverty and dirt. The books of this period, *Down and Out in Paris and London* and *The Road to Wigan Pier*, were experiments in the limits and possibilities of ethos. To write these books meant sleeping rough in London, working in terrible cafés in Paris, and living in dirty lodgings in Wigan. While *Down and Out in Paris and London* was provoked by Orwell's own poverty, *The Road to Wigan Pier* was commissioned by a publisher. Yet in some ways both books and the experiences that they retold were a response to his aesthetic auto-critique. Orwell returned to England after working for five years as a colonial police officer in Burma. He returned shameful of the despotism he had willingly taken part in; he was haunted, he said, by "innumerable remembered faces—faces of prisoners in the dock, of men waiting in the condemned cells, or subordinates I had bullied and aged peasants I had snubbed, of servants and coolies I had hit with my fist in moments of rage" (Orwell 1975, 129). Orwell recognized himself as divided between ethos (which was thoroughly bound by class) and what Bateson called "eidos"— the rational, logical, reasoning self (which was thoroughly convinced by socialism). In his own words he was "both a snob and a revolutionary." *The Road to Wigan Pier* is directed at the realization that rational argument misunderstands the hold that ethos has over each and every one of us. In describing the extensiveness of his own class ethos Orwell sees it as determining the very way he moves his body:

It is easy for me to say that I want to get rid of class-distinctions, but nearly everything I think and do is a result of class-distinctions. All my notions—notions of good and evil, of pleasant and unpleasant, of funny and serious, of ugly and beautiful—are essentially middle-class notions; my taste in books and food and clothes, my sense of honour, my table manners, my turns of speech, my accent, even the characteristic movements of my body, are the products of a special kind of upbringing and a special niche about half-way up the social hierarchy. (Orwell 1975, 114)

The experiments in rough living were undertaken because Orwell was faced with the evidence of class schismogenesis even (perhaps especially) among those who rationally wanted to see the end of class divisions. *The Road to Wigan Pier* is an odd and uncomfortable read. For one thing the feeling of ethological schismogenesis is performed through the address of the text: the book is only addressed to those outside the working class. Similarly, while Orwell is undertaking what might best be thought of as experiments in disgust, the reader is constantly being implicitly solicited on the matter of taste (this is disgusting, isn't it?), a solicitation that is designed to provoke the very reactions that he discusses as being so problematic for a progressive politics.

The mapping of ethos is undertaken along its contours and these contours have only one tone—revulsion. Reading across Orwell's writing, particularly his journalism and memoirs, you are faced with a figure that not only finds revulsion in others but is clearly compelled by self-disgust.[7] His early life, especially the boarding school he attended from the ages of eight to thirteen, taught him ethos through the deep pedagogy of shame and humiliation, and in this way internalized his feelings of self-disgust.[8] It is the pedagogy of disgust that is such an elemental figure in Orwell's work and provides a more effective class investment than the mere ideological beliefs that are usually associated with social class: "It may not greatly matter if the average middle-class person is brought up to believe that the working classes are ignorant, lazy, drunken, boorish, and dishonest; it is when he is brought up to believe that they are dirty that the harm is done. And in my childhood we were brought up to believe that they were dirty. Very early in life you acquired the idea that there was something subtly repulsive about a working-class body; you would not get nearer to it than you could help" (Orwell 1975, 112). This then might be both the starting point and conclusion of Orwell's "disgust experiment." In between is the work of encounter.

It becomes obvious that Orwell, in *The Road to Wigan Pier*, has not gone out to find an average working-class Wigan family to lodge with. He has gone out to find an exceptionally disgusting family to lodge with: these are the Brookers. The Brookers run both a lodging house and a "tripe shop." The shop has dead flies in the window and beetles crawling around the tripe. Tripe is the lining of a cow's stomach; it is cheap, nutritious, and notorious for its indigestible texture and the length of time required for cooking it. Mrs. Brooker is monstrously overweight and confined to a sofa, where she eats gargantuan meals and wipes her mouth with scraps of newspaper that she leaves lying around. Mr. Brooker does most of the work, which includes serving the lodgers food with filthy hands (bread always comes with dark fingerprints on its surface). Chamber pots are always full and remain under the kitchen table during meals. Both the Brookers complain incessantly, and their general bitterness adds to the disgust of the scene. Affect, sensorial experience, and perception congregate most particularly around Mr. Brooker and his bitterness: "In the mornings he sat by the fire with a tub of filthy water, peeling potatoes at the speed of a slow-motion picture. I never saw anyone who could peel potatoes with quite such an air of brooding resentment. You could see the hatred of this 'bloody woman's work,' as he called it, fermenting inside him, a kind of bitter juice. He was one of those people who can chew their grievances like a cud" (Orwell 1975, 11).

Bitterness is what feeds Mr. Brooker, his sense of injustice, his spite (he chews it, like a cow). But it is also bitterness that seems to feed off Mr. Brooker: at one point Orwell describes Mr. Brooker's sense of injustice as a worm living in his bowels. Mr. Brooker's potato peeling seems to infuse the food with bitterness (clearly all of the meals were indescribably revolting), and the sense of this work being an infringement of gender roles further intensifies the bitterness.

Orwell didn't need to stay with the Brookers. They are representative neither of the class that Orwell is looking at nor of the lodgings available in Wigan. Orwell's disgust experiment is, in the end, aimed directly at himself. The bitterness that drives Mr. Brooker mimes the bitterness that drives Orwell and is most evident when he is writing about his own childhood humiliations. What starts out as an investigation of complementary schismogenesis (the intensifying of difference through class distinction) turns out to be symmetrical schismogenesis—where mutual bitterness is the affective ingredient that drives class division. Orwell's bitterness is, in the end, self-reflexive and it is that that proves the only possible way out of the stranglehold of his own ethos. To get there required a season in hell.

Vindaloo

While disgust, disdain, and repulsion might evidence the borderlands of ethos and the most fertile grounds for the work of schismogenesis, it would, I think, be wrong to think of schismogenesis as only taking place as a form of rejection. Schismogenesis also takes place (more awkwardly) in forms of intense, sensual enthusiasm. Voracious eating, especially of food experienced as "foreign" (though often its provenance is distinctly local), has occasioned a very specific form of schismogenesis in the United Kingdom as might be associated with, for example, Anglo-Celtic men ordering the hottest food on the menu as a display of macho bravado. This scene of schismogenesis has occasioned forms of popular culture such as the English football anthem "Vindaloo" as well as cultural replies by British Asian comics where the schismogenesis is imaginatively reversed. *Goodness Gracious Me*, a TV series starring Sanjeev Bhaskar, Kulvinder Ghir, and Meera Syal, spoofed the culture of aggressive relish by transforming the stereotypical scene of restaurant eating by inebriated British "lads." Their sketch "Going for an English" begins by mimicking U.K. cinema advertising of the 1970s (by using badly filmed and heavily scratched images), urging customers to eat at the Mountbatten restaurant in Bombay for "the authentic taste of England right here in India." Inside the restaurant a raucous group of Indians is getting ready to order. When they ask themselves why they come here every Friday, one of them replies, "You go out, get tanked up on lassis, and go out for an English. It wouldn't be Friday night without going for an English."

The scene of white English lads going for "an Indian" is, at once, mythic and actual. The ingredients of this scene of schismogenesis usually require the following: that the Anglo-Celtic men (the customers) should be inebriated; that the male South Asian waiters should be endlessly patient and polite; that the customers should be entirely ignorant of anything to do with South Asian culture (food culture, in particular); that they should be racist but in an offhand manner rather than confrontationally; that the customers should order the hottest dish on the menu and not balk at its spiciness; that the customers should carry on vociferously drinking alcohol. Actuality is usually more complex than myth.

This is Javed, who is remembering a time (unspecified) when he owned a restaurant in Bradford (probably during the late 1970s and into the 1980s). He is remembering one particular night when a customer demanded a particularly strong curry:

He was accompanied by a group of friends. He asked [the] waiter for a vindalu dish. I was listening to him. I went to my chef and asked him to make a special vindalu dish for him. You know a vindalu dish is made by pouring lemon juice over lots of green chillies so that the dish becomes strong and bitter. So we gave him the dish. But he complained and told that the dish was not hot enough. I was astonished. I asked my waiter to bring back the dish. Then I poured a big tablespoon full of chillies. My chef and other persons started to say, "Oh uncle! Are you mad! Do you want to kill him!" And I said, "Oh no he is not going to die." I swear I put so much red chillies and then green chillies as well. I added lemon juice and some garlic as well because garlic is also hot. So when he was eating that dish, his friends were laughing at him. After finishing his meal he came towards the counter. He was completely wet with his sweat. He asked who had cooked that dish. I pushed my chef backwards because I thought he might fight. You know it was one o'clock in the morning. I told him that I had cooked that dish and I asked him whether he had any complaints. He moved forward, shook hands with me and told me that he had never eaten such a strong dish in his entire life. He told me that he had really enjoyed eating that dish. And finally he thanked me very much. I told him that it was alright. But in my heart I said, "Son you go to your home tonight and then you will come to know" [laugh]. He came back after two weeks and asked me [laugh], "For God's sake, don't give me that poison again." Then I asked him who had told him to eat those vindalu dishes. I mean I told him that these were not even our own words. These chillies should have been used in a way that these dishes tasted mild and that was it. That was not even our food that he was eating. And I told him that he himself seemed very fond of eating these dishes. (Jamal 1996, 23)[9]

Javed's account is thick with affect; it is laced with intimations of violence and peppered with touches of humor; flavors and feelings are knotted together in complex and contradictory ways; pleasure and pain, politeness and cunning animate the production and consumption of sensual culture. The account is an example of social aesthetics at its most entangled. At a basic level the account tells the tale of a male customer enjoying what seems to be a bodily challenge of immense proportions, a challenge that at the end of the night he feels he has won, but on returning two weeks later has to admit defeat. There seems little animosity in either the victory or the defeat, though there is clearly enough insensitivity on the part of the customer for the waiters and the restaurateur to feel the threat of violence. The food itself has become a form of aggression (which seems to be a source of sorrow for the restaurateur, though he is the one telling the tale) and it is "spice" that in the end defeats the customer.

How would we unpick this scene to make it understandable as a scene of schismogenesis, of social aesthetics? At one level I think "unpicking" is the last thing that is required. The affective density of this scene, what makes it resonate so awkwardly, is the threading of such intense gustatory relish, with the almost nuclear burning of the spices, with the bodily effects of copious perspiration. What though is the mood of this scene, what is its tone? I think (and of course this is merely speculation) that it is necessarily multi-tonal. No doubt there is a vector of bitterness-aggression that drives this gustatory relish. Within the general (and mythic) culture of this scene the potential racist inflection is played out across gender and class. While South Asian restaurants and takeaways in Britain are often run on the basis of self-exploitation (whereby both owners and waiters earn minimum wage or less, and only earn money by working much longer hours than the customary forty hours a week), they signify as part of entrepreneurial and aspirational culture. For many working-class Anglo-Celtic British, eating an "Indian" may well be experienced through the mottled glass of class envy.[10] For this vector the masculinity of the restaurant (most of the South Asian restaurants in the United Kingdom are run by Muslims whose heritage is Bengali, Bangladeshi, or Pakistani, and most are run exclusively by men) and its status as both restaurant and affordable would be crucial.

Yet the bitterness-aggression vector might not be working alone. Across this, and driving gustatory relish in another direction, might be a vector animated by xenophilia-openness. Is this vector harder to substantiate? And if so, why would that be? Ambiguity surrounds the choice of the dish vindaloo. Mythically it is the most violent of dishes, the one that is the "strongest." But if the association is that spiciness is equated with Indian-ness, then the more spicy the more "Indian." Vindaloo is a working-class choice (proof of an unsubtle palate), but it is also the choice most outward looking (within this logic, at least). Bateson acknowledged that ethos was achieved through pedagogy (the training of the senses, of affect, of the orchestration of aesthetic life). But this also means that change of ethos requires sensual, affective pedagogy. The Indian restaurant, then, is always a scene of sensual pedagogy. This customer might well be driven by bitterness, but he might also be a learner: a very strict autodidact, willing to undergo sensual realignment as quickly as possible.

... And Politics?

In this essay I have been promoting an attentiveness to affect through the wider lens of social aesthetics. In doing this I was keen to emphasize the connections between affect, sensual and sensorial culture, perception, and so on. Occasionally I have hinted at the longer tradition involved in thinking about the aesthetics of social life; and once or twice I have offered concrete examples of this tradition (Bateson, and in a different vein, Orwell). Bateson's term for the dense weave of aesthetic propensities that might be shared (at some level) by a group is "ethos." Other writers have tried out different terms. For Ruth Benedict, for instance, it was the "pattern" or configuration of culture that mattered; for an ongoing French tradition, which would include Marcel Mauss and Pierre Bourdieu, the term for this wider sense of cultural disposition has been "habitus."[11] This social aesthetic work has provided some wonderfully fleshy sociology; it has also at times offered trite, mechanistic, and overly normative accounts of lively culture. A commitment to descriptive entanglement is hard to sustain for long and harder still to shape into something approaching academic conclusions. But if the academic payoff for social aesthetics might seem, at times, ambiguous and uneven, the political utility of such an approach must seem even more dubious.

In the world of affect, of social aesthetics, is there a place for politics? Clearly if there is it wouldn't be one that could hitch its flag straightforwardly to a sense of determinable outcomes. For a start, the complexity of these intermingling registers seems to guard against predictable effects and affects. If politics is envisaged as a form of rational persuasion for progressive ends, say, then the realm of social aesthetics might seem to be a significant hindrance for it. In Orwell's writing it almost seems as if ethos is an impossible foe, a prison house that can accommodate you but from which you can't escape. This is the rationale of his argument. Yet the performance of the work and the performance of the life suggest something else: the transformation of ethos through experiments in living. Here politics is a form of experiential pedagogy, of constantly submitting your sensorium to new sensual worlds that sit uncomfortably within your ethos. There is hope here: social aesthetics points to the mutability and dynamism of ethos and habitus, as well as their conservatism. Just as there is no necessary progressivism in this realm there is no essential defensive resistance either. The vindaloo eater (whether he likes it or not) is engaged in a form of sensorial pedagogy:

whether his lessons reaffirm his ethos or expand it in empathetic directions is hard to tell. It seems clear though that if our "affect horizons" are the result of deep pedagogy, then an affective politics that wanted to expand the aesthetic realms of communities would need to champion an affective counter-pedagogy. What would this look like? If this politics was dedicated to opening up the affective, sensorial tuning and retuning of the social body—then it would need to be exorbitant. But it would also need to reverberate at the level of the everyday. You could imagine such an approach politicizing school dinners in a way that wasn't simply dedicated to the instrumentalism of nutrition, but oriented to the communicative pedagogy of multicultural food. This would be a modest, everyday politics, a politics of the gut as much as the mind, oriented more toward ethos than eidos.

Notes

1   See, for instance, Feher, Nadaff, and Tazi 1997.
2   For contemporary work in this area, see Fisher 2002, Ngai 2005, and Altieri 2003.
3   For a recent addition to the literature, see Heller-Roazen 2007.
4   There are exceptions, and exceptions too numerous to mention here. Feminist aesthetic engagement has been much more attentive to our creaturely life: see, for instance, Armstrong 2000.
5   See Simmel 1968, Rancière 2004, and Dewey 1934.
6   For Bateson's discussion of ethos as a problematic term, see Bateson 1972, 73–87.
7   For evidence of this, see Miller 1997. Miller quite rightly dedicates a chapter to Orwell in his book on disgust and shows the complexity of Orwell's disgust. I'm indebted to Miller on this.
8   See Orwell 1952 for an account of his early school years orchestrated through humiliation, shame, and disgust.
9   Ahmad Jamal's ethnographic study of food consumption in Bradford (U.K.) was undertaken in the mid-1990s with informants from British Pakistani and Bangladeshi and Anglo-Celtic communities.
10 There is not the space here to provide a full account of the class dimensions of the British South Asian restaurant and its reception. A history of this diasporic cuisine and its various class inflections can be pieced together from the following sources: Choudhury 1993, Collingham 2005, Monroe 2005, and Visram 2002.
11 See Benedict 1934, Bourdieu 1977, and Mauss 2006, for relevant work. Clearly this is far from being a homogenous tradition; nonetheless the potential and problems that I would want to point at here do run through most work that has tried to gather together the threads of a living culture and speak about them at a general level. I would argue that critical inquiry into cultural affect tends in two directions—on the one hand there is a centripetal tendency to draw all the threads together to form a knot—on the other hand more specialized work has moved centrifugally, untangling

these threads and isolating particular strands. Research in this area feels the pull of these centrifugal and centripetal forces. The idea of stressing "entanglement" in this essay is my attempt to mitigate these forces. Benedict, Bourdieu, and Mauss navigate between these forces as they move from concrete specificity to theoretical abstraction. The ability to remain "entangled" is clearly visible in this work, if inconsistently.

Félix Guattari on Affect and the Refrain

Lone Bertelsen & Andrew Murphie

> The aesthetic impact of a floating red hulk on the
> horizon facilitated the televisual modulation of mass
> sentiment.—Angela Mitropoulos and Brett Neilson,
> "Exceptional Times, Non-governmental Spacings, and
> Impolitical Movements"
>
> How quick this becoming is in many cases, . . . territory
> is constituted at the same time as expressive qualities
> are selected or produced.—Gilles Deleuze and Félix
> Guattari, *A Thousand Plateaus*

If you work in advertising, or propaganda, you know that Jean-Luc Godard was only half right when he declared "it's not blood, it's red."[1] The color red always bleeds. It summons up an unusually wide ranging—but often *open, ambiguous*—power to affect and be affected. Even in images, red bleeds into our real life, our real blood flows. Red bleeds and blood flows involve a literal affective contagion. It's a bleed in which "body meets image" (Massumi 2002, 46ff).

This essay begins with an image that bled into the power to affect and be affected by that collection of bodies included in, or excluded from, "Australia." This was an image (think of it) of *a red ship—a huge freighter—on the horizon*. The repetition of this image did not just *illustrate* a complex political event. It helped *bring it into being*.[2] Taking our departure from the constituting power of this image, our more general concern will be with Félix Guattari's "logic of affects" (Guattari 1995a, 9). This logic will be taken as the basis for Politics with a capital "P," for the micropolitical events of everyday life, for their analysis, and for the modes of living made possible. This will require us to develop a more *technical* understanding of *the constitutive role of refrains*—as found in the repetition of the image of the red ship. Refrains structure the affective into "existential Territories" (Guattari 1995a, 15). If, as we will suggest, affects are intensities, then refrains are affects "cycled back" (Massumi quoted in Deleuze and Guattari 1987, xv).

If we have remained vague so far about this red ship on the horizon, this has been deliberate (the ship was part of the "*Tampa* crisis" of 2001 involving a Norwegian freighter, the Australian government, and over four hundred asylum seekers). Although this is often forgotten later, affects—and political events—often begin vaguely. Or rather, affective events begin in a *powerful indetermination*, one "on the horizon." The force of this indetermination—a chaos that soon begins to press upon a context—calls for refrains to fold the chaos into the beginnings of structure, to bring a little order (Deleuze and Guattari 1987, 311). This is a crucial moment in the constitution of affective territories. Refrains constitute what will always be fragile, no matter how benevolent or virulent, territories in time. These allow new forms of expression but render others inexpressible.

This essay's main purpose is to sketch the relations between refrains and Guattari's "logic of affects," especially as put to work in the current struggles over affective distribution at the core of political and everyday life. It is hoped that this sketch might provide a small contribution, among many, to a letting go of "archaic attachments" to often hierarchical "cultural traditions" (Guattari 1995a, 4) in favor of a "subjective pluralism" (Guattari 1996, 216). This is a pluralism that might escape an increasingly conservative "Politics," in favor of the infinity of little affective powers available to everyday life.

We will need some quick preambles. First, we should note that we are not considering the refrain as a new kind of signifier. Rather, its reorganization of affective forces involves a "molecular rupture" of the system of signs, of given ranges of expression, of the "already classified" (Guattari 1995a, 19–20). Refrains may sometimes be drawn from the discursive, but they break up the logic of discursive frameworks, at first in an imperceptible fragmenting of frameworks via affective intensity. This affective intensity is "capable of overthrowing" (Guattari 1995a, 19) the entire order of discourse in favor of transformation and the new modes of living with which we will conclude.

Second, this approach to politics and everyday life differs from those that tend toward a more direct analysis of signs and discourses, rights and rationales, within what is often at best a clash of given frameworks. If territories are usefully, often aggressively contested in these approaches, it is only *after* they have been formed. This essay, however, no longer accepts "a thesis . . . *which tends to make aggressiveness the basis of the territory*" (Deleuze and Guattari 1987, 315). There will be plenty of aggression after. That comes, literally, with the territory. First, however, the territory—its expressive basis—*must be formed*. Even then, territories are always falling apart. Then there is the additional problem of affective communication between territories, a *transduction (transformation) of forces rather than transmission of signs*. We will see the affective power of a red ship on the horizon as that of a transducer of affective forces, a refrain, not really a sign.

Third, we are assuming three different aspects to affect. The first is affect as transitive (Guattari 1996, 158), as the movement of impersonal, or we could say "pre-personal" forces (Guattari 1995a, 9), in which we are caught up (global warming makes this crystal clear). This is affect as the "limit-expression of *what the human shares with everything it is not*: a bringing out of its *inclusion* in matter" (Massumi 2002, 128). The second aspect is affect as more personal, literally more familiar. The terms vary but this is affect as emotion or feeling, the folding of broader affective intensities into the nervous system, eventually to become recognizable as the *register*, eventually the representation, of the ongoing folding of self and world, *as* the person. Emotion involves physical states (heat and increased heartbeat in anger, trembling in terror). Feelings are complex strings of ideas traversing emotions as they remap them (Damasio 2004, 28). The third aspect of affect perhaps lies in between the other two. This is the Spinozan "power to affect and be affected" "by which the power of acting of the body itself is increased, diminished, helped, or hindered, together with the ideas of these affections" (Spinoza 1952, 395). Affect is again "transitive," in constant variation, not so much a state as the ongoing "passage from one state to another" (Deleuze 1988a, 49). This is the fulcrum of politics micro and macro.

Fourth, conservatives sometimes seem to have found the presence of affect in politics easier to work or refrain (Massumi 2002, 2005a; Buchanan 2003). For nearly a hundred years, for the conservative, one of the main tasks of politics has been to attempt to capture and control affect (Lippmann 2007, Bernays 2004, Curtis 2002), if in the service of a rational(ist) elite somehow above the chaos of affective forces. The episode of the red ship thus has a long heritage.

Guattari wishes to reclaim the affective for a different agenda. For a start, he allows for no position outside of, certainly not above, affective forces. *One could almost say that for him affect is all there is.* What follows is an *aesthetic* approach to politics, meaning that Guattari acknowledges the primary importance of both sensation and creation. Of course, Guattari is opposed to more conservative attempts to mobilize affect, only in the service of its subsequent capture in a reductive and elitist "logic of delimited sets" (Guattari 1995a, 9). He opposes this with the idea of social practices or analyses with flexible and open-ended methodologies (metamethodologies) (Guattari 1995a, 31) that enable a "subjective pluralism" engaging with the complexity of affective events (exactly what the conservative capture of the events involving the *Tampa* was designed to avoid). Furthermore, Guattari's embracing of affect in social practice is *ethical* in that it evaluates practices of living. In sum, his is an "ethico-aesthetic paradigm." Guattari proposes this as an alternative to the more common *pseudo*-"scientific paradigms" traditionally employed in "the human sciences and social sciences" (Guattari 1995a, 10). In ethico-aesthetics "to speak of creation is to speak of the responsibility of the creative instance with regard to the thing created, inflection of the state of things, bifurcation beyond pre-established schemas, once again taking into account alterity in its extreme modalities" (107).

The modern signals a constant innovation as much in the developments of regimes of sensation as in those of rationalist modes of thought. Both increasingly tend to micro-colonize the infinity of little affective events that make up our everyday lives. Guattari's response is to take the everyday infinities and powers of affect very seriously, and to develop a creative responsibility for modes of living *as they come into being*.

A Red Ship on the Horizon

In 2001, just weeks before September 11, events involving a red, Norwegian freighter and 438 mostly Afghani refugees changed the political territory of Australia. How this occurred has been an enormously important question for many Australians, one that has received many detailed and intelligent responses.[3]

A red ship appeared on the horizon. The geographical horizon was north of Christmas Island in the Indian Ocean (2,600 kilometers northwest of Perth, close to Indonesia). The political horizon was that of a desperate conservative government (that of John Howard and his coalition of Liberal and National parties) facing an election and almost certain defeat. The Australian government used the incident of the red ship (and others—such as the "children overboard affair"[4]) to turn likely defeat in an election into a "dark victory" (Marr and Wilkinson 2003).

In the images that provided the "aesthetic impact of a floating red hulk" (Mitropoulos and Neilson 2006), this was first and foremost *a* red ship on the horizon—that is to say, a singular, intense "red shipness" on a general horizon. Hidden within this "red shipness," however, was no ordinary cargo. On board were 438 refugees (mostly Afghani) who had been rescued by the Norwegian freighter *MV Tampa* on August 26, from a small, Indonesian fishing boat.

The Australian government had known that the Indonesian fishing boat carrying the asylum seekers was "in trouble" for at least "20 hours" before a call for rescue was relayed. It "wanted Indonesians to take responsibility for the problem" but "the delay put the lives of 438 people in terrible danger" (Marr and Wilkinson 2003, 3). Once the people had been successfully rescued by the *Tampa*, the Howard government denied "the Tampa permission to enter Australian Territorial waters" (Maley 2004, 154). Eventually, on August 29, for the sake of the health and safety of everyone on board, the *Tampa*'s captain, Arne Rinnan, decided to enter Australian territorial waters near Christmas Island. His ship was eventually taken over by Australian special troops.

The asylum seekers were then transferred to the island of Nauru as part of a wider operation the government called the "Pacific solution."[5] From this time, refugees arriving by boat to claim asylum in Australia were picked up at sea before they could reach Australian territory. They were taken to Nauru or Australia's northern neighbor, Papua New Guinea. Both had received millions of dollars from Australia.

We need to separate three features of the *Tampa* event: the emergence of territory via the refrain, the emergence of new functions within this territory, and the further refraining of this new territory and new functions. First, in Deleuze's and Guattari's terminology, there is the emergence of the event as a territory, the red ship as its refrain or its mark. The *MV Tampa* is defunctionalized (Deleuze and Guattari 1987, 315) (as, in another way, were the refugees themselves), removed from the sign systems and material processes involving regular international shipping. It becomes the mark, the possibility of a new *event* (a new *virtual potential* for things to happen differently), of a new set of *physical territories* (actual borders, detention centers, ship's decks, islands, *bodies*), and of a new set of *existential territories* (these include virtual potentials, physical places, new modes of living, new laws, new sign systems, discourses, rhetorics, new emotions and feelings, new powers to affect and be affected). In sum, a new field of expression arises, a refrain that potentializes other refrains.

Prefiguring what is now a wide range of legislated censorship of the media with regard to government activity, the government would not allow the media, or even the Red Cross, on board. There was to be no visual evidence of defenseless and desperate people or leaky little fishing boats (Burnside, n.d.). *The red ship provided an entirely different aesthetic.* The image remained that of a large imposing red hulk, often shimmering in the heat on the horizon. Personalization was resisted, giving the event a very different feel. Refrains are a looping of "pre-personal" affective forces into a variable temporal "texture"—what Stern calls a "temporal contour" (Stern 2004, 62). The image of the *Tampa* had a slow, drawn-out contour, an almost immobile intensity. Its refraining—in tabloid newspapers, the nightly news—created an insistent, unresolved stubbornness: a redness sitting on the horizon that would not easily go away. It could have been a metaphor for threat or rescue, invasion or refuge, "Asia" (Afghanistan, Indonesia) or even "Europe" (Norway and those overly maternal Scandinavians with their welfare states), the simultaneous threat of globalization and the isolation so key to Australia. It was all of these and more, but *first* it was an uneasy and persistent redness sitting on the horizon.

It was the event's temporal texture that allowed for a considered reorganization of a territory that had become increasingly inhospitable to a conservative government. In Australia, it would come to complement the very different "temporal contour" of the repeated images of the attacks of September 11. Here was a contour—a refrain—in which something shocking happened quickly, out of nowhere, again and again. The interaction of these two contours in Australian politics would dynamize a full range of repressive governmentalities for years to come.

The second feature of the *Tampa* event involves the *new functions* that emerged within the new *existential* territory marked by the red ship. A range of at times quite contradictory forces was made available to new expressive powers. A staging of powers to affect and be affected was provided, on the ship's deck, the ocean, and in the media. A cast emerged to be taken up by these powers: asylum seekers, merchant sailors, soldiers, several nations, the United Nations, maritime and international law, and of course, political parties. A new range of affective dynamics began to play its part, and in turn this led to new social forms, new laws, the red ship refrain now bleeding into what was becoming a culture entrained to be wary of anything that hinted at "softness." It is true, there *were* some acts of compassion, but these found little visibility in the new territory. New forms of aggressivity, however, did. "Politics" was constituted precisely as a visible but abstract, even disembodied, contest. In taking over the ship, a rehearsal of Iraq, attack was constituted as defense. The aggressivity began to be played out against a series of abstract targets held in place by the red ship: "refugees," international laws and obligations, international shipping, compassion. Like all aggressivity, it was polarizing. Everything became a matter of attack and defense. *Everyone had to have an opinion.* It was at this point that signs and discourses, frameworks and orders, fully emerged. Opinions and arguments matter of course, but *it perhaps matters more that an opinion has to be had.* A new territory had opened for political contest on terms much more suitable not only to the Australian government but to conservatives around the world.

The *Tampa* affair could have been worked out differently. However it was, as David Marr and Marian Wilkinson have suggested, a "dark victory." It allowed a remix of "border protection" and "national security" that densely interwove the psychic and the social, the legal and the geographic. The red ship made further refrains possible. In its wake, the prime minister brilliantly, darkly, victoriously stated, "We decide who comes into this country and the circumstances in which they come" (in Marr and Wilkinson 2003, 277). This was a classic discursive refraining of ambiguous affective powers within an increasingly broad and enduring existential territory. It confused an increasingly presidential-style "fathering of the nation" with a "we" that was itself an open assemblage of a political party, a government, and a fairly homogeneous image of like-minded "real" citizens (from which of course many were excluded). Despite, or because of, the slow "temporal contour" of the image-refrain itself, it was a disturbingly dynamic time. Laws were changed (Ross 2004, Frow 2007) and states of exception proliferated (Buchanan, 2003). William Maley suggested that the "demonisation of asylum seekers, with an emphasis on border protection, was perfectly calculated to play on [swing voters'] fears" (Maley 2004, 161).

The third feature of the *Tampa* event concerns the way it enabled a further refraining of affective dynamics. It arguably helped toward a general strengthening of states of exception in the increased demonization of ethnic groups, unions, the unemployed, intellectuals, artists, and anyone else not appearing to be completely mesmerized by Howard's "opportunity society." More directly, it provided the ground for the implementation of harsher, better funded, and more secretive "new border control technologies" in "Operation Relex" (Mitropoulos and Neilson 2006). Australia's borders were literally moved, with the excision of Christmas Island and others from Australia's migration zone. Mitropoulos and Neilson explain that, "while formally, the right to seek asylum remains, these laws remove the ability of migrants who arrive on certain Islands and reefs to seek asylum" (Mitropoulos and Neilson 2006).

From the Outside

If a refrain is a gathering of forces, these are forces that, like a red ship on the horizon, like refugees, *come from the outside, as a challenge to established forms*. The red ship provided a political opportunity precisely because it seemed, in its stubborn redness, to lie on the border between force and the creation of a new form of (political?) expression. It was not quite yet a content.

The red ship shows us that affect is not form. Affects are *transitions* between states (Guattari 1996, 158). A "logic of affects" might even argue that "states" are themselves slow, refrained, or looped affects—in short, passages. As transitions between other transitions, passages in a field of relays, affects have actual and virtual sides. They are *actual* for example in sensations or emotions as a kind of coming into being that is nevertheless always in transition (Massumi 2002, 35, 207). They are *virtual* in that they carry "un-actualized capacities to affect and be affected" (DeLanda 2002, 62). None of this finds final form except in the refrain, with its looping of "temporal contours" and resonances. The form of a refrain is not, therefore, a stable distribution of "formed" affects. It is an erratic and evolving distribution of both coming into being and the power to affect or be affected. This is its power. The refrain is a particularly useful way of negotiating the relations between everyday infinities of virtual potentials and *the real (that is, not just theorized) operations of power*. Refrains enable modes of living in time, not in "states."

The cry of many since the *Tampa* has been an attempt to understand this power: "how did it come to this?" Guattari might have said; "yes, and how could it have been, how can it be different?" This requires a somewhat technical answer.

The Temporal Resonance of Affect

It is often forgotten that refrains are not just closures but openings to possible change. They allow us "to join with the forces of the future" (Deleuze and Guattari 1987, 311). Refrains join with future forces by stitching themselves into them. They are able to do this because affects, as transitions or passages, are able to link up across senses, across events, across "temporal contours," between or within different aspects of refrains. They are "cross-modal" (Stern 2004, 65). One aspect of this is that, as Massumi writes, "affect is synesthetic, implying a participation of the senses in each other." Again, variation is power: "the measure of a living thing's interactions is its ability to transform the effects of one sensory mode into those of another" (Massumi 2002, 35).

Affect is, similarly, *cross-temporal*, implying a participation of "temporal contours" in each other, singly or in the looping of refrains. This cross-temporality constitutes the movement of experience into the future (and into the past, as memory). On a macro scale an example is the refrained slow "threat of refugees" resonating with the refrained ongoing threat of inflation. A different example, in Australia at least, has been the cross-temporal linking into the future of the crushing slowness and suspension of the *Tampa* crisis with the speed and suddenness of September 11. To understand this on the micro scale, we can turn to Daniel Stern's discussion of the "vitality affects" developed in "temporal contours." This allows us to begin to understand the "micro-temporal dynamics" of "direct experience" (Stern 2004, 62).

Stern initially introduced the idea of "vitality affects" in order "to explain the mother's affective attunement to her infant, as an early form of inter-subjectivity." However, Stern suggests that "the idea has wider application." Here we can clearly define a "temporal contour." It is "the objectifiable time-shape of a stimulus . . . [that] impinges on the central nervous system from within or without." He gives the pleasing example of a smile, noting that "a smile seen on another's face has a distinct temporal contour that takes time to form. . . . There is an analogic unfolding, not a sequence of discrete states or events. . . . Everything we do, see, feel, and hear . . . has a temporal contour. . . . We are immersed in a 'music' of the world at the local level—a complex polyphonic, polyrhythmic surround" (Stern 2004, 62–64).

The specific contours matter. As Stern puts it, "there are a million smiles" (63). Imagine two similarly structured smiles from a friend, but one much faster than usual, one very slow. They affect you very differently.

Vitality affects are the "subjectively experienced shifts in internal states" that "are the complement to temporal contours" (Stern 2004, 64). They are different from "categorical affects" (simply put, recognizable emotions, like "fear" or "anger," that we find easier to pin down). In fact, in Stern's view *vitality affects (and temporal contours) work across and between more "cate-gorical affects"* (64). Think of the friend's strange smile—is he or she happy or angry or *perhaps something in between*? Think of the red ship's unusual refrained contour, of the work it can do. "This micro-temporal dynamic" is the very stuff of everyday—and political—life. It is affective, "analogic," and, crucially for politics and social life, *open to switching modalities* (between emotions, "states," different senses, images, other "temporal contours"). It is primarily relational. "Because of our capacities for cross-modal translation," writes Stern, "a vitality affect evoked from one modality can be associated to a vitality affect from any other modality, or from any other time or situation. *Vitality affects lend themselves to the formation of associative networks*" (65, emphasis ours).

The nation feels more alive in such a crisis as that of the red ship precisely because there are very new "temporal contours," a shifting and destruction of habits, a wealth of new "cross-modal" communications. It is this that makes such times so productive for politics, in the meeting of macro- and micro-political life.

In sum, we have "vitality affects" and "temporal contours" emerging via events, gathered into refrains, diagrammed with other refrains, and stimulating the nation's nervous systems. That this process occurred in a kind of slow motion in the case of the red ship only made it all the more effective. This process is accompanied and extended out of situations via varied individual emotions, the latter more narrowly defined as individualized and "categorical" in the normal sense (*my* fear, *my* anger), and eventually via feelings, complex thoughts arising from emotional experience. It is only with feelings perhaps that micro-experience evolves into narrative and story, and what is often regarded as "real Politics" or "real" social life begins. Even then, there is an ongoing "crossing of semantic wires" (Massumi 2002, 24) in affective intensity.

For Massumi, affect is precisely a matter of how intensities come together, move each other, and transform and translate *under or beyond* meaning, semantics, fixed systems, cognitions. Part of the assumption here is that— even in the most reactionary of circumstances—*nothing happens if affective intensity has not already paid us a visit*. This refines our understanding of why territory—spatial and temporal—is always "existential territory." It is as much a territory that enables movement as something that keeps everything in its place. It is movement itself. For Guattari, territory is "never given as object but always as intense repetition" (Guattari 1995a, 28).

However, in political life, in theoretical life, and in everyday life, attempts are often made to particularize and stabilize this intensity, and to pacify affect, to reduce it, classify it, and quantify it. In a sense, affect often finds itself in a situation like Pavlov's dogs, harnessed up in the laboratory, given electric shocks, but then reduced to the functioning of their salivary glands (and what came to be called "experimental neurosis"). Yet affect escapes (Massumi 2002, 35). This is troubling, for governments, for experts, perhaps for theorists sometimes. The more affect escapes, the more governance, or indeed much of contemporary life, seems an attempted but impossible management of "temporal contours" as they "impinge upon the nervous system." Massumi writes, for example, that once the color-coded terror alert system in the United States was deployed "affective modulation of the populace was now an official, central function of an increasingly time-sensitive government" (Massumi 2005b, 32).

It is important to note that an overemphasis on emotions or feelings will miss the extended dynamics of affective events, in politics or elsewhere. In the first place, as Massumi writes, "emotion and affect . . . follow different logics." Affect's logics are not those of "received psychological categories" (Massumi 2002, 27). Moreover, emotion is "qualified intensity" while affect is "unqualified" intensity. It is "crucial to theorize the difference" (28). Neither is there a natural or necessary progression from affect to emotion or feeling. Deleuze makes this clear in his writing about the work of the painter Francis Bacon. Deleuze even suggests that in Bacon's work (and we assume elsewhere) "there are no feelings . . . there are nothing but affects; that is, 'sensations' and 'instincts' " (Deleuze 2005, 39). In sum, we do not have to feel an emotion with regard to red ships, refugees, the World Trade Center, and planes in order for refrains and "affective modulation" to do their work. Indeed, such events might render us numb to feeling. Yet they still bring us forces or take them away, acting via a reorganization of sensations and instincts. If we live out a micro-fascism within everyday life (Foucault in Deleuze and Guattari 1983, xiii), this is via the passage of sensations, both with *and without* feeling, with *or without* our agreement or disagreement.

Refrains and Nervous Worlds

With this in mind, we can begin to diagram a categorization of affects and refrains according to Guattari, although not in a way in which one type of affect or refrain would exclude another, or there would be stable structures of relation between them. It is rather a question *of degree of composition* within a rhizome of refrains.

For Guattari *simple affects* are *"sensory affects"* (Guattari 1996, 163), for example, a light in my eyes, a red ship on the horizon, a picture of a red ship on the front page of a newspaper. These accord with what he calls the *"simplest" refrains* (Guattari 1995a, 15), such as birdsong, a child singing a little song in the dark (Deleuze and Guattari 1987, 311), a repetition of images of a red ship.

Mostly, however, things are not simple. At any given moment for real beings there is (for a healthy subjectivity) a "polyphony of modes of subjectivation" and *"a multiplicity of ways of 'keeping time' "* (Guattari 1995a, 15)—a multiplicity of simple refrains in action. The multiplicity of relations between these refrains (and times) expresses itself in what Guattari calls *"problematic affects"* (1996, 163). These accord with *"complex refrains,"* a mix of simple refrains that "marks the intersection of heterogeneous modes of subjectivation" (Guattari 1996, 199). One example Guattari gives is that of television viewing (1995a, 16). Perhaps the television is showing the red ship, stationary, on the horizon. A newsreader is reading the news in that special tone of voice. Then follows a prime minister I think will save me (or can't abide another second). Eyebrows trimmed, he drops his voice lower and talks with those special movements of his chin. I drink tea (another temporal contour). I've just meditated. I'm breathing slower than normal. A complex refrain, a problematic affect envelops me, *with or without* my feelings, in accord with my opinions or not.

In a further layer of composition there are *"hypercomplex refrains,"* with *"hypercomplex problematics."* These bring highly absorbing *singular* "universes" (Guattari 1995a, 16) like mathematics into lived experience. Hypercomplex refrains sometimes transport one to an abstract, "interior" world, into the "incorporeal universes" of music or mathematics perhaps. They sometimes involve a "massive affect" that "plunges us into sadness or indeed, into an ambience of gaiety and excitement" (Guattari 1995a, 16). I feel I live in the world of red shipness and border control. I am plunged into the sadness of "Howardism" or what Melissa Gregg and Glen Fuller call "the refrain of the righteous" (Gregg and Fuller 2005). I go out with friends to hear music, and we are immersed in a world of "gaiety and excitement."

Overall, we face a powerful mix of simple, sensory, problematic, and massive affects, given some structure in time by simple, complex, and hypercomplex refrains in varying processes of composition and decomposition. These perform a reorganization of sensation and instinct, of temporalities, of resonances within or across nervous systems, involving the likes of global-

ization, neoliberal economics, global warming, the war on terror, mathematics, love, music. Massumi makes the political stakes explicit when he
writes, "Affect holds a key to rethinking postmodern power after ideology. . . . This makes it all the more pressing to connect ideology *to its real
conditions of emergence*" (Massumi 2002, 42, emphasis ours). In this, the
refrain's power (and here we must think far beyond music [Guattari 2000,
46]) resides in a powerful, creative, self-organizing *transversality*. Refrains'
work with affect is *cross-modal, intertemporal*. As with the *Tampa* refrain,
the problem is the need, faced with the power of the refrain, for absolute
closure (for border control in fact).

From "Archaic Attachments" to "Subjective Pluralism"

In 1992, Guattari's outline of situations such as that of the red ship on the
horizon was prescient. He wrote of a world increasingly and often problem-
atically "dominated by rising demands for subjective singularity" (Guattari
1995a, 3). Events such as the red ship are foundational in a new round of
"quarrels over language [for example, English-language tests for citizen-
ship], autonomist demands [the demand by Australia and the United States
for their independence from the Kyoto Protocol concerning global warm-
ing], and issues of nationalism and nation [possible "Australian values" tests
for citizenship]," which manifest themselves in "a *conservative* reterritorial-
isation of subjectivity" (Guattari 1995a, 3, emphasis ours). This is narrowly
prescribed and reinforced. For Guattari it consists of a "mixture of archaic
attachments to cultural traditions that nonetheless aspire to the technological and scientific modernity characterising the contemporary subjective
cocktail" (1995a, 4).

An obvious example of this is the "archaic" potential for racism in Australia, which, drawing on a number of deeply resonating refrains in the
constitution of Australian life, feeds into the new technologies of border
control and detention (Mitropoulos and Neilson 2006). Some commentators have pointed to a new existential territory of insecurity (economic or
otherwise) that plays into the "paranoid" revival of archaic attachments to
xenophobia and racism (Hage 2003).

Guattari stresses that "the economy of collective desire goes both ways, in
the direction of transformation and liberation, and in the directions of
paranoic wills to power" (1995b, 15). However, taking affect seriously, not
only as a means to a hierarchical end, might be the beginning of *an experi-*

mentalism in social and cultural life (24). It is here that Guattari situates his concept, ethics, and practice of a "subjective pluralism" (1996, 216).

This begins with the acceptance of the very notion of a pluralism in subjectivity, of a mix of partial temporalities, of dissensus, even "multiplicity within oneself" (Guattari 1996, 216), of the necessary shifting complexity of analysis and social practice (262–72). This pluralism is a *multiple mobility of processes, events, intensities*, from the red ship's refrain or color-coded alert systems creating "central nervousness" (Massumi 2005b, 32) to a cup of coffee, to falling in love, to suddenly feeling tired, or the persistent resonance of "archaic attachments," perhaps all of these resonating together: a "polyphony" of refrains (Guattari 1995a, 15).

In the next section of this essay, we will examine what is at stake in repositioning affect with regard to "subjective pluralism." Currently much of social control is an attempt to close down "subjective pluralism."

"A Logic of Affect Rather Than a Logic of Delimited Sets"

In a short interview, Guattari argues that in contemporary society "we try through various means, such as the mass media and standardized behavior, to neuroleptize subjectivity" (Guattari 1996, 215). A neuroleptic is an "antipsychotic drug." It literally means "capable of affecting" or "taking hold of" our nervous system. Guattari sees a more general cultural neuroleptizing accompanying the politics of "central nervousness"—an intense reactive reworking of affective life between neuroleptics and "central nervousness." This appears in contemporary capitalism and the mass media's "infantilizing subjectivity" (Guattari 1996, 272). It is this that leads to repression, "the rise of religious fundamentalism," exploitation, racism, "and the oppression of women" (266). It was such infantilization that aided Howard's "dark victory."

For Guattari the first "important ethical choice" (1995a, 13) in response is between "scientism" and the aesthetic. For Guattari, "either we objectify, reify, 'scientifise' subjectivity, or, on the contrary, we try to grasp it in the dimension of processual creativity" (13). As concept and practice, the refrain is responsive to the ethico-aesthetic paradigm, a creative alternative to "universalist reductions to the Signifier and to scientific rationality" (30). With the refrain, one can "think 'transversally'" (Guattari 2000, 43) about subjectivity, in tune with "its idiosyncratic territorial couplings . . . its opening onto value systems . . . with their social and cultural implications" (1995a, 4). The intensity of transversal connections (that is, affect) across difference is un-avoidable here. Affective intensity is literally the life of territorial processes. A territory is its differential intensities—conflict and/or compassion—and cannot be reduced to "delimited sets" (9).

To be fully ethical, Guattari's transversal connections must "allow the acceptance of the other, the acceptance of subjective pluralism" (1996, 216). The *ethico-aesthetic* paradigm is therefore also the "*ethicopolitical*" (104). The links between the two are clear in the events involving the *Tampa*. Discussing the *Tampa* and related events, Rosalyn Diprose has stressed the importance of maintaining "the difference between bodies necessary to the expression of meaning" (Diprose 2003, 36; see also Mitropoulos and Neilson 2006).

The affective "engine" (Guattari 1996, 159) makes all the difference here. Real bodies need to be in affective relation (that is, real refugees and real members of the Australian public) in order for this difference—*as meaning, as a shift in existential territory*—to arise. In the case of the Howard government, the refugees were nowhere to be seen because the "difference between bodies" was between a ship, a government, and an abstract electorate. This was further reduced visually to the conflict between two refrains in conjunction—the red hulk on the horizon, and closeups of the prime minister in front of the Australian flag, chin out, magically invoking the nation in his conflating "we," along with the "delimited sets" via which "Australia" was to register. In this it was not only the refugees that were nowhere to be seen. The electorate had disappeared as well, abstracted into the face of the prime minister whose main differential relation was with a huge red ship. We begin to see why "subjective pluralism" is not just a nice aim, but the lifeblood of community, very different to the leader-intoned "we." Diprose puts the problem acutely: "Community lives from difference, on the touch of difference of other bodies that cannot be assimilated to mine. . . . A politics of exclusion presents a picture of community with which community cannot live" (Diprose 2003, 39–48; see also Diprose 2005).

For Guattari, an affective community requires that it is not only the unified "we" that needs to be fragmented from within. It is also the "I," which is always already a "multiplicity within oneself" (Guattari 1996, 216). Gary Genosko writes that Guattari develops "a conception of the individual as fundamentally . . . a group subject" (Genosko 2000, 156). Guattari himself explains: "It is a matter not only of tolerating another group, another ethnicity, another sex, but also for a *desire for dissensus, otherness, difference*. Accepting otherness is a question not so much of right as of desire. This acceptance is possible precisely on the condition of assuming the multiplicity within oneself" (1996, 216, emphasis ours). This multiplicity can be excessive and generative, precisely in that it is mobilized by affective intensities and refrains. It acknowledges an affective sociality of embodiment—Guattari suggests that "we cannot live outside our bodies, our friends, some sort of human cluster" (1996, 216).

However, the multiplicity of intensities overlaid within a body means that, "at the same time, we are bursting out of this situation" (Guattari 1996, 216). There is always an excess of affective intensity (Massumi 2002, 217) to be invested in a red ship, a prime minister's face, or the stories of refugees surviving a ship's sinking, and for this to be folded into, to actively resonate within, the "group subject." This group subject, whether our selves or larger social groups, is never some reasonably known—delimited—"human cluster," delimited by "key performance indicators" or "customer feedback." Affect always carries subjectivities elsewhere, to new territories and a dismantling of the old, ever toward the infinite possibilities and powers contained within our bodies, our friends (and our foes?), and their ecological contexts (Guattari 1996, 215–16). Each event, each body, carries the "affective potential" (Manning 2006) for things to turn out differently, as they inevitably will (despite the "logic of delimited sets"). We live affective transitions, the sensations of events as they come into being. At the same time, we live the affective carriage of future potential, affect's transversality through different temporalities—affect's *virtuality*.

The virtual is the pool of *relational potential* from which the affective event is drawn (see Massumi 2002). It is this virtuality that allows for an ongoing "re-singularization of subjectivity" (Guattari 1996, 202). However, as we have seen with the *Tampa* refrain "the politics of the virtual . . . does not necessarily belong to the left" (Gregg and Fuller 2005, 152). Or at least, all political forms at times involve a desire for openings, if only often to revivify "archaic attachments" and closures in the process. The pool of "relational potential" includes racism and fear. This is why, when Guattari talks about the importance of a "politics of the virtual," he specifically points to "an *ethics* and politics of the virtual" (Guattari 1995a, 29, emphasis ours), to which we will return shortly. This virtuality also inhabits signs. Guattari suggests that, just as bodies are not reducible to their given contexts, so signs, in their affective dimension, burst out of "strictly linguistic axiomatics" (1995a, 4). Driven by affect, signs exhibit a "non-discursive" aspect, one that acts beyond the constraints of discourse (Guattari 1995a, 1–31).

No subjective event—whether directly embodied or discursive—is reducible to "neuroleptized" affect or the "logic of delimited sets." All subjective events—including the discursive—have a "non-discursive" "pathic" dimension (Guattari 1995a, 25–30). There are always affective paths between elements (red ships, prime ministers, my own group subject). Or, more correctly, elements and subjectivity emerge from these pathic events. A prime-minister-red-ship-my-group-subject-abstracted-refugees-abstracted-SAS-soldiers-nightly-news assemblage emerges as a complex refrain through which other affective events pass (all kinds of different affects—an infinity in fact). The emergences and passages of the pathic/affective subjective mode are prior to "the subject-object relation" (Guattari 1995a, 25; see also Massumi 2002, 217). With "pathic subjectivity" (Guattari 1995a, 25) it is a question "of co-existence" (30). However, "in rationalist, capitalist subjectivity" (26), and in scientistic paradigms, "pathic subjectivation" is "systematically circumvent[ed]" (26). Or at least, such a circumvention of the pathic and affect is constantly *if impossibly* attempted.

At the same time, the impossibility of avoiding the dynamism of affect is crucial. It means that "an affect is . . . not, as the 'shrinks' commonly wish to represent it, a passively endured state. It is . . . *the site of a work, of a potential praxis*" (Guattari 1996, 166, emphasis ours). The work of capitalism and scientistic paradigms—their ongoing attempts to tame affective intensity—will never be completed. The "system" never succeeds in the way that scientist paradigms and "delimited logics" often claim.

A New Social and "Subjective Music"

There has been an understandable tendency in the analysis of events such as the *Tampa* and September 11 to pose the social as now controlled by the right of politics. This is largely *technically* correct. There are new media controls via the technics of neoliberal management practices. Legal frameworks—new logics of delimitation—have been redrawn and legal institutions re-stacked with more conservative judges. Significant legal changes involve the management of population via the likes of new refugee visas. There are also new technological drives toward border control, surveillance, the performance management of education, and so on.

However, all of this is as fractured as it is effective because it only acknowledges affective intensity to then attempt to re-cage it within (new) "delimited logics." It assumes—it has to—a knowable socius, one that can be reduced to its delimitations. Guattari suggests that to defeat this, social theory needs to acknowledge that, as with bodies and language, *social prac-*

tice implies engaging with an excess to the social, strictly speaking. Here Guattari points out that the "term 'collective' should be understood in the sense of a multiplicity that deploys itself . . . beyond the individual, on the side of the socius" and "before the person, on the side of preverbal intensities" (Guattari 1995a, 9).

Daniel Stern is again of great interest to Guattari because Stern conceptualizes a "trans-subjective" side of subjectivity. Stern develops (alongside "vitality" and "categorical affects") the notions of "sharable" and "non-sharable affects" (Guattari 1995a, 6). Sharable affects indicate "the inherently trans-subjective character of an infant's early experiences, which do not dissociate the feeling of the self from the feeling of the other." There are ongoing "dialectics between 'sharable affects' and 'non-sharable affects'" (Guattari 1995a, 6). In other words, there is an ongoing assemblage between more and less open aspects, or more and less structured modes of individuation, within the group subject. Guattari also includes "non-human" aspects in this ongoing assemblage, which "share" their own "temporal contours" and affective logics. These include art, music, computer technology, educational and other institutions, and the media. Indeed, the "non-human prepersonal part of subjectivity is crucial since it is from this that its heterogenesis can develop" (Guattari 1995a, 9). A consequence of all this is that the subject/society opposition (Guattari 1995a, 1) no longer makes sense. Rather there are complex affective and intensive exchanges, situated in the broader ecology of the world (Guattari 2000).

Once again we see the central importance of affect. Massumi suggests that affect is "trans-situational . . . the invisible glue that holds the world together" (Massumi 2002, 217). For Guattari, "affect sticks to subjectivity, it is a glischroid matter" (Guattari 1996, 158). It "sticks" to the "speaker" as much as the "listener," it sticks in empathy, in desire, in the general "transitivist character of affect." It is from this that a complex and open affective knowledge emerges in "multi-polar affective compositions" (158).

Guattari places his hopes for "new . . . social practices" (272) in this "multi-polar affective" sociality and a broad-ranging "ontological pluralism" (216). He insists on "a subjectivity of difference" and its promotion (272), remaining firmly democratic while arguing for "an ethics of responsibility" (Hans Jonas, quoted in Guattari 1996, 271). However, as is the case in his conception of subjectivity, Guattari does not argue for an overarching or fundamental unity to social relations or to forms of political resistance. Rather his ethics is one of immanent engagement with the affective in situ. The affective is *mapped out* in an ongoing way by specific, non-totalitarian "cartographies." Each one of these "represents a particular vision of the world which, even when adopted by a large number of individuals, would always harbour an element of uncertainty at its heart. That is, in truth, its most precarious capital" (Guattari 1996, 271).

It is in fostering this element of uncertainty that the refrain becomes ethical. The refrain in itself is pragmatic not ethical. Yet its pragmatism forces it to deal with the uncertain. Even in the attempt to create rigid "certainties" or borders, as in the *Tampa* events, the refrain must work the affective in real time, immanently. More ethical refrains preserve a degree of uncertainty, an opening to affective infinities and powers, while making the affective more livable. This is why the "logic of affects" needs the refrain. If affects are deterritorialized and "non discursive" then they are still "awaiting their existential completion" (Guattari 1996, 158) and it is here that the refrain has to do its work. It is refrains that can keep Guattari's pluralist subjectivity functional, by "keeping time" (1995a, 15) in an aesthetic practice of duration, repetition, and difference engaging with the affective world.

Here Guattari writes about the importance of a "renewed form of sociality." He does not talk about this in terms of "relations of opposition." He writes that "it is a matter of forging polyphonic interlacings between the individual and the social. Thus, a subjective music remains to be thereby composed" (Guattari 1996, 267). More complex refrains might structure this subjective music into new, singular "universes of reference" (169), which again need not be closed. In turning "reference around on itself," refrains give "not only a feeling of being—a sensory affect—but also an active way of being—a problematic affect" (Guattari 1996, 167). The ethical question concerning this active way of being is, "How does one go about producing, on a large scale, a desire to create a collective generosity?" (Guattari 1995b, 24). Guattari argues that this "takes work, research, experiment" (24) but that "it is possible to envision different formulas organizing social life" (25). Again Guattari stresses uncertainty: "Not only must I accept this adversity, I must love it . . . seek it out, communicate with it, delve into it, increase it. It must get me out of my narcissism, my bureaucratic blindness, and will restore to me a sense of finitude that all the infantilizing subjectivity of the mass media attempts to conceal . . . responsibility emerges from the self in order to pass to the other" (Guattari 1996, 271–72). Massumi writes of a politics of a differential "*caring for* belonging" (2002, 255)—not assuring the borders of the nation, or the future of the political party, but rescue at sea.

We began this essay with an analysis of affects and refrains in the case of a singular red ship on the horizon. This allowed us to understand the complexity with which a conservative politics was able to turn the powerful indetermination of affect to its advantage. However, thinking in terms of affect has a power beyond critique. Here we need to remind ourselves that behind the redness of the red ship event, and outside of national politics, was an ethical encounter—that of sailors and refugees in a rescue at sea. The ethics of such encounters hinges on the extent to which the everyday infinity of affective powers themselves can be accepted. Too often this is not the case. The nation, Politics, or even disciplinary analysis deems that affective powers should be returned to an "infantilizing subjectivity" masquerading as cultural maturity or even sound critical judgment.

Notes

1   This was Godard's response when he was asked why his film *Pierrot le Fou* exhibited so much blood onscreen.

2   We are not, of course, saying this image was solely responsible for the events surrounding the *Tampa*.

3   See Buchanan 2003, Ross 2004, Maley 2004, Mitropoulos and Neilson 2006, Marr and Wilkinson 2003.

4   Shortly before the same election, in October 2001, facing criticism of its handling of the *Tampa*, the government knowingly misrepresented photographs of children in the water next to another boat full of asylum seekers. These photographs were supposed to show that the "unprincipled asylum seekers" would do anything to get into the country, including throwing their own children into the water to be "rescued." In fact, the asylum seekers' boat was really sinking.

5   One hundred and fifty refugees were taken in by New Zealand.

PART THREE   INCORPOREAL/INORGANIC

Morale in a State of "Total War"

Ben Anderson

Attending to affect has come to promise much to cultural theory: offering ways of understanding the genesis and maintenance of the relations that make up the cultural and directing attention to the conditions under which novelty is produced, while anticipating the goals and techniques that could compose new forms of cultural politics based on inducing, amplifying, and transmitting capacities to affect and be affected (for example, Seigworth 2007b, Massumi 2002, Probyn 2005, Sedgwick 2003). Affects are understood as impersonal intensities that do not belong to a subject or an object, nor do they reside in the mediating space between a subject and an object. So the key political and ethical task for a cultural politics of affect is to disclose and thereafter open up points of potential on the "very edge of semantic availability" (Williams 1977, 134) by comprehending the genealogies, conditionalities, performativities, and potentialities of different affects.

If the emergence of an affective cultural politics is promissory it is simultaneously an imperative that emerges from a nascent recognition that affect is modulated and transmitted in forms of power addressed to "life" (Hardt and Negri 2004;

Thrift 2005). A range of work has mapped the imbrication of different affects in power formations that modulate the circulation and distribution of affects by intervening and directing ongoing processes—rather than exclusively through the prescriptive normalizations of forms of disciplinary power (Deleuze 1992). Here it is precisely the transmission of affect, its movements, disruptions, and resonances, that forms of vital or life power can come to harness. These forms of power do not prevent and prescribe but work in conjunction with the force of affect, intensifying, multiplying, and saturating the material-affective processes through which bodies come in and out of formation.

Both the promise and imperative of attending to affect in cultural theory center, then, around claims to a relation, of some form, between excess and affect. It is this relation the essay addresses because it discloses a productive paradox that animates the current conjunction between affect and the political. On the one hand, claims to the unassimilable excess of affect over systems of signification or narrativization provide the ontological foundation for the promise of a new way to attend to the social or cultural in perpetual and unruly movement, whether codified in terms of the "autonomy" of affect (Massumi 2002) or the "immeasurability" of affect (Hardt and Negri 2004). On the other hand, it is claimed that the transitive excess of affect is precisely what is targeted, intensified, and modulated in new forms of power—forms of power that themselves function through an excess of mechanisms that saturate and invest life, whether named as "control societies" (Deleuze 1992) or "biopower" (Hardt and Negri 2000). The promises and imperatives of cultural theory's current engagement with affect resonate together around the theme of excess and, moreover, the relation that modalities of power in the present conjuncture have to affect's excess. Nevertheless, drawing them together raises a set of questions. How to attend to, welcome, and care for indeterminacy, for affect's virtuality? How, in short, to realize the promise that is attached to affect? And how to simultaneously bear witness to forms of power that function through this indeterminacy, not by reducing it but by saturating or intensifying it? How, put differently, to respond to the imbrication of affect in an excess of knowledges, procedures, and techniques without being enamored of a power that acts without limit or outside?

These questions take on an added importance when we remember that the problematic of how to respond to the perpetual becomings of affect has longer roots and complicated routes that entangle multiple affect theories.

This is a troubled genealogy. It may include intellectualist discourses about affect and its ability to escape, shatter, and seduce reason. It may also evoke a still too present equation between emotion and the gendered figure of the irrational woman or the classed figure of the angry crowd. Equating affect with excess is risky, even if it is far from new (albeit increasingly common) as a refrain across many contemporary affect theories. Hence, claims of excess have also been central to the disavowal of affect theory. Despite this troubled genealogy, addressing the equation between affect and excess is necessary because it opens up a question for a politics of affect: how to think the intricate imbrication between the unassimilable excess of affect and modalities of power that invest affect through an excess of techniques?

This essay explores this problematic through a case study of how morale emerged as an object for specific techniques of power as part of changing relations between the state and the population at the start of the Second World War. I focus on the example of efforts to create and control "morale" under conditions of "total war" because it offers a case study of an excessive state apparatus that functioned by tracking and synchronizing the excesses of affect. Such a focus might seem to jar with recent attention to the indeterminacy of affect. For there is, on first reflection, nothing ambiguous about an object of power, nothing that resonates with the multiplicity, fluidity, and openness that the term affect provokes cultural theory to think with. To describe how a named affect becomes power's object is, on this account, to describe yet another way in which the opening of affect is closed, reduced, and contained in familiar processes of naming and classifying. Two qualifications are, therefore, necessary regarding my use of the term "object of power," or "power's object." First, an "object" of power names the surface of contact for modalities of power and thus acts as a hinge between a desired outcome and the actions that make up the exercise of power. Yet, any exercise of power need not have an object in the sense of "object" as the passive, reduced effect of processes of abstraction, limitation, and reduction. If we look at the etymology of the word "object," we find a more unruly sense of object—object as an obstacle, something "thrown in the way of," or "standing in the way of" (Boulnois 2006). How an object of power shows up is, then, an open question. Second, establishing a surface of contact for power offers a solution to the problem of how to extend action into the future. Such hopes, expectations, and promises animate the processes of knowing, naming, and acting on an object of power. Identifying the anticipatory structure of power leads, then, to a question in relation to morale in "total war." Under what conditions did tracking and synchronizing morale accumulate a hope —the hope of securing mass mobilization for mass destruction?

The essay proceeds as follows. The first half develops the problematic of affect's excess by describing how the expansion of the political to include affect operates as a productive paradox: affect is taken to be saturated by forms of power that work "from below" while also marking the limit of power itself. Through this discussion we face a pertinent question for cultural theory's emerging engagement with affect: how to be political when the excess of affect—its expressive and differential capacity—is imbricated with the excessive workings of power?

The second half of the essay develops this argument by focusing on the case study of how morale emerged as a target to be protected on the eve of the United States' entrance into the Second World War. Mobilizing morale promised to synchronize affect-as-excess with the excessive workings of a "providential" apparatus defined by relations of prediction, relief, and repair and a "catastrophic" apparatus defined by relations of destruction, damage, and loss.[1] The conclusion goes on to argue that the case of morale complicates the blend of imperatives and promises that surrounds the contemporary turn to affect by disclosing a longer genealogy of the imbrication of affect-as-excess and excessive modalities of power(s). This complication suggests that affect must exist as a perpetually deferred promise on the horizon of cultural theory rather than a stable ground or excessive outside.

Affect and the Political

The point of departure in addressing affect and politics is that affects are an inescapable element within an expanded definition of the political, rather than a natural dimension of life to be recuperated and recovered or a secondary effect of the secret ideological workings of power. This broad assertion of the reciprocal determination of affect and the political exists within a range of contemporary affect theories. It resonates with, for example, longstanding feminist engagements with emotion as an indeterminate conversion point between subjective ideality and a world (Terada 2001). The focus in this essay is on one of the trajectories that a politics of affect has subsequently taken: the development of a vocabulary specific to affect as a response to new power formations emerging as part of what Massumi (2002, 43), after Ernst Mandel, terms "late capitalist cultures" or what Hardt and Negri (2004) term, in part after the autonomist tradition of Marxism, "the real subsumption of life."

What is unique about this trajectory, and why it is my focus here, is that it is based on a claim that attention to affect in cultural theory is not only necessary but contemporaneous. It occurs in parallel to a set of economic and cultural developments that aim to invest and harness the productive powers of life. The turn to affect is therefore legitimized as timely because it provides a way of understanding and engaging with a set of broader changes in societal (re)production in the context of mutations in capitalism. These changes include the advent of new forms of value and labor centered around information and images; the emergence and consolidation of biopolitical networks of discipline, surveillance, and control; and the development of the molecular and digital sciences (Clough 2007, Parisi and Goodman 2005).[2]

From within this context, affect is taken to be one, but not the only, object of forms of power that invest in the production and modulation of "life itself" (Thrift 2005). Augmentations and diminutions of the body's capacity to affect are modulated through multiple techniques of power and known through multiple forms of knowledge (including neuroscience, the various psy-disciplines, the molecular sciences, and systems theory). This contemporary power formation has been given the name "control" to denote the shift Foucault anticipated from the molding of individual subjects in mass formations (disciplinary power) to the modulation of what Deleuze (1995) terms "dividuals"—sub- and trans-individual arrangements of intensities at the level of bodies-in-formation (see Hardt and Negri 2004, Massumi and Zournazi 2002). Here categories of the biological and cultural are mixed and scrambled in the invention of new material/immaterial hybrids. What Foucault (2003, 242) termed "Man-as-living-being" is not simply addressed and ordered in terms of biology (or the ratio of births to deaths, fertility, reproduction, and so on). Instead, in what could be understood as an extension of Foucault's (2007) discussion of the public as the affective pole of population,[3] attention is focused on the emergence, distribution, circulation, and mutation of pre- and post-individual capacities to affect and be affected (Massumi 2002, Hardt and Negri 2004).

The first move is, therefore, an expansion of politics to include affects alongside an ambivalent, often hedged, claim as to the role of affect now. Perhaps this can be summarized in Berlant's (2000) pithy, deliberately provocative but conditional formulation that "the impersonal is also political." As such the turn to affect is not only timely but imperative if the present conjuncture is to be adequately grasped, witnessed, and intervened on. Alongside these moves has been a second, potentially more disruptive move that understands affect as the limit to the effective functioning of power *even when it is its object*. This can be succinctly summarized in the following way: if power takes affect as its object, this guarantees that power—in whatever political formation—can only ever be a secondary, reactive, reduction of affect. Affect is the limit to power because it is limitless. As affect acts as a "point of view" on an unspecified outside (of which one name is the virtual), it discloses life as expressive and differential: expressive, because affect is in perpetual formation rather than existing as a secondary instantiation of an a priori discursive or ideological order; differential, because this process of formation generates unforeseeable newness in the ways that affects are actualized. Affect has, in short, come to name the aleatory, open nature of a social that is always in the midst of being undone. Hence the intense focus in work on affect and ordinary life on the creative opening to an outside in moments of rupture, instances of discontinuity, or flashes of passage (Anderson 2006, Lim 2007, McCormack 2005).

There exists a productive paradox in which affect is a paradigmatic object of forms of vital or life power in the political formation named as "control" but is, simultaneously and without contradiction, the best if not only hope against it. The treatment of affect in Hardt's and Negri's (2000, 2004) theses on the status of "living labour" after the "real subsumption" of life by capital dramatizes the double status given to affect. Hardt's and Negri's brief, speculative, but important comments on "affective labour" open up the implications for thinking politically, but also illustrate some of the problems of making affect synonymous with an excess to power.[4] Affective labor is a subset of immaterial labor that "produces or manipulates affects such as feelings of ease, well-being, satisfaction, excitement, or passion" (Hardt and Negri 2004, 108). As this definition indicates, what affect is and does is left fairly undetermined. Nevertheless, what gives affective labor such a pivotal position is that as it is bound up with "new and intense forms of violation or alienation" (Hardt and Negri 2004, 67), it is also claimed to be both "outside" *and* "beyond" measure. Affective labor exceeds measure in part because of affect's status as what Negri terms, following Spinoza, an "expansive power" of "ontological opening" that is a "power of freedom" (1999b, 77).

Affective labor is thus an integral component of the creative and indefinite process of biopolitical production that is given the name "multitude." In a short piece, "Value and Affect" (1999b), that provides much of the basis for the sections on affect in *Empire* and *Multitude*, Negri provides the clearest expression of how affect exceeds measurability. The exposition makes affect the ground for what elsewhere he terms the all-expansive creativity of living labor (Negri 1999a, 326). "If in fact affect constructs value from below, if it transforms it according to the rhythm of 'what is common,' and if it appropriates the conditions of its own realization, then it is more than evident that in all this there resides an expansive power [*potenza espaniva*]" (1999b, 86).

Affect is here not only the guarantee of the aleatory, that is the incessant irruption of the contingent, within the political. More specifically, affect is integral to the material force of associative, cooperative, form-giving labor. This is not, we should note, the only way of framing the relation between affect and the political. Elsewhere affect, in the guise of "passion," acts as an index of the political as a sphere of contestability and dissensus (see Laclau and Mouffe 1985). Here the interruptions and transformations of affect act as a ballast against any account of the primacy of power over life. There is always already an excess that power must work to recuperate but is destined and doomed to miss. It is that excess that is central to the creativity of biopolitical production and thus the power of naked life (Hardt and Negri 2004, 348). Beginning from the point of view of affect, in the context of a wider argument about living labor and its anteriority to capital, affirms that processes of transcendent capture (power as *potestas*) are fragile, secondary responses to affect as *potentia* (Negri 1991). Power is therefore doomed to miss or fail if the first condition of affect is that it flees and frees (Nancy 2006).

This is, however, only one way of framing the relation between the excess of affect and the productive yet ultimately reductive workings of power. Massumi (2002) offers another more nuanced version as he affirms both the investment of affect by a power that creates and improvises and affect's intimacy with "a never-to-be-conscious autonomic remainder" of thought and life (Massumi 2002, 25). Massumi has a much stronger sense than Hardt and Negri that power *in*forms and so is not exclusively a form of transcendent measure (223). Nevertheless, power is described as a calculation of affect, and thus a productive limitation of the ambiguous openness that the term "affect" names (223). Notwithstanding these differences, this second move is more radical than a simple expansion of the political because it installs affect as the limit to the efficacy of power as command, capture, or limitation. Attending to affect becomes, therefore, synonymous with a promise. Affect's promise is that a movement of creative production is primary even as we bear witness to the productive effects of power "from below." If only we find the right techniques, sensibilities, or concepts reality's openness can be variously affirmed, tended to, or experimented with (whether that finds its expression in a spontaneously emerging multitude or in an affirmation of everydayness as synonymous with the potential for things to be otherwise).

But invoking the excess of affect becomes problematic when we turn back to arguments that an excess of techniques now saturates and invests affect as part of the political formation named variously (but also interchangeably by Hardt and Negri) as "control" or "biopower." There have, of course, long been attempts to regulate the force of affect. Think only of the careful cultivation of specific virtues that have an affective basis (from political affects such as fraternity, military affects such as glory or honor, or scientific affects such as wonder). What is argued by theorists of the present conjuncture is that the excess of affect is now not so much regulated as induced, not so much prohibited as solicited. Modulation replaces constraint. In short, power works through what Massumi (2002) terms the "unownable" or "trans-situational" dimensions of affect. But if this is so then making affect the limit of transcendent forms of capture leads to a problem; if affect is the limit of the political that exceeds transcendent capture then an a priori separation is installed between affect (as constitutive or *potentia*) and power (as constituent or *potestas*). This separation has different consequences; either an antagonism is assumed between affect and power as transcendent measure or affect acts as the limitless outside to a productive power that can only ever be reductive. Notwithstanding these differences, the separation makes it difficult to engage with and understand the productive workings of forms of power that come to function through affect-as-excess. How do forms of power establish the disruptive openness of affect as their referent object? How is that remainder or supplement named and known? How do the techniques and technologies of power function in relation to the transitive excess of affect? How, if affect is its object and/or medium, do modes of power function?

Addressing these questions involves comprehending how different affects —rather than a mysterious and general substance termed "affect" (Probyn 2005)—are imbricated with mutable and variable modes of power that differ in their targets, desired and actual outcomes, hinges, and spatial forms (Nealon 2008). The first step would be a suspension of epochal arguments that affect is now a paradigmatic object of power in the contemporary conjuncture. Such arguments should be presented at best equivocally for two reasons. First, recent work disrupts the argument that modernity is founded on either a purging or regulation of disordering passions. Susan James (1997), for example, demonstrates that seventeenth-century political philosophy took the excess of passions to be an overbearing and inescapable part of human nature that a politics must harness and address. To paraphrase Spinoza's famous declaration: not only do we not know what a body can do, we do not know what a body has done or could have done. The result would be suspending the a priori celebration of affect as a creative power that exceeds capture as the limit to power as well as refusing the a priori lamentation for the loss of either authentic affect or affect per se in the present.[5] Second, research has begun to describe the imbrication of the openness of affect with specific, varied modalities of power. Modes of power such as domination or discipline involve different relational ties and have specific effects (Allen 2003). This work brings into question either a totalization of the contemporary or any neat chronological movement from forms of power based on centralized, intentional domination to forms of vital power. The lesson is that affects are constantly in conjunction with forms of power that coexist, resonate, interfere, and change rather than simply replacing one another.[6]

The example of the modulation of morale in "total war" offers one example of how the excess of affect over qualification is tracked and synchronized through forms of power that are themselves excessive in that they aim to extend throughout life without limit or remainder.

"Total War" and the Intensities of War

In the context of the emergence of "total war," governments invented ways of targeting and destroying morale and ways of protecting and harnessing it. The term "total war" was first popularized by Erich Lunsdorrf in a pamphlet, "Der totale Krieg," during the First World War. But its first use was by French civilian leaders in the Great War who coined the terms *guerre totale* and *guerre integrale* (see Chickering, Förster, and Greiner 2004). "Total war," as used to designate a concrete historical phenomenon rather than ideal type of war, involves two changes that make war "a war of nerves" that alters the "character of peace" (Park 1941, 360). The first involves an expansion of the "front line" of war through the advent of new extended technologies of destruction and damage that reduce the distance between home front and frontline, folding the two into one another. Strategic bombing, for example, involved an asymmetry between the destructive capacities of the bomber and the vulnerability of the bombed. It opened up the possibility of "occupation by air" (Lindqvist 2002). Psychological operations, slightly differently, involved techniques such as rumor or misinformation that aimed to shape and mold perception. These worked through and subverted the various channels of information that made up daily life (such as radio, posters, newspapers, and so forth) (Virilio and Lotringer 1997). Second, distinctions between civilian and soldier, combatant and noncombatant, tend to fade or be eliminated as mobilization for war is "total." War extends throughout the spaces of the economy or leisure and, consequently, comes to rest on the participation of populations. The battlefield is extended. A "home front" is established that is made up of new actors such as "industrial workers" or "domestic workers." These are variously protected (through the architecture of shelters, for example) and targeted (in area bombing or by rumor generation). These two changes make war "total" in the sense that the apparatuses of the state aim to expand to every sphere of life and all of life must, consequently, be mobilized for, and subordinate to, the war effort (Van Creveld 1991).

A set of intensive socialities accompanies these changes in the spatial form of war, of which morale is but one part. These include the pleasures and passions of the destructive activities of "total war" and the various attempts to regulate those passions through ideals such as "honor" or "glory" or through disciplinary practices such as the drill (Ehrenreich 1997, Burke 1999). They also extend to the traumatic experiential geographies of suffering or loss that can haunt the victims and sometimes perpetrators of the multiple relations and forms of violence that make up "total war" (Hewitt 1994). While normally considered to be a pacifist maneuver—as it makes present the horrors of war—it is also worth noting that understanding the "total" battlefield as a site of swirling, resonating affects has been central to fanatical praise of "total war" as the revelation of inhuman forces that undo and disperse the fragile form of the human (Toscano 2007). Ernst Junger's call for "total mobilisation" in his fascist memoir *Storm of Steel* of 1920, for example, finds in war's sundering of the comforts and habits of individuality what Toscano critically terms an "intensity-in-movement devoid of any intrinsic organic armature, a vitalism that only appears at the very limits of organism, whether this be physiological, political, or aesthetic in nature" (2007, 189).

The spaces of "total war," from the battlefield to the home or trenches, are spaces of affect and this has long been recognized in forms of military thinking. Morale, though, is unique both because it is born in the emergence of a new dimension of war—"intense fellow feeling" as part of warfare (DeLanda 1991)—and because it has subsequently accumulated a promise in

Western military thinking, as the indeterminate and indefinable target that, whether destroyed or protected, would enable the activity of war to carry on the momentum of its own enforcement. A certain anticipatory tone has long infused and animated discussion of morale—a sense of possibility that we could name as hopefulness. The following two sections trace one episode in the history of this promise, describing how morale emerged as a diffuse potentiality to be secured as part of the excess of providential and catastrophic actions that make up "total war."

Threat and Morale as Resource

A special issue of the *Journal of American Sociology* from 1941 on "Morale" exemplifies how the threat of future losses or damages to morale was brought within the state's horizon of expectation to emerge as a problem. The psychologist Harry Sullivan links the status of morale directly to the expansion of techniques and technologies of destruction. There is no limit or outside to war. War is everywhere. War is "total" then because it involves a "total" mobilization. This mobilization extends to the affective realm and makes morale a key resource of the nation-state to be "secured": "The circumstances of modern warfare require the collaboration of practically everyone. Ineffectual persons anywhere in the social organization are a menace to the whole. The avoidance of demoralization and the promotion and maintenance of morale are as important in the civilian home front and the industrial and commercial supporting organizations as they are in the zones of combat" (Sullivan 1941, 288).

The turn to secure the morale of a given population is intimate, therefore, with the recognition by the state of new forms of vulnerability and new ways of wounding. The special issue classifies the multiple techniques that threaten the domestic population and demonstrates how the state imagined ways in which morale could be damaged or destroyed. It is worth citing the terms used by the authors at the time to gain a sense of the catastrophic imagination through which morale was perceived to be under threat: violence functions through "the quasi-factual," the "ideological," and the "analytical" (Estorick 1941, 468); the "disorganization of effective central control" (Sullivan 1941, 289) directed against individual communities; and the direct demoralization of individuals by techniques that "communicate a feeling of recurrent suspense, each new wave of which the victim finds himself less able to tolerate" (290).

The anticipation of a threat to morale calls forth forms of action to prevent or prepare for it. Morale is acted on, then, in anticipation of its dissolution. The entity threatened in the context of "total war" is the population. Let's unpack how the population is understood, given the multiple ways in which forms of biopower target and work through "population." Discussions of "population" in relation to "total war" begin from an explicit understanding of "population" as a collective that pertains to a given territorial unit. This is either a specific area or region within the nation-state or the state as a bounded geographical entity. Here the meaning of population is very close to late sixteenth- and early seventeenth-century understandings of a "people or inhabited place" (Legg 2005). From this starting point, the "population" is considered to be composed of a mass of affective beings. Although morale itself remains indeterminate, as I will discuss in more detail below, it is assumed to be scored across a range of interpersonal psychological factors (such as "combativeness, rivalry, initiative, fellow-feeling, gregariousness, docility, infectious gaiety" [Landis 1941, 332]) and the biochemical substrate of the body (such as "dehydration of the tissues of the body" [284] or "the obscure biochemical effects which come from undercooling" [285]).

However, the population that makes up morale is not simply a collection of individuals grasped in terms of a preconscious, autonomic, bodily affectivity. The population is itself an affect structure. But how? There is no unanimity. Quite the contrary. Versions of the relation between collectivity and morale proliferate. In one case, morale is described as a property of occasions and gatherings: "One of the most pervasive forms in which tension and will manifest themselves in individuals and in society is in moods. Every occasion, be it a funeral or a wedding, has its characteristic atmosphere. Every gathering, even if it is no more than a crowd on the street, is dominated by some sentiment" (Park 1941, 369). In another, morale is a property of groups or associations: "But the characteristic problems of morale belong to group temper, and it is to group mentality that the term is most characteristically applied. *Esprit de corps* is definitely a group phenomenon" (Hocking 1941, 311). Elsewhere, morale is a property of a collection of minds that is given the names "publics" or "crowds": "It is not a state of mind existing in one man alone, but in many. It is not a state of mind to be enjoyed, for itself, but to serve as a spring of action. It is not a uniform state of mind—the same under all circumstances—but is relative to the end in view" (Landis 1941, 331).

The target is the population seen from one direction, its affective life—an affective life that is dispersed from the subject to, on the one hand, an affectively imbued bodily substrate and, on the other, to various types of collectivity. The pertinent space to act overextends from the biophysical body to the taking place of gatherings or happenings.

While there is no unanimity about the form of the collective, what is threatened is the unity or coherence of those collectives and, thereafter, how collectives are mobilized as part of "total war." Destroying morale threatens to create a break or interruption in the life-world of a population and thus disrupt the centrifugal movement of "total mobilization." Threats to morale have a particular force, just as efforts to secure it do, because they assume a very specific relation between morale and the action of a population. Morale is the basis to action because it exceeds present diminishing affections of the body. It is a "spring" of action (Landis 1941, 331) or a "gift" to action (Hocking 1941, 303) because it is "prospective" and organized around a "faith in the future" (Park 1941, 366). Elaine Scarry (1985) hints that the basis to the promise of morale is a suggestive association between morale and the creative founding, enabling, or making of future worlds. But morale is also the motive force that enables continued mobilization under the catastrophic conditions civilians may find themselves in during "total war," specifically conditions of "hardship" or "suffering" (Landis 1941, 333) in which the body is potentially affected by "weakening influences from within (fatigue, reluctance, anxiety, irritability, conflict, despair, confusion, frustration) and from without (obstacles, aggression, rumors of disasters)" (Estorick 1941, 462).

Under a "total" mobilization of life and property and "total" methods of destruction, where boundaries between civilians and the military erode, civilian bodies are exposed to a myriad of events and conditions that damage. Morale promises, therefore, to enable bodies to keep going *despite the present*, a present in which morale is either targeted directly or threatens to break given the conditions of "total war." And what threatens is an unpredictable, uncertain, future "crisis" in which morale suddenly breaks or shatters, bodies are exposed to the conditions of the present, and the movement of "total" mobilization fails or ends. The threatening other to morale— feared by those imagining a future crisis in morale—is given the name "panic." Unlike in the early cold war when forms of cybernetics became central to generating "versions" of panic (Orr 2006), here panic is understood according to early behaviorist psychology as a form of *dis*organization (see McLaine 1979). Panics differ in intensity, but they are commonly understood as the dissolution of order emerging from disruptions or disturbances. These disruptions or disturbances are described in the following terms:

"an event suddenly shows that the universal does not make sense and one finds one's self badly demoralized" (Sullivan 1941, 282) or "any grave threat of insecurity or of cutting off all of one's satisfactions is perceived under circumstances which prohibit rational analysis and the synthesis of that wonderful thing which we call an understanding of what has happened" (282).

Destroying or damaging morale threatens to turn something interior and necessary to total mobilization—a group of bodies, a frequently repeated activity, rational analysis, understanding—into a devastating, destructive force (Orr 2006). An indicative "panic-provoking situation" that would generate a crisis in morale is one in which the individual as an affective being is disorganized. This is described by one of the contributors to the special issue on morale. Note how the body to be protected is described in terms of concrete visceral and proprioceptive phenomena (sensation, the skeletal system, and so on) that underpin conscious perception and deliberation: "There will be a ghastly sensation from within, from all over within; there will be nothing remotely like reasoning or the elaboration of sentience; there will be a tendency to random activity, but practically no movement of the skeletal system because it is inhibited by diffusion of stimulus and contradictory motor impulses. As you recover, and the intense cramps which have developed in the viscera relax, you find yourself exhausted, tremulous, perhaps without control of your voice" (Sullivan 1941, 279).

Unlike the disordering of panic, then, the promise of securing morale is that it enables bodies to coalesce despite the persistent presence of affections that may diminish or destroy bodies. Acting over morale offers the dream of a "certain island of predictability" in the "ocean of uncertainty" that is "total war" (Arendt 1958b, 220). Put differently, morale promises that the "total" mobilization of citizens can continue despite the excess of devastation and damage in "total war." It promises a means to intervene and break the relation between the capacity of an individual or collective body to be affected (through some form of diminishing encounter induced by the techniques of "total war") and that body's capacity to affect (in this case to continue with the activities that define being a civilian in "total war"). Morale becomes linked to "world making" in part, then, because it is assumed to be separable from the affections of the body and, somehow, to exceed them. Morale "tends to have an aura of the spiritual, to signal some capacity for self-transcendence or form of consciousness different from physical events" (Scarry 1985, 106).

Virtualization and the Promise of Morale

Establishing morale as a target of power promises a way of mobilizing a mass for mass destruction. It enables the otherwise unimaginable heterogeneity or bewildering abundance of modern societies to coalesce into an undifferentiated whole—a whole that thereafter acts in concert even as it resists clear and stable form. In short, morale as a property of a population is addressed as a fundamental component of a state's potential power in the state-versus-state dynamics of "total war." Morale encourages factory productivity. Morale underpins agricultural labor. Morale sustains belief in democratic ideals. Morale powers the war economy. As the hinge of action, morale exists as a target in "total war" in the complicated sense that Weber (2005) argues the word "target" originally had. Although its roots are uncertain, target probably comes from "targa," meaning shield (specifically a light and portable shield carried by archers). Remembering these defensive origins means that "hitting" or "seizing" a target or targets is "linked to a sense of danger, to feelings of anxiety and fear, and to the desire to protect and serve" (Weber 2005, vii). The providential apparatus established on the eve of war is future-oriented in that it is animated by fears and anxieties that a "crisis" in national morale is looming. The future anticipated is characterized by the *inevitability* of loss and damage. Suffering will happen. The question is how to deal with it. In the shadow of the catastrophic future the need to secure morale therefore becomes a necessity for the state and civil society. Morale must be mobilized if this disastrous future is somehow to be lived through and the state is to endure. The promise of maintaining morale is that it enables "total mobilization" and so morale must, in turn, be secured whenever and wherever it takes place.

As we learn from Derrida (2006, 89), promises are *restless*: "a promise must promise to be kept, that is, not to remain 'spiritual' or 'abstract,' but to produce events, new forms of action, practice, organisation and so forth" (cited in Bennett 2005). Promises call forth, demand, present action. To realize the promise of targeting morale the prewar period witnesses the extension of a state apparatus of prediction, preparedness, and repair that takes the morale of collective populations as a target to be secured. Hence, it is precisely the motive power of morale that is predicted through various techniques that aim to know what morale is in order to secure it, harnessed through techniques that aim to generate and maintain it, and repaired through techniques that mitigate the effects of its loss (most notably civil defense).[7]

At the heart of this apparatus, and the catastrophic apparatus of air power, are attempts to track the current state of morale in order to render it subsequently securable. But because of a combination of its indeterminate relation with action, and its indeterminate location, morale—as an object of knowledge—becomes a vague, but actionable "something more" that is made ever more diffuse and ubiquitous to life. Here Hocking, a psychologist, wonders if "it" can be singled out: "Morale, then, is something else than physical preparedness for an enterprise, something additional but not separable. . . . Morale itself, however, is something more than awareness of capacity, and a high morale may exist when capacity is low. Can we single out this something more?" (Hocking 1941, 303).

The period before America's entrance into the Second World War witnessed a multiplication of techniques of measurement and calculation that attempted to track this "something else" and thus make it subject to intervention and action. In the United States this included now ubiquitous techniques for referring to and evoking affective publics such as the "social survey" (Estorick 1941) and the "public opinion survey" (Durant 1941) that later become central to attempts to know the effects and effectiveness of bombing morale (see United States Strategic Bombing Survey 1947a; 1947b).[8]

What is known through these techniques was not, however, considered to be the "true nature" of what morale is. Remember, morale exceeds attempts to establish it as a thing in itself. As Major James Ulio summarizes when discussing how techniques for maintaining morale in the military can be used in relation to civilians: "It [morale] is like life itself, in that the moment you undertake to define it you begin to limit its meaning within the restrictive boundaries of mere language" (1941, 321). Instead the focus is on the "conditions operative in morale formation" (Durant 1941, 413) through a measurement and calculation of the actions of the population as an aggregate of sociobiological processes. Because morale is "like life" and "exceeds" as a "something more," it must be tracked indirectly. With the exception of observational methods—such as the use of mass-observation (Hamsson 1976)—morale was tracked through its various and varying traces. Traces which could be found throughout life. Any aspect of life could potentially reveal the presence or absence of morale, so techniques of knowledge must know all of life without limit or remainder. Morale is everywhere. It is in excess of any qualification or containment in particular activities. In the United Kingdom, for example, morale was understood through the frequency, extent, and duration of strikes, industrial output, convictions for drunkenness or drunken driving, and crimes against property (Durant 1941, 411–12). In France "bad morale" was known through "political tension, public violence, repudiation of existing regime by large bodies of citizens, exaggerated individualism, general passivity, demographic factors, and susceptibility to panic and despair" (Durant 1941, 408). While in China morale was known through "dependence on American and British aid, the relations of the 'return to the coats' school with the 'new hinterland' school, the price of grain, the absence of medical facilities, and the treatment of Manchurian troops by the central government" (Durant 1941, 408).

If these lists initially seem arbitrary at best, they nevertheless tell us two important things about the type of object of power that morale becomes. First, neither morale nor these other factors are what Foucault (2007) terms the primary datum. Instead it is the interaction between the two. Morale is related to the price of grain. Morale is related to demographic factors. Morale is related to convictions for drunkenness. In short, morale varies. What techniques of knowledge do is track this movement by surveying its changes and establishing its changeability rather than simply establishing the presence or absence of morale per se. Second, and because it is like life itself, morale is not transparent to techniques of knowledge. It is not a stable object that can be identified and classified. Techniques of measure and calculation must engage a range of factors seemingly unrelated to morale in order to intimate its scope and effects. The result is that the governance of morale becomes the governance of life. Governance becomes "total." It must be found throughout life. Morale is expanded to the extent that the urban sociologist Robert Park could argue that "we must recognise morale as a factor in all our collective enterprises. It is a factor in the operation of the stock exchange, quite as much as it is in the activities of the Communist party" (1941, 367).

The very presence or absence of morale becomes undecideable or indeterminate. It is only knowable in its many and variable effects. This is the second sense where morale serves as a promissory note, not simply as an "isolated island of certainty" (Arendt 1958b, 220) offering the state in "total war" its sovereign capacity to "dispose of the future as if it were the present" (245). But further, morale becomes the horizon of governance rather than an object of governance, an endlessly deferred absent presence that can only be inferred from a seemingly arbitrary list of activities that are diffused throughout the whole of life. Paradoxically, securing morale involves the virtualization of morale. As the target and hinge for action in "total war," morale exists as a virtuality that comes to be known only through its varied traces. This is virtualization in Pierre Lévy's sense of "an 'elevation to potentiality' of the entity under consideration" (Lévy, cited in Weber 2004, 284). Morale is no longer an actual entity locatable in observable affective beings or affect structures through procedures of observation or experimentation. To secure morale is to elevate it to an indeterminate "something more" that is cause and effect of an unruly excess of activities, processes, and events. This elevation can be understood as a process of movement from the actual to the virtual. Thus, "instead of being defined principally by its actuality (as a 'solution'), the entity henceforth finds its essential consistency in a problematic field" (Lévy, cited in Weber 2004, 284). Morale promises, therefore, because it escapes, comes to be equivalent to life, and is thereafter absent as a delimited object. Yet, neither is morale a rare inassimilable other, akin to a punctual experience that shatters and disrupts. Instead it is commonplace, a dimension of all activities. Potentially all of life must be acted on in order to protect an exposed population, a move that echoes the emergence of a "target rich" environment—*life*—as the object of the catastrophic state apparatuses of aerial bombing or rumor formation in which morale was taken to "break," be "lost," "vanish," or "collapse" (see Douhet 1972, Kennett 1982, Pape 1996).

If the taking place of morale has regularities but takes on the structure of a promise, and yet total war exposes all of life to new threats, then how, thereafter, can government action foster a prospective "readiness" for action (Estorick 1941, 462)? How does acting on morale become part of the "total control" of populations? Given that morale is under threat the key problem becomes the "development, protection, and maintenance" of morale (Sullivan 1941, 282) and the pragmatic question becomes "what are the methods of control by which good morale is created and preserved?" (Landis 1941, 331). But this poses a problem. Morale does not offer a graspable hinge for action. It is both everywhere, being found throughout life, and nowhere, being like life in that it escapes definition. The response is found in the development of techniques that act over the *population* seen from the angle of its corporeal and collective affective life, variously named as the "collective temper of a people" (Lindeman 1941, 397), "group temper" (Hocking 1941, 311), or "underlying solidarity of the people as a whole" (Sullivan 1941, 300). Acting over the population involves two types of techniques. The first involves addressing individuals directly as affective beings primarily through forms of communication. Radio, the press, movies, theater, and educational institutions are described as the "principal morale building agencies which are available in a democracy" (Angell 1941, 352). The second involves acting over a range of factors and elements that seem far removed from morale but nevertheless implicate the collective as an affect structure. For example, how often should news of casualties be given? How can democracy move from an ideal to a fact passionately felt by subjects? How should housing be designed to ensure physical comfort? What level of physical activity should be incorporated in a national recreation plan?

In the case of acting over morale in "total war" we find that the activities of power resemble what Foucault (2007, 326), discussing the sixteenth- through eighteenth-century assemblage that in French was named police (and in German, *Polizei*), termed "an immense domain . . . that goes from living to more than just living."[9] The site of action is a "full" version of life, or as Ojakangas (2005) puts it, a plenitude of life in its becoming, in which mobilization of morale is "total" in the sense that it aims to extend across all of life without limit or outside. Because morale is scored across all life, action to mobilize morale must also occur across all of life. Consider, for example, discussion of the use of radio to generate morale as an exemplar of the intersection of techniques that act over affective beings and a population as affect structure.[10] Radio is one of several techniques of communication that promise to harness what Robert Park (1941) terms the "magical power" of morale through means that would enable the idea/ideal of democracy to live "in men's minds and hearts." Radio is valorized for the immediacy with which it enables certain collective affects—including the warmth of voice— to be communicated at a distance. An executive at the National Broadcasting Company valorized radio along three criteria: "(1) the immediacy of its conveyance of news; (2) the vast mass of persons thus reached, many of them having only delayed access, if any, to the newspapers, and not a few being unused to reading, or incapable of it; (3) the psychological appeal of the living human voice as contrasted with cold type—even when accompanied with the barrage of photographs now so universally employed by the press" (Angell 1941, 355).

While the technique addresses the individual as an affective being, a being who will be moved by the living human voice, morale is an indirect effect of other variables. Integral to the efficacy of radio is that it promises to enable a diffuse, heterogeneous population to coalesce into a defined public that sparks into being around issues. Radio is valorized, therefore, because it promises to synchronize a heterogeneous population through the attunement of bodies at a distance. News, by contrast, is dismissed as an appropriate technique for "developing" or "maintaining" morale due to its relation with the innovation of newness and thus its supposed "tendency is to disperse and distract attention and thus decrease rather than increase tension" (Park 1941, 374).

Morale is not governed through techniques of power such as radio by establishing a direct relation of obedience or consent between a sovereign and a subject. Indeed various techniques are dismissed because they are asserted to rely on a crude "manipulation" of morale through techniques of prescription or prohibition. It is worth comparing the use of radio as a providential technique with rumor generation as a catastrophic technique to give a sense of how "total" methods of affective modulation work. Rumor formation was a central technique of the "morale operations" branch of the Office of Strategic Services Planning Group (OSSPG), and rumors were designed to act affectively—spread confusion and distrust, stimulate feelings of resentment, and generate panic (Herman 1995). A briefing note of the OSSPG from 1943 established the "Doctrine Regarding Rumors." It contains discussions about what a rumor was and how it worked by propagating through a population. The key question was how to enable a rumor to spread while retaining its original content—the properties that supposedly enabled this type of circulation included plausibility, simplicity, suitability to task, vividness, and suggestiveness. If this was the case then rumors could subsequently act affectively in three ways. This was summarized by the Office of Strategic Services:

1 Exploit and increase fear and anxiety amongst those who have begun to lose confidence in military sources.
2 To exploit temporary over-confidence which will lead to disillusionment.
3 Lead civilian populations to precipitate financial and other crises through their own panicky reactions to events. (OSSPG 1943, 4)

Both rumor and radio act affectively. But neither guarantees to produce a direct effect since both act by becoming part of the complex, living conditions that form and deform morale. The targets for rumors return us to the population understood affectively discussed above, including "Groups or classes of people that lead monotonous lives which favour the use of fantasy" (OSSPG 1943, 8). Or "Groups or classes of people that have become fearful and anxious about their personal wellbeing. Focus on 'information' that confirms the pessimistic expectations of the group involved. Extreme rumours designed to produce open panic should be timed with military action" (8).

The relation of each technique—radio and rumor—to the affective surface of emergence is not simply negative. Both techniques aim to be generative of new affects of morale or panic. So rumor is designed to act by producing an "open panic," while, in contrast, radio is valorized for how it may enable "good morale" to emerge, circulate, coalesce, and feed into the action of the state.

In the case of radio and rumor, morale cannot be brought into being directly, only indirectly through techniques that are becoming part of life. Such techniques function by acting on and becoming part of the same reality as both processes of morale formation and other mechanisms of morale generation. Rumor and radio therefore check and limit certain circulations of morale and panic by catalyzing and directing others. As such they exemplify the expansion of the scope of techniques of power once the target becomes ever more diffuse. Both are "total" in the double sense that they extend to all of life and, to be successful, must become indistinguishable from the dynamic whereby that life unfolds.

Conclusion: Affect and Power

In "total war," morale is targeted as an indefinite potentiality through two types of processes—tracking and attuning—that when taken together aim to synchronize the excess of affect with the excessive mechanisms of a providential and catastrophic state. These processes combine to produce what I would term a *logistics of affect* that aims to mobilize the potential of a mass formation and transfer that potential into processes of mass destruction (Virilio and Lotringer 1997, 24). In this way, we can see that the promise of targeting morale returns in the geo- and bio-political present. The current "global war on terror" involves both providential and catastrophic techniques that take affects, including morale, as both their object and medium. "Shock and Awe," a network-centric air-power doctrine and perceptions management operation, is but the most high-profile recent example of what, after the German Zeppelin and Gotha bombing raids over England during the First World War, has been known as the "moral effect" or "terror effect" of bombing from the air. Echoing with everything from the Kantian sublime to electric shock treatment, the effects of "Shock and Awe" are designed to create forms of affective harm and damage, named as "comatose and glazed expressions" (Ullman and Wade 1996, 20), "feeling of impotence" (61), "fear of his own vulnerability and our own invincibility" (62), and "frustration, collapsing the will to resist" (64). The link between "total war" and the "war on terror" is the extensive apparatus of "psychological warfare" in the cold war (see Robin 2001, Simpson 1994). But even as there are resonances between these historically specific formations and their processes of militarization, there are also differences. In "total war," acting over morale promises that the state will be able to harness the motive power of a mass and sustain that motive power in the future. Mass mobilization of the state's potential is enabled for mass destruction. In "network-centric war" morale is understood as a property of complex, adaptive networks rather than a mass and is thus targeted by creating specific "effects" that will become immanent to how that network holds or comes together. Networks target networks. Notwithstanding these and other differences, what is shared is the hope that victory will be achieved by targeting morale as a diffuse potentiality.

Here we return to, and affirm again, that while attending to affect promises much for cultural theory it is also simultaneously an imperative that follows from a recognition that affect is modulated in multiple modalities of power. But if affects are targets for modes of centered or dispersed power they are not simply available to be smoothly shaped, normalized, and instrumentalized at will. This is not to say, either, that affect acts as a point of view on an immeasurable excess. As discussed in this essay, morale exists as an object and medium of power because it escapes the excess of attempts to demarcate its scope and effects. Morale is grasped and handled as a diffuse potentiality instead of a fixed, locatable target. What it is and does multiplies and varies as a hope is invested in knowing, harnessing, and repairing it; morale is equivalent to life itself, morale is part of gatherings, morale is a function of the biophysical condition of the body, morale is an object of strategy, morale is . . . The result of this proliferation is that there is no such thing as morale "itself." Versions of what morale is and does coexist without coalescing into a single account that would name and classify its invariant nature. Or, to put it differently, it is precisely the aleatory, indeterminate existence of morale that is cultivated through and becomes indistinguishable from the excess of techniques that make up "total war."

Two conclusions follow regarding the relation between affect and power. First, the mechanisms discussed in this essay do not simply reduce the excess of affect, but aim, in different ways, to know and act on affects as collective phenomena intimate with life's indeterminacy—an indeterminacy that is itself indeterminately located, pertaining to both the affective substrate of life and to how populations form and deform. Power is not necessarily secondary to and parasitic on an insubordinate life the affective potential of which power struggles to command, control, and ultimately reduce. In the case of targeting morale, power virtualizes, endlessly proliferating what should be acted on, and modulates, hoping to sustain the motive power of a mass through catastrophic and providential action that becomes indistinguishable from life as it unfolds. It cannot then be assumed that affect automatically opens up to a limitless outside if such mechanisms function through and generate excess by knowing and precipitating emergence. Modes of power differ in their targets, hinges, practices, and desired outcomes in a way that disrupts a distinction between power as *potestas* and power as *potentia*, and undoes an antagonism between a domination over life and the savage insubordination of life.

Second, and in distinction from arguments that maintain that affect is an object of new modalities of power given the name "control," affect has long been imbricated with multiple modes of power that coexist, resonate, and interfere with one another (rather than replace one another in a relation of succession). In this essay these have included forms of sovereign power (of the state in "total war") and forms of vital power (in how radio functions, for example). There are, have been, and will be others. There is then a long genealogy to forms of power that know, synchronize, and track the circulation and distribution of affects. The question of the status of affect "today" is, then, a problem of understanding the emergences, changes, and shifts in modes of power. While the current interest in affect is often placed in the context of the emergence of a politics of "life itself," or in terms of the "real subsumption" of life under a certain stage of capitalism, the case of morale opens up a longer genealogy that implicates knowledges such as social psychology, types of behaviorism and cybernetics, and techniques such as rumor formation or early radio.

Cultural theories of affect promise sociopolitical insight by simultaneously naming a new object of power and the unassimilable limit or outside to power. Perhaps once we begin from the conjunction of affects and power, rather than their a priori separation, affect will itself come to operate in the promissory mode as an endlessly deferred horizon for inquiry rather than a stable ground. Since "something promises itself as it escapes, gives itself as it moves away, and strictly speaking it cannot even be called presence" (Derrida 1992, 96–97), the question of what affect is and does can only be answered by following the intricate imbrication of different affects with variable and mutable modes of power.

Notes

1   See Ophir 2007 on the "providential" and "catastrophic" state.

2   There is no consensus about the nature, extent, and importance of these changes. In addition, it is important to remember that multiple claims are made for why cultural theory should attend to affect. These include to understand how and why ideologies are only sometimes effective (Grossberg 1992), to recover and give voice to hitherto marginalized subjects and histories (Cvetkovich 2003), or to better attend to the ongoing composition of everyday life (Stewart 2007).

3   Although it has received less discussion than his focus on population-biological processes (birth rates, mortality, etc), we should remember that Foucault argues that the "public" is the population seen from one direction: "[u]nder the aspect of its opinions, ways of doing things, forms of behaviour, customs, fears, prejudices, and requirements" (Foucault 2007, 75). The "pertinent space" of biopower extends from human species-being to the public. This is consistent with his comments that the population intervened on from the end of the eighteenth century includes "[t]he biological or *biosociological processes* characteristic of human masses" (Foucault 2003, 250, emphasis added).

4   The focus in this section is on Hardt's and Negri's use of the term "affective labour" because of the pivotal role they give to an equation between affect and excess. There are, however, multiple sources for Hardt's and Negri's use of the term as a subset of "immaterial labour." Two lineages are particularly important. The first involves different types of Marxist feminist research on the nature and value of emotional labor for waged and unwaged economies. This includes work on activities such as flight attending, prostitution, and housework (Fortunati 1995, Hochschild 1983). The second involves the writings of Italian "Workerism" (*operaismo*) on the "immaterial" character of post-Fordist productive processes, and, more recently, on the complex "emotional situation" of the multitude (see Virno 2004 on "opportunism" and "cynicism").

5   See Jameson 1991 on the "waning of affect" or Virilio 2005 on "the threat of a democracy of emotion."

6   See, for example, Stoler 2004 on affect and disciplinary power in colonialism or Allen 2006 on seduction and urban governance.

7   On the origins of civil defense, see Oakes 1994.

8   Techniques in the British context were similar. From May through October 1941 daily reports on morale were produced that were then summarized in weekly and monthly reports by the British Ministry of Information. These were supported by mass-observation research and also drew on a variety of other sources such as postal censorship, the police, and W. H. Smith newsagents. Beginning in 1941 the Ministry

of Homeland Security commissioned a number of surveys of public mood (see Jones et al. 2006).

9   "Police" is discussed by Foucault as one assemblage of political technologies from the end of the sixteenth century to the end of the eighteenth century concerned with "taking care of living" (Foucault 1994a, 413) by "manipulating, maintaining, distributing, and re-establishing relations of force within a space of competition that entails competitive growth" (Foucault 2007, 312). Police is "the ensemble of mechanisms serving to ensure order, the properly challenged growth of wealth, and the conditions of preservation of health 'in general' " (Foucault 1994c, 94, referring to *medizinische polizei*). The fundamental object of police was the good use of the state's forces (the state's "splendour") by acting on all the forms of "men's coexistence with one another" (Foucault 2007, 326). Police includes everything, but seen from a particular point of view—live, active, productive man (Foucault 1994a, 412; see also 1994b).

10   Occasionally governing morale becomes a problem of fixing and demarcating the normal from the abnormal. The one exception to the focus on "democratic" techniques is the psychologist Harry Sullivan. Sullivan proposed "[a] civilized version of the concentration camp" (Sullivan 1941, 294) to house those who threatened the nation's morale "by reason of personality distortion, mental defect, or mental disorder" (294).

Sympathy, Synchrony,
and Mimetic Communication

Anna Gibbs

Contagion is everywhere in the contemporary world. It leaps
from body to body, sweeping through mediatized populations
at the speed of a bushfire. No longer confined to local outbreaks
of infectious disease or even of hysteria, contagious epidemics
now potentially occur on a global scale and, thanks to electronic
media, with incredible rapidity. Consumer economies actually
rely on contagion for everyday functioning, connecting people,
money, goods, resources, ideas, and beliefs in global flows of
communication and exchange in ways that fundamentally alter
relations in the process. This calls for a new understanding of
what I term "mimetic communication." By "mimetic communication" or mimesis, I mean, in the first instance, the cor-
poreally based forms of imitation, both voluntary and involuntary (and on which literary representation ultimately depends).
At their most primitive, these involve the visceral level of affect
contagion, the "synchrony of facial expressions, vocalizations,
postures and movements with those of another person," producing a tendency for those involved "to converge emotionally"
(Hatfield, Cacioppo, and Rapson 1994, 5).

This essay examines several phenomena (sympathy, synchrony, and the various forms of mimicry and imitation we might reassemble under the broad heading of mimesis) and argues that together these provide a starting point for theorizing mimetic communication. At stake in this is the tension between humanist and nonhumanist forms of thought, between those who argue for the necessity of understanding formations of the subject and those for whom thinking is a practice that should extend us beyond the known forms of the subject. Mimesis is rather like an image in which figure and ground can always be reversed, so that sometimes subjectivity is in focus, while at other times it recedes into the background, leaving something new to appear in its place. Rather than privileging one view over another, the task of theory may then be to know through which optic it is most productive to look at any given moment. Or—perhaps more difficult—to learn how to oscillate between these views, neither of which can simply be discarded. How might we, then, learn to think across the plurality of domains in which we are (and need to be) organized as subjects but in which the very process of subjectivation also produces potentials that may open unsuspected possibilities for new ways of thinking, being, and acting?

Mimetic communication can be conceived as an example of synchrony, as a pervasive "sharing of form" that seems to be "the fundamental communicational principle running through all levels of behaviour," through both human and animal bodies, and connected to other rhythmic processes in the natural world (Condon 1984, 37). But it might equally be conceived as a contagious process that takes place transversally across a topology connecting heterogeneous networks of media and conversation, statements and images, and bodies and things. These mimetic connections are a result of contagious processes in which affect plays a central part. Or, at least, this is the aspect of affect with which the humanities and cultural studies have mostly been concerned in recent years. Here it takes on a broadly Spinozan-Deleuzian sense, emerging as an asubjective force in a perspective from which the human appears as an envelope of possibilities rather than the finite totality or essence represented by the idea of the individual organism. This is the view from which Brian Massumi can describe affect as an energetic dimension or "capacity" and emotion as a selective activation or expression of affect from a "virtual co-presence" of potentials on the basis of memory, experience, thought, and habit (Massumi 2003). What this view leaves out is the highly differentiated work performed by the "categorical" or "discrete" affects opened by the work of the American psychologist Silvan Tomkins. Tomkins derives his view of the affects as innate in large part from

Darwin's germinal observations in *The Expression of the Emotions in Man and Animals*. Although Tomkins's work has been put to serious use by both Eve Kosofsky Sedgwick and Adam Frank, who introduced it to cultural studies in 1995, it remains relatively little taken up in the United States and virtually unknown in Europe, although it has generated an exciting and heterogeneous field of thought in Australia.[1]

Both ways of conceiving affect understand it as intricately involved in the human autonomic system and engaging an energetic dimension that impels or inhibits the body's capacities for action. But, while affect in the Deleuzian sense is asubjective and anti-representational, operating across the boundary between the organic and the nonorganic, Tomkins's affect theory enables the specification of the energetic dimension of affect in very precise ways. It provides us with a differentiated account of the neurological, physiological, and expressive profiles of each of the nine affects it recognizes, allowing finer distinctions than the traditional psychoanalytic concentration on the degrees of arousal of anxiety and aggression. It delineates an affect dynamics that specifies which affects are likely to be called up in response to which others and why, and a systems-oriented, nonteleological way of thinking human development as affective responses are patterned—or organized—by ongoing processes of script formation. Although these two broad ways of conceiving affect doubtless begin from very different philosophical assumptions, they are both essential, it seems to me, in the overarching intellectual project of rethinking the human in the wake of a sustained critique of Western rationality.

Beyond these two major affect theories, there is widespread disagreement both between and within the various disciplines that claim a stake in affect— psychology, the neurosciences, biology, sociology, cultural studies, anthropology, and so forth—about whether to conceive of affect as innate or socially constructed, how to formulate its relationship with cognition, emotion, and feeling, and what these sorts of decisions might entail theoretically and politically. There are obvious risks in an interdisciplinary approach to affect theory, which must contend with the sheer mass of thought about it, and with incommensurabilities between and even within disciplines. Thus, what appears as the same object from one optic to the next is often not, and the conviction that attends a sense of discovery continually dissolves into doubt. Mimesis is as much contested as affect. Mimetic communication in the cognitive sciences names an ensemble of modes in a hierarchy of sophistication: mimicry, emulation, imitation, and mimesis. Distinguishing between them is important, especially in the empirically based cognitive sciences, which need to specify exactly what they mean to accede to the standards of sound experimental design, and in ethology, where, by virtue of doing so, various animal and human capacities can be compared. But too often these distinctions become one more expression of a certain Platonically derived Western ambivalence about mimesis as a form of copying giving rise only to the fake or the second rate, and which therefore wants to see mimesis as essentially the preserve of children, "primitive" peoples, and animals. For example, in one of several important discussions of mimesis, Theodor Adorno refers to it as at once part of "biological prehistory" and as "the repressed of the Enlightenment" (Horkheimer and Adorno, cited in Potolsky 2006, 144). In part because of this, I want to argue here that these distinctions may be less important than what these various modes of mimesis have in common, since affect is a powerful vector in all of them, and taken together and considered as a phenomenon apart from philosophical prejudice, they may open the way to a new "epidemiology of affect" that sees continuities between things that were once held to be discrete, and discontinuity and difference where once there was sameness (Gibbs 2001). Ultimately, this may also facilitate a rethinking of theories of mimesis and the practices associated with them developed in non-Western cultures and referred to by Western anthropologists as "magic," a concept that, as Adorno foresaw, may have far greater purchase in contemporary Western societies than is usually realized (Horkheimer and Adorno 1972, Gibbs 2008; for theories of magic, see, for example, Mauss 1972 and Frazer 2000).

The interdisciplinary process is especially fraught when crossing between the humanities and the sciences. Rey Chow (2002) comments that perhaps the most far-reaching analysis of mimesis as both natural and cultural phenomenon in Western thought—that of René Girard—has failed to be productively taken up because it lacks empirical or scientific justification. This may be so, but if in what follows I sketch a rough map of the recurrent concern with mimesis in various kinds of empirical work, it is not to provide an empirical "grounding" or legitimation for a rethinking of mimetic communication. Rather, what I am suggesting is that theory needs to adopt a heuristic function, drawing creatively on different forms of knowledge to ask *what if* one conceived the world in this way? What then becomes possible in the space opened up by such a "passionate fiction," to borrow a term from Teresa de Lauretis (1994)?

If human mimesis—in its complex imbrication of biological capacities with sociality—is to be properly understood, a multidisciplinary approach drawing on the sciences as well as the humanities is required. There is now a renewed interest in the biological foundations of human life, and a new curiosity about the permeability of boundaries between human and animal life as the possibility of organ transplants from animals to humans (for example) becomes part of our daily awareness. Mimicry is both nature and culture: Michael Taussig sums up the intricacy of this relation when he calls mimicry "the nature that culture uses to create second nature" (1993, xiii). As Mary Bateson puts it, "the acceptance of parents as appropriate models for imitation is certainly based on biological patterns, and then the culture elaborates on that by inventing school teachers and psychoanalysts" (1979, 67–68). And although culture is predicated on certain biological capacities, it seems clear that the biological body marks a constraining, rather than a determining, influence on the nature of the human. And—in part by virtue of constraint—it also actively enables certain kinds of development. It is now not so much a question of trying to work out what is nature and what second nature, but rather to see that the question of nature versus nurture is an artificial one, once we recognize the complex ways in which the human organism and its environments are "mutually unfolded and enfolded struc-tures" (Varela, Thompson, and Rosch 1993, 199) and are each recomposed in and through their exchanges.[2] For in fact evolution demonstrates the muta-bility and malleability of biology as against its permanence (think of the way the functional architecture of the brain alters with the advent of literacy in certain cultures), and, in another temporality, the biological is rewritten by culture with the aid of technology from drugs to pacemakers or by the outbreak of epidemics of hysteria or multiple personality disorder (each of which can be seen, at least in part, as contagious mimetic phenomena, as Ian Hacking (1998) has argued of the latter, and Juliet Mitchell (2001) of the former).

"Mimicry is a very bad concept," write Deleuze and Guattari (1987, 11).[3] But is there, then, also another way to think mimicry, that form of embodied copying that also serves as a kind of hinge between nature and culture? If the importance of mimesis in everyday forms of culture and communication has failed to be properly understood in Western culture in part because it has been associated with infants and animals, is there something now to be gained from paying attention to serious explorations of it by ethologists and researchers of infants?[4] And why might it matter to do this? A move in this direction would allow us to begin to rethink mimesis not as simple mimicry or copying dependent on vision (monkey see, monkey do), but as a complex communicative process in which other sensory and affective modalities are centrally involved. What we have to gain from this is a better understanding of the role of mimetic communication in social processes, and especially of the making—and breaking—of social bonds. These form the basis for a sense of "belonging," and, ultimately, of the polis, as what forms the affective bases of political orders.[5]

At the heart of mimesis is affect contagion, the bioneurological means by which particular affects are transmitted from body to body. The discrete innate affects of which Silvan Tomkins speaks are powerful purveyors of affect contagion, since they are communicated rapidly and automatically via the face, as well as the voice. This is because the distinct neurological profile of each affect is correlated with particular physical sensations, including muscular and glandular and skin responses. Of particular interest is facial expression's activation of a mimetic impulse in response to the facial expression of observers, tending then to elicit the same affect in them. It is very difficult not to respond to a spontaneous smile with a spontaneous smile of one's own, and one's own smile provides sufficient feedback to our own bodies to activate the physiological and neurological aspects of joy.[6] Central to the working of affect is the fact that "affects are not private obscure internal intestinal responses but facial responses that communicate and motivate at once both publicly outward to the other and backward and inward to the one who smiles or cries or frowns or sneers or otherwise expresses his affects" (Tomkins 1966, vii).

People are expert readers of faces, and these communications are more often understood than not, even though they often take place outside awareness. So the face plays a central role in the expression and communication of affects, and its importance has only been amplified by the pervasiveness of media in everyday life (see Gibbs 2001, and Angel and Gibbs 2006). The face is ubiquitous in the realm of the image, where it conjures both the discrete affects and the frequent attempts to mask them ("backed up affect," as Tomkins terms it), which television soap actors are especially good at signaling. But the human face also seems to diagram itself onto the sensuous qualities of other images in which it does not explicitly appear: landscapes, houses, foods, animals, skin, and choreographed bodies, so that the world can be facialized even in the absence of faces from the image. Magazines as well as television make use of facialization in this way to conjure more complex representations of mood, including those sustained complexes of affects elaborated as emotions that may vary greatly culturally and historically.

But the face is not the only vector of mediatized affect contagion. Consumers of media are also conscripted into its flows at a level we might term—following Gilbert Simondon—"preindividual" (1992, 302). Increasingly, the graphic signs of logos like the Nike swoosh, or the soundbite-sized musical signatures of McDonald's, or the brief arrangements of notes with which our computers and mobile phones greet us, function at this level. These signatures, or logos, whether in sound or image form, generate feelings that mobilize the body's capacity for synesthesia, in which affect seems to act as a switchboard through which all sensory signals are passed. Toyota's "Oh, what a feeling!" maps the image of a jump in slo-mo and ends with a freeze frame onto an arrangement of notes that mirrors the jump's rising contours and then seems to cruise out over an edge *Thelma and Louise*–style, before evoking the thrill of the G-force with the falling scale of "Toy-ota." Both sound and image trace the typical pattern of arousal and plateau of the discrete affect of joy.

Logos, whether visual or aural, evoke the "elusive qualities . . . captured by dynamic, kinetic terms, such as 'surging,' 'fading away,' 'fleeting,' 'explosive,' 'crescendo,' 'decrescendo,' 'bursting,' 'drawn out' and so on," which the infant researcher Daniel Stern identifies as the activation contours of the discrete affects (Stern 1985, 55–57). These activation contours *qualify* the discrete affects, corresponding to the pace of rising and falling levels of their arousal: he offers the example of a rush of joy or anger. Whether an affect is coming or going is information that is then conscripted into semiotic systems of meaning: joy arriving means something very different from joy departing or deflating. But, according to Werner's theory of physiognomic perception, which shows that a series of simple two-dimensional diagrams reliably elicits a restricted number of categorical affects ("happy, sad, angry"), the same falling line that signals joy departing or deflating will usually be read as sadness (Stern 1985, 53). Similarly, a slight lengthening of the line that composes the "sadness' diagram will tend to animate it, so that the temporal dimension is again brought into play because the line then evokes the kinematics of gesture, in the same way we are able to infer a flourish from a certain signature, which then lends the signature a particular significance since we take it to say something about the person who produced it.[7] Visual and musical logos orchestrate the activation contours of the discrete affects both to incite our own bodies into immediate mimetic response, and, in the same moment, by the same movement, to conscript affects into signification.

Stern's work is of enormous importance to both kinds of affect theory, adding a new dimension to Tomkins's thought about the apprehension of the affects, and enabling Massumi to forge a crucial connection with Walter Benjamin's concept of "nonsensuous similarity," which is "tied to the senses but lacking in sense content," able to be "directly perceived"—but only "in feeling" (Massumi 2003, 142).[8] In thinking about the role performed by what he comes to call "vitality affects," Stern concludes that affect functions as the "supramodal currency" into which experience in any sensory modality may be translated (Stern 1985, 53).[9] For Massumi, vitality affects are amodal; they can "jump not just between situations but also between sense modes," producing "nonlocal" correspondences in which forms appear as "the sensuous traces of amodal linkage" (Massumi 2003, 148). This precisely describes the work of mimesis, even at its simplest level, in mimicry.

Mimicry may represent the desire to disguise what one is (an animal avoids its predators; an Internet predator pretends to be a teenager), or the desire to become something else (a human infant identifies with its parents). It can mean either homage or hostility; it might signify sympathy, seduction, deception, defense, or aggression.[10] It may serve the serious purposes of learning and those of pleasurable play, which seems to be at least partly what Walter Benjamin has in mind when he writes in his essay "On the Mimetic Faculty" that the "child plays at being not only a shopkeeper or a teacher but also a windmill or a train" (1979, 160). But at the heart of mimesis is the immediacy of what passes between bodies and which subtends cognitively mediated representation, which it does not ever entirely replace or supersede. It is not analyzable within a semiotic model, nor does it require an "I": it is essentially asubjective even though it plays a crucial role in the formation of subjectivity. Mimesis can morph bodies, changing color, odor, form, or movement; or it might choose words or clothes or cars or even ideas as its medium. But what it signifies and the medium in which it operates is less important than its mode of operation. Mimicry is not a representation of the other, but a *rendering*—a relation between things in "which, like a flash, similarity appears" (Foucault 1973, 24).

Mimicry can be understood as a response to the other, a borrowing of form that might be productively thought of as communication. By "communication" in this context, however, I do not mean the transmission of information, but, rather, action on bodies (or, more accurately, on aspects of bodies)—as, for example, when reading fiction produces new affect states in us, which change not only our body chemistry, but also—and as a result— our attitudes and ideas as we shape from narrative a structure of meaning (see A. Gibbs 2001, 2006). This sharing of form comprises information in the pre-cybernetic sense: it represents the organization or communication of relationships (which might be spatial, temporal, tonal, energetic, logical, causal, and so on) through temporary captures of form by way of mimesis. Not reducible to bit units, information of this kind is a "life process whereby difference [or pattern, relationship] is discovered in the environment" (Yoshimi 2006).

Mimesis, like affect, is not necessarily best thought of as occurring at the level of the individual or of the organism. It is not a property of either subject or object, but a trajectory in which both are swept up so that forms can be seen as "the sensuous traces of [the] amodal linkage" between them (Massumi 2003, 148). Another way of thinking about this would be to say that mimesis abstracts some (but not all) aspects of what is copied from the other, making use of vision, hearing, olfaction, morphology, or behavior, or several of these. But it is not simply a question of subject and object relations between mimic and model, or of the active mimic and passive model. Rather, evolutionary ecology speaks of a "mimicry complex" that includes mimic, model (which could be a different species from that of the mimic), and "dupe" (the receiver of the deceptive signal), and this dupe may be a third species, if we take the example of the predator. And while mimicry often operates to the mimic's advantage and the model's disadvantage, this is not always the case. Caillois's famous essay critiquing the idea of mimicry as a device for survival makes this abundantly clear when he describes the dangers of disguising oneself as a leaf when that is what members of your own species actually eat (Caillois 1987, 67). However, the mimicry complex does nevertheless exert a transformation of both parties—an "a-parallel evolution" as Deleuze and Guattari (1987) have it.

Perhaps the best example of the effects of mimicry on the model is given by Deleuze and Guattari in their discussion of the asymmetrical co-evolution they term "becoming." The famous case of the wasp and the orchid makes this very clear: the orchid imitates the wasp so that for a moment the wasp becomes part of the orchid's morphology and its reproductive system, while the orchid in turn becomes part of the wasp's alimentary system. The form of reciprocity involved here is asymmetrical, but both parties to the process are "de-territorialized."[11] I return to this particular example because it was recalled to me as I read a newspaper story about a researcher, Anne Gaskett, who had discovered that wasps got wise to the orchids over time, but that the orchids seem to develop more alluring scents, intense colors, and beautiful forms in order to stay ahead of them (Macey 2007). Although the article about her work doesn't say this explicitly, the only parts of the orchid affected by this "arms race" are its scent and form, while only the wasp's "bullshit detectors" change to try to keep pace with them. (Or it could be the other way around in the race, since it is not possible to say which party is ahead at any given moment.) This is communication not so much between a wasp and an orchid per se, as between the wasp's alimentary system and the orchid's reproductive system (Massumi 1992, 165). Mimicry is very selective in its use of sensory channels—in this case the ones used are olfactory, visual, and morphological.

Human mimicry, too, is selective (and, like the relationship between the wasp and the orchid, implicates cross-species desire), as when we put on floral perfumes or animal fur to enhance our powers of attraction. But this selectivity also has another very particular significance in human mimicry, which hijacks it in the service of the formation of that crucial site of organization, the self. Daniel Stern describes how, when a nine-month-old girl becomes excited about a toy and is able to grasp it, she "lets out an exuberant 'aah!' and looks at her mother. Her mother looks back, scrunches up her shoulders, and performs a terrific shimmy with her upper body, like a go-go dancer. The shimmy lasts only about as long as her daughter's 'aah!' but is equally excited, joyful and intense" (Stern 1985, 140).

What Stern's account of the mother's cross-modal imitation—or translation —of the baby's squeal of delight into a dancing shimmy corresponding with its length and rhythmic contour also makes clear is that similarity is crucial, but so too is the difference produced in this sensory translation. For it is the *difference*, or the correspondence—isomorphism without identity— produced in the translation from one sensory mode into another that, from within the optic of the formation of the self, facilitates the infant's gradual recognition of the interiority of the other (as well as of itself). In the infant's increasing awareness that experience can be communicated and shared, two subjective worlds come into momentary contact, even though the meaning of this contact and its function in the subjective worlds of mother and baby will be different for each of them. The accuracy of the translation—especially the matching of the infant's degree of arousal—is crucial to its success, and Tomkins's affect theory helps us chart this with some precision. Surprise (rather than startle) is provoked by the novelty of the change of sensory channel implicit in the sufficiently congruous (that is, not shocking) translation. Surprise at this level of arousal is a positive affect, directing the baby's attention to engagement with the mother and helping to sustain her interest in it, while startle (the same affect at a higher level of arousal) would have been frightening for the baby.[12]

This process of translation between different sensory modalities is what initially enables experience to be ordered into familiar patterns, including the formation of "affective scripts" designed to manage punishing negative affect and maximize rewarding positive affect (Tomkins 1962). These emergent constellations of experience operate largely outside of awareness but form an experiential matrix for ongoing affective responses to and constructions of the world. In producing difference by means of cross-modal translation, affect *organizes*, both intra- and inter-corporeally, though it does so in very different ways in different cultures. It is this organization of the self into an ongoing and more or less flexible process patterned by affect that facilitates a relatively high degree of cohesion and a sense of continuity in time, even as the self continues to undergo both analeptic and proleptic reshaping by the work of memory and anticipation. The self—whatever form it may take in different cultures and however a sense of agency may be distributed between it and the world in any given culture—then becomes a complex and ever-evolving social interface.

Mimetic knowledge may be the earliest form of knowledge of both self and other, as the infant researchers Meltzoff and Moore suggest, and this is a knowledge made possible by the work of feeling: "Because human acts are seen in others and performed by the self, the infant can grasp that the other is at some level 'like me': the other acts like me, and I can act like the other. The cross-modal knowledge of what it *feels* like to do the act seen provides a privileged access to people not afforded by things" (1995, 55, emphasis added).

"Feeling" in this context seems to cover a range of meanings, from the sense of proprioception and affect in Massumi's sense of "capacity" to a sense of understanding that seems to be the basis for empathy. The same is true of the kind of feeling generated by the "embodied simulation" made possible by the operation of the mirror neuron system. When we watch someone performing an action, the mirror system in human beings evokes both the "sensory description" of the stimuli and the motor schema of the action itself (Gallese 2007).[13] In other words, when we see an action performed, the same neural networks that would be involved if we were to perform it ourselves are activated. In fact we may actually experience something of what it *feels* like to perform the action, as when we watch someone jump and feel our own body strain toward the movement. Darwin (1998, 40) describes this as the motor sympathy between two bodies.

The organization of relations between bodies enabled by mimetic communication and the development of the self also facilitates one's sense of agency. When researchers of infants slowed down films of interaction between mothers and babies, they noticed that the babies' apparently random kicking and wriggling happened in time with their mothers' vocal rhythms as they talked the language that came to be called "motherese": a highly expressive, patterned, and repetitive way of speaking with exaggerated changes in pitch and intonation that seems to be designed to capture the babies' attention and to meet and match the babies' preferred sounds and movements in their particular rhythm, pace, and intensity. This synchrony is an important prerequisite for the "mutual affective regulation" of mother and baby. It means that the mother is able to respond to the baby's needs because, for example, she is attuned to the level of a baby's distress or she knows how to hold its interest. She can modulate the infant's distress and amplify its enjoyment, and this forms the baby's earliest experience of the regulation of affect states. It is the basis of the baby's eventual capacity for the affective self-regulation that will afford it a measure of autonomy. The baby also knows how to solicit the mother's attention, without which it will not survive—experience in Romanian orphanages showed even more graphically than Harlow's controversial psychological experiments on monkeys during the 1950s that babies, even when fed adequately, died if they did not receive sufficient human comfort.

But this mimetic capacity for synchrony (and the affective attunement facilitated by it) is not just a feature of infancy, or of the relationship between mothers and babies. This phenomenon, also referred to as the "entrainment" of one person with another, as when someone's gestures and movements are synchronized with their speech, or when an attentive listener's or an audience's almost invisible movements are synchronized with the speech rhythms of the person to whom they are listening, so bodies come to "move in *organizations of change* which reflect the microstructure of what is being said, like a car following a curving road," as Condon writes (1984). But it may not be possible finally to locate agency in one person rather than another, because all aspects of behavior are "both sequentially and hierarchically continuous at the same time" (Condon 1979, 135). Behavior is "all organized together and each aspect is discriminated as a pattern of relationship in contrast to the rest" (Condon 1979, 135). One aspect of behavior may entrain others both in one's own body and in that of someone else. Here research involving infants, which normally takes the development of the self as its object, actually enables an understanding of relationship closer to Massumi's understanding of mimesis—as a movement that assembles relations as it traverses bodies, leaving form as a trace in its wake, rather than being a property of bodies themselves. Nevertheless, the operation of the self, assembling affect with cognition and so enabling a certain "freedom of the will," complicates human synchrony.[14] Human beings are perhaps as likely to fall out as to fall in with someone else.

The complexity of the relationship between affect and cognition that characterizes the human, and the dependence of cognition on affect and the senses, comes more clearly to the fore when we start to think about the way language—in the very process of making meaning—is implicated with rhythm and movement. There is a musical aspect to infant entrainment in the repetition of short "phrases" by the mother, and later on (when the infant is about two) her play tends to turn rhythmic, and games are shaped by rhyming and other forms of melodic patterning. In considering these elements of entrainment, Colwyn Trevarthen speculates about an inherent time sense that seems to be built into the human brain. This is a "shared pulse" that can be used for either synchrony or alternation—for example, turn-taking in conversation. Trevarthen asserts that pulse or rhythm and affective sympathy are the two main components of attunement between mother and infant. Rhythm (or "pulse"), like affect, *organizes* (1999/2000). As Condon writes, "There is an inner unity and integrity to the sustained relationship [between different body parts moving at the same time, even at different speeds and in different directions]. [It is] as if the body parts were obeying a pulse or wave train which organized them together. . . . Body motion appears to be an emergent, continuous series of such pulse-like, organized forms" (1984, 42).

Both animal and human bodies move in bursts of polyrhythmic expression that allow "intricately timed pulses of muscular energy in harmonious pulses of plastic transformation that push against the environment" (Trevarthen 2002).[15] Similarly, speech and writing may also be entrained by rhythm. The turn-taking or alternating vocal forms of mother-infant interaction were identified as an important means of organizing communication and termed "proto-conversation" by Mary Bateson (1971), who in earlier work emphasizes the complementarity of conversation in interaction with other modalities:

The essence of conversation is in fact the possibility, provided in ordinary conversation by kinesic behaviour and paralanguage, of organization into units larger than the syntactic sentence, so that both participants are included in an ongoing pattern. Infant gazing is the precursor of adult gazing, infant gesticulation a precursor of adult gesticulation, and infant vocalization a precursor of adult vocalization. But would learning in each of these types of signalling occur if they were not juxtaposed and their communicative functions were not complementary? (Bateson 1979, 72)

They are not only complementary but also analogous, and translatable. They are capable of substituting for each other and of corresponding to each other. And they are also, on occasions, capable of contradicting each other. Mother-infant communication involves participants who use different codes coordinating their behavior in a common performance (as also happens in cross-cultural communication), but adults are capable of using a number of different codes and sometimes the code-switching that governs performances is a result of complex contexts (Bateson 1979, 7).

Movement, sound, and rhythm are all anterior to symbolic verbal communication, and provide a prototype for it: verbal conversation is formally predicated on the rhythms of nonverbal behavior, which it does not ever entirely replace or supersede. Movement, sound, and rhythm are neither vestigial to language, nor unorganized accompaniments to it. Gesture, for example, is a "forceful presence" in language (Agamben 1999, 77). It seems to actively facilitate thought and speech, lending form to the sweep of an idea, helping to draw it out. Writers don't deliver messages, they make gestures, as Merleau-Ponty puts it (1974, 60).

Gesture, then, is "a 'material carrier' that helps bring meaning into existence" (McNeill 1992).[16] So sympathetic modes of communication not only persist alongside linguistic modes: they also inhabit and actively shape them. These are not rudimentary, infantile, or so-called primitive modes of communication: rather, they are the essential prerequisites for, and working collaborators with, verbal communication. They are not noise in the system: they are part and parcel of it.

Mimesis is an entirely holistic, analogue mode of communication in which "the world is apprehended as variation on continuous dimensions, rather than generated from discrete elements" (Bucci 2001).[17] While language involves both serial and parallel modes of processing, it can also be thought of as a form of serial processing of experience that has already been parallel-processed. This parallel processing is performed via the distributed modes of input from the various different senses. Information from each of the senses is compared with memories of previous experience in each modality before being combined. Of course all of this happens in an instant and is always ongoing. In Tomkins's terms, this represents an informational compression that is necessary because consciousness is "a limited channel" (Tomkins 1992, 287). Such compression condenses affective, sensory, and so-called cognitive forms of knowledge, creating procedural (or more broadly, nondeclarative) memory. This is the domain of habit without which we can't function. It comprises motoric, perceptual, and cognitive skills as well as complex emotional patterns such as the one Tomkins codifies as affect scripts. These and other automatic forms of knowledge are what allow us to engage in complex multitasking, as when we think about something else while driving through a familiar streetscape.

This process of compression prompts a rethinking of just what is meant by cognition at all, especially when it is routinely associated with language. Tomkins insists on the complexity of what he calls "the cognitive system," given the importance of it to sensory and motor modes of knowledge that not only "operate outside consciousness and permit consciousness to restrict itself to other objects of knowledge," but which—in the case of sensory knowledge—give rise to a plethora of different kinds of knowledge, beyond the different senses: drive, affect, and muscle sensations, as well as the proprioceptive sense (Tomkins 1992, 16). In elaborating on the different kinds of knowing produced by these various functions, Tomkins makes clear that they are all integral to the cognitive system, which would include all of the above. He suggests that cognition has been at once too narrowly defined and too easily imagined as an independent "high command mechanism" that would assess and arbitrate other ways of knowing. Instead, he argues against the existence of a separate cognitive mechanism at all, and for "a more democratic system with no special mechanism completely in charge or, if in charge, able to endure as a stable mechanism" (Tomkins 1992, 17). What results from this picture is a "distributed authority" that makes cognition "as elusive to define as the 'power' in a democratic form of government or the 'meaning' in a sentence" (Tomkins 1992, 17).

At the limit, then, Tomkins makes clear that there can be no "pure cognition," no cognition uncontaminated by the richness of sensate experience, including affective experience. Aspects of this level of experience cannot be translated into words without doing violence to the totality of awareness, for example, to the simultaneity of various sensory experiences that renders them indivisible, as when, sitting by the window in a café watching the busy streetscape with the warmth of the morning sun on my back, I smell the delicious aroma of coffee and simultaneously feel its warmth in my mouth, taste it, and can tell the choice of bean as I listen idly to the chatter in the café around me and all these things blend into my experience of "being in the café." But the holistic nature of everyday perception can't be directly translated into language and to express something of this in words I must split it into sensory components and list them in succession, which implies a hierarchy of importance—and so on. Of course, language also enables a reflective handle on experience, opens new forms of agency, articulates temporal relations, and links things distant in time or place.[18]

According to Walter Benjamin, language is "the highest level of mimetic behaviour . . . [it is] a medium into which the earlier powers of mimetic production and comprehension have passed without residue, to the point where they have liquidated those of magic" (1979, 163). Speech and writing both comprise "an archive of non-sensuous correspondences" (162) in which what Massumi calls "felt relations" can be shared "at any distance from the sensuous forms they evoke" (Massumi 2003, 148). Yet, if language is action at a distance on the forms it connects, it nevertheless acts directly on the body.[19] Metaphors not only often derive from bodily processes (Lakoff and Johnson 1999), but they excite a "sympathetic" response in the form of embodied simulation in much the same way as mirror neurons do (see R. Gibbs 2006).[20] This simulation is not voluntary, nor is it a form of pretense: it is "automatic, unconscious and prereflexive" (Gallese 2003, cited in R. Gibbs 2006). Because simulations are shaped by somatic memory, they have specific consequences for how metaphors (but also many types of nonmetaphorical language) can be understood. Language is in fact highly dependent on the body's physical capacities for its effectivity. It is also very selective, concentrating on evoking experience in one sensory channel at a time: in this respect, it treats the body not as a unified and indivisible whole, but as an ensemble of potentialities that can—and must—be selectively activated. The body, then, is not so much a medium as a series of media, each of which connects in its own way with technological media, including writing. Mimesis produces the virtual by enabling the reassembling of these disparate media, giving rise to what is "real without being actual, ideal without being abstract," as Proust writes of dreams (1992, 906).

Merlin Donald suggests that from an evolutionary perspective, mimesis makes symbolic thought possible, since symbolic thought originates in "externalised acts" (like the act of reading aloud, rather than silent reading, the capacity for which is developed later). These acts are predicated on "a brain capacity that allows us to map our elementary event perceptions to action, thus creating, at a single stroke, the possibility of action, metaphor, gesture, pantomime, re-enactive play, self-reminding, imitative diffusion of skills, and proto-pedagogy, among other things" (2000, 33).

Mimesis operates at every level of experience, from the most immediately corporeal to the most abstract. Understanding the corporeal, nonverbal dimensions of mimetic communication is crucial to explaining its pervasiveness in human social relations and its centrality to cultural forms such as cinema and performance, which aim to bind spectators into complex forms of sociality, including story, cinematic spectatorship, and audience membership. We tend to think of vision as the most important sensory mode for mimicry, especially in the age of the image. However, although sight is in fact neurologically dominant in the so-called higher primates, it rarely operates in isolation from the other senses, and its dependence on them indicates the importance of sensory cross-modalization—or synesthesia—in mimesis.[21] To reconfigure mimesis as cross-modal mimetic communication enables a transformation in thinking about vision and visuality. Visuality appears not only as a biophysical phenomenon but also as a social process, a way of relating to what is seen. Mimesis can then be understood as the primary mode of apprehension utilized by the body, by social technologies such as cinema, television, and even the Internet, and by the cultural processes involving crowd behavior, fads, celebrity, and pandemics of anorexia or depression, as well as the processes by which rapid shifts of social and political attitudes may occur.[22] A better understanding of how mimesis is involved in these processes is important because mimetic communication contributes to the generation of the "affective social tie" (Borch-Jacobsen 1988). It is the cement of parent-child, peer, friendship, and love relations, and, under certain conditions, fleeting fellow-feeling between strangers. It also forms the affective basis for ethical dealings with others.

The whole of human culture, then, is, perhaps, predicated on imitation, in which difference and innovation are as central as reproduction and similarity. Yet—in part precisely because of this—the innate human capacity for mimesis gives rise not only to vastly different and often incommensurable modes of lived emotion but also to completely different ways of producing and archiving the nonsensuous similarities that comprise both the very qualities of lived experience and the forms of abstract knowledge in different cultures.[23] Massumi enjoins us to remember the "duplicity of form," which participates "spontaneously and simultaneously in two orders of reality, one local and learned or intentional, the other nonlocal and self-organizing" (Massumi 2003, 151). It is this duplicity that necessitates an oscillation between two perspectives. On the one hand, a certain strategic humanism viewed through the optic of representation that focuses on the culturally plastic and historically changing forms of subjectivity still seems indispensable if we are to remember that what we call "the human" can never be more than an image and will always tend to exclusion and prescription. On the other hand, the world of "nonlocal," asubjective becomings in which these forms appear simply as momentary traces of other movements promises to give rise to envisionings beyond the already known, even as their discovery threatens to produce a universalizing discourse that elides the crucial specificity and particularity of differences, especially cultural and sexual ones. The "passionate fictions" of writing, and art more generally, seem to offer a way of working in both dimensions simultaneously, and contemporary theoretical writing is increasingly borrowing the techniques and methods of fiction to this end, interlocking sensation with story and in the process recreating the essay as a heuristic for innovation.[24]

Notes

Earlier versions of sections of this work were delivered to "Between the Cultural and the Clinical" (University of Sydney, 2001); the NMLA (Hartford, Conn., 2001); the International Literature and Psychology Conference (Arezzo, 2002); and the "Theorising Affect" conference (Durham University, 2006).

1   In particular, I have in mind work in cultural studies by Elspeth Probyn, Jennifer Biddle, Melissa Hardie, Maria Angel, Jill Bennett, Melissa Gregg, Megan Watkins, Sue Best, Cristyn Davies, Gilbert Caluya, and Kane Race.

2   In other words, both must be thought as relations, not terms.

3   I take them to mean that it requires rethinking.

4   After years of debate about whether or not animals actually did imitate or merely emulate, there seems to be increasing agreement that many do really imitate. For example, Gisela Kaplan (2007) argues that Australian magpies possess large vocal repertoires for which neither a reproductive nor a purely territorial function can be identified and which may possibly comprise a rudimentary form of language called referential signaling. Pepperberg (1990) makes similar arguments about parrots, and Herman (2002) about dolphins.

5   It has been argued that being mimicked makes human beings more pro-social (Van Baaren et al. 2004). However, the opposite is also possible (Gibbs 2008).

6   This is so because the activation of one part of the response (here, facial expression) is sufficient to activate the others.

7   "Ludwig Wittgenstein said that when one sees something beautiful—an eyelid, a

cathedral—the hand wants to draw it" (Scarry 1997). Of course, painting involves a gestural dimension that relies on our capability to translate the curve we see before us into a loving caress. See Hommel et al. 2001 for citations of a number of empirical studies about the inference of kinematics from the trace.

8 My thanks go to Greg Seigworth for alerting me to this extremely helpful essay and for his very helpful editorial comments.

9 Cytowic (2002 and 2003), adduces neurological evidence for the intrication of affect and synesthesia.

10 "At all stages of animality, mimesis tends to produce differences as well as to efface them, to make signs appear and make them disappear. When we interpret, for example, what we call the mimesis of certain insects now as 'intimidation,' now as 'camouflage,' it is in all appearances to this double property that our interpretation returns" (Girard 2000).

11 Or, as Deleuze and Guattari specify, this process of de-territorialization involves a "co-existence of two asymmetrical movements that combine to form a block, down a line of flight that sweeps away selective pressures" (1987, 293–94).

12 Here I adopt Tomkins's identification of surprise-startle as a discrete affect provoked by novelty that interrupts what has been ongoing and functions to "re-set" attention (1962).

13 Much commentary on mirror neurons focuses on vision, but mirror neurons also exist for hearing (Kohler et al. 2002). Moreover, as Wolf et al. point out, "Fneurons, which are visual/motor neurons, represent a subset of a larger group of neurons designated as multimodal neurons (Graziano and Gross 1994, 1031) because they contain within them the capacity to be directly activated simultaneously by different sensory modalities, for example, auditory, somatosensory, and visual" (Wolf et al. 2001).

14 I refer to Tomkins's wonderful account of how the structure of the affect system both constrains and enables freedom of the will (1962).

15 Trevarthen argues that this may form the basis of narrative orchestration and he sees the apprehension of time in what he calls the intrinsic motive pulse as central to this (1999/2000).

16 In fact Rizzolatti and Arbib argue that gesture (rather than subvocalization) is the evolutionary precursor to symbolic communication (1998). And the mirror neuron system in human beings may have facilitated this process:

> Consider a PET study conducted in humans by Bonda and colleagues in 1994 that indicates that there are also significant hand movement representations in Broca's area. The implication is that this area is specific for the expression of language developed from a gestural communication region and highlights again the consideration of the significance of a mirror neuron system in 'the capacity to make and interpret facial communicative gestures and the capacity to emit and understand "verbal gestures"' (Rizzolatti 1994, 139). *This ultimately links gesture to verbal communication.* It is important to keep in mind that the connections to the limbic system are wired to apply an emotional valence to the behaviors that, in part, are governed by the mirror neuron system. This enables humans to appreciate affective subtleties in communication. (Wolf et al. 2001, emphasis in original)

17 "Subsymbolic processing . . . is experientially immediate and familiar to us in the actions and decisions of everyday life—from aiming a piece of paper at a wastebasket or entering a line of moving traffic to feeling that rain is coming, knowing when the pasta is *almost* done and must be drained to be 'al dente,' and responding to facial expressions or gestures. [It] accounts for highly developed skills in athletics and the arts and sciences and is central to knowledge of one's body and to emotional experience" (Bucci 2001).

18 For a fuller discussion of the relationship between language and the senses, see Angel and Gibbs 2009.

19 See A. Gibbs 2006 for an extended discussion of this aspect of language.

20 Massumi refers to this phenomenon as it occurs more broadly in reading as "incipient action" (2002, 139).

21 As Massumi writes, synesthesia and the separation of the senses are "co-primary, since the potential for each conditions the actual exercise of both" (2002, 282–83).

22 It is in the context of the diffusion of innovations that the work of nineteenth-century French sociologist Gabriel de Tarde now takes on renewed significance, and I take this up in Gibbs 2008.

23 In this essay I have drawn exclusively on the Western forms I know best.

24 See Schlunke 2006 for a wonderful discussion and demonstration of writing as mimesis.

9   THE AFFECTIVE TURN

Political Economy, Biomedia, and Bodies

Patricia T. Clough

When in the early to mid-1990s, critical theorists and cultural critics invited a turn to affect, they often did so in response to what they argued were limitations of poststructuralism and deconstruction. As Rei Terada would suggest, there was a growing sense that poststructuralism generally but deconstruction in particular were "truly glacial" in the pronouncement of the death of the subject and therefore had little to do with affect and emotion (2001, 4). More accurately, as Terada goes on to argue, the turn to affect and emotion extended discussions about culture, subjectivity, identity, and bodies begun in critical theory and cultural criticism under the influence of poststructuralism and deconstruction. Affect and emotion, after all, point just as well as poststructuralism and deconstruction do to the subject's discontinuity with itself, a discontinuity of the subject's conscious experience with the non-intentionality of emotion and affect. However, the turn to affect did propose a substantive shift in that it returned critical theory and cultural criticism to bodily matter, which had been treated in terms of various constructionisms under the influence of poststructuralism and deconstruction. The turn to affect points instead to a dynamism immanent to bodily matter and matter generally—matter's capacity for self-organization in being informational—which, I want to argue, may be the most provocative and enduring contribution of the affective turn.

Yet, many of the critics and theorists who turned to affect often focused on the circuit from affect to emotion, ending up with subjectively felt states of emotion—a return to the subject as the subject of emotion.[1] I want to turn attention instead to those critics and theorists who, indebted to Gilles Deleuze and Félix Guattari, Baruch Spinoza and Henri Bergson, conceptualize affect as pre-individual bodily forces augmenting or diminishing a body's capacity to act and who critically engage those technologies that are making it possible to grasp and to manipulate the imperceptible dynamism of affect. I want to argue that focusing on affect—without following the circuit from affect to subjectively felt emotional states—makes clear how the turn to affect is a harbinger of and a discursive accompaniment to the forging of a new body, what I am calling the biomediated body.

I will explore the technical frames of the biomediated body, specifically "biomedia" that make possible the mass production of genetic material, and "new media" where digitization makes possible a profound technical expansion of the senses. I will argue that the biomediated body challenges the autopoietic character of the body-as-organism that, by the late nineteenth century, had become the model of what a body is. Because the body-as-organism is defined autopoietically as open to energy but informationally closed to the environment, thus engendering its own boundary conditions, Luciana Parisi and Tiziana Terranova have argued that the body-as-organism befits the disciplinary society of late nineteenth-century industrial capitalism, "where the fluids which were circulating outside and between bodies . . . are folded onto themselves in order to be channeled within the solid walls of the organism/self/subject" (2000, 4). The body-as-organism is organized for "reproduction within a thermodynamic cycle of accumulation and expenditure; and trained to work" (5).

Like the body-as-organism, the biomediated body is a historically specific mode of organization of material forces, invested by capital into being, as well as elaborated through various discourses of biology and physics, thermodynamics and complexity, metastability and nonlinear relationality, reconfiguring bodies, work and reproduction. The biomediated body is a definition of a body and what it can do—its affect—that points to the political-economic and theoretical investment in the self-organization inherent to matter or matter's capacity to be informational, to give bodily form. But if what has allowed us to "see" matter as informational or as self-organizing "is the advance in technology that materially supports (nonlinear) mathematics, and with it mathematical technology" (DeLanda 1992, 134), then the biomediated body is not merely technological all the way down. More importantly, the biomediated body exposes how digital technologies, such as biomedia and new media, attach to and expand the informational substrate of bodily matter and matter generally, and thereby mark the introduction of a "postbiological threshold"[2] into "life itself."[3] Therefore, while I am drawing on critical discourses on new media and biomedia that define these media as technically expanding what the biological body can do while, however, remaining biological, I also am pointing to the postbiological threshold as the limit point of these discourses.[4]

In offering a sampling of some scholars who are critically engaging affect, biomedia, and new media, I want to take the affective turn beyond the body-as-organism that the discourses of affect, biomedia, and new media still often privilege. I want to do so in order to elaborate the historically specific mode of organization of material forces that the biomediated body is, both in relationship to what I will discuss as capital accumulation in the domain of affect and the accompanying relations of power in the shift of governance from discipline to biopolitical control, a shift that depends on a certain deployment of racism.

The turn to affect in critical theory and cultural criticism provides the opportunity for so expansive an exploration precisely because the cultural critics and critical theorists engaged with affect, especially those to whom I am about to turn, have treated affect both in terms of what is empirically realized and in terms of the philosophical conception of the virtual. It is at the crossing of the empirical and the virtual that the postbiological threshold inserted into "life itself" is both exposed and shielded from view. At this threshold the virtual is the potential tendency of biomedia and new media to realize the challenge to autopoiesis of the body-as-organism that the biomediated body poses. It is here too that the virtual is met by the reach of political economic capture.

Affect, Bodily Capacities, and the Virtual

In what has become a canonical text about affect that links it to the philosophical conceptualization of the virtual, Brian Massumi defines affect in terms of bodily responses, autonomic responses, which are in excess of conscious states of perception and point instead to a "visceral perception" preceding perception (Massumi 2002).[5] But if this reference to autonomic responses seems to make affect the equivalent of the empirical measure of bodily effects, registered in activity such as the dilation of pupils, the constriction of intestinal peristalsis, gland secretion, and galvanic skin responses, Massumi uses such measures for a philosophical escape to think affect in terms of the virtual as the realm of potential, unlivable as tendencies or incipient acts, indeterminant and emergent.

So, for Massumi the turn to affect is about opening the body to its indeterminacy, the indeterminacy of autonomic responses. It is therefore necessary for Massumi to define affect in terms of its autonomy from conscious perception and language, as well as emotion. He proposes that if conscious perception is to be understood as the narration of affect—as it is in the case of emotion, for example—there nonetheless always is "a never-to-be-conscious autonomic remainder"; "a virtual remainder," an excess of affect (2002, 25). Further, it is this excess out of which the narration of emotion is "subtracted," smoothing it over retrospectively "to fit conscious requirements of continuity and linear causality" (29). Consciousness is "subtractive" because it reduces a complexity. It is "limitative," a derived function in a virtual field where any actualization becomes, at that same moment of actualization, the limit of that field, which otherwise has no pre-given empirical limit. Affect and consciousness are in a virtual-actual circuit, which defines affect as potential and emergent.

Massumi's turn to the body's indeterminacy, then, is not a return to a "pre-social" body. Arguing that affect is not to be misunderstood as pre-social, Massumi proposes that it is "open-endedly social," that is, "social in a manner 'prior to' the separating out of individuals" (2002, 9). When there is a reflux back from conscious experience to affect, it is registered as affect, such that "past action and contexts are conserved and repeated, autonomically reactivated but not accomplished; begun but not completed"(30). There is an intensification of affect. There is bodily memory—"vectors" or "perspectives of the flesh"—what Massumi calls "memory without content," which, however, remains indeterminate, the indeterminate condition of possibility of determinant memory and conscious perception (59). Affect refers to the metastability of a body, where the unstable pre-individual forces, which make up the body's metastability, are neither in a linear relationship nor a deterministic one to it. The temporality of affect is to be understood in terms of thresholds, bifurcation, and emergence—the temporality of the virtual.

It is its participation in the virtual that gives affect its autonomy—its escape from the particular thing that embodies it. As such, affect refers to the openness of a body, an openness to participation in what Massumi, following David Bohm, refers to as the quantum indeterminacy of an "implicate order" (Massumi 2002, 37). As implicit form, affect is potential that as soon as it begins to take form dissolves back into complexity across all levels of matter, as quantum effects feed the indeterminacy appropriate to each level—the subatomic, the physical, the biological, and the cultural. As Massumi sees it, quantum indeterminacy puts affect at every level of matter such that the distinctions of living and non-living, the biological and the physical, the natural and the cultural begin to fade (37).

If Massumi's turn to autonomic responses of the body is in fact a way to think the sociality of metastability, it also brings materiality closer to the nonphenomenal, the incorporeal, through the philosophical conceptualization of the virtual played out against theories of nonlinearity and metastability, open systems and the quantum indeterminacy of implicate order. What is at issue in these philosophical-theoretical connections is not merely the affectivity of the human body but, I would argue, the affectivity of matter, matter's capacity for self-organization, its being informational. It is this understanding of matter as affective, as informational and self-organizing, that connects the autonomic responses of the body, or what Massumi calls the "infraempirical" experience of the human body, to the incorporeal, nonphenomenal complexity that is the condition of possibility of the empirical, what Massumi calls the "superempirical" (2002, 144–61). Just as the virtual falls away with each actualization, the superempirical falls away with the emergence of the empirical.

But if it is increasingly possible, as I am proposing it is, to register the dynamism of the superempirical as the dynamism of matter, it is because the superempirical is not only a philosophical conceptualization of the virtual but also a technical expansion that reveals matter's informational capacity. To get at this, it is necessary to return to Massumi's illustrations of affectivity in experiments measuring bodily responses and to notice the technology or technical framing required to make the experiments exemplary illustrations of affectivity. For example, one illustration involves measuring participants' verbal and physiological responses to images, which leads Massumi to distinguish the effect of an image's intensity, its affect, from the content of the image. Another illustration concerns monitored bodily reactions that show participants' brain activity to occur a half-second before they can consciously register the reactions. Another illustration involves a device that is used to strike the retina with the full spectrum of color in order to research the physical and physiological conditions of vision.

While for Massumi these experiments both illustrate the autonomy of affect and leave a trace of the superempirical, which he expands temporarily with a philosophical conceptualization of the virtual, I am proposing that these experiments are technical and conceptual framings of bodily responses that produce affect and reveal the capture of the virtual. Massumi's exemplary illustrations of the autonomy of affect not only show what the body can do; they show what bodies can be made to do. They show what the body is becoming, as it meets the limit at a postbiological threshold, which draws to it the dynamism of matter that had been hidden in oppositions held in place by the body-as-organism, between the living and the nonliving, the physical and the biological, the natural and the cultural. It is to this post-biological threshold, I want to argue, that the critical discourses taking up affect, new media, and biomedia are drawn and with which they are ambivalently engaged.

New Media and Biomedia:
The Technical Framing of Affect

In an impressive set of readings of poststructural thought and new media criticism, Mark Hansen revisits the relationship of technology, digitization, and the body (2000, 2004a). While recognizing the severe anti-mimesis of the digital image, whose infrastructure, after all, is only layers of algorithmic processing or a matrix of numbers that has severed all reference to an independent reality, Hansen surprisingly makes this the very possibility for rethinking new media, as he focuses on the relationship digitization invites between the digital image and the body's internal sense of its movement, its tendencies or incipiencies, which, following Massumi, Hansen refers to as affect (2004a, 7). Hansen argues that digitization engages bodily affect, inviting it to give information a body. Bodily affect is called to transform "the unframed, disembodied, and formless into concrete embodied information intrinsically imbued with (human) meaning" (13). While Hansen's treatment of new media is important in that it uniquely draws out the relationship of digitization and bodily affect, it does so, however, while shielding the autopoiesis of the body-as-organism from the challenge his treatment of digitization seems to pose.

For Hansen, the relationship of bodily affect and digitization requires that we rethink the image as informational. With digitization, he argues, the image itself has become a process, which not only invites the user's interaction but rather requires the human body to frame the ongoing flow of information. New media require the affectivity of the body, just as new media allow for an experience of affectivity by expanding the body's sense of its own affective indeterminacy. Returning to Bergson's treatment of the body as a privileged image or center of indetermination that in its movement draws out or "subtracts" perception from the world taken as an aggregate of images, Hansen argues that bodily affectivity, its capacity to act, to move, is central to, indeed "forges," the digital image. Thus, what links the subject and technology is bodily affectivity itself. For Hansen, focusing on the affective capacity of the body allows us to grasp the way in which technology enters the human subject first and foremost through the body, in the case of digital by "tingeing or flavoring the embodied perceptual present" (Hansen 2004b, 605).

Digitization engages this bodily sense of the present specifically by engaging the body's capacity to affectively sense the passing of time in the present. The digital image inserts a technical framing into the present, expanding bodily affectivity and thereby allowing us to experience "the very process through which our constitutive living present continually (re)emerges, from moment to moment—that is the selection from a nonlived strictly contemporaneous with it" (Hansen 2004b, 614). For Hansen, this nonlived that is contemporaneous with the present can be captured by the digital and, as such, the digital acts as a technological intensification or expansion of the nonlived, nonlinear complexity, or indetermination of bodily affectivity. For Hansen, affective capacity and digitization are a coupling framed by the body-as-organism.[6] Here, Hansen draws on Francisco Varela's discussion of affect and the neural dynamics constitutive of conscious perception that connect affect to the flux of time.

Hansen focuses especially on Varela's discussion of the abrupt perceptual shift or reversal of images in such phenomena as the Necker cube, pointing to "the depth in time" in neural dynamics that this shift implies (Varela 1999). Varela argues that this "depth in time," a depth of presence, makes the perceived reversal of the image possible "as a sudden shift from one aspect to the other, and not as a progressive sequence of linear changes" (Hansen 2004a, 250–51).[7] In that sudden shift or depth in time, there is "a stabilization," a vectored assembling of "the distributed cognitive system, while the 'depth' or 'thickness' correlates with the host of competing distributed neural processes from out of which this stabilization emerges" (251). This is to say, "the microphysical elements of a neural dynamics are selectively combined in aggregates (cell assemblies) that emerge as 'incompressible but complete cognitive acts'" (251). Varela concludes: "The relevant brain processes for ongoing cognitive activity are not only distributed in space, but they are also distributed in an expanse of time that cannot be compressed beyond a certain fraction of a second, the duration of integration of elementary events" (Varela 1999, 7). For Varela, there is a "frame" or "window of simultaneity" that corresponds to the duration of the lived present, in which aggregates assemble, emerging from complexity. This frame is "a horizon of integration," where integration, however, is always emergent and intrinsically unstable, a metastability (Hansen 2004a, 251).

This fraction of a second, this impossible timing of the present in the passing of time registered neurophysiologically, is not unlike the half second of brain activity before a subject indicates a conscious response to stimuli that Massumi points to. They are illustrations of affect as bodily capacity, or incipient act. Varela too treats this fraction of a second in which "the self-organization of elementary events" occurs as a matter of affect, arguing that implicated in this fraction of a second of organizing is affect's very nature as "tendency, a 'pulsion' and a motion that, as such, can only deploy itself in time and thus *as time*" (Hansen 2004a, 253). As Hansen sees it, Varela's analysis opens up "to the microphysical domain in an unprecedented manner" (250) and therefore shows the function of affectivity "in the genesis of time consciousness," as affectivity links "the striving of the human being to maintain its mode of identity with the embodied basis of (human) life. In sum, affectivity comprises the motivation of the (human) organism to maintain its autopoiesis in time" (250).

While Hansen recognizes that digitization challenges "the human to reorganize itself," nonetheless the affective body with which Hansen begins this reorganization remains the body-as-organism. In returning to the body's autopoiesis by finding it in the neurophysiological registering of affect, Hansen withdraws his treatment of new media from the larger technological environment that includes biomediation. What Hansen sees as the immateriality of information in this larger technological environment is matter's capacity for self-organization or its capacity to in-form itself—a materiality specific to information made visible and manipulable through digitization not only as a matter of new media art but political economy as well. At the crossroads of genetics and informatics, the body's being informational not only raises the question of the relationships being forged between biology and information, matter and information, "life itself" and information. It also raises a question about the productivity of these relationships, their materiality in political economic production.

Whereas Hansen's treatment of new media insists on the difference between the human body and human-machine assemblages, between bodily affect and digitization—differences that harken back to the differences that haunted constructionism—Eugene Thacker's treatment of biomedia reveals the informational substrate of the body and the impossibility of the distinctions Hansen seeks to maintain. Thacker argues that the body of biomediation is not merely a body-as-constructed, given that "constructionism formulates an ontological division between the 'bio' and the 'media,' such that the latter has as its main task the mediation of some unmediated 'thing'" (Thacker 2004, 12). Instead, Thacker defines biomedia as a technical reconditioning of biology, a technological framing that enables biology to perform in novel ways beyond itself, while remaining biological (14–15).

Thacker proposes that in thoroughly integrating the computational logics of computers and biology, biomedia produces a body that is informational. This is not merely a matter of technology representing DNA as information but rather understanding information as inhering in DNA as "a technical principle," as biology's computational capacity (Thacker 2004, 39). For Thacker, "information is seen as constitutive of the very development of our understanding of life at the molecular level—not the external appropriation of a metaphor, but the epistemological internalization and the technical autonomization of information as constitutive of DNA" (40).

Thacker is not endorsing the equation of biology or life with DNA, recognizing as he does the "the multitude of heterogeneous elements that collectively form an operational matrix," in which DNA is only a part (Thacker 2005b, 98). Rather, his focus on DNA is meant to point to the ongoing investment of capital and technoscientific discourses in the molecular level of the body as an informational body, the biomediated body. The biomediated body, therefore, is not disembodiment. Rather it is a recent complexification in bodily matter at the molecular level as its informational capacity is made more apparent and more productive. What is unique to biomedia, Thacker argues, is that it is biology that both "drives production" and is "the source material." Biology is "the process of production" and in replacing machines, biology "is the technology" (2005b, 201). In the technological framing of the "labor performed routinely by cells, proteins, and DNA," biomedia produces the biomediated body as a laboring body (201).

Biomedia, therefore, is the infrastructure of a political economy that aims to continually transform informatics-based products into "the long-term generation of information" (Thacker 2005b, 80). Thacker gives the example of genetic-specific drug development. On the one hand, the drug has potential for economic gain, for which the consumption of the drug is necessary, "connecting information to the biological body" (79). On the other hand, what is more lucrative than the sale of drugs is the "booming industry of diagnostic tests" and the production of databases. There is the economic gain sought in maintaining "the recirculation of products (pills, testing technologies) back into information (databases, test results, marketing and media campaign" (85). But in the development of "database management, data analysis, software design, infomedicine, and of course diagnostics," the bodies that consume these commodities, Thacker argues, will be touched "only to the degree the body and 'life itself' are understood in informatic ways" (85).

While Thacker has gone a long way in exploring the political economy of biomedia, he does not register how the biomediated body, in its appropriation of biology's capacity to mutate or create, challenges autopoiesis (characteristic of the body-as-organism) as biomedia introduces into "life itself " what Keith Ansell Pearson calls "a techno-ontological threshold of a post-biological evolution" (1999, 216). It is to treatments of the postbiological threshold in evolution and to the biopolitical economy of the biomediated body that I now turn.

Labor, Energy, Information, and the Body-as-Organism

If by the late nineteenth century the body of disciplinary industrial capitalism could be described as the body-as-organism, characterized by autopoiesis, it would not be until the late twentieth century that Humberto Maturana and Francisco Varela would theorize the autopoiesis of the organism in order to refuse genetic reductionism (1980). After all, in defining the organism as engendering its own boundary conditions, and therefore as informationally closed to its environment, Maturana's and Varela's theorization of the organism's autopoiesis gives more weight to the organism's drive to preserve its homeostasis and equilibrium than it does to its component parts or its genetic structure. Yet, in doing so, autopoiesis makes it difficult to think the organism in terms of evolution. N. Katherine Hayles has pointed out that the circularity of autopoiesis, preserved in every situation of the organism, is contradictory with evolution, where species evolve through continuity but also through change and genetic diversity (1999). Keith Ansell Pearson goes further than Hayles, situating his critique of autopoiesis in terms of what he calls "a 'machinic' approach to questions of evolution" (1999, 3).

Not only is autopoiesis inconsistent with the Darwinian theory of genetic diversity, but, as Pearson proposes, autopoiesis "blocks off access to an appreciation of the dynamical and processual character of machinic evolution," which "connects and convolutes the disparate in terms of potential fields and virtual elements and crosses techno-ontological thresholds without fidelity to relations of genus or species" (1999, 170). As Pearson sees it, the organism must be rethought as an open system that places it "within the wider field of forces, intensities and duration that give rise to it and which do not cease to involve a play between nonorganic and stratified life" (154). This would introduce into autopoiesis "the complexity of non-linear, far-from-equilibrium conditions," which bring the human to "a techno-ontological threshold of a postbiological evolution" (216). Pearson's rethinking of autopoiesis looks to the ongoing investment in the informatics of biology, an investment in the biomediated body's introduction of the postbiological threshold into "life itself." He also takes a look back to the evolutionary history of genetic reproduction.

In critiquing autopoiesis, Pearson draws on Lynn Margulis's and Dorion Sagan's theorization of endosymbiosis, which suggests that machinic evolution not only befits the biomediated body but also has a long evolutionary history (1986). Margulis and Sagan point to the parasitic and symbiotic relations that precede the appearance of reproduction through nucleic DNA, a process called endosymbiosis. They also point to the process of endosymbiosis continuing in the body of the cell, challenging the model of evolution based on linear or filiative evolution. Endosymbiosis, that is, involves cellular elements other than nucleic DNA, elements, such as mitochondria, that are captured in the cell body without losing the autonomy of their reproductive machinery, their own method of information transmission. Mitochondria reproduce symbiotically, in a bacteria-like way, assembling (through contact or contagion) across phyla without fidelity to relations of genus or species. As Luciana Parisi puts it, endosymbiosis adds turbulence—"microbial memories and cellular parasitism"—to reproduction through nucleic DNA (2004, 175). This turbulence links endosymbiosis and biomediated reproduction; both transmit information without fidelity to species and genus.

Parisi also links biodigital sex and machinic evolution to the philosophical conceptualization of the virtual. She suggests that there is political economic investment in the virtual, as biodigital sex is meant to stretch "the
unpredictable potential to differentiate beyond expectation," capturing "the
interval between states" (2004, 157). For Parisi, this means an investment in
the tendencies of recombinant information understood in terms of matter:
matter as informational, with the capacity to self-organize. Biodigital sex,
then, is an investment in a mapping of the "portals of immersion in the
swerving flows of matter" (165), an investment in the "ceaseless modulation
of information that follows the auto-transmutation of matter by changing
its activity of selection from one moment to the next" (133).

For this understanding of matter and information, Parisi points to the
various efforts to theorize the relationship of information, energy, entropy,
and "life itself," stretching from the nineteenth-century interest in thermodynamics and entropic closed systems to the late twentieth-century interest in dissipative structures and open, nonlinear systems under far-from-
equilibrium conditions.[8] This movement in the theorization of information
suggests that in a closed mechanical system, as the second law of thermodynamics states, the increase in entropy is inevitable as an irreversible process
of heat-death. Meanwhile in terms of open systems, irreversibility or the
passing of time is disconnected from heat-death or the entropic closed system, and it is understood instead in terms that extend and revise Claude
Shannon's take on entropy as the condition of possibility of information
(1948). Offering a mathematical theory of information, Shannon argued
that information is the measure of the (im)probability of a message going
through a channel from sender to receiver. Information, in this mathematical
account, makes meaning secondary to information; information is primarily
a matter of contact and connectibility, a modulation of attention or affect by
fashioning or reducing the real through the exclusion of possibilities.

Although Shannon's theorization of information in the late 1940s followed his dissertation dealing with "the algorithmic and combinatoric properties of genetic code," (Thacker 2005b, 52), Norbert Wiener's theorization of
information at around the same time was more directly linked to biology
and "life itself" (1950). Shannon had theorized information as positively
correlated with entropy such that the more entropy, the more improbable
the message being sent, and therefore, the more information. Wiener proposed that information was an organization or an ordering in the indifferent
differences of entropy or noise, and thus was to be understood to decrease
entropy. Information is a local organization against entropy, a temporary

deferral of entropy—that is life. Even as entropy increases in the universe as a whole, information can prevent entropic collapse temporarily as extrinsic resources of informational order or energy arise.

This understanding of information as a negentropic decrease of entropy, along with the understanding of information as positively correlated with entropy, makes it possible to theorize information once again, this time in terms of open systems, where information is connected both to the movement from disorder to order and from order to disorder in relationship to the irreversibility of time. If open systems are understood in terms of the nonlinear, nondeterministic relations of metastability, where the microscopic forces are ontologically defined as probabilities, then information's negentropic decrease of entropy can be understood to decrease information (or to increase the probability of the range of microscopic forces) at the same time that an increase of complexity or turbulence, a disordering of order, can emerge, thus increasing information (or the improbability of any particular microscopic force). This is what Ilya Prigogine and Isabelle Stengers capture in theorizing the dissipative structures that emerge by chance in far-from-equilibrium conditions, such that the dissipation of entropy is itself dissipated or temporarily reversed in the chance emergence of a dissipative structure (1984). Here information as contact or connectibility is not only a matter of the real arising in the exclusion of all other possibilities as the mathematical theory of information proposes. Rather theorizing information in terms of metastability under far-from-equilibrium conditions allows for the virtual, or potential emergence, that is, the deferral of entropy, or the dissipation of negentropic dissipation across different scales of matter, bringing into play their different dimensions, speeds, or temporalities.

Drawing on Prigogine and Stengers, Parisi argues that turbulence is the norm in the biophysical world, where now the "asymmetrical relationship between pre-individual and individuated multiplicities composing all assemblages of energy forces" is intensified (2004, 158–59). It is this turbulence out of which order and disorder emerge that is captured in the biomediated body with its potential for viral expansion or bacterial recombination of information, or where the "symbiotic assemblage of non-analogous modes of information . . . multiply the lines of transmission—stimuli and receptions— between all modes of communication: a virus, a human being, an animal, a computer" (134).

The shift in the relationship of the empirical and the virtual at the post-biological threshold also turns on what Parisi describes as the "real subsumption of all machines of reproduction" (including most recently the machine of biodigital sex, working at the molecular level) into capital (2004, 127–40), such that capital has begun to accumulate from within the very viscera of life, as "life itself" refers to some abstraction of life to some new unit for negotiating an equivalency between the cost of energy expenditure and its reproduction or replacement—an abstraction of life meant to control if not prevent postbiological evolution, as much as to provoke it. At the same time, the dynamic of capital itself becomes governable by immanent controls rather than by external criteria of fitness.

The Political Economy of the Biomediated Body

When the turn to affect was invited in cultural criticism and critical theory in the early and mid-1990s, the invitation had a certain resonance with the fast capitalism of an intensified financialization, as capital propelled itself around the globe along with the innovative technologies that made its lightning speed possible, while at the same time transforming ideological institutions—those of the state under the pressure of transnationalism, and those of the private and public spheres under the pressure of global expansion of commodity markets and media technologies. In cultural criticism and critical theory there was the accompanying celebration of border cultures, hyphenated identities, and queered subjectivities that yielded, however, in the latter half of the 1990s to the elaboration of melancholy, a focus on trauma, a worrying about memory that shifted remembering and forgetting to the body. In this context, the turn to affect, as Eve Kosofsky Sedgwick proposed, could lead cultural criticism from the "paranoid strong" theorizing of deconstructive approaches, while making it possible to reverse the effects of trauma (2003, 1995). It would do so because affect, it was argued, is "freer" than the drives as theorized in psychoanalysis, and therefore affect is more amenable to change.

In such accounts, the affective turn's privileging of movement, emergence, and potentiality in relationship to the body was often returned to the subject, the subject of emotion, as a surplus of freedom that could be aligned with what was referred to as globalization in the wake of the breakup of the Fordist-Keynesian regime of capital accumulation, a breakup thought to offer possibilities, even as its downside was foreshadowed in the focus on melancholy and trauma in cultural criticism and critical theory. There were, however, critical theorists and cultural critics who had turned to affect recognizing that the transformation of the Fordist-Keynesian regime into the turbulence and complexity that accompanied what David Harvey called "flexible accumulation" marked the passing from formal subsumption to real subsumption (1989). This transformation provided political, economic, and cultural relevance for taking the affective turn.

As a regulation of overaccumulation, the Fordist-Keynesian regime had overseen the drawing of laborers' reproduction into the exchange relationships of an expanding commodity market, a "formal subsumption," accompanied by the development of the state apparatuses of civil society aimed at the socialization of laborers, along with the expansion of mass media in facilitating mass consumption of the output of mass production. Subsumed into capital, the reproduction of the laborer becomes itself a force of production further motivating the appropriation of every aspect of reproduction and communication by technology, further widening the reach of mass media with the development of information technologies and further enlarging the service economy.

While formal subsumption was meant to be a solution to the problem of overaccumulation, it too produced overaccumulation as wages rose in response to laborers' demand for higher wages in order to meet the cost of reproducing themselves and their families through the market exchange in commodities and services. But they also demanded more in terms of quality of life, expressed as a frustration magnified in social movements of identity and recognition. By the early 1970s, as the relationship of work and life was restructured, the wage became a matter of political demand, severing the production of surplus value from the laborers' surplus production. On the one hand, there was an attempt to stabilize prices and wages through manipulating a basic resource of energy in the oil crisis of 1973. On the other hand, there was a drive to technological development that transformed the very function of media; there was a shift from selling products to manipulating affect, an expansion of the service economy and the technological autonomization of its functioning (Caffentzis 1992).

Social reproduction had become a matter of time, capital-invested time realized in images to be consumed by the consumer, for example, in watching television, but also in doing therapy or going to the gym (Dienst 1994). The function of the media as a socializing/ideological mechanism had become secondary to its continuous modulation, variation, and intensification of affective response in real time, where bodily affect is mined for value. There is a socialization of time as media makes "affect an impersonal flow before it is a subjective content," as Massumi would put it (1998, 61).

In this context, the circuit from affect to emotion is attached to a circulation of images meant to simulate desire already satisfied, demand already met, as capital extracts value from affect—around consumer confidence, political fears, and so forth, such that the difference between commodification and labor, production and reproduction are collapsed in the modulation of the capacity to circulate affect. If all this seems only to characterize first-world economies, actually formal subsumption necessarily had a global reach. The media and digital technologies that would allow for the outsourcing of capitalist production to regions all around the world beginning in the early 1970s, when they themselves globalized, set off financialization in various parts of the world other than the first world, bringing nations and regions, unevenly to be sure, into a worldwide capitalist economy.[9]

In this global situation, the connection of affect and capital is not merely a matter of a service economy's increasing demand for affective labor or media's modulation of the circuit from affect to emotion. Rather, pre-individual affective capacities have been made central to the passage from formal subsumption to the real subsumption of "life itself" into capital, as the accumulation of capital has shifted to the domain of affect. Whether appearing as the expansion of affective labor and media modulation of the circuit from affect and emotion, or as international exchange in body organs and other body parts, or as the demand for adherence to normative procedures for guarding life, such as human rights protocols, in order to control entrance into economic circuits (see Thrift 2005, Virtanen 2004, Chow 2002, Negri 1999b), capital accumulation in the domain of affect is seeking at a deeper level to measure energy, in the human body and "life itself" in terms of their informational substrate, such that equivalencies might be found to value one form of life against another, one vital capacity against another. With information providing the unit, capital accumulation in the domain of affect is an accumulation and an investment in information as the dynamic immanent to matter, and its capacity for self-organization, emergent mutation, and creation. In this passage from formal to real subsumption, the tendencies of capitalism are moved toward the techno-ontological post-biological threshold.

Biopolitical Racism and the Biomediated Body

If capital accumulation in the domain of affect means that there is an "assimilation of powers of existence, at the moment of their emergence (their phased passing)," this assimilation, Massumi argues, also serves biopolitical governance, as the powers of existence are made to pass "into a classificatory schema determining normative orbits around which procedural parameters for negotiation and advocacy are set" (1998, 57). Biopolitical control is not the production of subjects whose behaviors express internalized social norms; rather, biopolitical control is an effect and cause of the "normative" undergoing "rapid inflation, as classificatory and regulative mechanisms are elaborated for every socially recognizable state of being. . . . 'Normal' is now free-standing, no longer the opposite and necessary complement of 'abnormal,' 'deviant,' or 'dysfunctional,' as it was under disciplinary power, except in limit cases" (57). For Massumi, control transforms the subject of discipline into "generic figures of affective capture" that provide a "gravitational pull around which competing orbits of affect and thought are organized" (54). These figures are not individual subjects but rather what Deleuze referred to as "dividuals" (1995, 180), statistically configured in populations that surface as profiles of bodily capacities, indicating what a body can do now and in the future. The affective capacity of bodies, statistically simulated as risk factors, can be apprehended as such without the subject, even without the individual subject's body, bringing forth competing bureaucratic procedures of control and political command in terms of securing the life of populations.

The linking of control and political command with the risk factors of statistically produced populations is a form of power that Michel Foucault called biopolitics. In contrast to disciplining, biopolitics turns power's grasp from the individual subject to "life itself." As Foucault put it: "So after a first seizure of power over the body in an individualizing mode, we have a second seizure of power that is not individualizing, but, if you like, massifying, that is directed not at man-as-body but at man-as-species" (2003, 243). But biopolitics is not without any interest in the individual; biopolitics individualizes as it massifies. In linking biopolitics to biomedia, Thacker argues that "biopolitics accounts for 'each and every' element of the population, the individual and the group, and the groups within the group (the poor, the unemployed, the resident alien, the chronically ill)" (Thacker 2005b, 25). However, if populations, in this gradated approach, "can exist in a variety of contexts, defined by territory, economic class groupings, ethnic groupings, gender based divisions, or social factors," they do so "all within a framework analyzing the flux of biological activity characteristic of the population" (25). What makes the biopolitics of the biomediated body a political economy, then, is the break into biology or "life itself" by carving out various populations in order to estimate the value of their capacities for life, or more precisely, their capacities to provide life for capital. Foucault described this deployment of populations as racism (see Mbembe 2003).

For Foucault, racism permits a return of something like the sovereign right to kill in the context of biopolitics. As he put it: "If the power of normalization wished to exercise the old sovereign right to kill, it must become racist" (2003, 256). Although speaking to events of the first half of the twentieth century, even while remembering nineteenth-century colonialism, Foucault offers an important take on the racism at play in contemporary biopolitics. He argues that it is "far removed" from the racism that takes the "form of mutual contempt or hatred between races," or the sort of "ideological operation that allows states or a class to displace the hostility that is directed toward them or which is tormenting the social body onto a mythical adversary" (258). This racism deploys something like a crude evolutionism that permits the healthy life of some populations to necessitate the death of others, marked as nature's degenerate or unhealthy ones. Of course, the mutual hatred among races, or the projection of hate and fear onto a population that makes it into a mythical adversary, may come to function as a support of evaluations of populations, marking some for death and others for life (see Ahmed 2004b).

If this racism is central to the political economy of the biomediated body, it is because it is a racism that is deployed each and every time a differentiation is made among and in populations, constituting additional bodies of data. In contrast to the racism linked to the body-as-organism and its skin-morphology, the racism that Foucault points to gives the biomediated body its differences, even as the biomediated body gives racism its informatic existence. Although the visibility of the body-as-organism still plays a part, the biomediated body allows the raced body to be apprehended as information. Here the very technologies of surveillance and security, which presently operate to race populations, do so by monitoring bodily affect as information, ranging from DNA testing to brain fingerprinting, neural imaging, body heat detection, and iris or hand recognition—all are proliferating as "total/terrorism information awareness technologies."[10] The biopolitical racism of the biomediated body engages populations in terms of their "vulnerable biologies"—vulnerable not only to illness, life, and death, but also to national and international regulatory policies, military research programs, and a range of social anxieties concerning the level of threat (Thacker 2005b, 228).

Conclusion

In pointing to the devastating potential of biopolitical racism at the postbio-logical threshold, it is important to remember, however, that a threshold is indeterminate. It is the limit point beyond which there will have been change irreducible to causes. To elaborate the political economy of the biomediated body is not to determine the political economic as the cause of the biomedi-ated body or its potential. It is rather to offer a back-formed analysis of the conditions of possibility of arriving at this threshold—which will help to move thinking about political economy away from a retrospective analysis and toward strategies for what is to be done. While the political gain ex-pected of the affect turn—its openness, emergence, and creativity—is already the object of capitalist capture, as capital shifts to accumulate in the domain of affect and deploys racism to produce an economy to realize this ac-cumulation it is important to remember the virtual at the threshold. Beyond it, there is always a chance for something else, unexpected, new.

Notes

I want to thank the colleagues who generally supported me throughout the rewriting of this paper, especially Amit Rai, Jasbir Puar, Joseph Schneider, Anahid Kassabian, Jackie Orr, Una Chung, and Craig Willse. I especially want to thank Couze Venn and Gregory Seigworth for their helpful comments and edits.

1   For a recent review of the turn to affect in cultural and literary studies that takes up the difference of emotion and affect but which also exemplifies the way in which such criticism ends up with feelings and emotions, see Ngai 2005. Also see Clough 2007.

2   I am taking this term from Pearson 1999.

3   I am following Eugene Thacker who puts the scare quotes around "life itself" to indicate that there is no essence that is discoverable—as life itself. But since the term has been used by molecular biologists since the 1950s, Thacker keeps the term. I also argue that life itself is being abstracted through capital accumulation in the domain of affect (Thacker 2005b, 60–61).

4   Brian Massumi argues, "It is only by reference to the limit that what approaches it has a function: the limit is what gives the approach its effectivity, its reality." The reality the limit gives "is movement or *tendency*..." (Massumi 2002, 147).

5   Massumi argues that "visceral sensibility immediately registers excitations gathered by the five 'exteroceptive' senses even before they are fully processed by the brain.... The dimension of viscerality is adjacent to that of proprioception, but they do not overlap" (2002, 60–61).

6   Hansen has more recently revisited the question of the body and digitization and has

extended his argument to proposing that the body has a primordial technicity; nonetheless he still privileges the human body as that which gives meaning to digitized information. See Hansen 2006.

7   Hansen is drawing from Varela 1999.

8   My discussion of the following information draws on a number of sources besides Terranova 2004 and Hayles 1999, including Johnston 1998 and Taylor 2001.

9   I am borrowing here from David Harvey's (2003) discussion of "accumulation by dispossession," giving it my own spin.

10 I am drawing here on discussions with Jasbir Puar regarding her book *Terrorist Assemblages: Homonationalism in Queer Times* (2007).

PART FOUR   MANAGING AFFECTS

10 EFF THE INEFFABLE

Affect, Somatic Management, and Mental Health Service Users

Steven D. Brown & Ian Tucker

As psychologists trying to say something in public
about the causes and cures of human distress,
we have to stick to the effable, even though the
effable never tells the whole story—David John
Smail, "On Not Being Able to Eff the Ineffable"

Rick is attending a monthly meeting with his psychiatrist.[1] She sits adjacent to a desk covered in paper while she considers one particular sheet containing the test results of a sample of Rick's blood, which had previously been sent for external analysis. Rick currently takes a large range of prescribed psychoactive medication, following his formal diagnosis of schizophrenia several years ago. Today's meeting concerns one of these medications—Clozaril (the brand name of clozapine, an atypical antipsychotic drug). Rick had successfully argued at a prior meeting for a reduction in dosage from 400 to 300 milligrams. He would prefer not to take Clozaril at all, and this is unsurprising given the large range of uncomfortable side effects typically reported by clozapine users. His psychiatrist disagrees. In part her disagreement is fundamental. Any reduction in medication is a step away from "adherence." That is, the maintenance of a medical pharmaceutical regimen. Failure of adherence risks the return of visible psychotic symptoms and disorganized behavior. Going down this road opens up the very real possibility of Rick being sectioned (that is, legally held against his will in a psychiatric hospital facility). The psychiatrist considers the test results. She hears Rick's discomfort. If it were up to her, there would be no problem changing the medication. But unfortunately the test results indicate that there is a problem with the functional strength of the clozapine in Rick's blood sample. A further reduction in the dosage of Clozaril at this point could have unfortunate consequences, as there has to be a certain level of medication in his blood. Any reduction would take Rick below this "critical level," which in turn would risk undermining the whole treatment package. She has, she says, no choice. Rick must remain on the 300 milligrams dosage rate.

What are we to make of this scene? What does contemporary social science offer to our understanding of Rick's experience? In one sense matters are quite simple. We see the exercise of medical power in the figure of the psychiatrist, and the oppressive consequences this has on Rick. His legal and moral rights are here overruled by the diagnosis of schizophrenia. As a consequence Rick is marginalized, excluded from full participation in mainstream society and subject to the ultimate sanction of being deprived of his liberty on the say-so of his psychiatrist. A rich vein of work from the 1950s onward—including the writings of R. D. Laing, David Cooper, Franco Basaglia, Félix Guattari, and, not least, Michel Foucault—provides ample reference points for such an account. In formal terms we would say that this work allows us to analyze the modalities of the production of "abnormality" as a constituent part of the organization of the modern state, creating forms of "internal exclusion" for large swathes of the population who have the misfortune to become objects of medical concern.

There is then apparently very little that remains to be said about encounters such as the one above. Mental health service users like Rick are caught in an ever ramifying network of power relations in which psychiatric knowledge is mobilized and continuously reconstituted. We can describe the particularity of these relations in Rick's case (and here the manner in which the psychiatrist supposedly invokes the test laboratory as the ultimate arbiter of decisions concerning Rick, thereby displacing the authority by which she acts but nevertheless exercising power, is analytically very interesting).[2] But seemingly we can do little to better the overall thrust of the neo-Foucauldian logic that underpins the critical account of psychiatry.

Our concern in this essay is to gain some analytic purchase on the gap between subjectification and the broader aspects of Rick's experience that are not entirely subsumed in his positioning as a user of mental health services. Critical studies of mental health by both academics (for example,

Bentall 2009) and those involved in the mental health service user movement (for example, Newnes, Holmes, and Dunn 1999) have emphasized the systematic discounting of such experience in psychiatric encounters and in service use more generally. The very powerful accounts of the brute thereness of living with a formal diagnosis of mental health issues that abound in this literature seem to require little additional theorization. This creates something of a disconnect between the top-down analysis of power relations, knowledge practices, and subjectification that social science can offer, and the bottom-up accounts of the everyday lives of service users found in this literature. Both are united in their desire for a critique of psychiatric reductionism but seem to pass each other by when working out the terms (see Sedgwick 1982 for an early argument on this).

The dilemma is to find the means to describe the living, embodied encounter of a service user, suffering the aches and pains of routine medication, with his or her psychiatrist, who is able to marshal blood tests, dosage levels, and diagnoses, but who also grapples with the moral and ethical conflicts of providing care, in a way that does not lose sight of the complex dispositif (the health-care system, the legal framework, the pharmaceutical industry, the dense web of families and carers) that serves as the necessary condition of their meeting. To keep both in view seems to require a continuous gestalt switch, where foreground and background, experience and dispositif alternate.

From a social science perspective, we see parallels with the kind of conceptual difficulties that attended Foucault's latter work on "sexuality" (1979, 1990a, 1990b). As Foucault notes in the introduction to *The Uses of Pleasure*, the quotation marks have a certain importance here since what is being considered is a series of problematizations around bodies, pleasures, conduct, knowledge, and ethics rather than sexual matters per se (1990a). There can be, for Foucault, no historical account of sexuality that does not pass by way of the dispositifs through which the body and its pleasures become objects of concern. Yet this does pose the question of the status of pleasure. Can it have any sort of existence outside a given dispositif? Or put slightly differently, what is the productivity of pleasure, what does it and can it do such that it becomes an object of concern?

In an important short piece Deleuze takes issue with the use Foucault makes of "pleasure." He notes that pleasure seems already to be mediated and inflected by the determinations of the dispositif—"pleasure seems to me to be on the side of strata and organization" (Deleuze 2006, 131). To seek one's pleasures is to already know in advance something of how one wishes to take hold of one's desires. The "idea of pleasure" is then a strategic point that "interrupts the positivity of desire and the constitution of its field of immanence" (131). Hence, for Deleuze, desire must be the term for what passes into and becomes arranged in the dispositif (although he accepts Foucault's unease at the Lacanian inflection of desire as lack). Deleuze's Spinozist version of desire[3] implies no such negativity: "For me, desire includes no such lack; it is also not a natural given. Desire is wholly a part of the functioning heterogeneous assemblage. It is a process, as opposed to a structure or a genesis. It is an affect, as opposed to a feeling. It is a haecceity— the individual singularity of a day, a season, a life. As opposed to a subjectivity, it is an event, not a thing or a person. Above all, it implies the constitution of a field of immanence or a body-without-organs, which is only defined by zones of intensity, thresholds, degrees and fluxes" (Deleuze 2006, 130).

In contrasting desire with pleasure, Deleuze emphasizes that there is no question that desire can be natural. It is "wholly a part" of the dispositif (that is, "functioning heterogeneous assemblage"). But this does not mean that desire is thereby subjectified or otherwise put in its place, since as a process it participates with the virtual aspect of the dispositif that is "defined by zones of intensity" rather than by rational-conscious apprehension. There is an unfinished (and uninstigated) character to desire that it leaks outside of subjectification as ineffable singularity.

Deleuze's description of desire as "affect" seems then to hold together the subjectification of service users with the "displeasures" they experience but which are not entirely subsumed within their psychiatric diagnoses. What we wish to pursue is the ways in which displeasures—particular experiences that are in some part outside bounded consciousness—become intertwined with the formal process of psychiatric subjectification. Our argument in this essay is that the term affect, despite its polysemic constitutive vagueness, provides a way of engaging with "experience" shorn of some of its humanist garb. It allows us to begin to argue that experience is not singular, that it is, following Henri Bergson, a multiplicity of intersecting planes (1988). While some of these planes are indeed describable precisely in terms of relations of power, others are not. Indeed the sheer number of planes potentially at stake in any event renders the analytic dream of comprehensive description fatally flawed. If humanism rendered the subject as *imperium in imperio* because it was qualitatively different and extensively removed from the world (that is, as endowed with its own inner life and depth), then an attention to affect allows us to propose that persons differ from other creatures and things only quantitatively, by the number and complexity of the planes of experience that intersect, and intensively, through the particular connections and engagements that the human body is capable of supporting. In Bergson's terms, our human bodies differ from other bodies only insofar as "[we] know it from within, by sensations which [we] term affective, instead of knowing only, as in the case of other images, its outer skin" (1988, 61).

In what follows we first situate ourselves in relation to the Deleuzian aspects of the various threads that the "affective turn" has taken in social science. We then raise some concerns, following the recent work of Peter Hallward, around the virtual-actual distinction in Deleuze, and its ability to elucidate rather than evaporate the concrete conditions of experience. We then turn to some examples drawn from work with mental service users to illustrate how the notion of "somatic management," which draws equally on Deleuze and Michel Serres, allows us to make experience central without compromising on the analysis of relations of power that subtend it.

From Linguistic to Affective Turn in Social Science

Much ink has been spilled debating exactly why the linguistic turn in philosophy took hold quite so deeply across the social sciences. The general consensus is that the turn to the analysis of discursive and semiotic practices helped to create the common illusion that the grand dualisms of social scientific thinking—individual/society, body/mind, culture/nature—could be circumvented by treating them as linguistic resources with their own particular histories and occasioned uses. As John Law (1994) put it, the upshot was a "bonfire of the dualisms." In our own home discipline—social psychology—the promotion of the linguistic turn was a pivotal moment in rebutting the more reductive aspects of a neo-cybernetic model of mind (and society) that had come to dominance in the later 1970s, accompanied by the resurgence of a radical program of narrow experimentalism that seemed oblivious to the historical and cultural conditions of subjectivity (see Curt 1994, Potter 1996).

The linguistic turn has proved the forebear of a wave of critical thought with a seemingly insatiable appetite to "think" the human in the world as part of, and produced through, a multiplicity of context-dependent relations. But the irony of this effort is that it renders "discourse" into a kind of general purpose solvent, into which can be dissolved the very relations that are central to social scientific thought. For instance, the reception of the later work of Wittgenstein in social psychology, sociology, and science studies has given rise to the notion that social science is a form of philosophical anthropology (see Bloor 1983 or Harré 1991 for instance). Local sense-making practices can be analyzed in their particularity, but they cannot be enumerated or drawn together in any convincing fashion. While this "patchwork" approach serves as a necessary corrective to the universalizing tendency of structuralist social science, it also gives rise to the idea that there is a radical particularity to the study of social phenomena that needs to be pursued entirely in isolation to other epistemic endeavors. Conversation analysis, for example, adopts a rigid methodology for the study of individual sequences of interaction in detail, while refusing to connect its own micro-programs of research into broader debate across the social sciences. The outcome is akin to a series of detailed "snapshots" or frozen moments of social life.

We are struck by the similarity of this state of affairs with the problems that Brian Massumi (2002) points to in cultural studies. He points to the dominance of the "semiotic paradigm" as creating a kind of intellectual stalemate. The difficulty, as he sees it, is that analyses fashioned around the subject positions afforded by discursive practices end up withdrawing the very dynamics they were intended to capture. When subjectivities are understood as more or less clearly defined positions within a semiotic field, all flow and transformation is erased. The body is also viewed as a surface upon which discourse is inscribed rather than as something that is known "from within": "The idea of positionality begins by subtracting movement from the picture. This catches the body in cultural freeze-frame. The point of explanatory departure is a pinpointing, a zero-point of stasis. When positioning of any kind comes a determining first, movement comes a problematic second. After all is signified and sited, there is the nagging problem of how to add movement back into the picture. But adding movement to stasis is about as easy as multiplying a number by zero and getting a positive product" (Massumi 2002, 7). The argument that Massumi rehearses here is an updated version of one mounted by Henri Bergson at the close of the nineteenth century. In *Matter and Memory* (1988) Bergson famously attacks idealist philosophies constructed around the notion that the work of the mind is to cognitively elaborate and represent the properties of bodies extended in space around the perceiver. Bergson reasons that this "additive" model of representation is flawed since it would have us believe that there is "more" in mind than in the world. It is rather the case that mind "subtracts" or "extracts" aspects of extended bodies (or "images" to use Bergson's vocabulary). What is subtracted are anticipations of the possible forms of action or relations that might obtain between perceiver and perceived: "There is nothing positive here, nothing added to the image, nothing new. The objects merely abandon something of their real action in order to manifest their virtual influence of the living being upon them. Perception therefore resembles those phenomena of reflexion which result from an impeded refraction; it is like an effect of mirage" (Bergson 1988, 37).

There is always "more" in the world than can be apprehended by any given perceiver at any particular time. Bergson treats perception as a dynamic, adaptive process. It is akin to a kind of "searchlight" governed by our ongoing needs that "carves out" portions of "sensible reality" by identifying possible relationships that might serve as footholds in a mobile, ever changing reality (see Bergson 1988, 198).

The general form Bergson's argument takes is to see stability or clarity as a situated perspective that is extracted from overarching movement or change. This seductive reversal of terms slides neatly between idealism and realism, since it cuts the subjective down to size, but only on condition that we accept the "real" as constituted by a fluxional, ceaseless material movement that is fundamentally unknowable in its totality. In *Creative Evolution* (1913) Bergson applies a version of the argument to demonstrate that an understanding of evolution constructed around clearly defined evolutionary pressures and adaptive mutations amounts merely to a "superior mechanism" that is unable to grasp the movement and change of organic life for what it is. Massumi's renewal of Bergsonism for cultural theory accomplishes something similar. It reveals the semiotic/linguistic turn as a species of superior mechanism that cannot, in the final instance, reconstruct the reality of movement and change from its static terms. It cannot, for example, offer a good account of that part of Rick's experience that eludes fixity in the selection of semiotic terms in either the psychiatric lexicon or in the alternatives that exist in rival discourses (for example, "hearing voices"). Dynamism returns by focusing anew on the relation between perceiver and perceived, while recognizing that this relationship is situated, provisional, and emergent upon a prior material flux of bodies and relations that are to some extent pre-personal and most certainly pre-individual (that is to say, that a sense of individuality emerges from rather than conditions such arrangements of bodies). In this respect Massumi has the contemporary advantage over Bergson of being able to draw upon complexity theory as a stock of productive metaphors that lend the aura of scientificity.[4]

The significance of the term "affect" for Massumi's work follows directly from his use of Bergsonism. Take, for example, the following definition: "What is being termed affect in this essay is precisely this two-sidedness, the simultaneous participation of the virtual in the actual and the actual in the virtual, as one arises from and returns to the other. Affect is this two-sidedness *as seen from the side of the actual thing*, as couched in its perceptions and cognitions" (Massumi 2002, 35). Here Massumi draws upon Bergson's distinction between the virtual and the actual to point to the difference between an unfinished, material flux of reality and the concrete instantiations of this flux as perceptions and anticipated actions relative to a given relationship between perceiver and perceived. As with Bergson, what is genuinely astounding about this distinction is that it commands a belief that what is "real" here is the "continuous variation" (to use Deleuze's phrase) of the material flux itself. Contrastingly, our "actual" given perceptions, while "real" in the mundane sense of being indexically linked to our ability to act, are impoverished "snapshots" of living that are entirely relative to our current needs and situated concerns, and are hence different in kind to the inchoate, perpetually unfinished nature of the virtual.

Affect neatly links this "two-sidedness" in several ways. It proposes that analysis starts from the situated standpoint of *the actual thing* as it extracts a foothold in the material flux. It then reminds us that this foothold is *interdependent* with the relationships that the actual thing can apprehend with other bodies. Or put slightly differently, that there is a material arrangement of relations between bodies that allows for certain potentials to act. Since these relationships are by their very definition *open and unfinished* it follows that the actual thing can only *partially sense or feel* their possible character rather than render them subject to direct representation. Affect is then significant because it marks *a-cognitive* or *more-and-less-than-rational* modalities through which the actual thing engages in worldly activities. Moreover affect marks the *indeterminate* and *eventful* nature of concrete action as it expresses and further complexifies the material flux in which it participates.

The upshot of all this is that analysis ought to concern itself with two affective movements—the sensed "subtractive" movement of actualization and the vaguely felt "elaborative" movement of virtualization.[5] The former involves a preparedness to act and be acted upon in particular ways, while the latter implicates such actions into new possibilities for relatedness. In empirical terms, the study of both movements encounters very particular challenges. If the affectively mediated relation between the virtual and the actual is experienced, in part, as a-cognitive or more-and-less-than-rational then it follows that the rationalizing of such experiences in the flat language of social science analysis will rather miss the point. Hence Massumi develops an extraordinary procedure of roving between "experimental" sites (in the sense of both formal experiments and performance art) where something of either movement can be discerned through some kind of interruption or breakdown in the experimental procedure. What Massumi does is not so much explain or account for the phenomenon under consideration, but rather build practical-theoretical scaffolding around the interruption or breakdown that sets loose the affective movement. One connects to Reagan's film career, Stelarc's hangings, or the Katz color experiment rather than seeking a proper explanatory grasp.

Now Massumi's work is by no means the first occasion on which affect has been counterposed to rationalization. There is a long and rich tradition of just such thinking in psychology, which includes not only the increasingly well-known work of Silvan Tomkins, but also the earlier philosophical-experimental speculation of William James and Walter Cannon, through to the complex mapping of affective pathways in modern experimental psychology (see Izard 2007 for a useful summary). Indeed some work within psychology pursues just the same kind of exploration of "subject-less" pre-personal arrangements of body and mind that Massumi calls for. Brown and Stenner (2001), for example, elaborate the Deleuzian reading of Spinoza to extract a language of "encounters."

In summary, the affective turn most certainly (re)opens avenues of thought for those forms of social science that had become bogged down in the linguistic or semiotic turn. As Patricia Clough (2007) describes it, the most important aspect of this is that it demands that social scientists and practitioners of critical theory to some extent overreach themselves. If affect marks the necessity of thinking body and mind, along with the social and the technical, together, then the objects of study become infinitely more complex and unable to contain in a single academic discourse. For Clough this means seeking "an inadequate confrontation with the social, changed and changing, which exceeds all our efforts to contain it, even our efforts to contain its thought in the affective turn" (2007, 28).

It is this last aspect of affect—uncontainability—that we wish to focus upon and develop in the remainder of the essay, since it presents an enormous difficulty. If, with Massumi, we define affect as in essence beyond ordinary experience (this again, a key tenet of Bergsonism), then we are in effect pushing the motive core of affective phenomenon outside of analysis. The ineffability, the inexpressibility of affect becomes its key motif, to be ritually repeated throughout any form of empirical work. At the same time, since, as Clough points out, what can be contained is likely to defy easy summary in a singular discourse, then affect may become merely a convenient label for marking the limits of our expertise in understanding the actual mechanisms and processes at work.

Varieties of Empiricism

One of the crowning achievements of Deleuze's work is the deceptively simple definition of the task of philosophy as the invention of concepts (Deleuze and Guattari 1994). The practical task of philosophy is "always to extract an event from things and beings, to set up the new event from things and beings, always to give them a new event: space, time, matter, thought, the possible as events" (Deleuze and Guattari 1994, 33). "Things" and "beings" are of course *actualized* things and beings. They are what shows up as "sensible reality" for Bergsonian perception. To extract an event then means to return something of the actual back to the virtual, or to see sensible reality—ordinary experience (our situated and provisional knowledge of this and that driven by our ongoing needs and projects)—as one possible derivation extracted from a plurality, a multiplicity of potential relations. The thought of this plurality is named by William James as "pure experience" and by Deleuze as "pure immanence" (see Lapoujade 2000). For Deleuze, philosophy is necessarily charged with the invention of concepts because this pure experience/pure immanence exceeds and presents continuous challenges to ordinary experience. If Kantian philosophy responds to the threat of uncontainability by emphasizing the need for clarity in the categories of intelligibility, then Deleuzian philosophy makes the countermove of demanding that thought itself evolve through the crises wrought upon it through pure experience.

Pure experience appears to be a contradictory term, since it names a kind of experience that is outside of consciousness, an experience without a subject. As Lapoujade puts it, we must understand experience here "in a very general sense: pure experience is the ensemble of all that which is related to something else without their necessarily being consciousness of this relation" (2000, 193). He goes on to use the phrase "faire une experience" (meaning both to "have an experience" and "to conduct an experiment"). In the case of the crystallization of sodium and chloride, she or he who conducts the experiment is most certainly having the experience, but properly speaking it is sodium and chloride that undergo the experience of crystallization. Lapoujade's example is one where experience does not belong wholly to either subject or object, but is indexed instead to an "intermediary reality" (193). This is constituted by a weave of relations—the sodium and chloride becoming crystalline and the situated experimenter who is a participant in this event.

Following James, Lapoujade wants to position intermediary reality as primary.[6] Material relatedness and its potentials become the stuff out of which actualized "things" and "consciousness" emerge as such. Correspondingly, sensation or, as Massumi calls it, the "feeling of anticipation" or the "registering of potentials," which arises from the plurality of relations, becomes the primary mode of participation in intermediate reality (2002, 92). It is in this very specific sense that affect is to be understood as pre-individual and pre-personal "bodily capacities to affect and be affected, or the augmentation or diminuation of a body's capacity to act, to engage to connect" (Clough 2007, 2). In terms of bodily capacities what is ultimately perceived is only a selection, an extraction from pure experience. A vaster range of potential bodily *do*ings always lies beyond and before that which we are aware of. Whether we call it "intermediary reality" (James), "the virtual" (Deleuze), or simply "change" (Bergson), this ever-present excess of potential relatedness can be seen as a dynamic core of living: "When the continuity of affective escape is put into words, it tends to take on positive connotations. For it is nothing less than the *perception of one's own vitality*, one's sense of aliveness, of changeability (often signified as 'freedom')" (Massumi 2002, 36). Massumi sketches out something like a potential politics of liberation, grounded in the intangible "more" or reserve of experience/action, where there is an ever-present range of possibilities for action that exists in excess of what comes to be. As Massumi notes in his discussion of the neurological "half second gap" (2002, 29), this means that we can "feel" beyond our capacities to adequately experience. To this Clough adds that those technologies and technical augmentations that allow us to "see" and "feel" beyond the immediate limits of our "organic-physiological constraints" ought also to be considered in terms of how they are inserted into and offer possibilities for "felt vitality" (2007, 2).

In Rick's case, for example, we could begin by assuming that there are far more affectively mediated relations potentially in play than a narrow focus on subjectification would suggest. The Clozaril that Rick takes significantly affects his capacities to act. He is likely to be unaware consciously of many of these modifications—although he comes to feel some of them through his aching back. The back pain is then an actualized perception that is extracted from the plurality of possible relations between Rick's bio- and neuro-chemical capacities and the pharmacological potential of Clozaril. The value of affect theory here is that it might allow us to speculate on the range of other ways in which these relations might be actualized. The back pain need not be the only form of experience that could be extracted. Moving in the other direction, we can also see that Rick is affected by the distal judgments and procedures made in the laboratory that handles his blood sample. He is "touched" by their assessment of the functional strength of the Clozaril—that is to say it has a range of concrete effects on his capacities to act. The possible relations that are actualized in this meeting then expand way beyond the walls of the psychiatrist's office, although they are ultimately "infolded" in Rick's own ordinary experience.

The turn to affect theory does come with an attendant risk. Are the "potentialities" we have hypothesized anything more than artifacts that appear when we redescribe Rick's encounter with his psychiatrist in terms of affect? Or put slightly differently, how can we establish that these virtual, affectively mediated relations are relevant and productive for thought rather than mere theoretical adornments that are neutered in their analytic reach?

Peter Hallward's (2006) influential critique of Deleuze is worth briefly considering. For Hallward, the movement in Deleuze's own thought is continuously back toward the event of creation and away from what is created. Hallward claims that Deleuze's adoption of the Spinozist generative sequence, where immanent creativity is regarded as the core philosophical concern rather than the finite beings (or modes) that are the concrete expressions of this power to act, leads him to celebrate the virtual over the actual. The inchoate creatings that perpetually escape consciousness become valorized over the concrete conditions of human creatures. Hallward's conclusion is that the project of seeking freedom or liberty in a notion of the virtual amounts to "little more than utopian distraction" (2006, 162). Greg Seigworth (2007b) takes issue with Hallward's thesis, noting in particular that he appears to confuse a properly Spinozist notion of expression (where there is no division between what expresses and what is expression, the one being entirely immanent to the other) with "emanation" (where what is created is a residue, trace, or echo of a superior creative power). As a consequence Seigworth claims that Hallward fails to grasp the affectivity of the virtual in the actual—the myriad ways in which "creatures" sense and participate in "creations."

While we have some sympathy with Hallward's argument (notwithstanding the important correction provided by Seigworth), it seems to us that a more serious issue lies with the problematic relationship Deleuze bequeaths between social science and philosophy. As we have noted, philosophy is deemed the activity of creating concepts. These concepts are responses, mutations in thought made in response to the uncontainable movement of the pure immanence. In *What Is Philosophy?* (Deleuze and Guattari 1994), science and art are similarly dignified with their own distinctive creative endeavors (the constitution of functives and percepts respectively). But no role is given to social science. It is faced with the choice of positioning itself as either the underlaborer for philosophy (a kind of applied philosophical anthropology tasked with bringing authentic philosophical concepts into the world) or an inferior species of science (see Brown 2009). Matters are certainly not helped when Deleuzians such as Manuel DeLanda (2006) also instruct social scientists on how Deleuze's concepts provide a firm foundation for a coherent theory of society.

The problem is with knowing how to engage with the "transcendental empiricism" of Deleuze alongside the more mundane forms of empiricism that define social science. The Deleuzian version of affect does a powerful work of naming a particular philosophical problem (namely, how experience can be "subjectless"), but it cannot be translated wholesale into social scientific terms without considerable loss of analytic power. For example, the side effects that Rick suffers from Clozaril are diffuse. An empiricism that regarded Rick as merely incapable of offering a reliable self-report of his own condition and sought to sift his words for evidence of the officially established range of recognized side effects would obviously be in error, since it would have failed to adequately engage with the inchoate sensations arising from the encounter with medication. But the Deleuzian renaming of this ineffability as affect, and situating it in relation to, perhaps, the biopolitical management of medicated bodies is also problematic since it widens the circle of this ineffability without offering the tools to trace a way through the relations.

In the remainder of this essay we want to suggest that affect theory needs to be translated through a very particular procedure in order to gain purchase on the empirical objects of social science. We will call this the creation of "intermediary concepts." What we mean by "intermediary" is not some putative link between dualisms such as subject/object, but rather concepts that articulate the "middle space" of affective relations. These concepts should attempt to express the specific conditions of a given experience rather than general conditions. For example, in the case of Rick we require a concept that names the encounter of service users with psychoactive medication rather than any body with any ingested substance. It is further critical that an intermediary concept should make visible the loop between the actual and the virtual, the way in which actualized perceptions allow for an "acting back" on relations to allow for change (for example, self-practices made in response to medication that expand or transform experience). Finally, in an echo of Deleuze's treatment of philosophical texts, it is important that intermediary concepts should at no point diverge from the accounts offered by participants, even though they seek to reorganize and rearticulate such accounts.

Somatic Management

Meetings between mental health service users and mental health professionals (for example, psychiatrists, community psychiatric nurses [CPNS]) are complex social interactions. Service users are obliged to attend meetings and are bound by the outcomes that the professional determines (such as prescribing medication). At the same time, service users are placed under the expectation that they should offer up reliable self-reports of their thoughts, feelings, and behaviors. They are required to both "notice" and "report" their own conscious and physiological states. Mental health professionals then decipher these self-reports in terms of "symptoms" and "indicators" defined by standard diagnostic criteria (such as the *Diagnostic and Statistical Manual* or *International Classification of Diseases*).

Now while this process has been the subject of extensive critique in the antipsychiatric and critical psychological literature (for example, Boyle 2002, Droulout, Liraud, and Verdoux 2003, Harper 1994, Parker et al. 1995, Sadler 2005, Szasz 1974), what interests us here is the fundamental paradox involved in the encounter. It is the service user who "knows" his or her body from within, who has primary access to his or her feelings and thoughts. But the service user's knowledge is to some extent discounted, since it needs to be completed and properly deciphered by the mental health professional. One might see this as a sort of reversed Spinozism. Rather than affirming what a body can do, the meeting seeks to render the service user as a passive collection of dysfunctional affects that stand in need of careful management. The service user is then invited to focus on affective relations in terms of passions and deficits rather than active capacities and their expression. Consider the following example. Here Graham describes the outcomes of a series of meetings in terms of changes made to his medication:

> IAN: Have you ever had any, sort of side effects have you had things that you think may have been caused by your medication?
>
> GRAHAM: Um, when I was on the Chlorpromazine my skin used to burn and I used to feel er, like a tingling in my legs and it was *ever* so bad like, a er a restless feeling in my thighs on the Chlorpromazine. They gave me Procyclidine for that but um, they eventually put me on Benzexhol which stopped the er restless feelings, but my sk . . . skin still used to burn. They gave like a cream to put on and that but but I didn't really like it on my fa . . . you know skin and that. . . . (Tucker 2006, lines 231–38)

Graham first of all describes the side effects he perceived to be caused by Chlorpromazine. Note that Graham offers a series of very distinct feelings (burning, tingling, restlessness). In talking about how his skin *burned*, Graham uses a physical/thermal description. He also draws on a temporal dimension in using *tingling* to describe discomfort in the legs. Tingling is temporal as it refers to a rhythmic pattern of feeling: a tingle is a repetitive multilayered lightly felt "on-off" sensation (Scarry 1985). As a consequence Graham was prescribed Procyclidine and then Benzexhol. These are both anticholinergic drugs[7] typically prescribed to manage side effects, although each has its own range of extrapyramidal (that is, unintended) effects that may vary across users. Graham only reports effects in terms of decreased restless. His burning remained and was eventually treated with a cream, which he disliked because of the sensations it created on his skin and face.

What we see Graham doing here is offering up a set of heterogeneous actualized perceptions drawn from a potentially vast array of somatic events that he might conceivably have noticed. Burning, tingling, and restlessness are complex experiences that differ in their spatial and temporal qualities. Each successive meeting with a mental health professional results in a new intervention in Graham's bio- and neuro-chemistry. New affective modifications are made and are registered by Graham first in terms of the "restlessness" then in terms of the "burning." What is interesting here is the way that complex affective changes—how Graham's body is modified, how these modifications become expressed in terms of felt capacities to act—crystallize around particular feelings reported by Graham in his meetings with healthcare professionals.

We would like to describe this process using a term developed in the work of Michel Serres—"rectification." In an early piece entitled "The Origin of Language" (1982), Serres proposes to understand the human body as a vast system comprised of distinct interlocking levels. He then describes each level in informational terms as emitting both signals and noise to be received by a successive level. Serres then implicitly relies upon an observation formalized in the work of the biophysicist Henri Atlan—in biological systems, there is a real difference between what is emitted as signal and noise, and how this relation is received. What was simply background noise for one level may have informational value for the next level. Conversely, what is signal for one level may actually be received as pure noise. In Serres's words: "Each level of information functions as an unconscious for the global level bordering it, as [a] closed or relatively isolated system in relationship to which the noise-information couple, when it crosses the edge, is reversed and which the subsequent system decodes or deciphers" (1982, 80).

The upshot of all this is that the human body is in its totality a vast ocean of noise and signal. However, through a process of successive rectifications and integration, more refined or higher level couples of signal and noise appear as consciousness, in much the same way that Massumi talks of the subtractive quality of perception. But the key point for Serres is that the whole process is nonlinear—what emerges is the outcome of a chain of transformations where what is passed on is never equivalent to what is received and handed on in turn.

In the case of a body medicated with successive antipsychotic and anticholinergic drugs, the rectification process is likely to be highly variable and complex. The question then is how do a series of feelings such as burning, tingling, and restlessness emerge as the actualized perception (the final signal/noise couplet) from all these successive rectifications? One answer is to be found in the ways in which service users manage their own medication. All service users are expected to maintain formal "adherence" with prescribed drugs. However, in practice, many service users develop informal routines for taking medication that deviate from the recommended schedule. Such a form of "tailored adherence" is described by Roy in the following extract:

IAN: How often do you have to take that then?

ROY: Oh I take it every day.

IAN: Once a day or twice a day?

ROY: Supposed to take it twice a day but I always take it in the evening. I'm supposed to take four in a day, but because I take other medication as well, I sort of limit that to the evening, and the rest of the ones I do in the morning. So it sort of evens out in the same way. I know you're not supposed to do that but it does what it's supposed to do for me anyway.

IAN: So do you kind of, um how did you kind of work out that that was the best way to do it for yourself?

ROY: Well I noticed, I was doing that for a while and while I was doing that I thought I don't think it really matters. So long as I'm taking the four a day you know what I mean? Clozipine, and er, while I was doing that I found that it didn't really make much difference so long as I was just taking the same amount of medication.

IAN: So [you] had previously taken them in the morning and then in the evening? Like perhaps the CPN would say to do?

ROY: I was getting confused when I was taking them that way. When I found my own way of taking them it was it was doing the job, if you know what I mean? (Tucker 2006, lines 201–19)

What Roy describes here is a process of self-experimentation, of modifying his own bodily process—what we might be tempted to call, following Clough, ongoing self-managed somatic auto-affection, or more simply "somatic management" (2000). This is based around a process of modifying his medication regimen and engaging in close self-monitoring of his feelings and bodily states. The (provisional) outcome of his somatic management at the time of the interview was the conclusion that "it didn't really make any difference." But what though is this "it" that Roy is describing? Presumably at some level varying the mix and timing of medication really does make a difference—it affects Roy's body and offers different potentials for bodily capacities. We would reason though that the "it" Roy mentions refers to the kinds of feelings or states that might be deemed relevant to report to his psychiatrist. Varying his pattern of adherence doesn't matter so long as Roy does not end up producing experiences for which he might be subsequently held accountable (for example, hearing voices, suffering what are counted as delusions, experiencing extrapyramidal somatic effects). What Roy then omits from this "it" is the range of other background affective modifications that his somatic management produces.

In this way, we can see how the actualized categories of affectivity deployed by psychiatry serve as a possible grid of intelligibility in which the work of somatic management by service users is conducted. Roy varies his auto-affective states within the parameters of what he might be accountable for experiencing. Equally, we might observe that one reason why Graham focuses upon "burning" is that this feeling carries some currency in the psychiatric consultation while "tingling" apparently does not. Somatic management then includes psychiatry but not in the direct linear fashion suggested by an analysis of power relations. Rather the actualized affective categories of psychiatry mediate the process of reporting feelings (that is, of subtractively articulating distinct somatic states of affairs) and then correlatively direct the prescription of medications that result in further affective modifications. Somatic management then consists of a set of processes of *noticing and reporting* (the service user offers actualized perceptions to the psychiatrist), *diagnosing and prescribing* (where medication regimens are set and reviewed), and *modifying and monitoring* (as the service users experiment with their patterns of adherence). Every phase of the process involves a conjugation of signal and noise. For instance, the psychiatrist sifts the range of feeling offered by a service user such as Graham and selects only one to guide prescription. Similarly service users like Roy who are experimenting with their medication patterns will only consciously attend to those feelings and experiences for which they feel they are likely be held accountable.

In this last extract, from Beatrice, we see all these phases described at once. Beatrice recounts an episode where she had been experiencing severe muscle stiffness:

BEATRICE: The CPN says take two for now, and um, see how you go and
I did, and I almost recovered straight away. Well when I say
straight away, about half an hour, half an hour to an hour. I
felt really better you know. Whereas before then I was in bed
all the time, and I only got up if I really needed to, and even
then I wasn't feeling great. I didn't want to cook I didn't
want to clean, didn't want to do anything. But this Procyclidine really helped, and I thought oh I must be suffering
from the side effects of this drug. Anyway I took two more

the day after. And then I'd completely recovered. I told my
CPN who I saw, I see her on a Friday and it was the weekend.
So I think I rang her up on the Monday that was it, and told
her oh this Procyclidine, you'll have to get me some more.
(Tucker 2006, lines 466–76)

Beatrice here contrasts her experience following the change to Procyclidine
with her previous feelings of tiredness and fatigue. As with Roy, what is
interesting is that Beatrice organizes her experience around a category for
which she could potentially be held accountable. She does not describe what
affective modifications Procyclidine actually produces, but rather what it
does not do—it does not leave her tired and fatigued. Her experimentation
with the medication (under the blessing of her CPN—"see how you go"),
feeds into a new cycle of "noticing and reporting" structure. In this instance
it appears that Beatrice is able to reclaim some form of expertise over her
own experience, but only apparently on the condition that she displays a
hypervigilance over her own bodily states. What we can see here is the way
that service users are potentially able to make use of their own feelings and
bodily states as a means for reclaiming expertise over their experiences in
general, to the point where Beatrice is able to make recommendations to her
CPN about future patterns of prescription. Now admittedly this rather modest reclamation of personal experience is limited (Beatrice is not, for example, able to make recommendations about whether her treatment should be
discontinued altogether), but it does indicate a complexity and a fluidity in
the affective mediated relations between service users and mental health
professionals that is typically obviated in the antipsychiatric approach.

Affect Theory and Doing Social Science

Our opening quotation came from the British clinical psychologist David
Smail. As the head of clinical services in Nottinghamshire, Smail probably
did more in his career to genuinely affect the lives of mental health service
users than any jobbing social scientist could hope to achieve. Smail's academic writing on mental health (for example, Smail 2001b, 2005) demands
our attention because it is founded in practice, in precisely the attempt to
engage with and rethink the concrete conditions of living that Deleuze's
writing celebrates. Smail's position on mental health is that it is essentially
not a medical matter. Psychological distress is produced by the social conditions that emerge from the confluence of economic and political power.

As we understand it, much of the work that is fundamental to the affective turn in social science has sought a new space of liberty in the ineffable, in change itself, in affectively mediated relations that cannot be contained in the existing categories of critical thought. This is a properly philosophical move that draws on some of the most sophisticated attempts to overcome the abstractions of transcendence with the creative vitality of immanence. It also draws on a form of empiricism that offers the promise of breaking with the endless and pointless debate around subjectivity and objectivity in method. But Deleuzian transcendental empiricism, Jamesian radical empiricism, or Bergsonian intuition cannot be simply transported to the social and human sciences wholesale, not least because all of these versions of the near-identical method are ceded to philosophy alone by their originators. When they are simply transposed the results typically show blithe disregard for the particularities of doing social science and as a consequence create no new affects and no new experiences.

Should we then follow Smail's guidance in sticking to the effable? The context of his remark is interesting. Following Polanyi, he is quite happy to place ineffability as a modality of experience that has its place in the vast majority of human undertakings. His problem is whether or not this particular mode of experience ought to be a concern for mental health professions (and, as a consequence, subject to questions of professional training and accreditation). On balance then, Smail decides probably not.

Does his answer hold for social science in general? Here we have to disagree. The writings of Brian Massumi and of Patricia Clough, for instance, amply demonstrate that ineffability, in the guise of pre-personal affectively mediated relations, offers an analytic route out of the semiotic and post-Foucauldian slough of despondency into which millennial social science lurched. There is a conceptual innovation, a joyfulness, a creative fleetness of foot here—fast enough perhaps even to keep some pace with the relentless de-territorializing of modern capital.

But our enthusiasm has to be tempered. The intermediary concepts that social science invents cannot have the philosophical reach or ambition sought by transcendental empiricism. They must be more modest, better fitted to the concrete particularities of the objects we confront. Somatic management, the concept we have offered here to articulate the affective relations in play around mental health service users, is intended to do just that single job. It has no other utility or purpose, beyond perhaps serving as a kind of counterpoint to related concepts. This is what we would like to see from affect theory—a turn from the necessary philosophical labor of understanding experience beyond subjectivity toward the forging and unleashing of a plurality of highly particular and individually tailored concepts that explicate the complexities of experience threaded through contemporary sociocultural settings.

Notes

1 The extracts used in this essay come from a wider project involving interviews with mental health service users from a number of day centers in the East Midlands, United Kingdom (see Tucker 2006).

2 For a full analysis of this point, see Tucker 2006, chapter 6.

3 The derivation is from Spinoza's notion of conatus, or "endeavoring to persist in being." Although desire is extensively worked out as a concept with Guattari in *Anti-Oedipus* (1983), Deleuze's two full-length works on Spinoza offer the clearest account of the relationship to conatus (Deleuze 1988a, 1992).

4 This is not to say that Bergson was unaware of contemporary developments in the science of the day. Quite the reverse. His engagement was both direct and controversial, such as in the (in)famous debate with Einstein (see Durie 1999).

5 Bergson referred to the latter movement as "intuition" or the attempt to "recapture reality in the very mobility which is its essence" (1992, 32).

6 Lapoujade is here following in the tradition of "radical empiricism" that James inaugurates in his work. Put crudely, radical empiricism takes the relation as its central concern. In so doing the demarcation of subjects and objects is seen as secondary to an articulation of relationality (see James 2003). Radical empiricism must then yield to the mobility and fluidity of the relations it seeks to follow (their "ambulatory" character, as James puts it). This understanding of empiricism as outside the parameters of the subject-object dualism has not been well grasped within psychology, despite James's position as a foundational figure. For a contemporary attempt to develop radical empiricism as "reflexive foundationalism," see Brown and Stenner 2009.

7 These are drugs designed to lessen the side effects of antipsychotic medication.

11   ON FRIDAY NIGHT DRINKS

Workplace Affects in the Age of the Cubicle

Melissa Gregg

If you don't do this, you are headed for trouble.
—Dale Carnegie, *How to Win Friends and Influence People*

In the final season of HBO's *Six Feet Under*, Claire Fisher makes the transition from art school dropout to office temp in a desperate bid to support herself after the breakdown of her relationship with the troubled Billy. Claire's struggle to fit the straitjacket of corporate culture so soon after her dalliance with the bohemian world of sex, drugs, and artistic expression initially manifests in dreamscapes, such as the memorable scene in which her mindless singing to office Muzak develops into a fully blown desktop-dancing ode to some seriously constricting pantyhose.[1] However following the death of her brother Nate, Claire's comportment at work quickly moves beyond mere cynicism or bewilderment at the kitsch of Friday night drinks toward a self-destructive combination of substance abuse and verbal harassment of fellow workers. In contrast to recent social theory suggesting that the workplace is changing to mirror the schedules and priorities of the "creative class" (Florida 2002, 2005), Claire's spectacular fall from grace demonstrates a reverse movement, indicating the limited range of affective states and subjectivities permissible in workplaces dependent upon professional "cool" (Liu 2004).

Claire's character is a point of entry for this essay's discussion of the coping mechanisms workers use to withstand the drudgery of office life, as well as the shifts in middle-class status that are brought about by wider economic change. Many writers have noted that the privileges and security once distinguishing salaried jobs from manual labor are increasingly under threat, leading to the development of a new global "precariat" (Neilson and Rossiter 2005, Ross 2009), "cognitariat" (Berardi 2004), or "cybertariat" (Huws 2003) whose experience is structured by uncertainty.[2] The term "precarity" encapsulates this change and "refers to all possible shapes of unsure, not guaranteed, flexible exploitation: from illegalised, seasonal and temporary employment to homework, flex- and temp-work to subcontractors, freelancers or so-called self-employed persons" (Neilson and Rossiter 2005). Neilson and Rossiter are just some of the commentators who see political potential in this expressive identity, since erratic employment prevents citizens from attaining the state-sanctioned hallmarks of ontological well-being. The new moment of capitalism that gives rise to precarity "is not only oppressive," Gill and Pratt surmise, it also offers "the potential for new subjectivities, new socialities and new kinds of politics" that this essay will illustrate (Gill and Pratt 2008).

According to Alan Liu, we are now "on the scene of the abiding suspense of the contemporary middle class, which is even more structurally contradictory than the original white-collar class of the twentieth century" (2004, 19). Not only is this due to the international dynamics of offshoring, outsourcing, and contract hiring, the scale of which previous writers from Siegfried Kracauer (1998) to C. Wright Mills (1953) to William H. Whyte (1963) had little cause to anticipate. In today's workplace, employees who once positioned themselves as valuable assets to the firm based on the knowledge accumulated through length of service (Sennett 1998) or a demeanor that enhanced the pleasantries of a generally male business culture (Carnegie 1988) are likely to find such skills secondary to the more valuable traits of "flexibility" and "dealing with change."[3] To seek white-collar work in the current era "is to stake one's authority on an even more precarious knowledge that has to be re-earned with every new technological change, business cycle, or downsizing in one's own life. Thus is laid the foundationless suspense, the perpetual anxiety, of 'lifelong learning'" (Liu 2004, 19). These contradictory features Liu ascribes to salaried work also include the fact that employees are "simultaneously deskilled and encouraged to feel a deep emotional attachment to their work" (Moran 2005, 39).

Drawing connections between this experience and a longer history of queer phenomenology, Lauren Berlant describes precarity in terms of "animated suspension"; the general sensibility of neoliberalism as one of "impasse" (Berlant 2007c). This is "a space of time lived without a genre" in which people are variously "trying to gain a footing, bearings, a way of being, and new modes of composure" (Berlant 2007c). Berlant's reading of worker sentiment in the films of the French director Laurent Cantet provides a guide for the analyses that follow, which show a number of employees "getting, losing, and keeping their bearing" (Berlant 2007c) in the context of the office. The two examples I examine extend Berlant's project to highlight the difficulty of improvising etiquette, intimacy, and commitment when traditional narratives for happiness and contentment reach exhaustion. They indicate the fragility of middle-class professional "cool" and the need for a more encompassing political horizon for middle-class workplace affects.

Siegfried Kracauer's study of the "salaried masses" in Weimar Germany is another model for my approach. Kracauer demonstrates that cataclysmic events in world history are less influential for people's actions than "the tiny catastrophes of which everyday existence is made up" (1998, 62). The micro-encounters that appear online and onscreen in this essay provide focal points for transitory affects. As such, I will argue, they are both a hindrance to and a salvation from the more integrated and encompassing movement that is needed to confront the isolating working conditions of the present.

The Rise of Snark

Claire's temping role is one of several recent portrayals featuring the banality of office life. Joe Moran's consummate account of the BBC comedy *The Office* suggests that these depictions capture "the boredom of routine and the fear that even this impoverished existence, and its increasingly hollow claims to privileged status, might come to an end" (Moran 2005, 31). Beyond the television and movie screen, a growing number of platforms play host to this sense of fear, as well as the hopes and frustrations of those tethered to the LCD and keyboard on a daily basis. From webcomics to weblogs, gossip columns to newspaper feedback sections, the Internet access so vital to information jobs generates new communities of affiliation, many of which develop their own peculiar forms of humor based on surplus amounts of cultural capital (Wilson 2006). The cruel *knowingness* that underwrites both the privileged detachment of publications like *Vice* magazine and the politics of "snark" in blogging circles epitomizes this desk-bound subcultural humor.

While on one level its belligerent and typically condescending tone can be troubling, snark is best understood as a less than fortunate side effect of the copious ways the contemporary workplace relies on *simulations* of affect to maintain the bonds of capitalist enterprise. The anonymity of online culture can be the safe venting space needed to express the many negative affects that accompany office work, just as a list of easily accessible instant messaging buddies can offer more effective support than the face-to-face co-worker in the adjoining cubicle. Meanwhile, standardized displays of affection—from team-building morning teas to Secret Santa syndicates and Facebook friends —are the militantly obligatory and cloyingly positive tokens of appropriate collegial connection. These phenomena bear relation to, even if they do not fully mask, a culture of long working hours that often prevents workers from establishing more traditional friendship and community networks beyond the compulsory sociality of the office. As we will see, this phatic contact with "contacts" takes precedence while more private and personal issues are left to the solitude of the cubicle—even though the economic benefits of open-plan offices, with their mobile hot desks and movable "pods," render this space similarly invaded. Online and other communication platforms have become a means to escape the alienation of the office: they are a more constant and reliable place to give voice to the grievances that, in the name of teamwork and efficiency, the workplace tends to leave silent.

The vast proliferation of email amassing between corridors and across the floors of office buildings, business parks, and campuses of all kinds is the leading means by which spoken interaction between co-workers has been neutralized in office jobs. Email's storage capacity caters to the presumption that writing a message will avoid unnecessary interruptions and enhance productivity, despite the fact that the accumulation of multi-recipient messages and urgency flags contributes to a never-ending information flow with paralyzing effects of its own (Gregg 2010). With its casual address and relaxed punctuation, email can efface direct commands in hierarchical workplaces so that requests to act appear both friendly and discretionary. At the same time, companies use the same communication format to satisfy legal requirements and issue binding directives to employees. The medium is never the message: opening email remains a schizophrenic and unpredictable encounter.

Ultimately, where email doesn't succeed is in the affective aspects of message delivery—the communicative nuances that attend physical presence. Whether it is the courtesy behind an administrator's request, the shyness of a new employee, or the gravitas of the boss, email renders all its senders and receivers equal. In this sense, it is little wonder that it has become the preferred middle-class communication format. Email caters to the convivial fiction of equity in the workplace just as it requires a certain default literacy for it to act as a successful communication vehicle.

In "The Scriptural Economy," Michel de Certeau describes how the middle class learned to ensure its status and position through a superior mastery of language. Literacy enabled the power "of making history and fabricating languages": "This power, which is essentially scriptural, challenges not only the privilege of 'birth,' that is, of the aristocracy, but also defines the code governing socioeconomic promotion and dominates, regulates, or selects according to its norms all those who do not possess this mastery of language" (Certeau 1986, 139).

In the shift to a knowledge economy, Certeau's diagnosis takes on new connotations. Everyone from software coders to professional publicists challenges previous hierarchies of power, education, and privilege. The dominant class occupying jobs in today's lofts, offices, and boardrooms succeeds by making language its "instrument of production" (Certeau 1986, 139), which sets its members apart from the vast layer of service employees who are nonetheless crucial to their symbolic labor.

Certeau's description also helps to explain the phenomenal rise of email. Its textual properties favor those who may be good with words but less confident in person—those who are happy to write a smiley face but would struggle to provide "service with a smile" (see Liu 2004, 123). In office work—as in other parts of onscreen life—the emoticon is the default repository making up for email's tonelessness. The smiley face (or the signature kiss [x] among women) is a temporary resolution as much as it is an index of the problem of conveying affect through the screen. And yet for many employees, writing an email is preferable to using the phone because it avoids the messiness and time-wasting potential of human contact.

On the many occasions when textual communication falls short in the workplace, the results can be as humorous as they are concerning. *Passive-Aggressive Notes* is a website founded in 2007 that shows instances of just this kind of communication breakdown for entertainment value. This popular blog bears all the hallmarks of snark and cynicism outlined above, making visible some of the ambivalence and isolation of the information workplace. To spend just a brief amount of time on *Passive-Aggressive Notes* is to appreciate how tenuously the sense of security and contentment in middle-class life holds itself together. Further, it suggests some fault lines in the psyche of white-collar subjectivity that the competitive volume of witty one-liners in the site's comments sections cannot fully conceal.

Just a Friendly Reminder ☺ : Office Pass-Agg

By its own description, *Passive-Aggressive Notes* is dedicated to "painfully polite and hilariously hostile writings from shared spaces the world over." A typical post to the site consists of a brief narrative followed by one or two photographs of handwritten notes submitted quasi-anonymously by readers. The blog regularly attracts over a hundred comments in response to an entry, although RSS feeds and bookmarking websites register the actual readership as much larger. The original locations for the notes range from share-house kitchens to the inside of department store changing rooms, while the targets for notes range from roommates who fail to clean the house but do use your toothbrush to homeless people who should know better than to sleep outside the apartment blocks housing the blog's articulate, urban-dwelling demographic.

Though the tone of the site is resolutely tongue-in-cheek, it offers rich grounds for speculation about the number of tiny tyrannies taking place on any given day, that sequence of "miniature occurrences" to which Kracauer earlier referred (1998, 62). For the purposes of the site, a note writer is judged to be passive-aggressive if he or she is "a stubborn malcontent, someone who passively resists fulfilling routine tasks, complains of being misunderstood and underappreciated, unreasonably scorns authority and voices exaggerated complaints of personal misfortune." In reference to the notes on their site, the founders explain:

> some of these notes are really more aggressive in tone, and some of them are more passive—polite, even—but they all share a common sense of frustration that's been channeled into written form rather than a direct confrontation. it's barbed criticism disguised as something else—helpful advice, a funny joke, simple forgetfulness. as dr. scott wetzler, a clinical psychologist and the author of living with the passive-aggressive man, observed: "a joke can be the most skillful passive-aggressive act there is."[4]

Usually the relationship between note writer and reader means that a grievance must take the form of a polite entreaty that will draw attention to some offending behavior in (what is perceived to be) an inoffensive way.

The comedy of manners that ensues is what the site offers for voyeuristic amusement: standards of etiquette or performance are assessed, adduced, and reprimanded when they differ significantly from the consensus of the readership.

The yellow sticky note on the website's header indicates that the workplace is a key source for notes posted on the site. A number of archive categories are dedicated specifically to office life, as well as particularly grating group emails, notes emanating from shared fridges, and a surprising range of appeals affixed to toilet cubicles. Titles and tags added by the bloggers extend the humor, and posts often play to a theme, such as the "office anthropomorphism" entry that grouped together a range of notes depicting a talking sponge (use me!), door (shut me!), microwave (clean me!), and toilet (flush me!), all in workplace settings.[5]

Browsing the archives or the tagcloud is to be struck by the degree to which note writers are criticized or lauded for their use of language while making a pass-agg point. The categories assigned to file the notes include "bullet points," "CAPS LOCK," "ellipses-crazed," "exclamation-point happy!," "irregular capitalization," "smiley," "spelling and grammar police," "underlining," "unnecessary 'quotation marks'" as well as the use of "questionable logic" or a "rhetorical question." The strategies employed by note writers to express themselves are clearly designed to overcome both the constraints of the written word and the limitations on expressing affect in public. Yet the remarkable attention readers display to the writing, grammar, and composition of the notes suggests there is a certain pleasure in pointing out faults and peculiarities in language use. Other links on the site's blogroll reinforce a wider community interested in maintaining standards and taste ("Apostrophe abuse" and "The 'Blog' of 'Unnecessary' Quotation Marks" are just two sympathetic projects). The site is a haven for the literate and educated and its strong cohort of offensive commentators joins pedants and sticklers in displaying superiority through language.

Within the longer tradition of snark, this policing and mocking behavior bears similarities to the remorseless shaming techniques of more serious hacking subcultures—the punishing initiation rituals through which engineers and coders suffer critique when their work doesn't meet prescribed expectations (see Ullman 1996, Gilboa 1996). But what is also going on here is that the site gives voice to the exacerbation felt by many ordinary office workers in information jobs seeking to distinguish their own professionalism, competence, and "cool" from the amateurism, irrationality, and petty obsessions of co-workers. Subtle judgments are constantly being conferred in the process of categorizing the notes. Meanwhile, the online location of this classifying and demonizing behavior renders such practices virtually anonymous and safe from "real life" exposure or affront.

In each case, it is proficiency and competence with the written word that selects, rates, and regulates the behavior of others: first on the part of the note writer who seeks to affect the addressee; second on the part of the large, in-house community judging the note writer after the fact. The scriptural economy of the website has two dimensions. In the first instance, "the order thought (the text conceived) produces itself as a body"—a note—the posting of which to the website's heavy scrutiny creates successive "networks of rationality through the incoherence of the universe" (Certeau 1986, 144). Whether we focus on the initial decision on the part of the writer that a note is warranted or the secondary judgment of its status as "pass-agg," in Certeau's terms each act is an exercise in "producing an order so that it can be written on the body of an uncivilized or depraved society" (144).

Sometimes this "body" is more literal. It is not incidental that two of the most common locations for notes to be left around the office are the shared kitchen and bathroom. Both are places where, in contrast to the hypnotic screen to which workers are generally wedded, the materiality of others' bodies cannot be avoided. The range of creative descriptions of preferred toilet behavior in many notes (including volume of "pushing" to show courtesy to co-workers toiling near the facilities to "holding the handle down until everything disappears" to "show your respect for all of us") reflects the terms of etiquette and politesse of the public sphere—especially in the United States, where the majority of the notes originate. The almost ludicrous regularity with which notes appear documenting theft from the office fridge would itself seem a barometer of workplace atomization if it wasn't also symptomatic of the rise of flex-time and contract work. These factors leave many co-workers unknown to each other or sharing space at opposite ends of the day.

If the website's modus operandi is humor, one note from 2007 paints a more somber picture of one person's response to what is, in the conventions of this subculture, an apparently routine theft. The note read, in part (with formatting retained:

> It is Ok to steal food from people (I'm aggerating); but
> I am a MOTHER-TO-BE who starved because you
> Took a bite out of my lunch meat and cheese.
>
> Feel free to starve me, but not my baby!!!

Resorting to ALL CAPS to emphasize the point, the mother goes on to say:

LEAVE OTHER PEOPLES FOOD ALONE!!!

IF YOU NEED TO FIND A PLACE THAT WILL
PROVIDE YOU WITH FUNDS TO EAT OR A
BUDGET TO PROVISION PROPER FOOD
ALLOWANCES, THERE IS HELP FOR YOU ALSO.

PELASE DON'T LET ME CATCH YOU STARVING
MY CHILD (UNBORN OR NOT) BY TASTING,
EATING, OR STEALING MY FOOD

The description accompanying this note includes details of the "elaborate scheme" required to steal it from the fridge long enough to photograph and send it in to be published on the site. Humor is the main currency rewarded on the site beyond any notion of sympathy for the human sentiment evident in the notes. Some readers show support for the expectant mother in the feedback section, but the majority stick to the formula of admiring and rating the notes and make repetitive in-jokes. Threaded comments encourage such conversation, stimulation, and point scoring in this highly particular branch of the knowledge class.

Like the note writers whose messages are often directed to unknown others, the screen subcultures that make *Passive-Aggressive Notes* such a success arise from the experience of individuals whose employment conditions often mean they are a passing, transient presence in the lives of their colleagues. In this situation workers' sense of identity is performed and made meaningful through textual displays rather than encounters shared through physical proximity. In Certeau's terms, it is "mastery of language"— the residual authority of middle-class cultural capital—that allows a sense of collegiality to transpire online if not in person. All the while, these acts of demonstrable knowingness remain distant from local criticism or other embarrassing displays of affect that face-to-face confrontation might threaten.

In Liu's terms, *Passive-Aggressive Notes* is a leading example of the politics of the cubicle: "where cool people do act up—but oh so secretly, subtly, and undecidably (suspended between passiveness and activism, despair and hope)" (2004, 277). For Liu, the drive to maintain "cool" in the information workplace is a regression in the history of labor politics, for it "is almost unbelievably narrow in tone, incapable of modulation, cruel without compensating pathos, indiscriminate, inarticulate, and, above all, self-centred or private. Another way to say this is that at the moment of cool, knowledge workers (not to mention students training for knowledge work) regress to "adolescence," which is less a dismissive epithet than a structural description of individual as opposed to social archaism" (305).

The stakes in this turn to individualism in workplace politics are significant: "Even when knowledge workers have graduated and gone to work, 'cool' is how they instantly retreat to their mental 'room' instead of joining the broader, public history of peoples resistant to rationalization" (Liu 2004, 305). Liu is dismissive of screen-based subcultures because they remain isolated pockets of refusal, with no viable solution to the pressures affecting the white-collar workplace. Snark and cynicism may be symptomatic of the alienating conditions of information labor generally, but their short-term amusement value is of little use in aligning legitimate feelings of disaffection with a longer history of workplace resistance.

It is here that the character of Claire Fisher provides a fruitful if fictional contrast. As a precariously employed art-school dropout, Claire's experiments in refusing office protocol are some welcome admission of how regularly young people fail in the "winner takes all" cultural economy glamorized in a host of recent television series[6] and in the formulaic process of reality TV celebrity (Hesmondhalgh 2007, Turner 2004). The depiction of Claire's workplace shares visual cues for representing office life that, according to Joe Moran (2005), began with the film *Office Space*. Set against the meritocratic fantasy of NBC's *The West Wing*, the antics of HBO's *Curb Your Enthusiasm* or *Entourage*, and *Six Feet Under*'s own sometimes unbearably arch seriousness, the satirical humor in the scenes featuring Claire's workplace makes it uniquely interesting for being somewhere in between these preceding genre expectations.

For the uninitiated, Claire is the youngest child and only daughter in *Six Feet Under*, which pivots on the day-to-day running of a family-run funeral home, Fisher and Sons. The name of the business tells us that Claire was never likely to benefit from a clear career path or succession plan. Yet this patriarchal oversight and attendant structure of inheritance was thrown into disarray in the show's very first episode by the unexpected death of the father.[7] In a shift symbolic of the changing cultural composition of the United States in general and *Six Feet Under*'s particular Los Angeles setting, the life span of the show bore witness to a drawn-out struggle over changing the trading name of "Fisher and Sons" to "Fisher and Diaz"—a reflection on the increasing financial clout of the funeral home's chief embalmer and the show's main Latino character, Frederico.

Unlike the men in the series, Claire does not face the same dilemmas over whether to pursue the ambitions held for her by her father, and the narrative regularly plays witness to her lack of life direction as a young woman awkwardly positioned in relation to the forms of fulfillment available in a postfeminist culture (Gill 2007a, McRobbie 2004). Claire's eventual "awakening" as an artist is a consistently entertaining subplot for the show because she is an outsider to this, and indeed, *every* subculture. With few role models to guide her entrance to the art world, Claire is forced to learn how to gain and keep credibility on her own. An extended period exploring creative clichés of drug use, sexual experimentation, egotistical tantrums, and even showdowns over intellectual property has her beginning the fifth season in a volatile relationship with a schizophrenic photography teacher. Billy is conducting his own experiment in responsible neoliberal subject formation by attempting to stay on medication, to the detriment of his creative impulse. Growing bored with himself and missing the edginess that was central to his artistic genius, Billy's manic persona returns with a vengeance in the first few episodes. Claire is left running scared of her lover and all that his exciting world was supposed to represent.

Temp Is Short for Temporary:
Making Friends at the New Economy Hot Desk

When Claire is first depicted visiting a temp agency she explains to the desk clerk that she quit art school because there wasn't enough time to "be creative." She feels obligated to own up to her true aspirations, revealing that she's applied for a grant that she expects to get and she'll have to quit working "like, *immediately*" when it happens. This small gesture positions Claire as a genuine and honest soul entering the cutthroat reality of adult employment. Her cuteness is only exacerbated when the consultant replies to her generosity by saying, "Yeah well, temp is short for temporary." Turning to the computer database, the recruitment officer spends little time finding Claire a job, but warns that the firm is conservative: she'll need "a nice blouse, skirt, and hose."

We next see Claire making friends with a new office mate, whose collegial gestures (the supportive cliché "Having fun yet?," the invitation to sign a secret birthday card for Beverly) are key signifiers of the modern white-collar office.[8] When Claire protests that she hasn't met Beverly yet, figuring she shouldn't sign the card, she's assured that it doesn't matter, because no one ever reads them ("Last year I signed it Hitler and she didn't say anything"). This particular scene bears all the hallmarks of an initiation: site-specific jokes (like pass-agg notes, they are riddled with pathos); in-group language and rituals; tips on how to behave and treat people. What the viewer is led to discover is that in this situation friendship isn't much of a choice. You don't even need to know the person, you just have to participate. Moreover, the gifts exchanged among these compulsory friends have little meaning: they are pure gesture. What becomes comic is the expectation that there *would* be an appropriate affect accompanying it.

Another scene of confounded etiquette has Claire feeling obliged to thank her new cubicle colleague for sending an e-card with dancing puppies. Marking this convivial (textual) gesture then develops into an awkward moment as her colleague offers Claire a toilet pass so that she feels more a part of the team. In this instance too, workplace culture is shown to operate on the presumption that tokens of friendship will not be declined; invitations are never issued with the option of rejection. Listening to Claire's attempts to protest her meager gift is to recognize what Liu describes as the "eternal, inescapable friendship" of knowledge work (2004, 172), which Moran argues "undermines normal human relationships and then seeks to manufacture them after the fact" (Moran 2005, 38).

For despite the pleasantries of her co-workers, Claire is subject to some clear contradictions. As a temp, she isn't entitled to her own bathroom pass but she is expected to sign a card to fit in with everyone else. On several occasions throughout the season the rituals of the workplace evoke a reversion to high school hierarchies: one has to earn trust to get permission to go to the toilet. As it happens, this distinction proves to be important. The toilet becomes a key dramatic location in the narrative because it is the one site free from surveillance—it provides a temporary reprieve from the exhausting performance of professional cool.

Perhaps the ultimate act of friendship in office jobs is after-work drinks, and when she is invited early on, Claire seems unimpressed by the prospect of the nearby bar in the mall. She politely declines, saying she'll come next time. In turn, her colleagues accuse her of what an Australian would term "having tickets on herself"—or as one of Claire's co-workers puts it, in the Top 40 lingo of the moment, "What's the matter Claire, think your shit don't stink?" The suffocating attempts to draw her in to the world of pitchers, pool, and party pashing do ultimately have their effect, especially as Claire learns that her art grant application has been unsuccessful and her route out of temp work might be doomed.

In a rare confessional gesture during drinks, Kirsten tells Claire she is having a workplace romance with Ted, a suave-looking lawyer. "We're trying to be cool about it," Kirsten says, tellingly: "We didn't talk for a month; then fooled around in the boys' bathroom . . . We need to take it to that next level once he's dealt with some of his intimacy issues." Following this girly chat, Claire heads to the bar, where Ted himself appears to make an unsubtle play for her affections in a classic case of "making friends with the new girl." The two strike up an unlikely connection, especially given that on their first official date Ted acknowledges he is a Republican who voted for Bush junior and wholeheartedly backs the war in Iraq. Ted bypasses what he calls the "naïvete" of Claire's left-wing politics to argue that it's "human nature" to use violence to make progress. At this moment, which encapsulates the most significant ideological divide defining the show's political conjuncture, their conversation is interrupted by a phone call announcing that Claire's brother has collapsed.

Proving that Republicans can also be nice guys, Ted stays with Claire at the hospital through the long night that ensues. Despite their difference on issues involving the public sphere, Ted notices what has been missing from Claire's personal life for a long time. Against her protests ("You don't have to stay. I've got people here for support") Ted proves a comfort to Claire because he is able to see through her willful independence and recognize that her family has rarely been a source of support for her in difficult times.

Letting the Team Down

In the passage of time between Nate's funeral and *Six Feet Under*'s concluding episodes it becomes clear that despite Ted's careful attention Claire hasn't been coping very well with her loss and has failed to fully sublimate her bohemian habits in her new job. Of course, as a contract worker, Claire has no sick leave or benefits, and her inheritance has been blocked because she dropped out of school. Thanks to a diet of drugs and booze, Claire's temperament at work gradually proves too much for her colleagues, and Kirsten is finally compelled to confront her in the office toilet. Claire is clearly drunk (despite a mumbled protest that "you can't smell vodka") and yet Kirsten appeals to her with the same register of teamwork that has distinguished their relationship from the start.

"We're all really sorry that your brother died," Kirsten says. "I've told them all to give you a break." Interpreting her concern as lecturing, Claire inflames matters to the point where Kirsten resorts to bargaining: she "won't tell" human resources about all the bad behavior if Claire just goes home for the day. This ultimate act of best friend allegiance proves too close to school-yard theatrics for Claire, who throws both the paper towels and the offer of loyalty back in Kirsten's face. An even greater act of sisterly betrayal then follows as she announces that she has been sleeping with Ted all this time. Dragged down to the level of adolescent pettiness—a recurring affect in the office cubicles I have been discussing—Claire uses the only ammunition she has to hurt her so-called friend. Observe that in this case, as with the pass-agg notes, it is the actions of *bodies* that force colleagues to *feel*.

Much like high school, the office is shown to have strict rules of behavior that can result in punishment, discipline, and ostracism. Claire is forced to pack her belongings and does so in a beautifully obnoxious final exit from the office. Her inability to cope with the shock of trauma tries the patience of the team, which by its nature cannot accommodate extreme demands from needy individuals. To the extent that individualism *is* celebrated in this office culture, it is through the inane peculiarities of coffee and chai latte orders and the aesthetics of decorated IBMs. Succumbing to her grief, and seeing little point in holding it together any more, Claire's cool professional per-sona suffers a complete breakdown.

Arriving back at the funeral home, Claire's outburst gathers momentum. Taking note of an SUV parked in the driveway, she proceeds to verbally assault a new client of the family business. The crime? Daring to display a "Support our Troops" sticker on a car that demands so much of the oil that sparked war in the first place. "Support our troops? What a bunch of bull-shit," Claire says to the stunned female owner. As Ted tries to take her inside (as Claire notes, "we wouldn't want to *offend* anybody while they're support-ing our troops!") she breaks free and confronts the grieving woman with even more abuse: "Dozens of fucking Iraqis are dying every day. The whole world hates us for going in there in the first place and terrorists are going to be blowing up this country for the next hundred years and the best thing she can think to do about it is to put a sticker on that enormous shit box. American soldiers are still getting fucked up every day and they don't even tell us, and it's all so you can keep putting gas in this fucking car of yours to keep everyone feeling really fucking American!" Just as she deviates from the principles of appropriate workplace performance, Claire has no compulsion to abide by dominant liberal platitudes and suppress her anger at the war in Iraq. Drawing on Goffman (1971), we could argue that this insight into "the back region" of Democratic sentiment can only happen because Claire has lost any investment in a public "presentation of self." Freedom from the strictures of appropriate affect management allows her to see through both the superficiality of workplace friendships and mainstream political compromises. At this point, the only thing that finally quiets Claire is a reprimand from Frederico that the brother of the SUV owner just died. This knowledge has an instant impact because it registers at the same level of intensity that governs Claire's rage and anger. Away from the forms of investment that would require her to maintain the semblance of "cool," Claire responds to—because her outpourings ultimately arise from—the pain of losing a brother.

The links between the competitive metaphor of teamwork and Claire's greatest of workplace crimes, letting the team down, echo questions of loyalty to the nation that marked the political stakes of the presidency coinciding with *Six Feet Under*'s five seasons. The diagnosis offered by George W. Bush, "You are either with us or against us," provided the key barometer of patriotism at the start of the decade, and if morale is crucial to securing both business and military enterprise (see Anderson, this volume), Claire's collapse is partly due to the fact that these conventional forms of camaraderie were never really available to her—for reasons of gender, age, educational experience, and the sheer vicissitudes of fate.

Moran describes the appeal of *The Office* as based on empathy with the show's characters who are "both somewhere and nowhere, stuck in a notoriously dull place that is often the butt of their lame jokes but controlled by wider economic forces that they can neither influence nor understand" (2005, 42). By contrast, the sheer force of Claire's outrage against the inanities of her co-workers and her government is compelling to the extent that it *is* justified by an elaborate explanation of the wider economic forces dictating the terms for her experience of contemporary America. This latter portrayal actually suggests that it makes no difference whether citizens really understand the wider picture—simply telling people about their implication in the realities of contemporary geopolitics is about as effective as hitting an SUV with a handbag.

The significance of this climactic scene at the funeral home is heightened by the preceding, much more intimate encounter between Frederico and Claire's other brother, David. In a further exploration of workplace dynamics, the family values represented by Frederico (which loyal viewers recognize as hypocritical given his own extramarital affair) are pitted against those assumed of David, who comes to realize that his closest colleague does not, in fact, approve of his long-term relationship with a man. In this quite different representation of collegiality's limits, the friendship that has developed between the two men over many years still doesn't quite stretch to acceptance, and both are shown trying to "keep their bearing" in the knowledge of their own failings.

The poignancy of these closing plotlines is enhanced by their appearance following the death of the show's central character. In the episode featuring his funeral (for every episode features a funeral) Nate is described as someone who was "above all, an idealist." And so it appears likely that the abject despair, the unrelenting pain, and the claustrophobia that characterize the last season of *Six Feet Under* correlate with the affective state of a nation whose citizens had temporarily lost their capacity for idealism—which would explain why Barack Obama would require "audacity" to encourage fellow citizens to "hope" (Obama 2007).

In each of the texts I have mentioned, subcultural rituals, including tactics of group shaming, form the basis to overcome the anomie of the office cubicle. The virtual friendships of the networked employee complement and assuage the tenuous intimacies shared between co-workers who are variously subject to a range of petty rules and regulations. *Passive-Aggressive Notes* and *Six Feet Under* depict a workplace that supersedes both the alienation of the Fordist industrial era and the superficiality of corporate cool to what is now, in the information workplace, "the final drama": "a scripting that binds workers not just to the friendship system of corporate culture but, through their automatic participation in a universal environment of 'user friendliness,' to corporate culture as the stage of general culture, as the new model of general sociality, interaction, and communication. We don't need to be kind, generous, tolerant, accepting, sympathetic, or, in a word, social, anymore. We just need to be user friendly, which is the same as being corporate" (Liu 2004, 172).

The key directive for workers in office jobs is that "we not offend anyone," as Claire rightly observes. In these instances collegial relations are less a matter of striving for genuine communication or attachment and more a matter of maintaining a sense of ambivalent and polite detachment given the uncertainties of the employment landscape.

"Everything. Everyone. Everywhere. Ends."

In the final scene of *Six Feet Under*, Claire bids farewell to her family and a budding romance with Ted and hits the road, destined for New York City. Inspired by an entry-level position at New Image, a photo house (for which she was recommended by an old teacher—it just goes to show that in the art scene, like many others, the patronage system and "who you know" still helps), Claire is told while preparing to leave Los Angeles that New Image has gone into receivership. There will be no big break, no happy ending. Given what we know about start-up companies haphazardly employing willing artistic talent, the audience is left to assume Claire's destiny will be a competitive and unpredictable portfolio career, where investing in herself will come at the expense of any guarantee that she will arrive at a comforting destination: the stability and contentment of an ongoing, fulfilling job.

To live in conditions of precarity is to heed the existential lesson contained in the billboard promotions for *Six Feet Under*'s final season: "Everything. Everyone. Everywhere. Ends." Hence it is in this closing vision, of Claire driving alone on the highway, that she becomes a symbol for every other worker who has ever believed in this one modest hope, as well as the idea of America as the place of reinvention—the place where anyone can make it if he or she works hard and believes in the dream. As it has for decades in popular culture, the open road signifies the freedom to escape, to move on, to start again. And even if its image is both tarnished and emboldened following September 11, New York City retains its mythical status as the pinnacle of opportunity and rebirth. Reflecting on Claire's journey, as her road trip plays witness to the inevitable death of every character in *Six Feet Under*, is it not fitting to conclude that this imagery—of industry, of investment, of recognition for labor—might also be taking its last breath? What forms of reward and sustenance will apply in the new, flexible workplace?

The examples in this essay have shown some of the negative affects evident in the office environment. The implication all along has been that today's workers are missing a key legitimizing motive: the value system that William H. Whyte called "the social ethic" of the white-collar vocation. The rise of screen-based snark, set against a television drama motivated by questions of mortality and impermanence, signifies that something is wrong in the middle-class psyche. Old understandings of what it means to live a fulfilling life have lost some of their allure, with the politesse of office culture failing to mask the lack of intrinsic meaning people find in their work. Passive aggression and blatant hostility are cautionary warnings defying popular management principles that have already declared the triumph of the creative workplace.

In *The New Spirit of Capitalism*, Luc Boltanski and Eve Chiappello (2005) compare the tenets of white-collar work in the 1990s with those of the 1960s—the golden age of the bureaucratic firm and the morally charged sociological writing that accompanied it. They see the difference as follows:

"Now no one is restricted by belonging to a department or wholly subject to the boss's authority, for all boundaries may be transgressed through the power of projects. . . . With new organizations, the bureaucratic prison explodes; one works with people at the other end of the world, different firms, other cultures. Discovery and enrichment can be constant. And the new 'electronic relations' at a distance prove to be more sincere and freer than face-to-face relations" (90).

This reading reiterates the importance of mediated, online friendships in salaried work at a time when relations between physically present colleagues have become subject to instrumental commercialization. Noting the complicity between new media technologies and management techniques that target "human beings in their most specifically human dimensions" (2005, 98), Boltanski and Chiapello provide an important empirical contribution to affect scholarship, indicating the kind of critical accounts of the capitalist workplace that will be needed in future.

Passive-Aggressive Notes and *Six Feet Under* share the ominous historical juncture that Boltanski and Chiapello diagnose. As I finish this essay, a vastly different economic era is dawning. World financial markets are reeling and voting has started for a U.S. election pitched on hope for a better future. Perhaps this new moment will also encourage more optimistic stories to emerge from the solitude of the cubicle, to remind us of the solidarity we need to share in person as well as onscreen. For if it is true that lately we have been condemned to a feeling of "impasse," it is only by turning to our fellow workers that we may realize—as has been the case for every class formation that preceded it—this is not a condition we need to face alone.

Notes

1   Claire's reworked lyrics to "You Light Up My Life" fade into coherence as she grabs a stapler for a microphone and climbs on to her desktop singing: "You . . . ride up my thighs, you tug on my ass, you climb up my crotch . . . You ruin my day and fill my soul with hate . . ." As her finale gathers momentum ("It can't be right when it feels so tight") Claire's daydream is interrupted by a co-worker who asks if the music is bothering her and whether she should turn it down. Claire meekly responds: "Oh, yeah, maybe a little, thanks"—a neat passive-aggressive encounter of the type I discuss in greater detail below.

2   Despite the growth of writing on white-collar labor in recent years (see also Andresky Fraser 2001, A. Ross 2004, McKercher and Mosco 2007) it is worth noting that feminist studies predate this spike in interest by over twenty years. See, for example, Huws 2003, Crompton and Jones 1984, and Pringle 1988.

3   This change is amply demonstrated in the phenomenal success of motivational texts like *Who Moved My Cheese?* (S. Johnson 1998). Aside from strictly corporate work-places, a glance at my own university's staff development offerings for the current year includes courses on "living with change" as part of a desirable skill set for employees.

4   Small caps and loose formatting are retained here in the spirit of the web-based subcultures under discussion.

5   From 29 December 2007 post, http://www.passiveaggressivenotes.com/.

6   While their visual and narrative styles are very different, programs as diverse as *The L Word*, *Entourage*, *Curb Your Enthusiasm*, *Ugly Betty*, *Studio 60 on the Sunset Strip*, *Extras*, and *30 Rock* all operate at the boundary of participant/observer in a range of creative industries. In this way they suggest an audience that includes both the traditional connoisseur as well as the *producer* of creative content.

7   This narrative twist would be repeated in *Brothers and Sisters*, the subsequent vehicle for one of *Six Feet Under*'s main stars, Rachel Griffiths, as well as Calista Flockhart, who played one of the more memorable office workers of the 1990s and 2000s in *Ally McBeal*. Pertinent to my concerns here, *Brothers and Sisters*, screening on free-to-air ABC rather than HBO's cable subscription, staged a much more explicit confronta-tion between the liberal Democratic and "patriotic" Republican positions on the Iraq War that I discuss later in this essay. As the title implies, this narrative drama was structured within the more sentimental device of the middle-class family unit.

8   "Having fun yet?" is one of the stickers that comes with "Cubes" office toys. These desk-size Lego-like structures allow their owners to construct an office cubicle for a toy worker and decorate it with stickers that also include boring computer monitor screens, productivity flow charts, and holiday destinations. A whole set can be bought to create an office where "you're the boss." Thanks go to Heather Stewart and Michelle Dicinoski for supplying me with this knowledge, and my very own cube.

Megan Watkins

In studies of affect much is made of the ways in which it is distinct from emotion. Against the more social expression of emotion, affect is often viewed as a preliminary, preconscious phenomenon. A consequence of this is that affect is often conceived as autonomous and ephemeral. Its immediate impact is highlighted: the ways in which affect can arouse individuals or groups in some way but then seems to dissipate quickly leaving little effect.[1] While this distinction is a productive one for dealing with particular types of affective experience, it doesn't account for the distinction Spinoza makes between *affectus* and *affectio*, the force of an affecting body and the impact it leaves on the one affected. *Affectio* may be fleeting but it may also leave a residue, a lasting impression that produces particular kinds of bodily capacities. As Spinoza explains, "the body can undergo many changes and nevertheless retain impressions or traces . . ." (1959, III, Post. 2). It is this capacity of affect to be retained, to accumulate, to form dispositions and thus shape subjectivities that is of interest to me. It suggests that we grapple with this as a pedagogic process, whereby a sense of self is formed through engagement with the world and others and the affects this generates. In turning attention to the cumulative aspects of affect, however, I don't want to simply invert the focus of scholarly discussion. I am keen to explore both dimensions of affect, its ability to function as force *and* capacity, *affectus* and *affectio*. While a discussion of accumulation may seem to emphasize the latter, *affectio* is very much a product of *affectus*, and so affect as force or the processual aspect of affect is in fact embedded in a discussion of affective capacity. Affect is importantly a relational phenomenon and using an exploration of pedagogy to theorize affect highlights this relationality.

In this essay a particular type of pedagogic process is examined—primary or elementary education—in which the pedagogic relation is that of teacher and students. Drawing on key figures in the literature of child development —Donald Winnicott, Daniel Stern, and Lev Vygotsky—this essay will consider the ways affect is accumulated within this context and has an enabling effect for both teachers and students. As such, it addresses issues of both affect and pedagogic theory as each provides a useful mechanism for exploring the other. Also, while primarily a theoretical explanation of these issues, this essay makes reference to a study of teaching desire and classroom practice that illustrates some of these points. In doing so, it calls into question aspects of contemporary pedagogy, which, in placing emphasis on student-directed learning and online delivery, is experiencing a marginalization of the teacher at all levels of education. To those in charge of the "purse strings" this is a pleasing development. Through "independent learning," "personalized learning," "self-paced education," whatever the nomenclature, the teacher is being sidelined as learning is reconfigured as an activity independent of teaching or a body externally directing the process. This move is certainly cost-effective, but is it pedagogically effective? What is lost in limiting the teachers' role, refashioning them as facilitators or "learning managers" and conceiving learning as primarily an autonomous activity rather than a process of intersubjective engagement between teacher and student?[2] While this shift has been exacerbated in recent years by the impact of information and computer technologies and an economic rationalist drive to minimize teaching costs through the adoption of the online delivery of curriculum, the bifurcation of teaching and learning has a much longer genesis. To many, this rupture dates from a period in the early 1970s, if not earlier, in which psychology came to dominate educational thought, a discipline giving emphasis to students as agents of their own learning (Walkerdine 1984, McWilliam 1996, Vick 1996, Watkins 2005). The scientific "truths" framing psychology gave credence to the much older progressivist educational tradition that places a similar emphasis on the "natural" development of the child, viewing learning—as did Piaget—as primarily a function of maturation and discounting the effect of social intervention.

In exploring these issues I also want to give consideration to a notion of recognition that is a fundamental aspect of the pedagogic process. This is not simply in terms of a student desiring the recognition of his or her teacher but also the teacher desiring the recognition of his or her students. This pedagogic relation involves a process of mutual recognition realized as affective transactions that at one and the same time can cultivate the desire to learn and the desire to teach. It is interesting, therefore, that current pedagogic practice seems to want to minimize contact between teacher and student and encourage independent learning over whole-class instruction. While independent inquiry may be a long-term objective, with students having less reliance on the teacher as they move into the later years of school and on to tertiary study, independence in learning is something that is acquired over time and it is the teacher's role to help instill the knowledge and bodily capacity for students to work in this way. It does not seem an effective pedagogy for the early years of school or, for that matter, as the sole approach to learning in the later years. Teachers, whether at the kindergarten level or as Ph.D. supervisors, have a significant role to play in scaffolding their students' learning in the acquisition of more sophisticated levels of competence. This is a view shared by Probyn in her account of the affective dimensions of teaching (2004). In seeing herself as "first and foremost a teacher," she is critical of the impact of so-called progressive thinking on tertiary education and the relatively uncritical embrace of the online delivery of curriculum (Probyn 2004, 21). She refers to Brabazon's work in this area, which points out that, despite the flexibility of online learning, students ultimately "want to be taught in interesting ways by teachers" (Brabazon 2002). Given the current move away from teacher-centered instruction, however, in a recent study I conducted into these issues in the primary or elementary years of school, teachers were reluctant to foreground their role in their students' learning (Watkins 2007). Whole-class instruction, in particular, was not deemed "appropriate pedagogy" and yet, it became clear as teachers discussed their practice, their desire to teach was more obviously realized through this pedagogic mode; moreover, they also considered this a more effective means of delivering the curriculum. This suggests something about the role of affect and recognition in teaching and learning.

Before considering this in relation to one of the teachers in the study mentioned, I want to explore the connection between recognition and pedagogy more generally and to then draw upon the child development studies of Winnicott, Stern, and Vygotsky to examine the influence of affect, in particular the ways in which it accumulates in the process of learning.

Recognition and Pedagogy

Progressivist critiques of teacher-directed learning such as those provided by theorists of critical pedagogy, notably Giroux (1983, 1988) and McLaren (1989), tend to focus on issues of power and what they see as a misuse of teacher authority. Their vision of a transformative pedagogy is reliant on problematizing teacher authority and redirecting power into the hands of students, giving them responsibility for their own learning. Current perceptions of recognition within critical and cultural theory view power in a similar way. As Yar explains, "Recognition is taken as the instantiation of an economy of power which produces objectified and subjugated subjects, and/ or as the *sine qua non* of an ontology which reduces alterity, otherness and difference to the identitarian totality of the same" (Yar 2001, 57). While Yar's comments are a critique of the use of recognition in examinations of identity politics, they are of particular relevance to the negative perceptions of teacher-directed learning. A focus on a teacher's delivery of curriculum is seen to be at the expense of student learning with the teachers imposing their own knowledge upon students, limiting classroom interaction, and acting in a potentially abusive manner by exerting their influence in an attempt to gain the recognition of their students.

While little explicit treatment has been given to issues of recognition in discussion of pedagogy, where it is evident, as in the work of Bourdieu, it is viewed in a similarly negative light. To Bourdieu the search for recognition actually provides the motor for pedagogic work but to him this is problematic. He views recognition as a form of "symbolic dependence," "an egoistic quest" for the approval of others (Bourdieu 2000, 166). His central concern is for the child and the ways in which the symbolic capital associated with recognition "enables forms of domination which imply dependence on those who can be dominated by it" (Bourdieu 2000). The perspective taken here by Bourdieu, and others who share an equally pessimistic view of recognition, seems to confirm Yar's opinion that there is a tendency within critical and cultural theory to view Hegel's model of intersubjectivity in a negative light. As Kellner writes, "The Hegelian Master/Slave dialectic can help characterize relations between students and teachers today in which teachers force their curricula and agendas onto students in a situation in which there may be a mismatch between generational, cultural and social experiences and even subjectivities" (Kellner 2003, 67).

Of course there is always the potential for the abuse of power—it is the tension underpinning the master/slave dialectic—but this need not be the case. In a pedagogic context the dominant position a teacher exerts need not simply be read as a type of carte blanche for the maltreatment of students. This, however, is the perspective taken by progressivists who, in an attempt to neutralize this power and tip the balance in favor of the student, give emphasis to student-directed pedagogies. Jessica Benjamin explains, "Every binary split creates a temptation to merely reverse its terms, to elevate what has been devalued and denigrate what has been overvalued," but "what is necessary is not to take sides but to remain focused on the dualistic structure itself" (Benjamin 1988, 9). This seems a central point in understanding the pedagogic relation and the role of recognition within it: the relationship between teacher and student may not be an equal one but its success depends upon mutuality, a recognition of worth by both parties with this intersubjective acknowledgment being integral to their sense of self. Honneth (1995) takes a similar view in his account of recognition. With a more productive perspective on Hegel's master/slave dialectic, he describes how individual subjectivity is premised on the recognition of others. Power here is not neutralized. Rather, it can be conceived in Foucauldian terms as not simply repressive but enabling, with the moment of recognition involving at one and the same time a need for acknowledgment and a confirmation of self-worth. Integral to this process is the role of affect. Honneth explains, "Recognition itself must possess the character of affective approval or encouragement" (1995, 95). Affects, as such, are the corporeal instantiation of recognition, the sensations one may feel in being recognized, which accumulate over time, fostering a sense of self-worth. Moments of recognition, therefore, function as affective force, or in Spinozan terms, *affectus*.

While emphasis here is given to recognition as a positive process with the elicitation of positive affects, this may not always be the case. Recognition can also function in a negative way, carrying the resultant force of negative affects. In a classroom context this may involve a student being singled out for poor academic performance or behavior, which, if it is a common occurrence, may have a detrimental effect on the student's self-worth and desire to learn. Similarly, teachers' sense of worth can be shattered by the failure of students to behave and engage in the lessons they conduct, affecting their desire to teach. Negative affects, however, should not be viewed as all bad. In terms of subjectivity they may have what seems a contradictory effect. As Probyn explains in her account of shame, although it is a negative affect, it is only possible to feel a sense of shame if one possesses a degree of interest in the object that engenders this reaction (2005). Shame, as such, has a positive ethical dimension, an essential element of being human. Probyn bases this insight on the work of Silvan Tomkins (1962), who attaches considerable significance to negative affects in the process of learning. He provides an interesting critique of progressivist education in this regard and it is worthwhile to quote him at length on this point.

> Although the progressive education movement has stressed the importance of engaging the positive affects in education there has been a gross neglect of the significance of the mastery of negative affects. The reason is clear. Since the opposing philosophy of education had stressed rote, drill and discipline it was a natural assumption that the mastery of negative factors was restricted to this particular instance of puritanism and authoritarianism. But even a progressive philosophy of education must include prominently within its program the development of those abilities to tolerate negative affects. . . . (Tomkins 1962, 368)

At Tomkins's time of writing, progressivism was simply a movement. It was yet to achieve a position of paradigmatic dominance as has been the case in many Western countries from the mid-1970s.[3] Yet even at this point, prior to its mainstreaming as an educational philosophy, Tomkins was of the view that with an overemphasis on praise and positive reinforcement progressivism had failed to adequately equip students with the resources to counter, and perhaps more importantly accept, criticism, which is an important aspect of learning.

Recognition and Affect

A more positive interpretation of recognition that highlights reciprocity over domination and sociality over individuation is characteristic of much recent work in the field of child development studies, as in the work of Stern (1985)—as well as the earlier work of theorists such as Winnicott (1965, 1978, 2006) and Vygotsky (1986). Within a psychoanalytic framework there has been a shift in emphasis away from an understanding of the development of the infant psyche as based upon a Freudian model of "the drive-ridden ego" to one that relies upon interaction with significant others, especially the mother; it is a move, therefore, from the oedipal to the pre-oedipal, father to mother (Brennan 2004, 33). This shift within psychoanalytic thought has major implications for the study of pedagogy and, in particular, theorizing the nature of the pedagogic relation.

Yet notions of the solitary ego and an uncomfortable immersion in the social or symbolic prevail. Bourdieu, for example, ponders the move from "a narcissistic organisation of the libido in which the child takes himself as an object of desire to another state in which he orients himself towards another person, thus entering the world of object relations" (Bourdieu 2000, 166). In discussing this transition, Bourdieu refers to the "sacrifice of self-love" in which engagement in the social is represented as a loss, hence his negative perception of recognition as a loss of self. Given that Bourdieu's logic of practice is grounded in the notion of habitus, the embodiment of social structures that in turn structure individual action, this seems an unusual position on his part as it emphasizes reproduction over agency, the oft-made criticism of the habitus. Yet, as Noble explains, despite its usefulness, the focus of Bourdieu's construct is more about explicating social reproduction rather than examining subjectivity and interpersonal relations (Noble 2004). In positioning object relations as a phase following initial preoccupation with the self—the narcissistic ego—Bourdieu in a sense misrepresents Winnicott's perspective on child development.[4] Winnicott's theory of object relations is not about a move from an orientation of self to other. It is, in many respects, the opposite.

Winnicott's intention is to explain the process of differentiation. His focus is the move from what he views as complete union with the mother— hence his famous declaration that there is no such thing as an infant—to a position of independence as a separate self with his notion of transitional object mediating the process (Winnicott 1965, 39). In doing this, however, Winnicott gives emphasis to the interaction between mother and child with the development of self premised on intersubjective engagement.[5] Recognition is central to this process. As Kojeve points out, "The establishment of one's self-understanding is inextricably dependent on recognition or affirmation on the part of others" (1969, 11). In explaining the development of a sense of self, the issue for Winnicott is not simply how we become independent of the other but, as Jessica Benjamin explains, "how we actively engage and make ourselves known in relationship to the other" (1988, 18). Winnicott stresses that independence is premised on initial periods of dependence and that this dependence has actually grown out of what he terms "double dependence" (2006, 5). His reasoning here has much to offer pedagogic theory as it typifies the mutual recognition underpinning a productive conceptualization of the pedagogic relation of teacher and student. Another dimension to how such a connection with the other frames our notion of self is discussed by Honneth (1995, 99). Drawing on Winnicott, he refers to the ways in which infants gain a sense of bodily schema through the process of being held. Intercorporeality, skin acting on skin, the sense of touch, and the affective realm allows one to know one's body. A similar perspective is evident in Merleau-Ponty's phenomenology of the body: understanding our somatic selves through engagement with the world (1999).

In more recent work in the area of child development from the 1980s, Stern gives a similar emphasis to the role of intersubjectivity in the formation of the self. Yet his starting point and the way in which he maps development are quite different to those of Winnicott. To Stern there is no point at which the infant is confused in relation to a sense of self and other where development entails a process of differentiation. To Stern infants are "predesigned to be aware of self-organising processes" (1985, 10). He is interested in how different senses of the self manifest—an emergent self, a core self, a subjective self, and a verbal self—which, to Stern, are not successive phases of development. He explains that once acquired each of these aspects of self continues to function and remain active throughout one's life. These different senses of self are each a product of increasingly complex forms of relatedness beginning with the mother/child dyad as the primary relation of intersubjective engagement. This is an accumulation of self that seems dependent upon an accumulation of affect, which Stern alludes to in his account of mother/child interaction.

In discussion of this dyadic interaction and the ways in which infants engage with the world psychologists make reference to what is termed "contingent responsiveness," that is, the sense of pleasure an infant feels in response to a reaction of which he or she is the cause (Benjamin 1988, 21). This could involve pushing a ball or other toy and the joy that ensues in making it move. While the infant expresses joy in the response of the inanimate object, it proves to be more pleasurable if this is accompanied by a reaction from the mother or significant other. What becomes important in the repeated performance of this activity is not so much the action itself but the *re*action of another subject and the sense of recognition it generates. This acknowledgment acts as a spur for further action; the desire for recognition on the part of the infant instills a form of agency in the successful completion of the process involved in making an object move. In this instance the desire for recognition is not one-sided; it is mutual. The mother likewise desires the recognition of her child and gains fulfillment in his or her responsive play. So, despite the differential power relationship between mother and child, there is both a need to recognize the other and in turn to be recognized. In discussing this dialogic play between mother and child Jessica Benjamin refers to studies that provide a frame by frame analysis of the facial, gestural, and vocal actions and reactions of both parties that reveal a kind of "dance of interaction" (1988, 27). Benjamin explains that "the partners are so attuned that they move together in unison" with this play of mutual recognition seemingly fueled by affect (27).

This interaffectivity is a key concern of Stern. He points out that "the sharing of affective states is the most pervasive and clinically germane feature of intersubjective relatedness" (Stern 1985, 138). Elsewhere he stresses that it is only through the intensity of this form of interaction that infants are able to attain high levels of feeling (Stern 1993, 207). What the infant experiences, however, is not simply joy—this amplification of feeling has direct links with cognition. Prior to the work of Tomkins it was thought that affect and cognition were separate and unrelated functions, yet while affect can operate independently, Tomkins was able to demonstrate its impact on both thought and behavior, in a sense confirming the psychophysical parallelism expounded by Spinoza and also the relationality of affect (Angel and Gibbs 2006).[6] The interrelationship between affect and cognition and the difficulty in identifying the former's effect on the latter is perhaps best demonstrated by an examination of the affect of interest. Tomkins explains how in his work on the emotions Darwin overlooked interest altogether, confusing it with the function of thinking (1962, 338). To Tomkins, however, "the absence of the affective support of interest would jeopardize intellectual development no less than destruction of brain tissue" (343).

The relationship between affect and cognition and the heightening of affect that recognition can evoke are of particular importance to pedagogic theory in terms of what they suggest about the significance of the pedagogic relation of teacher and student: the ways in which a teacher's support influences a student's learning. While the focus of Stern's work is the interpersonal world of the infant, and so his argument about the relationship between affect amplification and interpersonal engagement relates to the early years of life, he is also of the view that while adults can reach high levels of joy when alone, this is largely dependent on an imagined other. Intensification of positive affects—as in interest—seems a function of engagement with others and, pedagogically, a significant other. The techniques teachers utilize in classrooms can act as a force promoting interest, which over time may accumulate as cognitive capacity providing its own stimulus for learning, a point I will return to below.

Accumulating Affect

In Stern's discussion of affect, however, he does not simply refer to categorical affects such as those identified by Tomkins. He also documents what he terms "vitality affects"—"those dynamic, kinetic qualities of feeling . . . that correspond to the momentary changes in feeling states involved in the organic processes of being alive" (Stern 1985, 156).[7] He explains: "They concern *how* a behaviour, *any* behaviour, *all* behaviour is performed, not *what* behaviour is performed" (Stern 1985, 157, emphasis in original). This notion of vitality affects seems to nicely complement specific categories of affect as together they can account for the ongoing interaction between self and other, self and world. These may peak at particular intervals with the experience of positive affects, such as joy or interest, or negative affects, such as shame or disgust, but, although the general flow of sensation—what Stern nicely terms "the interpersonal traffic of feeling"—is decidedly less intense, it still possesses an affective quality contributing to different states of being. Affect, as it is understood here, is not viewed as simply transient in quality. These states of being are not only momentary. Through the iteration of similar experiences, and therefore similar affects, they accumulate in the form of what could be considered dispositions that predispose one to act and react in particular ways.

In much of the quite diverse literature on affect, from psychology and philosophy to cultural studies and literary theory, this ability of affect to accumulate is either denied or rarely made explicit. Affect, as a bodily phenomenon, is typically conceived as fleeting, whereas emotion, with its cognitive dimension, is viewed as long-lasting, triggered on an ongoing basis throughout one's life.[8] Massumi, for example, sees emotion as the capture of affect given that the latter "escapes confinement" (2002, 35). Nathanson similarly explains that "affect lasts but a few seconds" (1992, 51). From his perspective "affect is biology whereas emotion is biography" (Nathanson 1992, 50). In making this distinction Nathanson does point out that "an organism" has the ability to retain and store information, but this storage capacity seems almost exclusively a mindful phenomenon, namely as memories that produce emotion. Affect, as such, is viewed as the biological component of emotion. While this may be the case, affect also operates independently, accumulating as *bodily* memory that, while both aiding cognition and inducing behavior, may evade consciousness altogether. This is perhaps best demonstrated by an example offered by Shouse (2005). He recounts the case of an elderly female patient of the neurologist Oliver Sacks who suffered an accident and lost all feeling in her legs for a period of three years. Continued therapy to help her regain mobility proved unsuccessful until Sacks noticed that her foot would tap in time involuntarily when she listened to music. After a change to music therapy, she eventually made a full recovery. Shouse uses this case to highlight how affect trumps will, with the recollection of music stored in the body prompting the woman's leg to move. He also thinks that it shows how affect always precedes both will and consciousness.

Something, however, seems to be missing from this analysis. While Shouse points out how the body is continually affected by numerous stimuli, which it in turn "infolds," registering them as intensities, this does not capture the ways in which affect actually accumulates in the body or the role of pedagogy in the process. This woman's involuntary tapping of her foot to music seems to indicate a lifetime of listening to music, perhaps learning an instrument or how to dance and embodying particular rhythms. Affect here does not so much *precede* will and consciousness, it simply evades or bypasses them, provoking habituated behavior stored in what could be termed "muscular memory," the "motor significance" of which Merleau-Ponty writes (1999).[9] This is not to suggest that affect always operates independently. As mentioned, affect provides a motivating force for consciousness. But while stressing their relationship, it is important to maintain an analytic distinction between mind and body, consciousness and unconsciousness, emotion and affect given the pedagogic implications of each category. Also, my interest is not so much the role of emotions within education but that of affect and the ways in which its accumulation within the body can promote the desire and capacity to learn.

Affect and the Pedagogic Relation

It is this ability of affect to accumulate and its relationship to recognition that I want to consider in terms of the interaction of teacher and students, particularly on a whole-class basis, and the ways in which teaching and learning seem fueled by these interconnected processes. Learning is generally conceived as a cognitive activity. While it has an affective dimension this seems to receive very little theoretical explication. The connection Tomkins makes between affect and cognition has been mentioned. Stern, similarly, is of the view that "affective and cognitive processes cannot be readily separated" and explains how "learning itself is motivated and affect laden" (Stern 1985, 42). This is a view shared by the early twentieth-century Russian psychologist Lev Vygotsky, a leading figure in the field of child language development. He was interested in the relationship between intellect and affect and remarked that "among the most basic defects of traditional approaches to the study of psychology has been the isolation of the intellectual from the volitional and affective aspects of consciousness" (Vygotsky 1987, 50). Within education Vygotsky is best known for his theory of the zone of proximal development or ZPD, which refers to the gap between children's actual development determined by independent problem solving and their potential development achieved when assisted (Vygotsky 1986, 187). Vygotsky was interested in the benefits of play and peer support in learning but attributed greater significance to the role of teachers and the support they provided students. He was actually a fierce critic of the progressivist free education movement prevalent in the Soviet Union during the 1920s (Van der Veer and Valsiner 1991, 53) and claimed, "Instruction is one of the principal sources of the schoolchild's concepts and is also a powerful force in directing their evolution; it determines the fate of [their] total mental development" (Vygotsky 1986, 157).

While Vygotsky gave some account of the influence of affect on language, due to his untimely death he was never able to elaborate his ideas about affect and learning (Vygotsky 1986). Given more recent developments in this field, as in the work of Stern, it seems that affect and interaffectivity could be especially useful in the theorization of pedagogic practice and engagement in learning, allowing for a more positive interpretation of the teacher's role in line with Vygotsky's notion of the ZPD.

These ideas came to mind as I was interviewing teachers as part of a study into teaching desire—a notion that can be understood as a double articulation of both the drive or motivation to teach and the engagement to learn that this can promote in students. As less and less emphasis seems to be placed on whole-class instruction, with a preference for independent and group-based learning, especially in primary or elementary school contexts, I was keen to investigate which pedagogic modes teachers considered the most effective and which gave them the greatest sense of satisfaction. The study involved interviews with twelve teachers and their principals in three schools within the Sydney metropolitan area of New South Wales, Australia. The teachers taught a spread of grades, from kindergarten to sixth grade, and ranged in age from twenty-two to sixty-four, possessing, therefore, a range of experience and understanding of the profession. The schools similarly represented a diverse group in terms of geographic location across Sydney and the socioeconomic status and ethnic mix of students. The focus here, however, is not so much the study, which is discussed in detail elsewhere (see Watkins 2007). Instead, I want to refer to a number of teachers' comments from both this study and an earlier investigation (Watkins 2006) and the account that one in particular provided of her teaching that exemplifies the affective dimensions of pedagogy presented here. My intention is not to present this example as empirical proof but rather to simply use it to lend support to the notion of an accumulation of affect and the ways in which more detailed analysis of the pedagogic relation could prove fruitful in explicating this point.

In interviewing the teachers I began by asking them about their practice and having them identify their pedagogy as being either more teacher- or student-directed. As with most of the teachers in this study, Nerida, a second-grade teacher, saw her approach to teaching as more student-directed or progressivist in design. Nerida was one of the mid-career teachers involved in the study. She had been teaching for thirteen years and trained at a time when emphasis was given to progressivist techniques of teaching and learning, a perspective still dominant within Australian teacher-training institutions. As Nerida explained, "They encouraged the teacher to be more of a facilitator rather than the person who stands up the front and gives information. Do you know what I mean? You are facilitating their learning. You are giving ideas."

Nerida displayed a reluctance to foreground her role in the classroom and her involvement in her students' learning. As the interview progressed, however, and she began to discuss specific examples of her practice, it became clear that her desire to teach was more obviously realized through whole-class instruction; the actual performance of teaching and engaging with students. While Nerida seemed unable to explicitly articulate this desire, there were a couple of teachers who reluctantly did so. For example, Sally, a more experienced teacher in another school, remarked, "I have to admit I like my place up front and centre for instruction." Two other teachers, commenting on what they considered the key ingredients for effective teaching, pointed out how important it was to get their students' attention. "I see it as performing," said one. "You need to perform, get them in, and keep them there. You need to be really animated I think to keep their attention." A colleague added, "To teach properly you really have to teach. You have to be a teacher out the front [*sic*]. I mean I still believe that, I really do. That's the one thing I'm a great believer in and really going around to kids on the spot."

While not acknowledging the centrality of her position in the classroom, Nerida took great delight in describing a lesson on syllable poems that had taken place on the day of the interview that exemplifies this. Nerida was teaching at Spring Hill Public School, located in the more affluent northern suburbs of Sydney with a student population high in socioeconomic status but low in the number with a language background other than English. Like most primary or elementary classes in New South Wales, Nerida's second-grade class of eight- and nine-year-olds was of mixed ability, though in terms of state averages in literacy and numeracy they were of a higher standard. In discussing this lesson she explained, "Today it was just one of those lessons where it was like, 'Wow,' I wish every day was like that. And, we made one up together and they were coming up with all these fantastic descriptive words and this whole year I've been drumming it into them."

She then provided more detail about her role in the lesson: "Well, we made it quite fun. Like I was hopping in and out of them and walking in amongst them and I'm going, 'Okay, what's another descriptive word about this?,' and then they would all cheer and I'd write it on the board. And do you know what I mean? I suppose it is your personality that comes through."

In explaining the effect of the lesson on both herself and the class, she pointed out that, "you have the same feeling I think as the kids because they are excited about a particular activity, or a particular experience and you think 'Oh!' You are excited for them because what you wanted them to learn is what they're actually learning . . . Yeah. And so they did it and it was just like you could see the kids' faces. I mean I know it's like the cliché thing, but you could just tell that they were so into it."

In this brief account of her lesson Nerida effectively captures the way in which her pedagogy has an impact upon her students. In teaching the class she was doing more than assisting students to arrive at a bank of words they could use in their own poems, with this input acting as an aid to cognition; the desire that was driving this teacher's performance seemed translated through the act of teaching into a desire to learn, a potent force or series of affects that her students embodied, prompting their engagement in the lesson. What is evident here is something akin to the dance of interaction between mother and child that Jessica Benjamin describes, a form of mutual recognition en masse that seems to captivate both teacher and students, heightening the learning experience and the effectiveness of Nerida's pedagogy. As she explains, "You have the same feeling." This affect attunement to which Stern refers is amplified here given the whole-class nature of the learning activity, as opposed to students working independently or in small groups (1985). This is not simply a dyadic relation of teacher and student, but rather the excitement and interest that are generated prove contagious with other students keen to be involved as part of the experience. This contagious nature of affect has been explored by Tomkins (1962) and more recently by Brennan (2004), who borrows the neurological term "entrainment" in discussing how the nervous and hormonal systems are activated by this process.

The contagion that seems evident from Nerida's account, and what she sees as the success of not only her lesson but the poems that the students produced both as a class and later individually, did not simply result from this singular affective experience. These effects, and in particular the quality of the writing that the students later produced, seem indicative of an accumulation of affect. While individuals are innately predisposed to affective response, much of what we respond to, and how we respond, is a consequence of learning: the repeated experience of similar affects accumulating in a dispositional tendency. As Nerida explained, she had spent "this whole year drumming it into them." Many of her students reacted the way they did as throughout the year she had encouraged an interest in writing, which this account of her lesson demonstrates, and this interest had fueled their desire to learn.[10] As Tomkins explains, "Interest has a physiological function as an aid to sustained effort" (1962, 337). In applying themselves as a result of the interest she promoted, Nerida's students had embodied the skills to write effectively. As with the mother/child dyad, however, the relationship between teacher and students is also unequal, yet this does not rule out the desire for mutual recognition. Despite her dominant position, Nerida seems intent on acquiring the recognition of her students and it is this that engenders her desire to teach. Similarly, the students' desire to please their teacher serves to promote their engagement in learning and further the interest already ignited, which, as Nerida recounts, is clearly evident in the expression on their faces, what Tomkins considers the primary site of affect.

Concluding Remarks

What this example suggests is that pedagogy plays an important role in the accumulation of affects that can generate a desire to learn. The role of the teacher, however, seems central to this process, as Vygotsky demonstrates in relation to his notion of a ZPD. Rather than emphasizing the potentially abusive nature of this relation, it is important to stay mindful of the insights provided by child development studies that emphasize the intersubjective nature of the formation of self and the important role of recognition within this. As Reed explains, "Becoming a self is something one cannot do on one's own; it is an intensely social process" (1995, 431). The social, however, as it is embodied as an ongoing series of affective transactions, needs to be conceived not only as a source of subjection but as a site of possibilities. It is cogent to conceive of teaching desire in much the same way: that is, as a force with productive potential. Giving emphasis to learning over teaching de-emphasizes the teacher's role and the potentially powerful ways in which recognition and interaffectivity can augment the pedagogic process. While power may be ever present, it provides the means through which agency is achieved. As such, the transformative potential of education can be more effectively theorized as for too long it has been clouded by the tired critique of both reproduction models and critical pedagogy that seek to downplay the role of the teacher and give students responsibility for their own learning, assuming power is only a force to be resisted rather than embodied as capacity with agentic potential.

Notes

1   There are exceptions to this interpretation of affect. Gregg, for example, examines the use of affective address employed by key figures in cultural studies, arguing that the writing technologies they employ do have a lasting political impact (2006).

2   In some cases online learning functions as an intersubjective experience between teacher and student but, given that the exchange is mediated by technology, the kind of affect that is produced is quite different.

3   For a historical account of the impact of progressivism, see Cope and Kalantzis 1993.

4   Piaget theorizes this move in a similar way as is evident in his examination of the transition from what he refers to as "egocentric" to "social" speech (1997).

5   In much of the child development literature reference is made to the mother/child dyad. Contact with the mother is viewed as the primary initial relationship of the infant. While in many cases fathers now take a much more significant role in raising children in contemporary Western society, the term "mother" is used here rather

than "caregiver" given that the mother generally retains a more significant role, particularly during the first six months, in which breastfeeding occurs. Also much of the research drawn upon here makes use of this term.

6   More recent work in neuroscience confirms the interaction between neural systems of emotion and those underlying cognitive functioning. On this point, see Phelps, who explains that "these interactions have prompted a reconsideration of the appropriate role of emotion in efforts to understand cognition" (2005, 52).

7   Stern actually makes reference to three categories of affect: categorical affects, vitality affects, and relational affects (1993). He explains that this third category or "register of feelings" operates in parallel with the other two and concerns the feelings of being loved, hated, secure, and so forth. While Stern is of the view that relational affects cannot be reduced to the categorical or vitality affects and so must form a separate type, I do not find this a particularly useful distinction as it could be argued that most affects are relational when they involve another animate body.

8   For a more detailed discussion of the distinction between affect and emotion, see Watkins 2006.

9   Maria Montessori makes use of the term "muscular memory," a form of bodily know-how required to successfully perform different tasks (1966, 145). To assist in the development of physiological movements she advocated that children perform certain exercises on a repetitive basis to ensure they habituated particular skills.

10   See Watkins 2006, which draws on observational data in a classroom with students exhibiting similar reactions to the techniques their teacher employed.

PART FIVE   AFTER AFFECT

13 UNDERSTANDING THE MATERIAL
PRACTICES OF GLAMOUR

Nigel Thrift

The affective moment has passed in that it is no longer enough
to observe that affect is important: in that sense at least we are
in the moment after the affective moment. That this is the case
can I think be demonstrated in several ways. One is the wealth
of studies that are now appearing that are concerned with the
analysis of specific forms of affect as a means of investigating
particular political-cum-cultural situations (for example, Berlant 2004, 2006, 2007a; Gallop 2006; Ngai 2005; Stewart 2007;
Thrailkill 2007). Another is the way in which specific theoretical and methodological traditions that have taken affect to be a
crucial element of their makeup have begun to deepen their
analyses, whether that be the case of the Italian *operaismo* tradition's use of the twinned notions of immaterial and affective
labor (for example, Berlant 2007b, Dowling, Nunes, and Trott
2007) or more conventional accounts of the hidden injuries of
class (for example, Reay 2005). Yet another is the way in which
the affective moment has begun to produce its own wares,
which are becoming an accepted part of the environment we
inhabit: in particular, I am thinking here of recent excursions
in installation and site-specific and conversational and par-

ticipatory art, which, though they take their inspiration from particular theories of affect, turn out to be much more than simple extensions of these theories (for example, Bishop 2005). Then, finally, there is the way in which affect has simply become an accepted background to so much work, a necessary part of the firmament through which the forms and shifts of any analysis are extruded.

This essay fits into this latter category. In particular, it follows the path first laid down by Gabriel Tarde in understanding economies as being about the generation of passionate interests (Barry and Thrift 2007). It follows from Tarde's account that economies must be engaging: they must generate or scoop up affects and then aggregate and amplify them in order to produce value, and that must involve producing various mechanisms of fascination. The economy is not, and never has been, a dismal science of simple profit and loss (although many of its effects are no doubt dismal). Tarde's account is only underlined by a situation of growing affluence wherein the difference between products and environments is often slight. In a crowded marketplace, the practices of aesthetics may be the only way to make a product or environment stand out from the crowd, especially given a growing emphasis on individual identity and individual style. In other words, the ability to generate a certain kind of secular magic that can act as a means of willing captivation becomes a key means of producing dividends.[1]

This essay is therefore concerned with how imagination of the commodity is being captured and bent to capitalist means through a series of "magical" *technologies of public intimacy*, most of them with long historical genealogies. Each of these technologies demonstrates the singular quality of *allure* through the establishment of human-nonhuman fields of captivation, for what seems certain is that many of the objects and environments that capitalism produces have to demonstrate the calculated sincerity of allure if people are to be attracted to them: they need to manifest a particular style that generates enchantment without supernaturalism. Currently, I argue, this quality of allure is being applied in all kinds of new ways, producing a more magical world that is also, at one and the same time, more calculated. In the process, new "intangible" value is being generated for industries that are already some of the world's key means of making money.

The essay is therefore structured in three parts. The first part establishes the ground for the argument by addressing the question of aesthetics as the hallmark of allure and one of the main means by which allure circulates, namely through the institutions of public intimacy (or what is sometimes called "extimacy"). The second part considers one particular form of the technology of allure, namely glamour. I will argue that this form of allure blurs the boundary between person and thing in order to produce greater captivation, in ways that are more often thought to be typical of certain Micronesian cultures where, for example, bodies do not exist as autonomous entities but have the capacity to act directly upon one another: persons are "fractal," able to incorporate others and parts of others (Bamford 2007). I will illustrate this contention by dint of two examples of colorful materials that cling to and transform glamour, respectively new designs of environment and hair. These examples both underline how the object world intervenes forcefully in the world's being there, as materials that occupy a zone that is neither alive nor dead, rather than being an exclusively human projection, and lead into the ways in which capitalism is currently involved in "worlding." Whether these developments are a matter for despair I leave until the concluding section of the essay, where I briefly address questions of aesthetics and morality.

Imagination and Aesthetics

Contemporary capitalism's magical powers arise from two intersecting imaginary forces, namely the force of aesthetic practices, honed now over a number of centuries, and the rise of so-called public intimacy, a series of practices with an equally long historical bloodline. Let me begin by touching on the *practical aesthetic imagination*.

It is crucial to note here that aesthetics is understood as a fundamental element of human life and not just an additional luxury, a frivolous add-on when times are good. Postrel puts it thus:

> Aesthetics is the way we communicate through the senses. It is the art of creating reactions without words, through the look and feel of people, places, and things. Hence, aesthetics differs from entertainment that requires cognitive engagement with narrative, word play, or complex, intellectual allusion. While the sound of poetry is arguably aesthetic, the meaning is not. Spectacular special effects and beautiful movie stars enhance box-office success in foreign markets because they offer universal aesthetic pleasure; clever dialogue which is cognitive and culture-bound doesn't travel as well. Aesthetics may complement storytelling, but is not itself narrative. Aesthetics shows rather than tells, delights rather than instructs. The effects are immediate, perceptual, and emotional. (2003, 6)

The point is that aesthetic pleasure has quality and substance that is generated by that side of sensation that is sheer formless enjoyment (Harman 2005). It is an *affective* force that is active, intelligible, and has genuine efficacy: it is both moved and moving (Thrift forthcoming). It is a force that generates sensory and emotional gratification. It is a force that produces shared capacity and commonality. It is a force that, though cross-cut by all kinds of impulses, has its own intrinsic value.

Aesthetic practices can take on a number of forms but among their chief expressions must surely be the vast spectrum of consumer objects that, as numerous ethnographies have shown, are able to produce all kinds of affective allegiances. Aesthetics is bound up with the discovery of new and alluring imaginative territories that reflect upon themselves. Though these territories are usually vicarious they are no less real for that. Goods are a substantial part of this process of imaginative exploration. From early on, goods have provided a sensual means of inhabitation that is also a *means of captivation.* As elements of aesthetic experience, they do not just provide evocations of times past or moral reckonings but affective senses of space, literally territories of feeling.

But in making such a claim about aesthetic enhancement, I want to go one stage further for I also want to claim that the aesthetic objects have their own existence. As Thrailkill puts it, aesthetic objects are "more than telegraphs of meaning that either are received as a form of penetration or possession ('sink[ing] right into your brainstem' as Walter Michaels writes) or remain forever unread, unreceived, and unrecognised ('we cannot know each other,' as Janet Malcolm puts this position)" (2007, 250). Thus, on one level, they are, as I have pointed out, connection machines, technologies that facilitate imaginary recognitions. But on another level they inhabit a separate existence. Qualities can belong to objects themselves rather than to our consciousness of them; they are not inert targets for our thoughts to animate (Harman 2005). In other words, I want to make space for the stuff of aesthetics as not just about human access to objects. Objects must be understood as involved in multiple overlapping negotiations with human being and not just as sets of passive and inanimate properties.

The power of objects is crucial to the account of aesthetics that I want to give, so I will expand upon this point. Objects are not there simply to furnish a human world as a feature of human perception that follows us around wherever we may be, only existing when chaperoned by a human subject (Harman 2005). They are a feature of reality itself that can be deployed at many levels at once, some of which intersect with the homeland of human presence and perception, some of which do not. They are a surplus. They are, as Harman (2005) would have it, "phosphorescent." Thus, the human contains all manner of objects within its envelope but it does not exhaust their presence, so that objects can signal in all kinds of ways that we may only partially perceive, or perceive as "magical" in that they provide associations and conjunctions, dissociations and echoes, that stimulate perception and imagination and, indeed, enjoyment. They allow us to create mental objects that can be briefly fixed, not only achieving a contouring of perceptions but also allowing these perceptions to ripple out as surges of affect (Stafford 2007). Contemporary art works have struggled precisely to illuminate these qualities, producing diagrams and animated tableaux that briefly stabilize a continuously mutating process.

While we need to be careful about arguing that more goods exist now than ever before or that they have increased in importance, something has changed in the last thirty years or so. Affluence has become much more general, in part because of the invention of lifestyle consumption, which stresses the expressive freedom of the individual and specifically an aesthetic economy that has generated ever-increasing value (Binkley 2007). This individuation of consumption, and the conformist nonconformity that arrived with it, produced not only a much greater emphasis on aesthetics in its own right but a number of other aesthetic results too. The first was the generalization of style. There is no one style of aesthetic expression that is now regnant. Rather, rigid hierarchies have broken down and a whole series of styles coexist. There is no one best way. A kind of aesthetic pluralism has become dominant. The second result was a much greater concentration on affect as a key to aesthetic design. As Postrel points out, "form follows function" has been supplanted by "form follows emotion" (2003, 9). The third result was an unparalleled aesthetic plenitude as once rigid style hierarchies have broken down. Fueled by rising incomes and falling prices, as well as more efficient methods of distribution and new product sources, something like a state of aesthetic abundance has been reached and that abundance reaches into the working class. Capitalist firms have both driven these developments with their attempts to produce market segmentation and customization and been forced to follow them: the attention recently to getting to know customers via the Internet is not just a commercial strategy but a sometimes desperate attempt to keep up with what customers' changing needs and wants may be. What follows is that we live in an expressive age in which aesthetics is both a key social moment and a key means of generating economic value (Lash and Lury 2007).

But, or so I will argue, my account cannot be complete without pointing to the evolution of another key imaginary force, namely the rise of *public intimacy* provided by the continuous development of new media forms. Again, I want to start back in the long eighteenth century with the decisive popular fusion of sensibility and taste, what would now be thought of as emotional susceptibility and aesthetic expression (Ellison 1999). The affective and the aesthetic were bound together by a code of intimacy, but it was a peculiar kind of intimacy. At this time the Western pact of intimacy was finally sealed.

In other words the public sphere is increasingly used to communicate what were once regarded as private passions. While once such a means of proceeding had been confined to the seventeenth-century stage, when both the prologues and epilogues of plays might allude to the sex lives of their renowned actresses offstage, thereby allowing both foreground and background to intermingle in a new combination, it has now become a routine form of sociability, amplified by the Internet and its numerous means of producing *synthetic experience*, experience that is fabricated to imitate or replace unobtainable realities and which, in the process, becomes a reality itself.

There are several ways of interpreting this state of affairs, of course. One is procedural: the always suspect divide between the social and psychological has broken down for good (Latour 2007). Another is based in critique: we live in a world of inward-looking consumer monads that are, as Sloterdijk (2007) puts it, "interidiotically" stable, endlessly repeating themselves in a frenzy of seemingly original but actually standardized affective gestures. Another is economic: public intimacy has a value and profit can be got from it. Whatever the case, there is evidence that public intimacy is now becoming an even more important impulse. We need to be careful in making such a historical judgment, of course, but the sheer weight of aesthetic machinery of public intimacy that is now available, the result especially of the preponderance of information technology, new materials that allow new surfaces to be produced, and new means of making connections, is currently of such consequence that it does more than intermediate. It generates the potential to produce a new range of means of sensing objects, not least by producing new forms of allure.

The result of the intertwining of these two imaginary forces is clear.

Aesthetics and public intimacy are being intertwined in new ways as part of what I call "*worlds*," spaces formed by capitalism whose aim is not to create subjects (as happened in the older disciplinary regimes) so much as the world within which the subject exists (Lazzarato 2004). These spaces can be understood as new forms of body with the capacity to alert us to that which was previously unable to be sensed—with the obvious corollary that certain objects can no longer be sensed—so producing the potential to generate new kinds of charm.

Now, by using the term worlds, I do not just mean the ability to produce customized environments, often designed down to the last tile, of the kind found in some malls, theme parks, and indeed computer games. I mean the ability to produce more generally *digestible* environments filled with objects that provide messages that employ all kinds of aesthetic norm. These messages are often diffuse because what are being brought together are things, not properties. But sometimes they cohere into a system that actively shapes intelligibility, what Harman calls a "cryptic totality" (2005). Such a viewpoint is akin to that of Max Black, who observes that the meaning of wolf is really "a wolf-system of related commonplaces." In other words, "In most cases there is not one wolf-quality in particular that catches our eye, since the metaphor leaves vague exactly what we are supposed to look at. Instead, there is a kind of electrical infrastructure of half-intuited wolf-marks and wolf-tokens" (quoted in Harman 2005, 119).

Thus, worlds have their own practices of *rendering prominent*, which bring together humans and nonhumans in all kinds of distributed combinations, giving rise to a particular style of going on that consequently focuses passions. These distributed combinations will be full of stock characters and icons, surfaces and colors, which feed on a particular historical unconscious. And they can trigger off all kinds of effervescent imitative behaviors, mimetic fields that can spread rapidly (Thrift forthcoming). But as the wolf example makes clear, worlds do not have to be designed down to the last detail or be complete and completed totalities, as once was often the case. And this means that their spatial character can be diffuse. It might be that sometimes a bounded space exactly corresponds to a world. More likely, though, a world will be a series of lines of association crisscrossing those of other worlds but occupying some of the same spaces, even if fleetingly.

In particular, the imagination can be captured and guided by a whole set of affective devices that are now able to be introduced into these worlds in ways that would have been difficult before—new kinds of cultural nerve, if you like, which build extra facets of "you." The invention of melodrama in the nineteenth century, the reinvention of the decisive moment as a result of photography and cinema in the early twentieth century, the allure of the extreme in the late twentieth century, all come to mind as examples of ways in which (if it is not a contradiction in terms) a *nondiscursive narrative intelligence* has gradually been developed, which allows the passions to be deployed to economic advantage by allowing consumer situations to be " 'moved' in the dual sense of emotionally engaged *and* repositioned with respect to the world" (Thrailkill 2006, 366, emphasis added). The restlessness of the imagination becomes an asset that can be valorized as everyday life becomes a cavalcade of aesthetically charged moments that can be used for profit, not least because *every surface communicates*.

In other words, I want to argue that nowadays the allure in allure is largely produced by the creation of worlds in which the boundaries between alive and not alive and material and immaterial have become increasingly blurred, so that what was considered as alive can become thing-like and what was considered as dead is able to show signs of life. I am not arguing that these lifelike objects are considered to be alive, but neither are they considered to be mere evocations. They are allowed a psychology (Turkle 2005). And because of their uncertain status, they are able to fascinate, that is to stimulate explorations of their nature and character because they are able to arouse repeated interest or stimulate curiosity. In the next section, I will attempt to illustrate the way that capitalism has played with these boundaries in order to produce semblances of life, likenesses that have a certain spectral quality that is undoubtedly about show and indeed calculation—and yet which still holds us in its grip.

Technologies of Glamour

So how does capitalism make its mark on the aesthetic sphere? What is the source of value? And how does it operationalize it? I want to pick out two technologies that act as crucial parts of the generation of allure, a quality that like other forms of charm limits and fixes our vision but also acts as a tool of exploration. Both technologies might be considered as magical in the sense that they seem to have a life of their own, part human, part something else. And that is exactly the point: they do. If we had to describe this kindred, magical quality, it might be better to describe it through the descriptor of style.

However, style does not consist of a list of factors that have to be ticked off, nor does it constitute a totality of meaning. *Style is a modification of being that produces captivation, in part through our own explorations of it.* Style wants us to love it and we want to be charmed by it; we want to emulate it, we want to be definite about it, we want to be absorbed by it, we want to lend ourselves to what it has become. Style, in other words, can be counted as an agent in its own right in that it defines what is at issue in the world that we can engage with (Harman 2005). With this minimal definition in play we can now move on to consider how capitalism captivates by addressing a specific style of allure, namely *glamour*.

Glamour

Glamour is a constant if fitful quality in consumer spaces, arising out of an environment that mixes human and nonhuman so as to produce captivation. But where did glamour originate from? How did it become an affective field that so many people feel inclined to explore? In this section and the next, I will recount a capsule history of glamour, and especially the role of theater, film, and performance, and try to set down why it has become more important and now has such a grip on Euro-American civilization.

Affluence brings with it the construction of the quality of glamour as a key imaginary in producing allure. In using the term "glamour," I am aware of a certain awkwardness of expression. But I need a term that operates in the everyday and as both an economic and an imaginative force, as (in its eighteenth-century meaning of magic or enchantment) a spell that is both erudite and occult but that can also encompass the nineteenth-century meaning of "a deceptive or bewitching beauty or charm" as well as its current usage, which denotes the spell cast by unobtainable realities. And glamour does this. For all its breathtaking qualities, glamour does not conjure up awe. It operates on a human scale, in the everyday, inviting just enough familiarity to engage the imagination, a glimpse of another life, utopia as a tactile presence: "lasting objects of perfection to be held in your hands" (Postrel 2005, 31). Glamour is about that special excitement and attractiveness that characterizes some objects and people. Glamour is a form of secular magic, conjured up by the commercial sphere. We might see it as a fetish, or as a means of feeling thought and tasting thought. What is clear is that we seek it out. And what is it that we are seeking out?

Glamour depends upon three cultural pillars. The first pillar is the object effect: an object standing for a world without troubles or with troubles you want. One way of understanding this effect is as displaced meaning (Mc-Cracken 1996). As sources of identity and hope every culture displays ideals that can never be fully realized in everyday life, ideals that "may uphold incompatible principles, deny the relations of cause and effect, require impossible knowledge, or demand more emotionally contradictory behaviour than human beings can sustain" (Postrel 2003, 31). But these ideals can be glimpsed in the imaginary realm, not least as worlds in which these ideals can be realized—as fleeting daydreams and fantasies, or as more comprehensively worked out paradises, utopias, and worlds to come—worlds in which stock characters, different stories of good or bad behavior, striking artifacts, compulsive geographies, and strong emotions make cherished imaginary abstractions seem attainable through their "unconscious poetry." "When they are transported to a distant cultural domain, ideals are made to seem practicable realities. What is otherwise unsubstantiated and culturally improbable in the present world is now validated, somehow 'proven' by its existence in another, distant one" (McCracken 1996, 106).

These worlds count as synthetic experiences that are both a repository and a generator of vicarious experience, experience that occupies an imaginary space but that is no less real for that. They are "fictions that have taken up residence in reality" (Wood 2005, 12). Imagination is itself lived experience. But to understand imagination as experience requires a greater understanding of space.

The second pillar is engaging alternate versions of "me" that can act as a particular imaginary norm, often speculatively and in parallel, in order to realize a particular form of character (McCloskey 2006). This is a reflexivity based on the centrality of play with an "episodic self" (Stafford 2007). It consists of knowingly engaging in self-representation and receiving affirmation from an audience, as an actor does. But this time the audience is the self. What we see, in other words, is the creation of worlds of virtual self-difference that allow "extra-yous" to thrive; these "extra yous" are "at once subject and object, knower and known, representer and that which is being represented" (Thrailkill 2006, 382). These new yous constitute "a productively divided state of being in which one seeks or receives insight into one's own perceptual experience" (Thrailkill 2006, 382). This state of being is restless and challenging. But it is also often pleasurable; the "you" takes pleasure in the "extra-you"—as in many cases of laughter where one is placed on good terms with oneself. And such a state of being comes with certain add-ons. The generation of "extra-yous" means that it is possible to be half-committed to a course of action while all the time commenting on it. Equally, it allows all kinds of worlds to exist, caught up with one another to a greater or lesser degree, each of which may have different cues.

Glamour's third pillar is calculation but it is calculation that must go unnoticed. It must appear as effortless. Glamour requires a courtier's nonchalance: "to practice in all things a certain sprezzatura, and so to conceal all art and make whatever is done or said appear to be without effort" (Castiglione 1959, 43). So glamour is selling. It is manipulation. It is seduction. It is a certain form of deception. But it is something more too. It is meticulous selection and control. "The creator must edit out discordant details that could break the spell—blemishes on the skin, spots on the windows, electrical wires crossing the façade, piles of bills on the kitchen counter" (Postrel 2003, 28). From out of these and other conventions comes the ability to generate "fake" feeling. So, glamour betokens making what is difficult appear easy, it requires vitality but also a sometimes steely accuracy, it demands envy but also identification. In other words, glamour is concerned with gaining a willing acceptance of manipulation through "fake" feeling, the result, in particular, of the work done on the so-called negative feelings like envy, anxiety, and competitiveness, which both frame it and provide an analysis of the social field, however crude (Ngai 2005, 2006).

Worlds that are supported by these pillars increasingly go beyond the sequential process to be found in stories and other linear cognitive tools (see Thrift forthcoming) and attempt to make appeals directly at the neurophysiological level by tapping directly into the interface with objects, whether these be carefully designed goods that feel right, images, icons, and effigies that tap into couplings of objects and cultural ideals, or other "enactive symbols" (Stafford 2007), which are, of course, more than symbols. Rather, they are forms of lived experience. In past consumer societies, the object world only very rarely was sufficiently populous that it could routinely produce atmospheres. But, I would argue that this kind of world making has now become an activity that involves much more than just the individual commodity. Rather, it involves the proliferation of performative object-fictions, in which sight, taste, touch, and the other senses combine to trigger cognitive heritages we are only vaguely aware of, the result of a vast increase in the palette of materials that are on offer that are able to produce marketable materiality. The obvious arena to which to point in this regard is the worlds that have become possible because of information technology. But, instead of following this particular aesthetic byway, I will point instead to the aesthetic possibilities that have arisen from new colored materials.

Glamorous Materials

There are many ways in which it is possible to produce glamour and I cannot fix on them all. Iconic experience like glamour is constructed from many building blocks. It can be sound. It can be the play of brilliant or subdued light. It can be powerful smells. It can be a haptic association. It can be pace. In this essay, I have chosen to alight on just one of the means of production of glamour, namely colorful materials. Straightaway, it is important to note that I take such materials as having their own resonance, not least because their appeal is mainly directly to the pre-personal domain in the form of movement sensations (Humphrey 2006). As Harman points out in discussing color, "There are qualities so free and nonteleological that they no longer even belong to specific things" (Harman 2005, 67) and color is one of these. Of course, color has a long history of manufacture and it is one of the key moments of aesthetics, understood as the sensual impression of light and color, whether found in Newton, Goethe, or the universal color symbolism of Berlin and Kay (Delamare and Guineau 2000, Leslie 2005, Pastoureau 2001). It may, indeed, be ingrained in us as a very part of how we are, as an element of archaic patterns of communication predicated on ritual and performance (Lewis-Williams 2004).

But what is at issue here is the ability to link certain colorful materials with the aesthetics of glamour in an unconscious poetry of substance. This is hardly a new phenomenon: but it has become a mass-produced phenomenon, especially since the first synthetic color was produced by Runge in 1833. Colored materials are, of course, central to the construction of worlds. Even computer-generated worlds attempt to animate texture and feel as key moments in generating a sense of reality. Much effort is expended on simulating surfaces like hair or fur, on getting particular liquids like milk or honey to flow properly, and on attaining accurate color effects. More generally, materials have been crucial to the generation of alluring spaces. Thus Benjamin's arcades, often thought (mistakenly) to be the prototypical capitalist spaces, depended upon the availability of materials like glass, artificial gems, and mirrors to work their secular magic (Leslie 2005).

But what would prove equally as important as the glamorous consumer phosphorescence that spaces like the arcades unleashed was the ability to produce colored materials, through an alliance of chemistry and art, thereby unleashing an "empire of colours" (Leslie 2005). We do not, I suspect, understand just how colorful our current civilization is, whether the colors are to be found on screens, in food, in plastics, and so on. Almost anything is now able to be colored or pigmented, often using computer technology, which is intent on reaching the limits of human color perception: the average human observer can readily distinguish some one hundred thousand colors (Delamare and Guineau 2000), many of which have affective and symbolic attributes. Thus, certain colors have historically been glamorous, at least for a time. Think of a dye like mauve, which when it was invented in the nineteenth century became linked for a time with glamour (Garfield 2001). Or, continuing in this vein, think of the first synthetic plastic, Bakelite, invented in the early twentieth century, which went on to become a glamorous material, at least for a short time, in the 1920s and 1930s. But what is different now is that aesthetic effects can be achieved on a near-routine basis. The range of effects that can be summoned up is enormous. Take the example of colored plastics. Postrel (2003) describes the enormous colored plastic banks held by some large firms: GE Plastics now has more than a million colored plastics banked in its custom color bank and since 1995 it has introduced more than twenty new visual effects into its compounds and resins, including mother of pearl, diamond, speckled glass, and various kinds of metal and stone.

In turn, by using new colored materials like these and combining them with other surfaces it becomes possible to construct environments that are the contemporary equivalents of the glamorous worlds of the nineteenth-century arcade or the staged staircases constructed by Morris Lapidus in his hotels in the 1950s or the first malls and that have now given rise to new disciplines like surface architecture. These are totally designed environments that can exude glamour because every single detail is designed without tradeoffs or compromises in order to produce brand push (Klingmann 2007).

The prototype for these environments is in all probability Rem Koolhaas's Prada "epicentre" store, which opened in New York in 2001, and which can be thought of as a spatial version of a brand. Koolhaas knowingly drew on various traditions of glamour to enliven these spaces, defining glamour as a means of capturing attention through the qualities of focus and clarity, the development of more intelligent objects, the power of tactile surfaces, and the use of unproductive, even excessive space (Koolhaas 2001). Prada stores based on these four principles have subsequently been rolled out in different incarnations, using different architects in some cases, across the world. They are often regarded as installations that explore the idea of consumerism—and they are—but they are something else too: prototypes for worlding. They depend upon a carefully designed backbone that, incidentally, pays homage to both the stage (each store actually has a small stage area) and to the aforementioned Lapidus staircases, as well as acting as a spine for all kinds of adaptable infrastructure. As importantly, every part of their aesthetic has been designed to produce allure, down to and including materials of all kinds. For example, the Los Angeles store uses black and white marble, aluminum, zebrawood, gel waves, polyester screens, silicone bubbles, laminated glass that fades from translucent to transparent, and a new material specifically designed for Prada, called "sponge," which can provide a porous artificial background. Equally, lighting has been carefully designed to interact with these materials. The eighty different kinds of light throw particular patterns and produce particular kinds of effect. The store is also loaded with information technology, which adds another surface. For example, dressing rooms are equipped with plasma screens that are invisibly built into the mirrored surface and allow customers to see front and behind, inventory screens linked to RFIDs display what items are in stock, and doors are made of glass that can switch from transparent to translucent. Then, finally, some of the surfaces move; for example, the lifts display goods while the showcases can move about.

But these spaces are now but a small part of practices of worlding: demonstrators whose concentration of innovations will gradually make their way into the smallest shop over time. What is more important about these spaces is the kind of ambition that they reveal. For they betray an ambition to produce spaces in which every surface communicates something (Thrift forthcoming). The kinds of colorful materials that exist will be part of this non-discursive writing. The combination of these colorful materials with other media has begun to make it possible to reliably activate all kinds of appeal, from the archaic to the newest inventions, thereby adding another layer of charm to glamour.

Glamorous Personas

Glamour is hardly just the domain of objects. It equally concerns persons, understood as fractal, that is as both singular and plural. A fractal person is never a unit standing in relation to an aggregate, or an aggregate standing in relation to a unit, but always an entity with relationships integrally implied. The person lies in between as a dividual rather than an individual. Persons do not exist as autonomous entities but have the capacity to act directly upon one another. And because persons are "fractal," they are able to incorporate others and parts of others, including objects. This becomes particularly apparent when we consider how glamorous personas are constructed.

Nowadays the glamorous persona is often associated with high-end fashion. It involves a combination of sex appeal, luxury, celebrity, and wealth. Historically, the social bearer of glamour was the aristocracy. Now, however, the bearers of glamour tend to be celebrities. Of course, celebrity covers a host of sins—it consists of all manner of species and levels. But I want to concentrate on just one form of celebrity, namely *charismatic celebrity* of the kind found among major stars of stage and screen, certain (and by no means all) politicians, some sports stars, some top models, and the like.

Celebrity is, of course, a massive source of value in the modern world but it can be argued that it has roots that go some way back in historical time and these need to be examined to understand the current phenomenon. Thus, Roach (2007) has argued that glamour in its modern form was discovered in the theaters of seventeenth-century London with the invention of celebrity. In these theaters, a new form of public intimacy developed that was based around the celebration of the magical persona, which in turn was based on an interaction between the characters invented by playwrights and the talents of performers: "persona and personality oscillated between foreground and background with the speed of innuendo, intensified by the personal chemistry of the starring actors, igniting the precinematic It-effect" (Roach 2007, 16). Before long, glamour had become an almost routine manifestation, the result of the parallel rise of publishing and print media. Glamorous actors and actresses started to become familiars. Of course, photography and cinema produced a step change in what was possible, transporting the personas of celebrities to new climes and producing a more intimate sense of acquaintance that could still be counted magical but that was everywhere to be seen. However, it is debatable whether as much changed in the transition to the screen as is often made out. But one thing did change for certain: images became crucial in transporting an effortless gaze of public intimacy that is the main hallmark of the glamorous celebrity. Of course, that gaze is calculated in every way—from the stance of the body to clothes and hair, even in some cases to the events of the course of life—but that makes it no less potent. Glamorous celebrity has four main characteristics (Roach 2007).

First, it is a key manifestation of public intimacy, premised on the illusion of availability since apartness is so much a part of what glamorous celebrity is. Second, it relies on synthetic experience, that is vicarious rather than direct experience of another's life. Third, it manifests mass attraction based upon a special allure made up of physical attraction, lack of self-consciousness, and a perceived indifference. Glamorous celebrity must be exercised effortlessly or not at all but, paradoxically, that effortlessness requires considerable effort. Fourth, it requires the ability to embody contradictory qualities simultaneously, thus producing an unresolved intensity: "Strength and vulnerability, innocence and experience, and singularity and typicality among them. The possessor of It keeps a precarious balance between such mutually exclusive alternatives, suspended like a tightrope dancer on one foot; and the empathic tension of waiting for the fall makes for breathless spectatorship" (Roach 2007, 8).

What is important to understand about glamorous celebrity is that it revolves around persons who are also things. They are a "something." They exist in the realm of mediated imagination, as stimuli promoting further exploration, stirring up the proverbial itch of urges, desires, and identifications that we can't help but scratch. They therefore need to be "small" enough to provide intimate connections to personal memory and "large" enough to satisfy the imaginary hopes and desires and needs of a public whose members often possess contrary expectations and who are united only by their need to explore, according to the principle that "the most charismatic celebrities are the ones we can only imagine, even if we see them naked everywhere" (Roach 2007, 22).

We can, of course, see various ways in which it has been possible to guide imagination historically, nearly all of them stemming from the religious notion of the effigy. The effigy was a thing that stood as a synthesis of an idea, for example divine rule, with often only the vaguest of connections to the person—saint, martyr, king, or queen—concerned.

But it is not just the substance of personas that changes. They become surrounded by an object world that confirms this model but also has its own existence. Thus seventeenth-century theater also saw the beginnings of the construction of elaborate object worlds in which the props could have lives of their own as unstable temporal contracts that temporarily crossed the divide between inanimate object and animate subject (Sofer 2003). This tendency has only increased since the invention of screened communication, especially with the advent of digital communication, reaching the next stage (quite literally) in the creation of worlds where celebrities are themselves accessories: "useless for all practical purposes but symbolically crucial to the social self-conceptions of their contemporaries" (Roach 2007, 55). In the celebrity worlds now being created, vicarious exploration of the affective fields of celebrity is a part of their captivation. More and more can be conveyed about these effigies through multiple layers of information that act to amplify interest and yearning, and to confirm or question certain self-conceptions.

The glamorous celebrity is neither person nor thing but something in between, an unobtainable reality, an imaginary friend, and an accessory, a mental image that can be conjured up in the imagination, explored, and made one's own, something that is at issue in the world. A celebrity's personality may contribute something to the celebrity's look and feel but so do a vast range of colorful materials, many of which exist on the boundary between alive and inert—clothes, jewelry, hair, skin, flesh all have their part to play. These colorful materials are a vital part of what glamorous celebrity is, lively fabrications that are telling in every sense; "what we at least think we see in the charming person is a certain total geography of objects, one that the charming agent acknowledges and inhabits to the exclusion of others" (Harman 2005, 138). Clearly, it is not possible to enumerate every one of the colorful materials that helps to make up these total geographies in a short essay like this one, so let me choose just one—hair. Hair occupies a borderline on the body, quite literally. It is the easiest part of the body to alter. It grows, and so must be cut. It can be curled, shaved, dyed, straightened, and greased. It changes color over the lifetime. "There is no longer such a thing as a 'natural' hairstyle. But was there ever?" (Cox 1999, 269).

Famously, Hillary Clinton's address to Yale University's graduating class of 2001 included the following bittersweet remarks:

> The most important thing I have to say today is that hair matters. This is a life lesson my family did not teach me, Wellesley and Yale failed to instill in me: the importance of your hair. Your hair will send very important messages to those around you. It will tell people who you are and what you stand for. What hopes and dreams you have for the world . . . and especially what hopes and dreams you have for your hair. Likewise your shoes. But really, more your hair. So, to sum up. Pay attention to your hair. Because everyone else will. (2001)

These remarks could be interpreted in all kinds of ways. As a feminist howl of anguish. As a condemnation of the superficial nature of modern politics and, indeed, of society as a whole. As the lesson that looks really do matter. As a further illustration of the fact that it is possible to be undone by your hair. But I want to approach them in a slightly different way: as a means of approaching the subject of celebrity. For Hillary Clinton found that "hair can exert a magical power even greater than that of accessories and clothes, in part because it functions as both simultaneously [and in part because] hair belongs (or appears to belong) to the body of the person who wears it" (Roach 2007, 117). Hair, in other words, as a synthesis of aesthetic object and a means of stoking public intimacy, can be charismatic (McCracken 1996).

Hair has a neglected history that is only just starting to be explored in detail. Yet hair has become a crucial moment in generating glamour, based in part on new technologies that allow hair to become more and more aesthetically expressive. Generally, hair has been subject to major technological shifts. For a long time the major hair technology was the wig. There is, of course, the long and involved history of the wig, which has now transmuted into the widespread use of many false forms of hair. But since the end of the nineteenth century, technologies have grown up that make it possible to do wig-like things with growing hair. To begin, hair can be colored. So, for example, although hydrogen peroxide was invented in 1818 it was nearly a century later that it started to be used for cosmetic purposes when the first commercial range of hair dyes was made available by L'Oréal in 1909 (Cox 1999). Initially, hair coloring was looked down on. Now, it is estimated that almost half of all women color their hair (Cox and Widdows 2005). Similarly, hair now has the capacity to be curled or straightened in ways that were not available historically. For example, producing permanent curls dates from the Marcel waves of *fin de siècle* Paris and from the invention of the permanent wave in 1909. Then, it is possible to cut hair in ways that before would have demanded a wig. Sometimes these inventions can interact: perming really took off in the 1930s when bob haircuts became fashionable. Finally, all manner of other hair technologies have become standard, from the hair dryer (which first arrived in 1920, although not becoming general until the 1950s) to shampoo (dating from the 1870s) and conditioner (invented at the end of the nineteenth century but first available in the modern form in the 1970s and 1980s).

Glamorous celebrity uses this technology to produce new surfaces that combine with other accessories to produce a particular look. Celebrities' hairstyles can often be seen as inventions in their own right, artifacts of the close correlation of clothes and hair that dates from the 1960s. Hairstyles have become a means of launching new celebrity faces and repositioning old ones, producing a signature that is a part of the glamorous celebrity sign system. In turn, that system can be explored by consumers. Thus "we try our best to ape [glamorous celebrities'] clothes and looks, and for many of us the easiest aspect to copy is their hair; taking on the cut of a star has a transformative power that sustains this feeling of identification long after the film or TV show has finished. Entering the salon with a photo of a star ripped from the pages of a glossy magazine is a rite of passage for many teenagers and has been ever since the existence of the star system in Hollywood" (Cox and Widdows 2005, 113–14).

Conclusions

In one sense, what I have outlined could be seen as another episode in what Sheldon Wolin (2008) called capitalist totalitarianism, recalling Arendt's definition of the driving force of totalitarianism as put forward in her book *The Origins of Totalitarianism*: "The aggressiveness of totalitarianism springs not from the lust for power . . . nor for profit, but only for ideological reasons: to make the world consistent, to prove that its respective supersense is right" (1958a, 458). But that would, I think, be to give that supersense too much force.

Equally, accounts of "ontological domination" (Lash and Lury 2007) seem to me to be too strong. It is surely the case that the new forms of capitalism may often seem all-encompassing. But the system cannot work unless there are loopholes through which the new and quirky can make their way. It may be that capitalism can use the power of aesthetics and the momentum provided by the consequential urge to explore in its favor, but that can only be with the accompanying risk that the exploration will move into hostile territory.

As importantly, this kind of account ignores the wealth of empirical research on consumers that shows that though there may be many who are attracted by glamour just as many use consumption as an integral part of gift giving and of sharing. Then again, many consumers do make attempts to link their consumption to ethical imperatives, sometimes half-heartedly, sometimes mistakenly, but certainly showing more than a slavish devotion to consuming for its own sake. It would be possible to see these kinds of practices as minor or subordinate but they have had sometimes considerable effects, ever since the original consumer boycott of sugar as part of the campaign against slavery in the eighteenth century (see also Trentmann 2007). Not everyone is taken in by the secular magic of glamour and other forms of allure, but sometimes even the most hardened feel its tug—in an impulse purchase, in some small sign of obeisance to a persona they can't help but fantasize about, in an object placed just so in a room.

So perhaps a better way of understanding consumer capitalism might be as part of a series of overlapping affective fields. Perhaps one of the most powerful means of setting up counterpractices might be to aesthetically modulate these fields. For example, Belk (2007) argues that sharing is a culturally learned behavior that can be disseminated in all kinds of ways and that with the rise of intangible goods like information, images, and ideas it ought to be possible to promote sharing on a much wider basis than currently, especially through the design of aesthetically pleasing objects that are predicated on precisely this kind of activity. Such goods can, of course, have their own allure. The challenge is to build that sort of charm, knowing that it can and must be done.[2]

Notes

I would like to thank Greg Seigworth for his comments on this essay, which is an extended and revised version of a paper forthcoming in the *Journal of Cultural Economy*.

1   The Left has always regarded this kind of magical pleasure as a fraud and a trap. That is not helpful. Such an attitude, located somewhere between complex forms of suspicion and simple snobbishness, makes it impossible to understand why this magic has a grip on people's lives and both overestimates and underestimates capitalism's magical powers. As Stengers puts it, "Is it not the case also that conveniently escaping a confrontation with the messy world of practices through clean conceptual dilemmas or eliminativist judgements has left us with a theatre of concepts the power of which, for retroactive understanding, is matched only by their powerlessness to transform? Naming sorcery as the power of what has been able to profit from any assurance our convenient simplifications entailed means that we may have something to learn from those practices we have eliminated as superstitious, the practices of those for whom sorcery and protection against sorcery are matters of serious practical concern. I do not claim we should mimic those practices, but maybe we should allow ourselves to 'see' them, and wonder" (2007, 15).

2   And it is. Think only of the way in which many artists today are intent on unsettling accepted aesthetic formations in projects that are political, analytical, and constructive all at one and the same time.

Rediscovering the Virtual in the Actual

Lawrence Grossberg
Interviewed by Gregory J. Seigworth & Melissa Gregg

In *Cultural Studies' Affective Voices*, Melissa Gregg describes
Lawrence Grossberg as "the principal figure" in cultural studies
to have recognized "passion, emotion and affect as the new
frontier for politics" (Gregg 2006, 105). Well before the current crop of writers and theorists exploring the possibilities
afforded by affect theory, Grossberg pioneered notions such as
"mattering maps" and "affective alliances" to understand the
significance of popular culture in daily life. In his most recent book *Caught in the Crossfire* (2005), Grossberg continues
to anticipate the ways in which U.S. neoconservatives seek to
exploit the vulnerabilities of U.S. citizens as well as aspiring
to win the "hearts and minds" of those further afield. There
is ample, multidisciplinary evidence that the co-editors of
this book have not been alone in embracing Grossberg's assertion, as expressed for instance in the introductory words of his
Dancing in Spite of Myself, that "the political intellectual has no
choice but to enter into the struggle over affect in order to
articulate new ways of caring" (Grossberg 1997b, 23). In this
extended interview (transcribed largely from a lively three-
hour discussion conducted in Larry's living room in April

2007), we invited Grossberg to reflect on his own trajectory through and around much of the conceptual terrain explored in this reader, and also to project what is next for affect theory.

GREGORY SEIGWORTH & MELISSA GREGG: How does your story intersect with affect? Do you recall when you first met affect? Was it through Heidegger? Freud? Nietzsche? Spinoza? Deleuze? Someone/something else? Further, has there been a progression in your understanding of affect and its modalities? And if so, how would you characterize these changes in your understanding?

LAWRENCE GROSSBERG: That's a good question. (*pause*) I suppose that I "met" affect, as it were, in Raymond Williams: the "structure of feeling." And in what Richard Hoggart addressed when he tried to define the question of cultural studies in terms of something like "what it feels to be alive" at a certain time and place. And through a kind of low-level engagement—I hesitate to say that they were "arguments" because I was neither confident nor educated enough to engage people in an argument—but my sense that the turn in cultural studies to questions of ideology and to notions of experience drawn out of Althusserian theories of ideology didn't actually address the problematic that Williams was addressing in the structure of feeling. I kept wanting to argue that somehow the notion—what Hoggart called "what it feels like" and Williams called "the structure of feeling"—was more than what the Althusserian notion of ideology and the extant theories of experience captured.

Now that was partly determined or shaped by two things. One was the early fact that I went to Birmingham with an interest in popular music. I was never interested in starting a field of popular music studies, but I was interested in finding out why music was so important in the counterculture. And by extension, why it was so important within the broader context of postwar youth culture. I was interested in how it worked, what it was doing, how it operated. When I got to Birmingham I more or less understood that somehow this had a lot to do with what Williams and Hoggart were trying to talk about as the structure of feeling. And that, in a way, popular music gave access to that perhaps more obviously than other forms of mediated culture.

So, my path was probably predetermined by the fact that I went into academic work with music as my object. Because I was convinced that theories of representation, of meaning, of ideology had little to offer any attempt to understand music. And in some of my earliest writings I started to talk about affect. Now, in looking back at them, I think that I had no idea what it was. But I think that I got it from Freud, because I had studied with Norman O. Brown as an undergraduate and we read Freud. Of course Brown's version of psychoanalysis was not like what we then get through Lacan. It was much more akin to Wilhelm Reich—and Deleuzian and Nietzschean ideas—than anything that we recognize today as psychoanalysis. But the notion of cathexis (the investment of affect) was there in Brown. So, I think that's some of what I was drawing upon.

But the other, I think, important determination here was that I left Birmingham before they discovered Althusser. So, their pathway was into the Althusserian arguments, and then from Althusser . . . well, I am not sure that some people have ever gotten out of those arguments to some extent. (*laughter*) Whereas when I went to Illinois to do graduate work with Jim Carey . . . I was with Carey reading pragmatism, and theories of habit, and Peirce, and then reading Heidegger as an alternative pathway to what they were doing in Birmingham. So, it was only sometime later that I reconnected with Stuart and the Centre for Contemporary Cultural Studies (CCCS), and he said, "Well, we've been . . . it's all Althusser. Here are some essays and books." And I had to sit down and read Althusser. But by then I was probably already tainted. I found Althusser overly rationalist, overly representational, and bound to a narrow notion of what we might call "regimes of signification." But we did reconnect, clearly, around Gramsci, and the Centre's rereading of his work.

I think Heidegger was crucial, bringing in notions of everyday life and a vague notion of experience (and of course the concept of modes of being-in-the-world) that was not simply ideologically determined. What Heidegger also brought in was Nietzsche. It strikes me that Brown was a Nietzschean of sorts. Anyway, the Nietzschean concept of the "will to power" and the concept of affect coming out of "will" probably served as the second source for me. And I think that it describes the space within which I have always been operating and still cannot resolve the issue. And that is: the Nietzschean space, like the Deleuzian space, of affect, is an ontological space and the psychoanalytic space is an empirical space. Is that the same as the relationship between "*affectus*" and "*affectio*"? One is ontological—and this is what Brian Massumi writes about all of the time: "affect as the ability to have affects and to be affected" [or "*affectio*"]—and that's the ontological nature of reality for Deleuze and for Nietzsche. But, actually, that's what I've *never* been interested in! I have been interested in some subset of forms of effectivity [*affectus*]—which I think is what Freud is doing in his earliest writings. The other thing that I think enters into all this, for me, is Paul Ricoeur. I went to study with Ricoeur for a year at the University of Chicago. And he was talking about what eventually became *The Conflict of Interpretations*, and his own reading of Freud. He gave me Freud's early essay on a hydraulic theory of the psychic apparatus . . .

GS & MG: So, then it was Freud's *Project for a Scientific Psychology* [1966] and . . .

LG: Right, and I loved it. And I thought that *that* was where it was all at. This was a notion of a kind of materialist investment that was simply irreducible to the ontological category. It was a system, a particular arrangement, or what I would call now a "machinic assemblage" that could take on various forms, and could be reorganized. A kind of range of possibilities. A virtual realm of machinic assemblages that organize the energy or investment in life. So, it all came together around that.

GS & MG: So, more specifically, about Deleuze. When did you first encounter Deleuze's work? At Illinois in the early 1980s, right?

LG: Yes, it was early at Illinois. The first time that I wrote about Deleuze was in 1982 or 1981. A bunch of us (Charley Stivale, Marty Allor, Jennifer Slack, and others) began to read Deleuze and Guattari together. We started with *Anti-Oedipus* [1983] and worked through it very carefully. And I liked it very much. I liked their work as a philosophy—as a radically anti-Kantian philosophy, a philosophy that articulated, although I could not have said it then, a different modernity, or rather the possibility of understanding the possibility of a multiplicity of modernities. And I liked it for the vocabulary, the tools, it offered me to begin to think through some of the empirical and theoretical problems of my efforts to understand cultural formations within conjunctural contexts. I'll admit that I do not really worry about whether my vocabulary, whether what I want to do with Deleuze and Guattari, is the "true" interpretation of their project. I do take them (and Foucault) and their work as providing a toolbox, which can operate at multiple "levels," so to speak. Unlike some people, I do not want to take just one tool and use it everywhere (my impression of at least some of the work of "governmentality"). But nevertheless it is a workable vocabulary that I can use theoretically and analytically to describe the different ways in which the real or, better, the actual is produced out of the virtual because I think that is the question that Deleuze and Guattari pose: what are the machines as it were that produce particular configurations of reality? And so, drawing on *Anti-Oedipus*, I started to think in terms of the differences between three modes of machinic assemblages: on the one hand, stratifying apparatuses that distribute and produce content and expression in Deleuze and Guattari's terms or, to put it loosely, the material and the discursive, and on the other hand, operating and organizing both content and expression, territorializing formations (producing and mapping places and spaces) and coding formations (inscribing differences). Each of these I understood to be not only multiple but constantly changing—involving, for example, not only territorializing but also de- and re-territorializing.

In a new essay that I have just written on "context," my argument utilizes these modes or machines to show that there are at least three ways of constituting a context. One is what I will call "conjunctural," which is the Marxist notion of a context of overdetermination. So, all of the variety of material, social, economic, cultural practices that form the relationality of a conjuncture, or what Williams called, in his definition of "cultural studies," the relations between all of the elements in "a whole way of life." For the moment, I am trying to think through whether it makes sense to describe this first context as primarily the result of, if you will, "coding machines," which establish a set of overdetermining relationships.

But that isn't the same as what Williams wants to "abstract" (for lack of a better word) out of such overdetermined contexts. Williams wants to re-describe that set of relationships as what he calls the structure of feeling, addressing in some ways the more phenomenological question of how you *live* those relationships. It also seems to me that this is the realm of "everyday life." Not in the sense that there is a singular everyday life that is always the same. It is not always the same, but a historical articulation of that realm of "how one lives." Everyday life is not simply the material relationships; it is a structure of feeling, and that is where I want to locate affect. This is what I call "territorializing." It is about how you can move across those relationships, where you can and cannot invest, where you can stop/rest and where you can move and make new connections, what matters and in what ways. It is what I called in *We Gotta Get Out of This Place* [1992] structured mobilities. Williams could not escape the assumption, however, that there was a correspondence between these two planes or dimensions of contexts.

And these are different from an ontological construction of a context. Here I want to, again, use Deleuze (but also Heidegger). Especially Deleuze's reading of Foucault, to say that machinic assemblages, in the first instance, are stratifying. They constitute the ontology of reality at a particular moment, a kind of historical ontology, which constitutes—in Deleuzian terms— the strata of content and expression or, in Foucauldian terms, "the sayable" and "the seeable," which exist, however, on the same plane. They constitute populations and the forms of conduct and, in so doing, a certain kind of relationality, if you will, of the discursive and the material.

As I have said, while I know the ontological use of the concept of affect, I want to locate affect in that second set of contexts, as territorializing. Obviously the full description of a specific context or reality should involve all of those contexts or "machines": coding, territorializing, and stratifying. That's always the question that I want to ask: what are the machinic apparatuses or regimes of discourse that are constituting the ways in which we live our lives? The possibilities of affect and their articulations to conjunctures and historical ontologies. And I think that there are a great variety of forms of affective apparatuses as well of their articulations.

This, I think, points to a common failure of cultural studies, and also of much of critical theory and analysis in some way: the failure both to separate analytically those contexts, and then to map their actual and virtual articulations. And this is where I have a disagreement with the way Deleuze and Guattari are often used in concrete work, where there is a leap from a set of ontological concepts to a description of an empirical and affective context. I think there is where my difference with people I admire like Brian [Massumi] and Nigel [Thrift] is located. But to use a different example, consider that some people in geography have argued that the concept of a flat ontology precludes the reality of scale as a vertical category. That seems to me to simply forget that most of the empirical work of Deleuzean analysis has to involve the plane of organization, where scale may not only be real but very effective as well.

Another problem for me (*laughs*) that comes out of this is that affect simply covers too much ground. Even in this second realm of lived realities or what I am now calling territories, affect still covers too much ground. There are too many forms, too many effectivities, too many organizations, too many apparatuses.

GS & MG: Yes, that's something that we were going to ask about: is it possible that affect itself has been overinvested by theory? Is there a way that affect lets one off the hook in the way, as you've sometimes argued, that theory does?

LG: Yes, I think that is a nice way of putting it. I do think that affect can let you off the hook. Because it has come to serve, now, too often as a "magical" term. So, if something has effects that are, let's say, non-representational then we can just describe it as "affect." So, I think there is a lot of theorizing that does not do the harder work of specifying modalities and apparatuses of affect, or distinguishing affect from other sorts of non-semantic effects, or, as I said, analyzing the articulations between (and hence, the difference between, as well as how one gets from) the ontological and the "empirical."

The last is a vexing problem, and crucial I think if we are ever going to sort out a theory of affect. It's like people who say the world is "rhizomatic." The world isn't rhizomatic! I mean, as virtual, the world is rhizomatic. On the plane of consistency then, the world is rhizomatic. But there is always a plane of organization and that's what you have to describe because that is what you have to de-territorialize and decode, and then of course it will always be re-territorialized and you will of course never get back to the plane of consistency.[1] And whether or not Deleuze and Guattari thought you could become a body without organs, I have never had the desire . . . and I see nothing particularly political about it anyway.

GS & MG: But is it that these planes (virtual/actual or consistency/organization) are so separable or is it that they persist alongside one another in the manner of Spinoza's monism? That is, is there another way perhaps to think the spatiality of their relationship?

LG: Yes, I do assume that these two planes are the same thing. It's like Nietzsche's will: it is the ontological condition of possibility of any empirical reality. But that doesn't mean that it is a description of any empirical reality. There is a difference between the transcendental condition of possibility and the actualization of those conditions. So, I think that sometimes affect lets people off the hook because it lets them appeal back to an ontology that escapes. And, it often ends up producing a radically de-territorializing politics that I have never been particularly enamored of anyway.

But it also lets me too much off the hook, because what we need to do is take up this work and rethink it. You know that brilliant chapter in *A Thousand Plateaus* [1987] where Deleuze and Guattari talk about regimes of signification, or what Foucault would have called discursive apparatuses, different forms of discursive apparatuses. Machinic assemblages produce different kinds of effects. We know that. Foucault would say that. Deleuze would say that. And Spinoza too, you know. Some of those kinds of effects are useful to group together and call affect. But then you have to do the work of specifying the particular regime of signification, and the particular machinic effectivity that is being produced.

In too much work done by people who talk about affect—or at least I get the feeling when reading some of it anyway—there is a kind of immediate effectivity of affect on the body. Despite constant denials, I can't escape the feeling that Brian Massumi's recent work, for example, on the color-coding of terror alerts reduplicates a kind of old-fashioned media-effects model. You know, you flash these lights at people and there is some kind of bodily response. Well, there isn't! Affect then becomes a magical way of bringing in the body. Certainly, there is a kind of mediation process but it is a machinic one. It goes through regimes that organize the body and the discourses of our lives, organize everyday life, and then produce specific kinds of effects. Organizations of affect might include will and attention, or moods, or orientation, what I have called "mattering maps," and the various culturally and phenomenological constituted emotional economies. I say it this way because I am not sure that emotions can simply be described as affect, even as configurations of affect. I have always held that emotion is the articulation of affect and ideology. Emotion is the ideological attempt to make sense of some affective productions.

So, I don't think that we've yet done the actual work of parsing out everything that is getting collapsed into the general notion of affect. Basically, it's become everything that is non-representational or non-semantic— that's what we now call affect. And, so, yes, I think you are right: it is letting us off the hook because then we don't end up having to find the specificity.

GS & MG: There is a strong body of feminist work on emotion and affect and, within affect theory itself, there are definite disciplinary differences within and across philosophy, psychology, critical race studies, and feminist standpoint theory—just to name a few. We're thinking especially of the way that women have historically been associated with emotion and hysteria as part of a wider effort to distinguish particular groups as incapable of rational thought and hence scholarly practice. Isn't part of the continued difficulty then in theorizing affect and emotion partly due to how the historical trajectory of both terms has been used to dismiss and trivialize others in the past, and even still today?

LG: There is a rich body of literature across disciplines and political formations as you point out. Some of it is very important and well theorized, and I have learned a lot from some of it, although I continue to think that much of it is undertheorized. Most of it involves either a kind of phenomenology of particular emotions, without much sense of what constitutes "emotionality" as a state or way of being in the world, that might be distinguished from other modes, or is based on extensions and elaborations of psychoanalytic perspectives, which seem to me to operate with too narrow a conception of affect, as if the only source and configuration of affect was, at base, libidinal desire.

On the other hand, there is an important question of why "affect" has been so consistently ignored, along with other concepts like emotion and the body, in the dominant traditions of Atlantic modern thought. I think that part of the answer is no doubt, as feminists have argued, the association of women as somehow inferior with the assumption that the sexual difference manifested itself through a series of binary differences: rationality versus emotion, mind versus body, and so forth. I think this is part of the answer but only part. On the one hand, the erasure of affect as a theorizable category is not limited to Euro-modernism, and on the other, there are moments, quite important moments, in Euro-modernism when the effort to theorize some notion of affect (usually broader than or other than simply emotions) has been a crucial interruption of the dominant traditions. I think we have to think this history in more complex and articulated ways.

GS & MG: Do you think then that part of the critique of Williams and his structure of feeling—especially the critique of Hall in his "Two Paradigms" moment—is that Williams couldn't quite finesse the connection, in a thoroughly convincing way, that you want to make between the ontological and the empirical? Or, another way to ask it: are there inadequacies that you saw (and continue to see) in "structure of feeling" that plague it still today?

LG: Well, you know I think . . . the simplest way to put it is that Williams was not a theorist. He never theorized "structure of feeling" so, in fact, we don't quite know what it is. But in the discussion that arises in the *Politics and Letters* (Williams 1979) interviews and his later work, he really does redefine the structure of feeling in radical ways and critiques his own earlier notions of the structure of feeling as the statement of homologies across the various dimensions and regions of social life. Now, the later work is much more interesting to me, where the structure of feeling is apparently more concerned with "the emergent." In *Politics and Letters* he talks about it as the relation between the livable and the articulatable, which for me echoes

Foucault's concept of the production of the relation between the sayable and the seeable. The structure of feeling is about the limits of signification, of representation, and (though I am loath to use the word) the kind of "excess" or "surplus" that is always there through discursive production that is not captured by notions of signification or representation. It is what Foucault in part was trying to get at, I think, by talking about discourse as non-semiotic effectivities. So, I think that the notion of a gap between what can be rendered meaningful or knowable and what is nevertheless livable is a more interesting place to start. And, for me, this connects up in very interesting ways with notions of modernity and everyday life.

GS & MG: Yes, the whole matter of affect intersects with your long-held interest in and critique of Kantian modernism. A key early essay, in this regard, is probably your piece from *Semiotica* in 1982, "Experience, Signification, and Reality" [collected in Grossberg 1997a, 70–102]. You seem to regularly circle back to this, to be looking for a way out or around certain of Kant's problematics.

LG: My theoretical efforts have always been directed at getting out of Kantian philosophy—which is, I believe, what Deleuze and Foucault were doing. It is of course common to critique Kantian philosophy for having universalized a specific set of understandings and knowledges, but I have been trying to argue that the deep structure, if you will, of Kant's influence remains largely in place, even in the work of such influential and important thinkers as Derrida. Across a range of issues, logics, and assumptions, I have been trying to consider the possibilities of other ways of thinking, built on notions of multiplicities and positivities, which would recognize the complexity of discursive effects, agencies, and mediations. And this has been parallel to or connected with my effort to think about the possibility of reconstituting the "future" of the United States (the West, the world, whatever) insofar as I think that part of the way that cultural studies works is to try to offer a description of a context that reconstitutes it, in part, as what I call a "context of hope." So, then, one sees what is embedded, or, that is, one can see the virtual in the actual as a Deleuzian might say—so, one understands that reality is making itself and it will continue to, and that therefore there is a contingency about the world that opens up possibilities. Not in the utopian way that leads to misunderstandings and accusations like you are a gradualist or something because you want to take it step by step to get "there." I don't really want to get *there*. I just want to take that one step, and hope that that one step makes the world a bit better, and then we'll figure out what that context is and take another step. And that always seemed to me—the virtual in the actual, as it were—to be both excluded and undervalued; it is erased in a sense both by the Kantian philosophy and by the way in which the West has constituted the theory of modernity. And that is the link for me—the notion that there is only one—Euro-American or North Atlantic—way of being modern and we cannot get out of it, nor can we think outside of its logics.

I think I always wanted to say, "Are there not other ways of being modern? And what would those be?" So, I want to say that Deleuze is a modern philosopher—it is just that he has another modernity in mind. In just the same way that I want to say that Spinoza is *the* most modern philosopher that the West has ever produced. But again it's a different modernity. It's a modernity with very different roots, a very different set of historical traditions, and a very different set of political and social histories . . . and, of course, with a very different set of futures that are unlike anything else that Europe produced.

GS & MG: To follow up on this exclusion that you were speaking about, of being unable to find the virtual in the actual: your most recent book, *Caught in the Crossfire* [Grossberg 2005], deals quite a lot with re-imagining imagination, and in many ways it is precisely about finding this affective virtual in the actual. It is a potential that is there, but it is being almost systematically erased—not only by Kantian conceptions of modernity but also by rather explicit political maneuverings from the Right. This too has been part of your work for quite some time: the rise of neoconservatism and its intersection with the popular and the popular imagination especially since the Reagan years. This critique was such a major argument in your *We Gotta Get Out of This Place* and, so, this critique . . .

LG: . . . was also a critique of the Left.

GS & MG: Oh sure, but your critique of the Left is so much more harsh in *Crossfire*.

LG: But even in *We Gotta Get Out of This Place*, the critique of the Left—both in terms of its economics and its politics—is reasonably harsh, and well, you know . . . (*laughter*) . . . maybe that's why no one is reading it! If the critique is even harsher in *Caught in the Crossfire*, I think that is because, in the more than a decade between the two books, I think the Left (yes, I know it is a problematic term) simply abandoned any effort at analysis, at working through what was going on as the basis for a strategic response. Consequently, it abandoned any attempt to think strategically, to connect to what I and others would call the popular, the logics with which people evaluate and calculate their lives and the world in which they live. And the Left abandoned any notion of conversation, a conversation in which they would have to risk both discovering their mistakes and transforming their assumptions. Instead, the Left just circled the wagons, comfortable in their certainty that they already understood what was going on, without requiring much work, and they continued to occupy the epistemological, political, and moral high ground. Despite claims of democracy, they continued to practice an elitist and vanguardist politics, or at least it seems that way to me. You can perhaps feel some of my anger . . .

GS & MG: Well, you end *Crossfire* with an un-ironic quote from Reagan, c'mon! Could you, though, say more about this notion of re-imagining imagination that you've now taken up?

LG: Yes, it is a kind of Deleuzian distinction—and as you know, I am a pragmatist: I tend to use theorists and I'm not so interested in "being Deleuzian" as much as I am in using Deleuzian concepts—but the distinction between possibility and virtuality is crucial, and I think that most theories of imagination have been theories of possibility. Of which, the utopian is the most obvious example. The result has been a politics that is almost never rooted in the present. But I think one must look to the present because it is in the present that you find the virtual, that you find the contingency . . . I think it is rooted in the possibility (if one can use that word) of reconceiving the imagination as intimately connected with the analytics of the empirical. Imagination is not separate from science, analysis, or description of the actual. Imagination has to be rethought as a rediscovering of the contingent, the virtual *in* the actual . . . and that it seems to me is a very different notion of the imagination than what the Left has ever had.

And this connects up much more with the pragmatists. I think that the way in which you enhance imagination is not to erase the present and allow your mind to rove free (as it were) but precisely to enhance your understanding of the present. A better understanding of the present is the condition of possibility for better imagination. Imagination involves empirical labor. At least this is what I have been trying to think through.

GS & MG: In your more recent work in *Crossfire*, youth is of course foregrounded—and, well, you've always been concerned with youth and youth culture, and the kinds of vitalities and intensities that attend to youth, especially around popular music and politics. And the recent book in some ways seems to offer a kind of privileged connection between imagination, affect, and youth. James Carey once had this line about your work where he saw it as wanting to bring "youth" as a category into the purview of cultural analysis in a similar way to, say, class or race or gender or ethnicity et cetera . . . that youth needs to be admitted alongside these in its own way and with its own particularities.

LG: Yes . . . (*long pause*) . . . well, I would hate to think of myself as adding another category of identity or subordination (even if there is some truth to it). I have been interested in youth, partly, because I thought that given its simultaneously privileged and ambivalent status in the United States it opened up unique ways of entering into and seeing what was going on. I do think that *Caught in the Crossfire* comes closer to putting forth a notion of youth as a political category that has to be taken account of than anything else I've written. Partly because there is, in that book, a certain kind of sense—however hypocritical it might be—of responsibility: a sense that I built a career by writing about kids, and it seemed to me that this is a moment in which it is incumbent upon some of us to advocate for the everyday lives of these kids, lives that are being transformed in profound ways. But . . . it was also a matter of thinking that perhaps, given that there is still an enormous affective investment in kids in the United States, there might be a way of articulating that investment to contemporary political struggles, to get people to reinvest in politics as it were.

GS & MG: But behind these kids in the crossfire, behind youth as a "category" (whether you refuse it as such or not) isn't there a way that this present crisis around kids is itself a kind of empirical marker for you, that there is something else, a larger claim about "youth" itself as a shrinking condition of possibility, as an affective virtual . . .

LG: Yes, I certainly think that's what I would now describe—and perhaps it is at least implicit in the book—as a certain configuration or articulation of modernity: where youth/affect/imagination are extraordinarily tied together.

Now, that's a fairly recent configuration of modernity that stretches back in my historical account of its emergence to post–Civil War America and goes up through the 1950s and 1960s (when it was dominant). So, if you go back to pre–Civil War America or if you go back to Europe in the seventeenth or eighteenth centuries, you won't find the same privileging of youth as a notion. You won't find any identification of youth with imagination. You won't find that special sense of the future that comes to emerge alongside notions of progress et cetera.

So, yes, I think that I didn't realize it at first—because I just thought I was describing the post-war context—but Foucault is right: you only get to describe realities as they are disappearing, when they are dying. Suddenly, for example, you can talk about "the subject" because the subject is disappearing. And what I didn't see was that this configuration, which had a history stretching back to the late nineteenth century, is now under attack and, by the 1950s and 1960s, was already indirectly under attack. People didn't realize that it was, and still is, under attack. Hence, you get what I take as the extraordinarily hypocritical position of baby boomers, who grew up living with the particular privilege of youth that partially constituted the dominant formation and embodied a slightly different structure of privilege in their own culture, who are now sitting by and watching the *de*-privileging of that same category for other generations because somehow they've been the transition point. I don't think boomers are to blame necessarily, but their lives have mapped out the changing regime of affect that is now, in part, disarticulating youth, affect, and imagination.

GS & MG: And, then, it seems that what articulates youth, affect, and imagination is, for you, in some way or another an economic or political-economic "abstract machine." Or, perhaps, we should ask: what is it that you see as having articulated youth/affect/imagination together in the first place?

LG: I suppose I would start by suggesting that this articulation is the result of a territorializing machine and involves a reconfiguration of social mattering maps and the structurations of everyday life. But at the same time, I have to say that this is the limit point, I think, of contemporary theorizing, isn't it? We, or, I should say I, haven't yet figured out a way to talk about, from one side, the totality and from the other side, the multiplicity of machinic assemblages.

So, let me explain *that* because I think it's crucial. Let me approach it this way: I think people have misread Williams for too long. Williams does not see himself in the culture and society tradition and does not see cultural studies as the continuation of that tradition. For Williams at least, the culture and society tradition, as one response to but also as one articulation of European modernity, starts with the separation and reification of the moments of the totality, and this fragmentation and reification of the social continues all the way through Althusser (where the levels—the economic, the political, the cultural—are separated). It is precisely what Deleuze then critiques too. You cannot separate the discursive and the material in this way, as if they existed in their own specificity, on separate planes or levels. They do not operate on separate planes. That's his flat ontology. This isn't about representation. This isn't about a transcendental economy of signification. Discourse and reality are on the same plane, so there is no separation of culture and society and I think Williams says that. And that's the import of cultural studies: it studies *all* the relations among *all* the elements in a whole way of life. And on that model, for Williams, cultural studies is not simply cultural criticism. It is not about reading the political significance off of a work, even with gestures toward its context. It is not about distributing works according to their politics or their political value, good and bad, progressive and conservative. It is not about studying popular culture or particular texts or subsets of popular culture; it is not about the political economy or even the ideology of popular culture. It is about reconstituting the totality, the complex set of articulations that make up the non-homogeneous totality of the context, or depending on how you understand the term, of the conjuncture. Only in this way can we open up the possibility of other ways of being modern.

It seems to me that one of the challenges that we now face is how to begin to rethink the notion of totality. I don't mean totality as a spatial totality as if it were a closed system but a totality that is the complexity of the machinic assemblages, of the reality that is continuously constructing itself. This is how I use conjuncture, as an articulation or condensation of multiple contradictions. There isn't a singular diagram that constitutes reality—that would be to fall back again into homology. But it seems to me that that's where a lot of work goes.

Maybe another way of putting this is that we are still trying to figure out how to talk about "determination" within a theory of articulation. I think the concept of overdetermination is a useful one, only insofar as it stops any fall back into simplifications and reductions. But I do not know that it gets us very far analytically (sort of like Williams's "all the relations among all the elements" . . . useful but impossible). I am struggling at the moment with this question. On the one hand, I think we have to follow Foucault to see the economic, for example, as the—no, rather as a—condition of possibility of other practices, but recognizing that culture is also a condition of possibility of the economic. So the concept of "condition of possibility" has to be further explored in terms of articulation. On the other hand, I am interested in the Spinozist concept of expression because it gives us back a relation to the totality. This is not a Hegelian notion of expression, but again, I do not think I have done enough of the work yet to offer a theory of articulation as expression. Or, is it expression as articulation? Clearly, I do not want to say that the political economy is producing youth in relation to affect and imagination et cetera. I want to say that this configuration is articulated, and the relation somehow works in both (and many directions), located with an articulated context of what I call liberal modernity under attack, a context that these relations are themselves implicated in and helping to produce. This is the theoretical and empirical work I tried to begin to do in the book, the actual work of mapping the complexity of articulations, of projects, of struggles, and of the lines of organization and flight.

But certainly, *Caught in the Crossfire* fails because it basically reproduces the Euro-modern fragmentation of the totality—here are the political, then the economic, then the cultural struggles and changes—and it can only put them together in terms of competing projects. As I said, I don't know yet how to organize such a project—and I only began to theorize how one might go about reconstituting the totality through a theorized empirical analysis of the struggle over modernity, as a complex set of struggles against "liberal modernity" and for other modernities.

GS & MG: Is part of the problem then that when we talk about affect in relation to modernity we are faced with new ways of thinking about the other or otherness? Taking account of affect seems to demand that we not dwell so much on questions of being, but rather on matters of belonging . . . and you've also talked briefly about this in more recent work of yours, often by way of Agamben, and as a way to route around certain problems raised by identity politics . . .

LG: Yes. My recent work has been interested in establishing the possibility of different actualizations of a kind of virtual modernity—"ways of being modern" in the virtual of which the North Atlantic vision of modernity is one actualization with its dominant machines of affect and dominant regimes of affect, and dominant structures of affect, and dominant ways of belonging.

I want to recognize that people live identity but ask whether you need to live belonging as identity where, at least in the current formations of modernity, identity is always bound up necessarily with difference and negativity (a very Hegelian logic that)? It's not that I am suggesting that such structures are not real in certain "modern" conjunctures: but I also do not believe they are necessary, that they are the only modern ways of belonging. I've always wanted to argue: no! There always has to be a way both to accept the reality that people live identity but also that there's always the potential for the actualization of other imaginations, of other ways of belonging, of identification, of community. And if you cannot theorize such possibilities, if you cannot see the present articulation as only one actuality among many virtual realities, then I do not think you can do the analytic and political work of understanding how one can move into another set of articulations.

So, one can imagine—as Paul Gilroy would say (and has for years)—you don't get rid of black people by getting rid of race. You get rid of racism and you reconstruct the ecology of belonging. It looks like a different modality of belonging because it won't be built upon notions of individuated identity, difference, and negativity. It won't be Kantian-Hegelian as it were. So, I think that seeing the relations between the ontological, the affective, and the conjunctural is key here. And of course there's a reason that I put affect in the middle—it is, after all, my privileging, the point that I want to see as "mediating"—not in a Kantian but a Deleuzean sense.

And I see this as connecting in quite interesting ways with "the popular." I'm trying to think through the notion of what the popular is. Here I can bring my argument about modernity to the popular. I've never understood arguments that popular culture is an invention of European modernity. Insofar as the popular is articulated within and to an economy of value and difference, yet, it may well be an invention of Euro-modernity.

My argument about the popular in a way reproduces my argument with Lefebvre's claim that everyday life is an invention of capitalist modernity; again, I want to say that it may well be true of *this* configuration but cannot we not imagine—and maybe even describe—other articulations? What would be alternative configurations of everyday life? We cannot imagine them again as only possible. We have to imagine them by looking at what there is, not just here but also in other places, and in the virtual.

I have the same argument about the popular—certainly people lived in the popular prior to Euro-modernity, especially when we realize that the popular cannot be reduced a priori to the category of popular culture. I want to distinguish specific historical articulations of the popular (without at the same time, and this is always the most difficult part, essentializing the popular, or defining it outside the specificity of its contextual articulations.

This is of course the important [point] of Gilroy's notion of the changing same, of anti-anti-essentialism, and of Hall's attempts to treat race and racism in radically contextual ways). But isn't this just the challenge—and impossibility—of cultural studies: to think contextually?

So, the question is, in its first inscription: what is the popular? Now I have been working with a group that includes some of my colleagues and grad students, as well as others from geography and anthropology. We refer to it as the "Rethinking the Popular" Group. It emerged out of a debate taking place here between two kinds of cultural studies factions. One is what I've traditionally been located in, which is built around a concern for hegemonic and state politics. But the other group, whose members think of themselves, rightly so, in cultural studies, committed to a kind of micro-politics, anarchist, world social forum, post-Zapatista and post-Seattle politics. It is sometimes referred to as the movement of movements. They want a political struggle that exists entirely outside of and independent of state politics, which they see as inherently contaminated. They want to imagine a politics that does not seek power. It is an experimental politics, as much about the styles and processes not only of politics but also of living as it is about resistance. I have to admit to having lots of sympathy for some of the arguments (especially at the level of micropolitics and its politics of the virtual), but I must also say that I think it is often historically naïve, that it fails to do the work of figuring out what is old and what is new, and that, in many ways, it echoes the politics of the 1960s counterculture, without taking that relationship seriously enough.

So one group was defending a kind of autonomous politics, and the other group was defending hegemonic politics. The former, at one meeting, was advocating bringing such autonomous and experimental politics, and even ways of living, to where we lived, while the other group said, don't you have to win people to such a project, and isn't that a hegemonic politics working on and through the popular? And we tried to have a conversation about the possibility of a rapprochement that would constitute a new post-autonomous . . .

GS & MG: And not post-hegemonic?

LG: . . . politics. Well, maybe you could also call it post-hegemonic; I am not so sure about that one. I think we might have to rearticulate the concept somewhat if it is to work in the present context. Anyway, I have to admit that the conversation has not gone as well, as productively as I might have hoped. (*laughter*) So, of course, I did as I always do. I created a group and said, "Let's think contextually about the popular." So we began by rereading Hall's "Notes on Deconstructing 'the Popular'" [1981] and we started to talk about it, and thought, what if we look at this essay as a particular intervention into a particular context. So, it was written in the late 1970s, and published in the early 1980s, and it's about the rise of Thatcherism, and it is one of those moments when there was—for Stuart Hall, John Clarke, and others—a kind of hegemonic struggle. What if we say that its understanding of what the popular is, and what the political is, and then what the articulation of those two is, is a result of its being a response to the context. What would you have to do to rewrite that essay in the present context? What would it mean to rethink the popular and the political and their articulation? So, it's a kind of Birmingham—collaborative (I hope)—project with two conversations going on: one is a general conversation about this, and the other involves each of the people in the group going about his or her own research. They are all trying to see it as a new contextual rethinking of the popular. After all, the popular is, for Hall, one of the places and, certainly, a key place, where the struggle for hegemony takes place, and there is that great ending to his essay where he says, "That is why 'popular culture' matters. Otherwise, to tell you the truth, I don't give a damn about it" [Hall 1981, 239].

So, the struggle for Stuart Hall is defined by what he already understands, as a result of his contextual labors, as the politics, but we need to continue doing all the work of explaining how the popular is the site of struggle as the conjuncture changes. What is it doing that enables the popular to be the site of struggle? All of my work has been toward understanding the popular in terms of affect, and its articulations into both actual and virtual politics, and what I am now trying to argue is—and, again I'll admit that I don't know if I am describing one kind of organization or regime of affect, or the totality— that affect is, in fact, the engine of articulation. Affect is what constitutes the relationality. So, that's why Williams was right to see that you couldn't separate the structure of feeling from the conjuncture. Because what makes the conjuncture *exactly what it is* are the affective articulations among the various overdeterminations. But Williams couldn't theorize it that way, although he was right to see it that way.

Now, we understand why the popular may still be a crucial site of struggle in the contemporary conjuncture. Even if the popular is not always or necessarily a site of resistance to or support of any particular position or practice, this is not to say that at certain moments, in certain conjunctures, it may organize resistance and possibility through any number of different forms of discursive effectivities. But the popular is key, I am hypothesizing, in the contemporary context, because it constitutes the relationalities among practices.

That's why Deleuze and Guattari can start off *Anti-Oedipus* with this notion of desiring production. Freudian desire becomes production. That's affect ontologically understood. But I have to say that it is "the popular" now—that it's the popular that creates the kind of relationality that leads desire here . . . here . . . here . . . here (*punctuating the air with pointed hand gestures*) along these notions. So, in that sense, just as Althusser would argue that there can be no society that does not have ideology, I would argue that there can be no society that does not have a "popular," because that's what organizes the *lived-ness* of life. Of course, it's that level at which Stuart Hall or someone else might say, "Isn't it the structures of meaning that make the relations?" I would say, "But, no, the difference is [that] you could have ideological interpellations but people do or do not *invest* in them." The meaning-structure has to somehow be affectively charged for it to constitute your experience. Now, it can be affectively charged involuntarily through forms of social machinery. It can be affectively charged unconsciously. But it is through the organization of the popular that the articulation of relationalities becomes possible. And that then opens up (I hope), the possibility of rethinking *where* the popular is.

GS & MG: Yes, this sounds hopeful, but isn't there a sense too in which something has increasingly gone in the breadth and variety of what's celebrated in contemporary popular culture? It seems like such a narrow pinch now: when, for instance, twenty-four-hour cable news leans more and more on financial reporting as the centerpiece of our collective existence . . . when the stock market serves as the ultimate barometer of well-being . . . the various financializations of the everyday . . . as life itself becomes increasingly articulated to capital.

LG: But what you are describing is a variety of different things, and again we need to separate them in order to then see their articulations. One is: it is certainly true that the economy has been affectively charged in new ways. Meaghan Morris (1998), after all, wrote an essay wondering about what made the minister of economics in Australia (Paul Keating) so sexy. Or why did Alan Greenspan become such a publicly recognizable figure? This doesn't mean that life is being reduced to economics but, rather, that something—some aspect or dimension of everyday life—is being reconfigured. And that's separate from other aspects, even economically: like the dominance of finance capital over industrial capital, which is still separate from the increasing commodification of everyday life. After all, Lukacs said this. Marxists have been saying this for more than one hundred years, that we are living in the time of reification, commodification, et cetera. This is Lefebvre's argument about everyday life. These things have different temporalities. They are different machines of the capitalist apparatus. And they have different effects. Some are more successful.

Yes, economics has become sexy but that doesn't mean that capitalism is helped in the end. Yes, capitalism is commodifying life. But capitalism commodified life before: now, we can commodify DNA. Yes, granted and it's horrible et cetera . . . but capital has always been biocapital. The slave trade: is that not the commodification of life? Can we not understand certain forms of gendered and sexual relations as involving a commodification of life? Yes, financialization has become dominant—and that has important effects. Certainly, there are lots of ways that we can talk about the changing status, presence, representations, forms, effectivities of the economy, but to reduce it to a single notion doesn't help. This is not only a matter of "historical" thinking, but also of finding adequate ways to do, and to theorize, politics/economics.

I have to say that I am very uncomfortable with the increasing sense, even among cultural studies people, that in the end, the bottom line is capitalism and that finally, however you describe what is new about capitalism (neoliberalism, post-Fordism, the knowledge economy, biocapitalism), it has finally achieved the status of totalizing control of our lives and reality. John Clarke's work, and the work of his group in social policy at the Open University, is so valuable here. I wish more people were reading it.

There are two things I want to say about the growing power of such interpretations, especially in the context of cultural studies. First, I simply do not believe the claims that all values are being reduced to market values et cetera, and I rarely see any evidence for such arguments. The reality of social existence, and of lived reality, is always more complicated, filled with multiplicities and contradictions, resistances and compromises. That does not mean that there are not forces pushing in one direction or another, and that in many circumstances, the range of our choices has been changed, even constrained, in new ways, pushed in new directions, And it does not mean that there are not significant changes happening in the fields and machineries of value, but I do not think it is all about capitalism alone and I do not think it is as simple as we often describe.

Second, I continue to believe that cultural studies must take economics seriously—not just to try to diagnose what is new about capitalism (based on its own already defined assumptions) or even to recognize that particular economic relations or apparatuses (such as markets) are constructed, but to rethink the very category of economies—to see it both discursively and contextually articulated within the totality of a conjuncture. We need to see it without fleeing from its complexity, its multiplicity and diversity of constellations, and its myriad relationalities and articulations. We need to see that the contemporary world is constituted as much by a struggle over what "the economy" is, and what constitutes something as "economic" as by any singular configuration, any simple diagnosis of Capitalism with a capital C, the latest version of a theory of, and fear of, the economic colonization of life itself. I think everyone should read Gibson-Graham's *The End of Capitalism (As We Knew It)* (2006), and then realize that the book is a challenge, not an answer. I might add that, in that effort, we need to take seriously not only the enormous variety of discourses that enter into the processes of articulating the economic, but also the work of economics as an academic and intellectual discipline. The discipline of economics, despite our oversimplifications, is not completely controlled by neoclassical and modeling theory; it is filled with a heterodoxy of positions, some of which (like the post-autonomist economics network) seem to be reaching for a cultural studies of economics as well.

Hence, I think we have to tread carefully when talking about the appearance of changing popular economies and subjectivities (such as those around the World Wide Web and other new technologies); we have to avoid rushing to conclusions without doing the theoretical and empirical work. Yes, I think we can assume that these changing organizations of popular culture (especially insofar as they are inserted into the dynamics of people's everyday lives) are producing new effectivities, but we sometimes seem too willing to assume that their effects can be read off of some description we have given of the changing apparatuses. Moreover, these effects are not the end of the story but the beginning for they are trajectories entering into extraordinarily complex terrains of lived realities, so their actual effectivity is always the result of further articulations. Do you see my point? I mean, I want to suggest, for example, that the media today are producing what for the moment I would call a structure of feeling or a mood (I am not sure which, but I do not think it is an emotion) of humiliation and this is a key to understanding much about the articulation of the popular and the political.

When I stopped writing about rock music, it wasn't because I stopped loving the music. It was because I was convinced that the entire context one had to construct in order to begin to talk about the work and power of the music had changed, not only in terms of the configuration of the musical apparatuses, but also in terms of the broader conjuncture. If my attempt to theorize the rock formation was, as I have always argued, a conjuncturally specific theory, then the question of how much of it continues to be useful is a question that has to be investigated and not taken for granted. I am pretty sure that some of my stuff on the affectivity of the music is still relevant, but whether the particular logics of affectivity, or the social logics that further articulated them, are—that I do not know. And I decided that I was not up to the task of starting over as it were, and besides, there were other, for me, more pressing tasks to be done. At least two of them are embodied in *Caught in the Crossfire*—first, to understand the changing conditions of growing up in the United States, and second, to continue to try to figure out "what's going on" in the broader conjuncture. A third task, what I am working on now, is to ask how cultural studies might be reconstituted, what sorts of concepts need to be (re-)invented to do cultural studies in the contemporary conjuncture.

GS & MG: Affect arrives, most explicitly, at the conclusion of *Caught in the Crossfire*, carrying this sort of feeling of hope against hope. In this very particular contemporary affective space, are you hopeful then?

LG: Well, I always see hope. I always see it because I believe the world did not have to be this way, and that it does not have to be any particular way in the future. I believe in the virtual. I believe that reality is always making itself and it's making itself with and *despite* humanity. That's why Deleuze, like Latour (though I'm not likely to be convinced into actor-network theory), decenter the anthropomorphic, not make the human the center of reality. Yes, we impact the world, and we do so sometimes in important ways and sometimes in devastating ways, but the world changes. And it will continue to change. So, I am hopeful at least in the sense, as my grandmother used to say, "This too will pass."

Am I hopeful in the more philosophical sense: somewhere between the Marxist naïve assumption that "human beings make history in conditions not of their own making" and the Foucauldian cynical assumption that "history is being made despite us whatever our intentions are"? . . . Well, yes, no, ahh-mm . . . (*laughter*) Stuart Hall once described himself as a political humanist and an intellectual anti-humanist. I am probably less of a political humanist than Stuart, but perhaps I am an ethical humanist. Anyway, I have to be hopeful. (*turning serious*) That hope does not fundamentally arise out of my being an intellectual, I think, but out of the rest of my life. I think at some point you stop being an intellectual only, and connect with what it means to be a citizen, to be part of a family, to be in a network of friends and acquaintances, to exist within a temporality of generations, et cetera.

What would it mean to live life without hope? It is why I think that there are limits to the intellectual's responsibilities, and to the intellectual's capabilities—I choose not to engage in the discourse of ethics, other than to say that politics is rooted ethics, and political change entails ethical discourse in complex ways. But I don't think that it's my duty as an intellectual to define ethics, nor am I particularly capable of it. And while there has certainly been significant intellectual and academic work on questions of ethics, in the end it is often difficult to see how this work articulates or even might be articulated into both the popular and the everyday.

Ethics transcends the intellectual enterprise. (I know I will get slammed for this!) Similarly, hope, in the end, transcends the political enterprise. Hope can be denied intellectually (that's a lesson of the Frankfurt School), but hope isn't defined intellectually. It's just that I don't think that it's the intellectual's responsibility to define the ethical position of the world. I think that begins to transgress what we are capable of. I want to appeal back to something like Foucault's "specific intellectual" and say "what constitutes you as experts?" After all, isn't that the Kantian trap? Wasn't it Kant who thought that we as intellectuals could constitute the ground of all ethics? I don't think that that's our task. It is part of the broader trap that I see many of my friends falling into, that because they are intellectuals, or because they study certain aspects of contemporary politics and culture, they can be called upon to comment upon almost anything. Is their insight so much greater than that of anyone else's, especially if they have not done the work of analyzing and theorizing what they are being called upon to talk about?

I do think that it's our task to help to create the conditions of possibility for reconstituting hope. I do think that it is the task of cultural studies to offer a better (re)description of the context it is analyzing (and that is what, ultimately, cultural studies is always analyzing; it is about contexts, conjunctures, not specific cultural forms or practices, in my opinion at least). And at least part of what makes a description better, for me, is that it does reconstruct the context as a context of hope, it does make visible the virtual inside the actual. It does open up the context to the possibilities of struggle, transformation, and, therefore, hope.

GS & MG: Your response here seems sympathetic to the argument one of us has ventured about the importance of affective voices in cultural studies [Gregg's *Cultural Studies' Affective Voices* (2006)]. The book argued that your voice in particular has been a prophetic one for cultural studies, a mobilizing presence with a distinct orientation toward or feeling for the future. Certainly your work has always opened on to the question of hope, even if now it is more immediately expressed as the need to re-imagine imagination. How does affect fit, as you see it, with the role of the intellectual and the act of, even the place of, speaking?

LG: Yes, there are a lot of ways of talking about that. One is that back in the 1960s, I met this person who claimed to be able to see your past lives. And who told me that, in a past life, I was a prophet. That is, I think that you are absolutely right, that's a voice that I . . . I am not sure that I necessarily chose it—but it is a voice . . . in a way, shaped at the intersection of Jim Carey, Stuart Hall, and my own kind of philosophical allegiances. I think people see a certain debt to Marxism, especially to Gramsci, and I have been very explicit about my effort to locate myself within a certain (anti-Euro-)modernist trajectory and to stand against the ways Euro-modern conceptions of cognitive labor dislocate passion from knowledge. My pragmatism has perhaps been less obvious, but I certainly inherited from Jim a deep faith in the fact that intellectual work is a conversation, and the conversation goes on. Conversations are not always peaceful—more often, they are noisy, passionate, and even reach the brink of or cross into violence, but still the conversation goes on. So, for me, people have always asked why I write so much and talk so much about cultural studies—that's partly what I hear you saying, Melissa: that I'm not only a prophet about the future, I am a prophet for cultural studies. And that's because I think it is a particular kind of intellectual practice that has something unique to offer, especially in a world in which the possibilities seem to be closed off.

As I said, I think cultural studies is an intellectual practice designed to produce hope because it is committed to context and complexity, because it refuses any reduction. Because even in the face of its failure, it reinvents itself. Precisely because it is so radically contextual, cultural studies' failure is never complete. It is never the end of the conversation. Intellectuals are always doomed to failure. We can never explain the complexity of the world. But the failure of cultural studies offers precisely the promise that it will reinvent itself. The fact that that theory always fails to some extent guarantees that cultural studies will reinvent itself in a new form, guarantees that cultural studies continues. That failure may be one of the few things that is guaranteed, since not only is the world changing around us, but those changes are characterized by the differing and multiple temporalities of different forms of effectivity. Certainly the effectivity of intellectual work is often slower than the temporality of changes taking place around it. Moreover, the reality is that quite often the virtualities we discover and imagine opening up to be realized are not actualized, and the task of analysis and imagination goes on. It may be the only thing that is guaranteed (thinking about Stuart's sense that cultural studies is always a refusal of guarantees), but the one thing it does assume is guaranteed is change, that change is the fundamental condition of reality. It's a theory that seeks, in its own logic, to recognize not only the contingency of its own production but also the contingency of that which it is producing: namely, the context. I think it's one of the few empirical/analytic projects that is radically open in that way. I think pragmatism fails in certain ways, and, in that sense of open-endedness, cultural studies is close to a Deleuzian model but as its more empirical side. That's why I've always thought there should be a way of bringing together elements of Gramsci with elements of Foucault, Deleuze, and Guattari.

GS & MG: The last essay in your collection *Bringing It All Back Home* [1997a] is about cultural studies and pedagogy. And that doesn't seem unintentional. Because there is a kind of inspirational tone . . . or perhaps one should say "passion"—cultural studies as passion—in your work that serves, in part, as a crucial pedagogical relay. There is a way that you bring cultural studies to students in the classroom—which is a very affective, intensely passionate relation to cultural studies' practice itself. Ken Wark once remarked that he thought that your greatest legacy to cultural studies would be your students. He, of course, didn't mean that at all as a slight against you or your writings but that you had produced a generation (or two) of folks—a remarkably diverse bunch doing work that barely resembles each other's, and almost none of it sounding like your own work very directly—but that one could tell that they had been your students (or, if not directly your students, at least close readers and fellow travelers), that they too embodied cultural studies as a passion.

LG: Well, that's good! But part of what you are describing is almost outside of my control. I have always been a passionate person. I never liked to get involved in anything that I didn't either love or hate. I have never liked the academic tendency to assume that passion somehow interferes with understanding. (Again, my attraction to both pragmatism and Spinoza). At Illinois, when they tried to stop me teaching my classes on popular music on the grounds that it was not a serious academic subject, some professors actually tried to argue that I should not be the teacher since I liked the music and the subject too much. Fortunately, just a small application of logic convinced them of where that argument might lead them. I have never been all that big a fan of pure logic, or of the notion that there is a single logic of truth, and it is certainly true that ever since I was in third grade (when I defeated my teacher in a mock trial defending my friend) I have realized that my power of persuasion is through pathos as much as logos. One cannot do without reason and evidence, but it is an illusion to think that they can or should rule without the passions.

As I said, I am committed to the practice of cultural studies. I think, if cultural studies as a practice is a fairly significant departure from the "normal" and dominant practices of the Western academy, it is a challenge in a number of ways. One being contextual. But two is precisely because it both recognizes "feeling" as part of its study, and also because it allows feeling as part of its practice, so in that way it has something over many forms of intellectual production. It doesn't seem odd when we look at feminists or critical race theorists that they have a kind of passionate commitment to their projects because we take for granted where that commitment comes from. Because cultural studies has no constituency (as it were) and no identity, the passion of its commitment is not transparent. Yet it has always been clear to me that the passion of that commitment is there in cultural studies.

I mean, I am proud if Ken says that one can look at my students, enough of them, and none of them look like me. None of them does the work that I've done. I've had a few students write about music but they don't write about it the way that I did. You know, and I am not even sure that I have any students who agree with me! (*laughter*) And sometimes I do wonder if it would be so bad if I had a few students, just one or two, who were pursuing my project with me, but I guess then I remind myself that many of them are, but in their own ways. They all are clearly my students. And that seems to me precisely what the lack of transparency of the source of that passion produces. It is not a kind of political passion of a constituency that reproduces itself in the constituency. And it is not the refusal of that passion of the academy that says, "Put your passion aside." Or rationalize it. It is a belief that the work you do matters: whether it is as a teacher—and I think cultural studies has produced good teachers, because it forces people to connect to their audiences in different ways and to seek out different pedagogies—or whether it is that the work you write somehow matters, not always in the short term necessarily, but there is just a faith.

Yes, I think my work matters (even if I am not sure that anyone reads it). Nevertheless, I think it matters. And if you ask me why: I don't know how. I don't have any evidence. Maybe the model is the guy stuck on an island who keeps throwing a thousand bottles out there (yes, I am echoing The Police). Does each one of those matter? Yes, because just one of those bottles needs to be picked up. I got an email just the other day from someone in Poland who is the director of a center there and he said that he didn't know cultural studies work, but he'd picked up a copy of *We Gotta Get Out of This Place* and it changed his intellectual and political life. Well, I am not sure I want the responsibility but, on the other hand, I have to think that you throw out these bottles and they have to make a difference.

And another part of that difference goes back to my understanding of the practice at the CCCS in the late 1960s, when I was there. Now I am not claiming origins, but for me at least that moment of institutionalization has a certain privilege and importance. And part of that was the commitment to a collaborative and collective project, and to collaborative and collective work. I know, people keep telling me, cultural studies is risky—because if you do it well, it is hard to stay completely grounded in and loyal to any single discipline, not only because it demands interdisciplinary work, but also because what questions one takes up and where they lead you to within the context may well change over time. And even more, collaborative work is doubly risky. That may be true, and I have only two answers. First, not being a big fan of the various risk theories circulating out there, I think taking risks has probably become a precondition of doing interesting and important work in the U.S. academy, so if you don't want the risk, don't claim the task. And second, perhaps we could start toward collaboration by simply trying to change the tone of our work—from what Meaghan Morris calls a culture of critique in which we build our reputations and our positions on the corpses of other scholars, condemning their inadequacies and their complicities with the dominant powers, to one in which we understand ourselves as working together, building on each other's strengths, however flawed and incomplete we may be.

Anyway, in the end, I have to think that, over the course of time and with the enormous body of wonderful and important work done by people, many people, including many of my friends and students, especially my friends and students, some of it will have its impact outside the academy as well.

GS & MG: In many ways, your work has long provided an ever-mobile map of the terrain for cultural studies thought. Sure, this map has its edges and undulations, and different people locate themselves on it differently, and move through it differently . . . but, surely, more than a few have stepped back from their own projects to look again at the terrain of cultural studies, and found that you've sketched out many of the parameters already.

LG: I think that's true of my intellectual work. One of the things that I enjoy and I think I am good at is mapping intellectual spaces. In some of my early articles, I was really just trying to lay out the map of certain kinds of theoretical work or the map of cultural studies work. Just so people could get a sense of the lay of the land—of what the problematics were, of what the various positions were—so that they could then navigate a place for themselves. It is one of the things that I always found useful for myself as well. And it is, I think, reflected somewhat in my pedagogical practice, where I think it is important to introduce people to the full range of positions and issues that constitute a field of discourse, before they focus in too narrowly on some question or position. Otherwise, how can they have made the choice that these are the questions they want to ask, that these are the positions from which they want to operate, except of course that they are either following their teachers quite literally, or else following some sense of academic fashion?

But, in the end, it all comes back to affect. In some way, you were right in your first question. It all began with affect. In fact, I was actually looking at a copy of my senior undergraduate thesis a couple of weeks ago, and although it doesn't use the word—it is all about affect. It is all about trying to figure out—and I didn't quite know it—a way to talk about affect. And not just to talk about it, not just to acknowledge it, but to realize that affect is produced, that it is always affected and effective in multiple and complex ways, and that it is always structured—existing in and produced by machines—in ways that cannot be separated from the articulations together of reality and power.

So, it began for me with questions that seemed to circle around affect: What does it mean? How does it get done? What was it in the 1960s that enabled music—that, really, for the most part, wasn't political—what made it bind a community together and articulate that community into political positions? What was it about the music that enabled it to give a generational identity, to organize a whole set of cultural and noncultural events into a coherent configuration of generational existence, as something more than identity? And I still haven't solved the problem!

And I am still trying to figure out how you talk about affect, and how you talk about the multiplicity of affect, and affect as multiplicity, about affect as machinic, and the machinic as territorializing, coding, stratifying, and, you know, how that connects to the larger totality. Without which, I don't know why one works. Because in the end, I still want to figure out what's going on. And I believe that giving the best answer one can, without simplification or reduction, even if it means giving up your favorite theoretical or political assumptions, is the responsibility of the intellectual and the most important contribution that the intellectual can make to the imagination and actualization of the virtual future. That is, to realizing that "another world is possible." That is what a context of hope is all about for me.

Notes

1   For Gilles Deleuze and Félix Guattari (1987, 506–8), the plane of consistency is the virtual co-presence of all elements of a totality in their real force-potential (both individual and collective). The plane of organization is the actual arrangement of elements in empirically describable and historically determined configurations (see also Deleuze 1988a, 128–29).

Worlding Refrains

Kathleen Stewart

What is, is a refrain. A scoring over a world's repetitions. A scratching on the surface of rhythms, sensory habits, gathering materialities, intervals, and durations. A gangly accrual of slow or sudden accretions. A rutting by scoring over.

Refrains are a worlding. Nascent forms quicken, rinding up like the skin of an orange. Pre-personal intensities lodge in bodies. Events, relations, and impacts accumulate as the capacities to affect and to be affected. Public feelings world up as lived circuits of action and reaction.

Critique attuned to the worlding of the refrain is a burrowing into the generativity of what takes form, hits the senses, shimmers. Concepts built in this way score the trajectories of a worlding's looping refrains, its potentialities, and attach themselves to the living out of what is singular and proliferative in a scene or moment, to what is accrued, sloughed off, realized, imagined, enjoyed, hated, brought to bear or just born in a compositional present.

This afterword is my refrain on the concepts gathering in the scenes of this volume. A repetition that underscores, overscores, rescores in a social aesthetics aimed at affect's moves and subjects jumping to invisible airs that waver and pulse.

These essays write affect as a worlding refrain all the way down. They hone critique to an inventory of shimmers. A sharpening of attention to the expressivity of something coming into existence. Here, affect is a gathering place of accumulative dispositions. What matters is not meaning gathered into codes but the gathering of experience beyond subjectivity, a transduction of forces, a social aesthetics attuned to the way a tendency takes on consistency, or a new regime of sensation becomes a threshold to the real.

Affect is the commonplace, labor-intensive process of sensing modes of living as they come into being. It hums with the background noise of obstinacies and promises, ruts and disorientations, intensities and resting points. It stretches across real and imaginary social fields and sediments, linking some kind of everything. This is why there is nothing dead or inconsequential in even the flightiest of lifestyles or the starkest of circumstances. The lived spaces and temporalities of home, work, school, blame, adventure, illness, rumination, pleasure, downtime, and release are the rhythms of the present as a compositional event—one already weighted with the buzz of atmospheric fill.

Everything depends on the feel of an atmosphere and the angle of arrival. Anything can feel like something you're in, fully or partially, comfortably or aspirationally, for good or not for long. A condition, a pacing, a scene of absorption, a dream, a being abandoned by the world, a serial immersion in some little world you never knew was there until you got cancer, a dog, a child, a hankering . . . and then the next thing—another little world is suddenly there and possible. Everything depends on the dense entanglement of affect, attention, the senses, and matter.

All the world is a bloom space now. A promissory note. An allure and a threat that shows up in ordinary sensibilities of not knowing what compels, not being able to sit still, being exhausted, being left behind or being ahead of the curve, being in history, being in a predicament, being ready for something—anything—to happen, or orienting yourself to the sole goal of making sure that nothing (more) will happen. A bloom space can whisper from a half-lived sensibility that nevertheless marks whether or not you're in it. It demands collective attunement and a more adequate description of how things make sense, fall apart, become something else, and leave their marks, scoring refrains on bodies of all kinds—atmospheres, landscapes, expectations, institutions, states of acclimation or endurance or pleasure or being stuck or moving on. Affect matters in a world that is always promising and threatening to amount to something. Fractally complex, there is no telling what will come of it or where it will take persons attuned.

Anything can be a bloom space. For my stepson, John, now, it is becoming homeless. An intimacy with the world's imperative. People like to simplify the situation of homelessness as if it is a self-evident process of abject poverty without a safety net or a subject of personal blame. But it is also a worlding, an attunement to a singular world's texture and shine. The body has to learn to play itself like a musical instrument in this world's compositions.

When he was in high school, John skipped classes every afternoon to play basketball with the guys even though it often ended in assault suffered. At night he would disappear to hang out with the budding neighborhood "gang" and no amount of talk or grounding would pull him back into the something of our household instead. Not even close. His buddies shaved gang symbols into his hair and painted the icons all over his arms and neck. He got thrown out of school under a no gang tolerance rule. He was arrested for trace amounts of marijuana possession—an event set off by him looking suspicious. And all of that was just the beginning. Take ten steps forward (alternative high schools; Job Corps and getting kicked out for fighting; enrolling in the military and having his enrollment set aside as fraudulent for failing to report his marijuana conviction even though it had been expunged from his record; getting trained as a nurse's assistant and getting a job and losing it after making it to the certification test but forgetting to bring his ID; living in group housing but getting kicked out for losing his job and not working his program to get another one; following someone he knew to a transitional housing duplex and just staying there until he got kicked out). Now he is on the street, learning the sensory labor of worlding as a homeless person. The walking, the finding places to sleep, the broken nose from rolling over on a rock, the encounters with the police, the talk— "I'm gonna get a place of my own with Jimmy, I'm gonna get my job back, I'm gonna get myself off the street, I won't be on the street for long, I give it ninety days. Give me thirty days and then I'll be back . . . It's not as bad as you think." He and his running buddy have a fight, split up, then reconnect; the counselor at the homeless shelter gives them the language of watching each other's backs. Their blankets are stolen. One night when it's below freezing someone throws a blanket over them while they sleep, wasted. It's like a miracle. He shows me what is different about him now; he has no hair on the insides of his calves because of all the walking they do to get food— Wednesday night it's on the east side of town at a church, Tuesday, Thursday mornings there's a truck down on the tracks, the Sally serves but no one likes the Sally, mostly they go to Lifeworks down on the drag—that's for the kids. But the drag rats are so grabby. He's had so much milk, no coffee, he's lost weight from not having enough to eat. He's proud of his new shirt—it's worth like twenty bucks—and he took a shower before he showed up on our steps this time. Every time he comes he has forgotten what he said last time, what he was planning. He says he looks good. He says he can't go into the army because of his feet and the swelling in his testicles. I say you need medical attention, these things can be fixed. Not these things, he says. Maybe the navy. The labored viscerality of being in whatever is happening renders choices and surfaces already weighty. Already the atmosphere you're literally attuning to. This kind of attachment can be easy to get into when the hard labor of attuning is pulled to the task. And of course it can be hard to get out of once you're in it.

John spends all of his time roaming to gather resources. He shows up at our house with Bluetooth headphones, a CD player, a radio, a huge stuffed Sonic character for his little sister. He went dumpster diving and only got twenty-one dollars. Can we do him a favor? Can we help him out financially? He'll be off the streets soon. He's working hard at being put into motion by a worlding that has arrived. Last night we got another call from the county jail. The caller was only calling to say that he had left his backpack when he was released the day before. We say we'll try to get word to him to go pick it up. But I'm sure he doesn't know how to get there by bus. A bloom space can catch you up and then deflate, pop, leave you standing, a fish out of water. Or, same thing, it can catch you in its moves.

A bloom space is pulled into being by the tracks of refrains that etch out a way of living in the face of everything. These refrains stretch across everything, linking things, sensing them out—a worlding. Every refrain has its gradients, valences, moods, sensations, tempos, elements, and life spans.

I was living in the coal mining camps in West Virginia when Reagan was elected. Right away everyone knew that something was happening, that we were in something. Right away the stories started about the people who were getting kicked off Social Security disability—why her? She's a widow with diabetes, no car, no running water, no income. Why him? He's crazy and one-legged; he's got nobody. Old people were buying cans of dog food for their suppers; you'd see them at the little rip store—just maybe six cans of dog food on the conveyor belt and that was it. Young people were living in cars; the stories traced their daily movements over the hills—where they were spotted parking, how the baby's dirty diapers were piling up in the back seat.

These were extreme stories—dense and textured stories that made a scene out of the end of the socially responsible state as it had been lived in this place until just yesterday. Sort of. None of this was a surprise, just a shock. Just the recognition. When things shifted in the political economy of coal, the big mines closed and people were getting killed in the deadly little punch mines. Then it was over. The union died one day in the middle of a strike. Word came down that the company wasn't negotiating. A feeling of stunned defeat settled on huddled bodies. The bodies wheezed. They reeled. They were hit by contagious outbreaks of "the nerves," people fell out; they said it was like they were being pulled down by a hand that grabbed them in the middle of the back.

The force of things would amass in floods of stories and in ruined objects that piled up on the landscape like an accrual of phantom limbs. This was not just some kind of resistance, or even the resilience of a way of life, but the actual residue of people "making something of things." It was the material, sensory labor of attending to a bloom space that stretched across the world as they knew it. People said the place smothered them and they "wouldn't never want to leave." The worlding of the place accreted out of opening events. A story, a gesture, a look, or an outbreak of the nerves would establish a trajectory and pick up crazy speed or disperse, or settle into a still life, or blanket the place like a premonition spontaneously generated in the lives of all those attuned.

The barer the life became, the more its worldings proliferated and accrued. The attending to what was happening became the direct materiality of people's shared senses. Intensity was the air they breathed. Bodies were on alert—marked, readily engaged, always talking, gathering the eccentricity of characters, exercising the capacity to affect and to be affected. Snake handling boomed in the churches whenever the economy went bust. For the sinners, there were drinking and drugs and sucking the gas out of other people's cars with a tube. Sometimes there were phantasmagorical eruptions, maybe a teenager going on a week-long burning spree and ending up living under a rock, or racist violence in the dark, in the woods, in a space of condensed displacement—a white on black rape, all men, an escape and a long night's walk back to the safety of a segregated camp. But never an official confirmation of any kind. Later, when the talk shows started, young people who were overweight or "didn't talk right" were flown to Hollywood to be on the shows. Fast food chains in town became the only place to work; the beat-up pickups went and the beat up Ford Escorts came. When the idea hit that the young people were going to have to leave and go to the city for work, the girls all started taking karate lessons in preparation, so now there are a lot of black belts in West Virginia and Cincinnati. Wal-Mart happened in West Virginia. Oxycontin happened. Tourism didn't happen. Falwell's Moral Majority didn't happen either; the little metal stands full of Moral Majority pamphlets appeared in the backs of churches, but after years of standing there untouched they faded away. The kind of utopian thinking that comes of hard drinking flickered on and off through it all like the blue lights of a TV set left on at night.

It was in West Virginia, in the heavy and diffuse social living I was doing there, that I got into the habit of watching things arrive in the company of others. Things like a shift in the sensorium, or the stink of some national transformation settling over the hollers, or the sheer weight of power coming down, or the weirdly giddy possibilities that popped up with the advent of a Wal-Mart over the mountains in Beckley. It was then that I began to think, along with others, that nameable clarities like family or friendship or love or collapse or laughing or telling stories or violence or place are all bloom spaces. They are all forms of attending to what's happening, sensing out, accreting attachments and detachments, differences and indifferences, losses and proliferating possibilities.

Bloom spaces are everywhere. You can start anywhere. The etching of the refrain can show up in the mundane and the material process of solving problems. The hinge between the actual and the potential can pop up as an object out of place, the sense of an absent-presence, a road block, a sticking point, or a barely audible whispering that something's up in the neighborhood.

Right now they're tearing up the roads in the neighborhood. Getting out to the main road means running an ever-changing maze of detours. Tires are squealing, coffeed-up drivers are throwing transmissions into reverse and banging lefts and rights. It's been months. A neighborhood "we" is tired of it. They'll have one road blocked for weeks. Then they'll open it again and move the work over one block. But a week later they're back, tearing up the road right next to the place they just spent weeks excavating. What are they doing? What do they think they're doing?

Some of us recognize a new social habit of making eye contact with other drivers when we get stuck at yet another road block. We're in it together, whatever it is. Some of us are wondering together, but only temporarily, we know, and it's not a close connection—as much dog-eat-dog as collective. Then the city sends us all a postcard telling us to stop pouring grease down our drains. Its public service voice says that even if you pour hot water down the drain after you pour the grease in, it will eventually cool and coagulate in a big collective clump somewhere down the road, making a big mess and a big problem. What? This doesn't seem right. It's too symbolic—a message about bad mechanical hygiene in this part of town. But still, for a minute we (could) all imagine the big clumps of grease gathering at those pipe junctures under the roads. I did, and I wondered who else was hearing this faint whispering that something was now "in" the roads and underneath. Some of us are thinking about the under-the-roads and the city's maybe not so great attunement to what's going on. Now it's the fourth time they've dug up this one section of road that stands between my home and office and I notice that this time they're just using hand-held shovels as if either they've given up actually looking for the "grease balls" (or whatever it is they're actually doing). Or maybe a body with a shovel now seems like a better method of attunement. It does to me. It's almost occult—the materiality of the looking and fixing, the almost audible whisper in the neighborhood that something's going on, that something's been going on for a long time, that we don't know, they don't know, it's annoying—the never-ending interruption of routes, it's a grating, a crankiness that has to be endured. It's a literal interval-making machine that blooms but never catches much sense.

Morning assembly at my daughter's elementary school is a buzz of bodies and tunes. Clusters of kids and their parents flow toward the cafeteria from a wide radius of streets and walking paths. There are bikes, skateboards, jump ropes, scooters. People are carrying lunch boxes and backpacks, school projects, coffee cups, cameras, papers to be turned in, other kids' stuff left behind at a sleepover. Tattoos are on display on arms, legs, peeking out of necklines and waistlines. Hair is tousled, sleepy, propped up, slicked. Some people are dressed up for work, but most work is casual dress or done at home. There are smiles in all directions, nods, greetings. Kids are calling out to each other, running over to each other and to their classroom lines, parents are finding their places against the walls near the others they speak to every day—"How's it going? . . . What'd you do this weekend? . . . Is that a cast on Max's leg? Hey, we have a project with our roof if you have time to look at it . . . This is the best part of my day. I know, me too. . . . Man, the allergies are terrible today! . . . Did you get that notice? . . . Are you going to Spring Fling? Oh, is that this week? Shit." Attention drifts to gazing at the others a little further out in the room, flipping gestures and hand signals that shoot trajectories across the space. "Hey, Costco Man! How ya like the heat! Summer's here, man."

When you enter the room you feel the angles flooding in, the luminescence of an ordinary but prized style of being present. A cross-modal force of synesthesia. A becoming sentient to a way of being, an experience of community in terms of what it makes possible. An intimacy tied to the mood of the place. A vibe (did I forget to mention that this is Austin, zip code 78704, known for its aging hippies, musicians, artists, do-it-yourselfers, and hipsters?).

The classes take turns going up on stage. Passing around the microphone, the kids recite the pledges of allegiance to the United States and Texas, in English and Spanish. Then it's "Get your snappers ready . . . Good, better, best, we will always do our best to make our good better and our better our best." They lead the school song: "It's so full of life, in this school there is no strife; Spirit in the air, teachers smiling everywhere . . . Here to make a difference, teaching peace and harmony; Zilker is a great place for kids!" The kids call for announcements, birthdays, sing "Happy Birthday" CHA, CHA, CHA!, and huddle on stage for the final cheer, "HAVE A MARVELOUS MONDAY!" Then everyone shoots off to their classrooms or back to the sidewalks and streets. The broad smiles linger on the faces. A powerful and fragile refrain accumulates over time, recomposes itself every day, and floats out of the auditorium attached to bodies.

The assembly takes ten minutes. It didn't take the new principal much longer to pop it like a balloon. He fumbled it for about a month, but we all knew on day one that assembly was dead when he took over the microphone and failed to remember the sequence, the lyrics, the repetition in Spanish. The parents were making eye contact—first bemused and then outraged. As a newcomer, unattuned to the rhythms and tempos of assembly's perfect machine, he thought he could make it more efficient. He tried half a dozen times to change where the students of each classroom stood and which direction they faced so that the kids could flow out of the room to their classrooms. The teachers were making contact and raising their hands to catch his attention as complexity turned to dead, shape-shifting chaos. It was as if he had thrown up the pieces of a puzzle hard wired into grooves and then panicked. There was no putting the scene of the assembly back together again. He didn't have the kids go up on stage, he didn't ask for birthdays, when he was reminded that we needed to recite in Spanish he would vaguely mumble, "Does anyone know Spanish?" (leaving the 30 percent of the room that was Spanish-speaking stone silent, looking at him). The kids were bored, embarrassed, waiting for the awkward impasse to come to an end. Finally the principal decided assembly should be only once a week. (The parents said "What about us?") Assembly went back into the hands of the teachers and the kids. But once a week is not a refrain that works its way into everyone's day. It's another something that has to be remembered, an option on Mondays. Not a scene of bonus pleasure.

Transitions can be hard. That's an understatement when you're old and frail and giving up your last home.

My mother was born to a life of hard transitions. Her father was one of a long and broad line of hard-drinking bricklayers and farmers. They built the big public works in the area—schools, bridges, banks. They disappeared into violent, abandoning drinking for weeks at a time. Beat their wives and/or kids and then spent days crying for forgiveness to their eldest daughters (like my mother). Hard transitions. Once her mother, Bea, walked off with all her little girls to live with a relative in another town. They walked all day. But they went back. Once her father dropped off all the girls at a school the next town over and never came back to pick them up. They waited and waited. They gave a girl a quarter to get them a drink but she never came back either. My mother laughs about it now—a lesson learned. She can't remember how they ever got back home; she'll ask her sisters. They were by then a pack of scared but competent girls who had each other's backs. The massive horses that plowed their father's fields filled them with horror; the girls worked behind them, alarmed senses laying down ruts. My mother learned to drive the farm truck when she was ten. It was the Depression. Bea told the girls not to tell anyone when they had only potato soup for supper, but my mother loved potato soup and ate it happily every day. Bea could play any song on the piano by ear after she heard it once. She hung her hand-washed laundry on the line in the field, sent the girls out to pick blueberries to make pies, made all their clothes, worked cleaning houses, taking in laundry. Later, when Jack was dead and the kids were grown, she went to work as a housemother at the nursing school of the hospital. As an old woman she was an aide in an institutional classroom for kids with muscular dystrophy and brain damage, lifting heavy bodies in and out of wheelchairs and onto toilets, cleaning houses on the weekends. She could draw.

There were strong and hard aunts. Uncles they hated. The girls walked over the fields and past Nunna's house to get to the school in town. Nunna's house was an old stage coach stop on the road to Newburyport. Now the little farm town is a bedroom community of Boston bursting with strip malls where ponds used to be. Aunt Mary loved kids (but not her own; she was mean to them); she would take the cousins (but not her own kids) to Boston Harbor on Saturdays in her old, wood-sided Beach Wagon. Her husband had died of a heart attack while carrying a bathtub over his head when she was pregnant with her fifth child. She took over his plumbing business, raised the five kids, and turned her big old house into a boarding house for working men.

Eventually the line of aunts and great-aunts who held the keys to learning and pleasure weakened and the hinge of potentiality snapped into raising children. A lot of them. My mother came from a line of hard, competent women barely attached (but attached) to men who meant long-term trouble and to kids (here the attachment was firm) who grew up in packs. The family was big. The women gathered on Saturdays to keep track of connections and losses as people married, had kids, got sick, had troubles, died. We cousins (if you included second and maybe third cousins) numbered over three hundred; we were a full half of any classroom in St. Michael's Parochial School. When we hit adolescence there were deaths among us—alcohol, drugs, fast-moving cars packed with kids on country roads. Air went out of the family. One sister broke off from the others after her oldest son died. Bea died. But the sisters had built a world. They had a habit and rhythm of putting one foot in front of the other. The labor of worlding. Looking back, they all say they don't know how they did it; that was just what you did in those days.

We were staying at my grandmother's house when the big house that belonged to my grandfather's family was struck by lightning and burned to the ground. My mother ran across the fields and stayed all night. She came back smelling of smoke. The fire had been so hot that the silver brought from Ireland had melted into a mass on the dining room sideboard. My mother still wonders how they got those nice things. There was lace, the silver, high ceilings, hiding places in secret passages, there must have been ten bedrooms, a pond. There must have been some money from somewhere. The men certainly weren't much good—not a one of them—though they had a big hand in all those courthouses and bridges that stand as monuments to an era.

Transitions. The big epochal ones you look back on are not so hard, at least not when you're looking back, their outlines etched as history on a landscape and a collectivity. Then you're not alone. You're part of the great generation or something. You're in it with others, going through something, a long line of somethings. When my mother looks back, she's just amazed at all the changes, as if the ground itself had shifted again and again and before you knew it, everything was unrecognizable, the force of things snapping into place as sheer transformation.

The old South Lawrence Irish families were like clans. They still are. They are completely closed except to their own. They're over at each other's houses every day; you'll see five or six cars parked at a time, coming and going. Things happen in those families. My mother taught poor Latino children who lived in burned-out North Lawrence. Every day there were stories about their lives. Bruises. Visits to apartments where there was no furniture or food. Violence. Sweetness. Great food. Beauty and loss. For forty years these families and their kids were for my mother an encounter with otherness that laid tracks of empathy, recognition, prejudice, despair, transcendence, amazement, labor, attunement, big and small achievements, and a lingering feeling of impotence.

Now all the sisters are gathered again, ritually, for the occasion of my mother's death. Not yet, but pressing. We sit them in comfortable chairs in my mother's living room, but they rearrange themselves around a table with tea and cookies. Suddenly they're loud. They're talking in rapid fire, over-lapping, stories that my sister and I have never heard before. They're piecing together the details that only some of them knew, had heard. They're scrap-ing the barrel. They hated Uncle Bill. They were afraid of him. (Which one was Uncle Bill?) They piece together good enough stories of events and characters by pulling on their individual senses. Shirley heard something once; Joan remembers a smell in a house; Tisha remains fearful of something that seems innocuous; Claire has a picture of him somewhere.

Afterward, my mother goes back up to the nursing home where she now lives. She's making the transition. Moving on, one step in front of the other, has a whole new meaning when you're blind and can hardly stand without the help of a walker. Yet she has the habit of a worlding. She is trying to find the rhythm of her new bodily life, to hit the reset button. She is laboring to literally fall into step with the pacing of The Meadows, to find lines of attachment, to become describable as a body by learning how to affect and to be affected in this world such as it is. She is looking for a track for a flourishing of some sort.

When she first came back from the hospital, her body could only cling to the bed sheets while feeling the vertigo of falling. I was sitting with her, trying to reassure her that she could wait now, things would get better. But when I would get up to leave for the night she would spring to a furtive standing position. "Okay, just help me get the label (l-a-b-e-l) on top of the walker. . . . Let's just do that before you go. Okay. Let's just figure it out. It's gold, it fits in your pocket, it goes over the . . . like a . . . table (t-a-b-l-e). Can you see it? Why won't you help? I just need you to do this one thing for me before you go." Then she would sink down, deflated. A few minutes later I would try to leave again. She would shoot up again, "Okay, let's just get this one thing done. . . ." It's a sheer repetition, a stab in the dark to discover a laboring rut that might include her.

The aides will slowly come to know her, know what she can and can't do. I will slowly learn to leave her to it. At first it's only an hour or two apart—an interval—and then we begin again with a report of what has happened. It's a sensory refrain pulling in events and scenes as if they were much-needed raw materials for a compositional grounding, a restart. She says this place is surreal. They have started to carry her down the hall to physical therapy. She says she saw small dogs in the hallway (the next day she discovers they were real). There is all this funny, cute equipment in physical therapy—red cylinders, something bluish you can sit in and move your arms around in, something like a robot that runs down the aisle. The occupational therapist was there on the first day, teaching her how to hold a fork again so she could feed herself. It's amazing what a difference a few teaching repetitions makes. I tell her this is a nice place; whoever knew it was here up on the second floor of Edgewood—big, lots of people, its own dining room and activities room. It's amazing. She asks me to tell her about her room. It's a cottage. She has a beautiful ash tree right outside her window, the snow is falling hard, beautiful, there's a full moon, the ground is covered, in the distance there is a huge dairy barn, there are still horses in the field, beautiful healthy horses in chestnut brown, they have wool blankets on and beyond the barn is Half Mile Hill where kids have always sledded and we went this afternoon. It was wild. We climbed to the top of the hill. Someone has left two Adirondack chairs and a table up there and you can sit and see the whole lake and mountain range. It's beautiful. Down below, tucked into the valley, Edgewood looks like a Scandinavian village. All white and collective. The Christmas lights are beautiful. Would she like some hot chocolate?

Then comes the time we have to leave at dawn. She's still very much alone and in the dark. She's in her bed. She struggles to find something a mother can still say. "Don't worry about me, I'm living the life of Reilly." I know this is somehow a surge to her prime and her Irishness, a fabulation that moves to find an earlier scoring. I look it up when I get home, just to do something. The *Life of Riley* was a popular American radio situation comedy series of the 1940s that was adapted into a feature film in 1949 and continued as a long-running television series during the 1950s, originally with Jackie Gleason. The expression "Living the life of Riley" suggests an ideal life of prosperity and contentment, possibly living on someone else's money, time, or work. It implies being kept or advantaged. The expression was popular in the 1880s, a time when James Whitcomb Riley's poems depicted the comforts of a prosperous home life. It could have an Irish origin. After the Reilly clan consolidated its hold on County Cavan, they minted their own money, which was accepted as legal tender even in England. These coins, called "O'Reillys" and "Reillys," became synonymous with a monied person, and a gentleman freely spending was "living on his Reillys."

Ten days later mother's language is much better. She loves the word-retrieval therapy. She's always had an amazing memory and a talent at picking up trivia. They tell her she's awesome. She passes the psychological evaluation with flying colors. The terrors have passed. They give her kisses on the cheek. Everyone loves her. She eats her meals in the dining room with the same two women and they have become her friends. Others come and sit next to her at activities. (Later the assessment team will call her the social role model.)

Another eight days into it, she's so happy. She knows everyone. She tells me stories on the phone every day (I call at 2 o'clock her time). Stories about the residents' histories, their connections, where they used to live, who their mothers were. And stories about the aides—their children, their education, their countries of origin. The aides touch her on the shoulder, they laugh with her. She can't remember names. She doesn't have to worry about anything. Like clothes. She doesn't mind taking their transportation to doctor's appointments rather than have one of us take her, but she's wondering if they can get someone to accompany her because when she went to see the neurologist that time before there were several buildings, snow, she had to take an elevator. She's wondering how she will make doctor's appointments, where her check book is, whether they're bringing up her mail. She wants to get her things organized, but they won't let her out of her chair without an aide. My job is to repeat over and over what detailed arrangements have been made in an effort to create tracks of recognition.

On the thirtieth day they kick her out of the Meadows. Medicare's payment period is over. She says she knows she's not ready to be back in her apartment but she'll try. She quietly does what she can to stay. She meets with the head of social services, reminding them that she is blind now. They take her back to her apartment in Edgewood. Aides visit to get her dressed, go the bathroom, bring meals . . . They come to get her for daycare for five hours a day but she doesn't take to it. She doesn't like some of the women in that group. They're all "oooohs and aaahs." The woman who is running the group was just about losing it today, rolling her eyes. Mom hates that sort of thing—a scene that's not working and people are losing it. She told them she didn't know how much she'd be coming back. But she had a good lunch. Sometimes they play memory games and she sparks up. Bad days she's reduced to the crabby figure instead of the one who "no matter what life throws at her, she gets up and puts one foot in front of the other every day."

She asks her friend Eleanor (who is blind) what her tricks are. Eleanor says she doesn't have any. My mother doesn't think Eleanor uses aides at all. She says she will never again eat in the big dining room at Edgewood. It's too much. People get dressed up. Even with an aide and her walker she has a hard time finding her way to a table and sitting down; she can't see her plate; she doesn't know how much food she's spreading over the table and her clothes. It's too much. She misses having her meals with the women in the Meadows.

But there are things that can be done. She has her sister go get her a new prism for the double vision in her one okay eye. Just in case. They take the door off her bathroom and replace it with a nice gauzy curtain. Now she can get in there herself with her walker but she's shaky. She has a number of episodes in only a few weeks. There are falls, cuts, fainting. Twice she ends up in the hospital. My brother Frank doesn't want her using the stove at all but she might have my sister Peggy get some little chicken pot pies. Frank says she can't even stand to make herself a sandwich.

She decides to cancel the dinners being delivered every night and set up for her (heated up, laid out). She doesn't want to have to clean up the Styrofoam containers the food comes in. There are so many of them and they need to be recycled. It's too much. Not right. But how will she eat? She's losing weight; she weighs one hundred pounds and she's so frail. She decides to start going to lunch instead of dinner in the big dining room. That would be better. She goes and makes a new friend. She wants to go back to physical therapy so she can learn to walk better, get some balance back. Once they bring her up to the Meadows for tea with her old friends as part of a walking therapy. But everything is pieced together. Claire keeps trying to shift things around, find something that works. It all ends when they find her one morning hanging off the bed, half under it, wrapped in her sheets and very disoriented. She's back to the hospital and then back, the very same day, to the Meadows. We get her a room of her own. We move her things up. We empty her apartment. It's a hard transition.

She's back to the work of being sentient to the world she's in. It is matter of literal contact, exposure to the rhythms, interruptions, bodies, pacings, and relations of a territory. A matter of being taken off, shown someplace else, catching on. A living through the transmission of affect, the restlessness of its promise, the relief of its continued mobilization, the anticipatory structure of power and obstacles. (If they would only let her get up for thirty minutes a day so she could find things in her drawers, remember where things are.) It is the production and modulation of "life itself" through worlding refrains. Synthetic experiences become generative repetitions of care and potentiality—the movies on Friday nights, the great food, bright colors, hats, festive occasions, sing-alongs. An accumulation that scores.

"ADM (Aéroports de Montréal) soutient que la sécurité des passagers a été améliorée." 2005. *La Presse* (Montreal). May 10: A7.

Agamben, Georgio. 1999. *Potentialities: Collected Essays in Philosophy*. Stanford, Calif.: Stanford University Press.

———. 2002. "Security and Terror." Trans. Carolin Emcke. *Theory and Event* 5(4).

———. 2004. *The Open: Man and Animal*. Stanford, Calif.: Stanford University Press.

Ahmed, Sara. 2000. *Strange Encounters: Embodied Others in Post-Coloniality*. London: Routledge.

———. 2004a. *The Cultural Politics of Emotion*. Edinburgh: Edinburgh University Press.

———. 2004b. "Affective Economies." *Social Text* 79: 117–39.

———. 2006. *Queer Phenomenology: Orientations, Objects, Others*. Durham, N.C.: Duke University Press.

Aidoo, Ama Ata. 1997. *Our Sister Killjoy*. Harlow, Essex, U.K.: Longman.

Allen, John. 2003. *Lost Geographies of Power*. London: Blackwell.

———. 2006. "Ambient Power: Berlin's Potsdamer Platz and the Seductive Logic of Public Spaces." *Urban Studies* 43(2): 441–55.

Altieri, Charles. 2003. *The Particulars of Rapture: An Aesthetics of the Affects*. Ithaca, N.Y.: Cornell University Press.

Anderson, Ben. 2006. "Becoming and Being Hopeful: Towards a Theory of Affect." *Environment and Planning D* 24: 733–52.

Andresky Fraser, Jill. 2001. *White-Collar Sweatshop: The Deterioration of Work and Its Rewards in Corporate America.* New York: W. W. Norton and Co.

Angel, Maria, and Anna Gibbs. 2006. "Media, Affect, and the Face: Biomediation and the Political Scene." *Southern Review* 38(2): 24–39.

——. 2009. "On Moving and Being Moved: The Corporeality of Writing in Literary Fiction and New Media Art." In *Literature and Sensation*, ed. Anthony Uhlmann, 162–72. Newcastle, U.K.: Cambridge Scholars Publishing.

Angell, James. 1941. "Radio and National Morale." *American Journal of Sociology* 47(3): 352–59.

Arendt, Hannah. 1958a. *The Origins of Totalitarianism.* 2nd ed. New York: World Publishing.

——. 1958b. *The Human Condition.* Chicago: University of Chicago Press.

Aristotle. 1976. *Ethics.* Trans. J. A. K. Thomson. London: Penguin Books.

——. 1998. *Nicomachean Ethics.* Ed. William Kaufman. New York: Dover Publications.

Armstrong, David F., William C. Stokoe, and Sherman Wilcox. 1995. *Gesture and the Nature of Language.* Cambridge: Cambridge University Press.

Armstrong, Isobel. 2000. *The Radical Aesthetic.* Oxford: Blackwell.

Ashbery, John. 2005. "Filigrane." *New Yorker* Nov. 7: 89.

"Attacks Were Most Important Historical Events in Our Lives: Poll." 2007. *Montreal Gazette*, Sept. 11: A17.

Badiou, Alain. 2001. *Ethics: An Essay on the Understanding of Evil.* Trans. Peter Hallward. London: Verso.

Bajaj, Vikas. 2005. "Bloomberg Cites 'Specific Threat' to NY Subways." *New York Times*, Oct. 6: 5.

Bamford, Sandra C. 2007. *Biology Unmoored: Melanesian Reflections on Life and Biotechnology.* Berkeley: University of California Press.

Barbalet, Jack M. 1998. *Emotion, Social Theory, and Social Structure: A Macrosociological Approach.* Cambridge: Cambridge University Press.

Barber, Lynn. 2002. "Life: Look Who's Talking." *Sunday Observer*, April 14.

Barrow, Robin. 1980. *Happiness and Schooling.* New York: St. Martin's.

Barry, Andrew, and Nigel J. Thrift, eds. 2007. "Special Issue on Gabriel Tarde." *Economy and Society* 36(4).

Barthelme, Donald. 1976. "I Bought A Little City." In *Amateurs*, 51–60. New York: Farrar, Straus and Giroux.

Barthes, Roland. 2005. *The Neutral.* Trans. Rosiland E. Krauss and Denis Hollier. New York: Columbia University Press.

Bateson, Gregory. 1935. "Culture, Contact, and Schismogenesis." *Man* 35: 178–83.

——. 1958. *Naven* [1936]. 2nd ed. Stanford, Calif.: Stanford University Press.

——. 1972. *Steps to an Ecology of Mind.* Chicago: University of Chicago Press.

Bateson, Mary Catherine. 1971. "The Interpersonal Context of Infant Vocalization." *Quarterly Progress Report of the Research Laboratory of Electronics* 100: 170–76.

——. 1979. "The Epigenesis of Conversational Interaction: A Personal Account of Research Development." In *Before Speech: The Beginning of Interpersonal Communication*, ed. Margaret Bullowa, 63–77. Cambridge: Cambridge University Press.

Baumgarten, Alexander. 2000a. "Aesthetics" [1750]. In *Art in Theory, 1648–1815: An Anthology of Changing Ideas*, ed. Charles Harrison, Paul Wood, and Jason Gaiger, 489–91. Malden, Mass.: Blackwell.

———. 2000b. "Reflections On Poetry" [1735]. In *Art in Theory, 1648–1815: An Anthology of Changing Ideas*, ed. Charles Harrison, Paul Wood, and Jason Gaiger, 487–89. Malden, Mass.: Blackwell.

Belk, Russell. 2007. "Why Not Share Rather Than Own?" *The Annals of the American Academy of Political and Social Sciences* 611: 126–40.

Belpoliti, Marco. 2001. "I Am a Centaur." In *Voice of Memory: Interviews, 1961–1987*, by Primo Levi, ed. Marco Belpoliti and Robert Gordon, xvii–xxvi. Cambridge: Cambridge University Press.

Benedict, Ruth. 1934. *Patterns of Culture*. Boston: Houghton Mifflin Company.

Benjamin, Jessica. 1988. *The Bonds of Love*. New York: Pantheon Books.

———. 1994. "What Angel Would Hear Me? The Erotics of Transference." *Psychoanalytic Inquiry* 14: 535–57.

Benjamin, Walter. 1979. "On the Mimetic Faculty." In *One Way Street*, 160–63. London: New Left Books.

Bennett, Jane. 2005. "The Agency of Assemblages and the North American Blackout." *Public Culture* 17(3): 445–65.

Bentall, Richard. 2009. *Doctoring the Mind: Is Our Current Treatment of Mental Illness Really Any Good?* New York: New York University Press.

Berardi, Franco "Bifo." 2004. "What Is the Meaning of Autonomy Today?" http://www.makeworlds.org/ (accessed 10 September, 2006).

Bergson, Henri. 1913. *Creative Evolution*. New York: Henry Holt.

———. 1988. *Matter and Memory*. New York: Zone Books.

———. 1992. *The Creative Mind*. New York: Citadel.

Berlant, Lauren. 1997. *The Queen of America Goes to Washington City: Essays on Sex and Citizenship*. Durham, N.C.: Duke University Press.

———. 2000. "The Subject of True Feeling: Pain, Privacy, and Politics." In *Cultural Studies and Political Theory*, ed. Jodi Dean, 42–62. Ithaca, N.Y.: Cornell University Press.

———. 2001. "Love, a Queer Feeling." In *Homosexuality/Psychoanalysis*, ed. Tim Dean and Christopher Lane, 432–51. Chicago: University of Chicago Press.

———, ed. 2004. *Compassion: The Culture and Politics of an Emotion*. New York: Routledge.

———. 2006. "Cruel Optimism." *Differences* 17(3): 20–36.

———. 2007a. "Slow Death (Sovereignty, Obesity, Lateral Agency)." *Critical Inquiry* 23: 754–80.

———. 2007b. "Nearly Utopian, Nearly Normal: Post-Fordist Affect in *La Promesse* and *Rosetta*." *Public Culture* 19: 273–301.

———. 2007c. "After the Good Life, the Impasse: *Time Out, Human Resources*, and the Neoliberal Present." Unpublished paper.

Bernays, Edward. 2004. *Propaganda* [1928]. Brooklyn: Ig Publishing.

Binkley, Sam. 2007. *Getting Loose: Lifestyle Consumption in the 1970s*. Durham, N.C.: Duke University Press.

Bishop, Claire. 2005. *Installation Art: A Critical History*. London: Tate Publishing.

Blackman, Lisa. 2008. "Is Happiness Contagious?" *New Formations* 63: 15–32.

Bloor, David. 1983. *Wittgenstein: A Social Theory of Knowledge*. London: Macmillan.

Boltanski, Luc, and Chiapello, Eve. 2005. *The New Spirit of Capitalism*. Trans. Gregory Elliott. London: Verso.

Borch-Jacobsen, Mikkel. 1988. *The Freudian Subject*. Trans. Catherine Porter. Stanford, Calif.: Stanford University Press.

Boulnois, Oliver. 2006. "Object." *Radical Philosophy* 139 (September/October): 123–33.

Bourdieu, Pierre. 1977. *Outline of a Theory of Practice*. Trans. Richard Nice. Cambridge: Cambridge University Press.

——. 1984. *Distinction: A Social Critique of the Judgment of Taste*. New York: Routledge.

——. 2000. *Pascalian Meditations*. Trans. Richard Nice. Cambridge: Polity Press.

Boyle, Mary. 2002. *Schizophrenia: A Scientific Delusion?* 2nd. ed. Hove, East Sussex: Routledge.

Brabazon, Tara. 2002. *Digital Hemlock*. Sydney: UNSW Press.

Braidotti, Rosi. 2002. *Metamorphoses: Towards a Materialist Theory of Becoming*. Cambridge: Polity Press.

Brass, Marcel, and Celia Heyes. 2005. "Imitation: Is Cognitive Neuroscience Solving the Correspondence Problem?" *Trends in Cognitive Sciences* 9(10): 489–95.

Brennan, Teresa. 2004. *The Transmission of Affect*. Ithaca, N.Y.: Cornell University Press.

Brown, Steven D. 2009. "Between the Planes: Deleuze and Social Science." In *Deleuzian Intersections in Science, Technology, and Anthropology*, ed. Casper Bruun Jensen and Kjetil Rödje, 101–20. Oxford: Berghahn Books.

Brown, Steven D., and Paul Stenner. 2001. "Being Affected: Spinoza and the Psychology of Emotion." *International Journal of Group Tensions* 30(1): 81–105.

——. 2009. *Psychology without Foundations: History, Philosophy, and Psychosocial Theory*. London: Sage.

Browne, Sir Thomas. 2007. *Religio Medici* [1643]. Whitefish, Mo.: Kessinger Publishing.

Bucci, Wilma. 2001. "Pathways of Emotional Communication." *Psychoanalytic Inquiry* 21: 40–70.

Buchanan, Ian. 2003. "August 26, 2001: Two or Three Things Australians Don't Seem to Want to Know about 'Asylum Seekers.'" *Australian Humanities Review* 29. http://www.australianhumanitiesreview.org/ (accessed Nov. 1, 2007).

Bullowa, Margaret. 1979. "Research in Prelinguistic Communication." In *Before Speech: The Beginning of Interpersonal Communication*, ed. Margaret Bullowa, 1–62. Cambridge: Cambridge University Press.

Burke, Joanna. 1999. *An Intimate History of Killing: Face-to-Face Killing in Twentieth-Century Warfare*. London: Granta.

Burnside, Julian. 2002. "Refugees: The Tampa Case." *Postcolonial Studies* 5(1): 17–28.

Bush, George W. 2005. President's Radio Address. June 18. http://georgewbush-whitehouse.archives.gov/ (accessed 3 June 2006)

——. 2007. "Graduation Speech at West Point United States Military Academy, June 1, 2002." In *U.S. Presidents and Foreign Policy: From 1789 to the Present*, ed. Carl C. Hodge and Cathal J. Nolan, 408. Santa Barbara, Calif.: ABC-CLIO.

Bynum, Caroline. 1995. "Why All the Fuss about the Body? A Medievalist's Perspective." *Critical Inquiry* 22: 1–33.

Caffentzis, George. 1992. "The Work Energy Crisis and the Apocalypse." In *Midnight Oil: Work, Energy, War, 1973–1992*. Brooklyn: Autonomedia.

Caillois, Roger. 1987. "Mimicry and Legendary Psychasthenia." In *October: The First Decade*, ed. Annette Michelson, Rosalind Krauss, Douglas Crimp, and Joan Copjec, 58–75. Cambridge, Mass.: MIT Press.

Campbell, Melissa. 2006. "The Affect of *Vice* Magazine." Conference paper delivered at the annual conference of the Cultural Studies Association of Australasia, UnAustralia, University of Canberra, December.

Carnegie, Dale. 1981. *How to Win Friends and Influence People* [1936]. Revised ed. North Ryde, Australia: Eden Paperbacks.

——. 1988. *How to Win Friends and Influence People* [1937]. Middlesex, U.K.: Eden Grove Editions.

Carter, Sean, and Derek McCormack. 2006. "Film, Geopolitics, and the Affective Logics of Intervention." *Political Geography* 25(2): 225–45.

Castiglione, Baldassarre. 1959. *The Book of the Courtier*. Trans. Charles S. Singleton. New York: Anchor Books.

Certeau, Michel de. 1986. "The Scriptural Economy." In *The Practice of Everyday Life*, 131–53. Berkeley: University of California Press.

Chickering, Roger, Stig Förster, and Bernd Greiner, eds. 2004. *A World at Total War: Global Conflict and the Politics of Destruction, 1937–1945*. Cambridge: Cambridge University Press.

Choudhury, Yousuf. 1993. *The Roots and Tales of the Bangladeshi Settlers*. Birmingham: Sylheti Social History Group.

Chow, Rey. 2002. *The Protestant Ethnic and the Spirit of Capitalism*. New York: Columbia University Press.

Clinton, Hillary. 2001. "Yale Class Day Speech," in Kate Zernike, "Commencements: At Yale, Mrs. Clinton Ponders Hair and Politics," *New York Times*, May 21: B4.

Clough, Patricia. 2000. *Autoaffection: Unconscious Thought in the Age of Technology*. Minneapolis: University of Minnesota Press.

——. 2004. "Future Matters: Technoscience, Global Politics, and Cultural Criticism." *Social Text* 22(3): 1–23.

——. 2006. "Sacrifice, Mimesis, and the Theorizing of Victimhood (A Speculative Essay)." *Representations* 94: 131–49.

——. 2007. Introduction to *The Affective Turn: Theorizing the Social*, ed. Patricia Clough with Jean Halley, 1–33. Durham, N.C.: Duke University Press.

Collingham, Lizzie. 2005. *Curry: A Biography*. London: Chatto and Windus.

Colwin, Laurie. 1989. *Family Happiness*. New York: Harper Perennial.

Comfort, Max. 1997. *Portfolio People: How to Create a Workstyle as Individual as You Are*. London: Random House.

Condon, William. 1979. "Neonatal Entrainment and Enculturation." In *Before Speech: The Beginning of Interpersonal Communication*, ed. Margaret Bullowa, 141–48. Cambridge: Cambridge University Press.

——. 1984. "Communication and Empathy." In *Empathy*, ed. Joseph Lichtenberg, Melvin Bornstein, and Donald Silver, 35–58. Hillsdale, N.J.: Analytic Press.

Connolly, William E. 2002. *Neuropolitics: Thinking, Culture, Speed*. Minneapolis: University of Minnesota Press.

Cope, Bill, and Mary Kalantzis. 1993. "Histories of Pedagogy, Cultures of Schooling." In *The Powers of Literacy: A Genre Approach to Teaching Writing*, ed. Bill Cope and Mary Kalantzis, 38–62. London: The Falmer Press.

Copjec, Joan. 1994. *Read My Desire: Lacan Against the Historicists*. Cambridge, Mass.: MIT Press.

Cox, Caroline. 1999. *Good Hair Days: A History of British Hairstyling*. London: Quartet Books.

Cox, Caroline, and Lee Widdows. 2005. *Hair and Fashion*. London: V & A Publications.

Crompton, Rosemary, and Gareth Jones. 1984. *White-Collar Proletariat: Deskilling and Gender in Clerical Work*. London: Macmillan.

Csíkszentmihályi, Mihály. 1992. *Flow: The Psychology of Optimal Experience*. London: Rider.

Curt, Beryl. 1994. *Textuality and Tectonics: Troubling Social and Psychological Science*. Buckingham: Open University Press.

Curtis, Adam. 2002. *The Century of the Self*. London: BBC.

Cvetkovich, Ann. 2003. *An Archive of Feeling: Trauma, Sexuality, and Lesbian Public Cultures*. Durham, N.C.: Duke University Press.

———. 2007. "Public Feelings." *South Atlantic Quarterly* 106(3): 459–68.

Cytowic, Richard E. 2002. *Synesthesia: A Union of the Senses*. 2nd ed. Cambridge, Mass.: MIT Press.

———. 2003. *The Man Who Tasted Shapes*. Cambridge, Mass.: MIT Press.

Damasio, Antonio. 2004. *Looking for Spinoza*. New York: Vintage.

Darwin, Charles. 1998. *The Expression of the Emotions in Man and Animals*. Ed. Paul Ekman. London: HarperCollins.

Dawesar, Abha. 2005. *Babyji*. New York: Anchor Books.

Delamare, François, and Bernard Guineau. 2000. *Colour: Making and Using Dyes and Pigments*. London: Thames and Hudson.

DeLanda, Manuel. 1991. *War in the Age of Intelligent Machines*. London: Zone Books.

———. 1992. "Nonorganic Life." In *Incorporations*, ed. Jonathan Crary and Sanford Kwinter, 129–67. New York: Zone Books.

———. 2002. *Intensive Science and Virtual Philosophy*. London: Continuum.

———. 2006. *A New Philosophy of Society: Assemblage Theory and Social Complexity*. London: Continuum.

Deleuze, Gilles. 1988a. *Spinoza: Practical Philosophy*. Trans. Robert Hurley. San Francisco: City Lights Books.

———. 1988b. *Bergsonism*. Trans. Hugh Tomlinson and Barbara Habberjam. New York: Zone Books.

———. 1989. *Cinema 2: The Time-Image*. Trans. Hugh Tomlinson and Robert Galeta. Minneapolis: University of Minnesota Press.

———. 1991. *Empiricism and Subjectivity: An Essay on Hume's Theory of Human Nature*. Trans. Constantin V. Boundas. New York: Columbia University.

———. 1992. "Ethology: Spinoza and Us." In *Incorporations*, ed. Jonathan Crary and Sanford Kwinter, 625–33. New York: Zone Books.

——. 1995. "Postscript on Control Societies." In *Negotiations, 1972–1990*, trans. Martin Jaoughin, 177–82. New York: Columbia University Press.

——. 1997. *Essays Critical and Clinical.* Trans. Daniel Smith and Michael A. Greco. Minneapolis: University of Minnesota Press.

——. 2005. *Francis Bacon: The Logic of Sensation.* Trans. Daniel W. Smith. Minneapolis: University of Minnesota Press.

——. 2006. "Desire and Pleasure." In *Two Regimes of Madness: Texts and Interviews 1975–1995*, trans. David Lapoujade, 122–34. London: Semiotext(e).

Deleuze, Gilles, and Félix Guattari. 1983. *Anti-Oedipus: Capitalism and Schizophrenia.* Trans. Robert Hurley, Mark Seem, and Helen R. Lane. Minneapolis: University of Minnesota Press.

——. 1987. *A Thousand Plateaus.* Trans. Brian Massumi. Minneapolis: University of Minnesota Press.

——. 1990. "What Is a Minor Literature?" Trans. Dana Polan. In *Out There: Marginalization and Contemporary Cultures*, ed. Russell Ferguson, Martha Gever, Trinh T. Minh-ha, and Cornel West, 59–69. Cambridge, Mass.: MIT Press.

——. 1994. *What Is Philosophy?* Trans. Hugh Tomlinson and Graham Burchell. New York: Columbia University Press.

Derrida, Jacques. 1992. *Acts of Literature.* Ed. Derek Attridge. London: Routledge.

——. 2006. *Specters of Marx: The State of Debt, The Work of Mourning, and the New International.* Trans. Peggy Kamuf. London: Routledge.

Dewey, John. 1934. *Art as Experience.* New York: Minton, Balch and Company.

Dienst, Richard. 1994. *Still Life in Real Time: Theory after Television.* Durham, N.C.: Duke University Press.

Diprose, Rosalyn. 2003. "The Hand That Writes Community in Blood." *Cultural Studies Review* 9(1): 35–50.

——. 2005. "Community of Bodies: From Modification to Violence." *Continuum* 19(3): 381–92.

Donald, Merlin. 2000. "The Central Role of Culture in Cognitive Evolution: A Reflection on the Myth of the 'Isolated Mind.'" In *Culture, Thought, and Development*, ed. Larry P. Nucci, Geoffrey B. Saxe, and Elliot Turiel, 19–38. Mahwah, N.J.: Lawrence Erlbaum Associates.

Dorrien, Gary. 2004. *Imperial Designs: Neoconservatism and the New Pax Americana.* New York: Routledge.

Dougherty, Kevin. 2007. "Province to Rid Schools of Junk Food: Youth Obesity a Pandemic; Couillard." *Montreal Gazette*, Sept. 14: A8.

Douhet, Giulio. 1972. *Command of the Air* [1927]. New York: Arno Press.

Dowling, Emma, Rodrigo Nunes, and Ben Trott, eds. 2007. "Immaterial and Affective Labour: Explored." *Ephemera* 7(1): 1–7.

Droulout, Tiphaine, Florence Liraud, and Hélène Verdoux. 2003. "Relationships between Insight and Medication Adherence in Subjects with Psychosis." *Encephale-Revue De Psychiatrie Clinique Biologique Et Therapeutique* 29(5): 430–37.

Durant, Henry. 1941. "Morale and Its Measurement." *American Journal of Sociology* 47(3): 406–14.

Durie, Robin. 1999. Introduction to *Duration and Simultaneity*, by Henri Bergson, trans. Leon Jacobson, 1–7. Manchester: Clinamen Press.

Eagleton, Terry. 1990. *The Ideology of the Aesthetic*. Oxford: Blackwell.

Ehrenreich, Barbara. 1997. *Blood Rites: Origins and History of the Passions of War*. New York: Metropolitan Books.

Eliot, T. S. 1980. "Ash Wednesday." In *T. S. Eliot: The Complete Poems and Plays: 1909–1950*, 60–67. Orlando: Harcourt Brace and Company.

Ellison, Julie K. 1999. *Cato's Tears and the Making of Anglo-American Emotion*. Chicago: University of Chicago Press.

Estorick, Eric. 1941. "Morale in Contemporary England." *American Journal of Sociology* 47(3): 462–71.

Feher, Michel, Ramona Nadaff, and Nadia Tazi, eds. 1997. *Fragments for a History of the Human Body*. New York: Zone Books.

Fisher, Philip. 2002. *The Vehement Passions*. Princeton, N.J.: Princeton University Press.

Florida, Richard. 2002. *The Rise of the Creative Class: And How It's Transforming Work, Leisure, Community, and Everyday Life*. New York: Basic Books.

——. 2005. *The Flight of the Creative Class: The New Global Competition for Talent*. New York: HarperBusiness.

Fortunati, Leopoldina. 1995. *The Arcane of Reproduction: Housework, Prostitution, Labor, and Capital*. Trans. Hilary Creek. London: Autonomedia.

Foucault, Michel. 1973. *The Order of Things: An Archaeology of the Human Sciences*. New York: Vintage.

——. 1979. *History of Sexuality*. Vol. 1. Trans. Robert Hurley. New York: Vintage.

——. 1990a. *History of Sexuality*, Vol. 2, *The Use of Pleasure*. Trans. Robert Hurley. New York: Vintage.

——. 1990b. *History of Sexuality*, Vol. 3, *The Care of the Self*. Trans. Robert Hurley. New York: Vintage.

——. 1994a. "The Political Technology of Individuals." In *Power: Essential Works of Foucault 1954–1984*, ed. James Faubion, 3: 403–17. London: Penguin.

——. 1994b. " 'Omnes et singulatim': Towards a Critique of Political Reason." In *Power: Essential Works of Foucault 1954–1984*, ed. James Faubion, 3: 298–325. London: Penguin.

——. 1994c. "The Politics of Health in the Eighteenth Century." In *Power: Essential Works of Foucault 1954–1984*, ed. James Faubion, 3: 90–105. London: Penguin.

——. 2003. *Society Must Be Defended: Lectures at the Collège de France, 1975–1976*. Trans. David Macy. New York: Picador.

——. 2007. *Security, Territory, Population: Lectures at the Collège de France 1977–1978*. Trans. Graham Burchell. London: Palgrave Macmillan.

——. 2008. *The Birth of Biopolitics: Lectures at the Collège de France 1978–1979*. Ed. Michel Senellart. Trans. Graham Burchill. New York: Palgrave McMillan.

Franzen, Jonathan. 2001. *The Corrections*. London: HarperCollins.

Frazer, Sir James George. 2000. *The Golden Bough: A Study in Magic and Religion*, Vol. 1, Part 1, *The Magic Art of the Evolution of Kings*. Chestnut Hill, Mass.: Adamant Media Corporation.

Freud, Sigmund. 1957. "Mourning and Melancholia." In *The Standard Edition of the Complete Psychological Works of Sigmund Freud*, ed. and trans. James Strachey, 14: 237–58. London: Hogarth.

——. 1966. *Project for a Scientific Psychology.* Ed. and trans. James Strachey. London: Hogarth.

Frow, John. 2007. "UnAustralia: Strangeness and Value." *Australian Humanities Review* 41. http://www.australianhumanitiesreview.org/ (accessed Nov. 2, 2007).

Gallese, Vittorio. 2003. "The Manifold Nature of Interpersonal Relations: The Quest for a Common Mechanism." *Philosophical Transactions of the Royal Society of London B* 358: 517–28.

——. 2007. "The 'Conscious' Dorsal Stream: Embodied Simulation and Its Role in Space and Action Conscious Awareness." *Psyche* 13(1): 1–20.

Gallop, Jane, ed. 2006. "Special Issue on Envy." *Women's Studies Quarterly* 34 (3 and 4).

Garden, Nancy. 1982. *Annie on My Mind.* New York: Farrar, Straus and Giroux.

Garfield, Simon. 2001. *Mauve: How One Man Invented a Colour That Changed the World.* London: Faber and Faber.

Gatens, Moira. 2004. "Privacy and the Body: The Publicity of Affect." *Privacies: Philosophical Evaluations*, ed. B. Roessler. Stanford, Calif.: Stanford University Press, 113–32.

Genosko, Gary. 2000. "The Life and Work of Félix Guattari: From Transversality to Ecosophy." In *The Three Ecologies*, trans. Ian Pindar and Paul Sutton, 106–59. London: Athlone.

Ghent, Emmanuel. 1990. "Masochism, Submission, Surrender: Masochism as a Perversion of Surrender." *Contemporary Psychoanalysis* 26: 108–36.

Gibbs, Anna. 2001. "Contagious Feelings: Pauline Hanson and the Epidemiology of Affect." *Australian Humanities Review* 24. http://www.australianhumanitiesreview.org/ (accessed Jan. 30, 2007).

——. 2006. "Writing and Danger: The Intercorporeality of Affect." In *Creative Writing: Theory Beyond Practice*, ed. Nigel Krauth and Tess Brady, 157–68. Tenerife: Post Pressed.

——. 2007. "Horrified: Embodied Vision, Media Affect and the Images from Abu Ghraib." In *Interrogating the War on Terror*, ed. Deborah Staines, 125–42. Newcastle, U.K.: Cambridge Scholars Publishing.

——. 2008. "Panic! Affect Contagion, Mimesis, and Suggestion in the Social Field." *Cultural Studies Review* 14(2): 130–45.

Gibbs, Raymond W. 2006. "Metaphor Interpretation as Embodied Simulation." *Mind and Language* 21(3): 434–58.

Gibson-Graham, J. K. 2006. *The End of Capitalism (As We Knew It): A Feminist Critique of Political Economy.* Minneapolis: University of Minnesota Press.

Gilboa, Netta "grayarea." 1996. "Elites, Lamers, Narcs, and Whores: Exploring the Computer Underground." In *Wired Women: Gender and New Realities in Cyberspace*, ed. Lynn Cherny and Elizabeth Reba Weise, 98–113. Seattle: Seal Press.

Gill, Rosalind. 2007a. "Postfeminist Media Culture: Elements of a Sensibility." *European Journal of Cultural Studies* 10(2): 147–66.

——. 2007b. *Technobohemians or the New Cybertariat? New Media Work in Amsterdam a Decade after the Web.* Network Notebooks 01. Amsterdam: Institute of Network Cultures.

Gill, Rosalind, and Andy Pratt. 2008. "In the Social Factory? Immaterial Labor, Precariousness and Cultural Work." *Theory, Culture, and Society* 25(7–8): 1–30.

Ginzburg, Carlo. 1992. "Just One Witness." In *Probing the Limits of Representation: Nazism and the "Final Solution,"* ed. Saul Friedlander, 82–96. Cambridge, Mass.: Harvard University Press.

Girard, René. 2000. "From Ritual to Science." Trans. Trina Marmarelli and Matthew Tiews. *Configurations* 8: 171–85.

Giroux, Henry A. 1983. *Theory and Resistance in Education: Towards a Pedagogy for the Opposition.* London: Heinemann.

———. 1988. *Teachers as Intellectuals: Toward a Critical Pedagogy of Learning.* South Hadley, Mass.: Bergin and Garvey.

Giuliani, Rudolph. 2007. "Towards a Realistic Peace." *Foreign Affairs* 86(5): 8.

Goffman, Erving. 1971. *The Presentation of Self in Everyday Life.* Harmondsworth: Penguin.

Graziano, M. S. A., and C. G. Gross. 1994. "The Representation of Extrapersonal Space: A Possible Role for Bimodal Visual-Tactile Neurons." In *The Cognitive Neurosciences,* ed. M. S. Gazzaniga, 1021–34. Cambridge, Mass.: MIT Press.

Greenberg, Karen L., and Joshua L. Dratel, eds. 2005. *The Torture Papers: The Road to Abu Ghraib.* Cambridge: Cambridge University Press.

Gregg, Melissa. 2006. *Cultural Studies' Affective Voices.* New York: Palgrave Macmillan.

———. 2010. *Work's Intimacy.* Cambridge: Polity Press.

Gregg, Melissa, and Glen Fuller. 2005. "Where Is the Law in 'Unlawful Combatant'? Resisting the Refrain of the Right-eous." *Cultural Studies Review* 11(2): 147–59.

Grossberg, Lawrence. 1984. "Another Boring Day in Paradise: Rock and Roll and the Empowerment of Everyday Life." *Popular Music* 4: 225–58.

———. 1986. "Is There Rock after Punk?" *Critical Studies in Communication* 3(1): 50–74.

———. 1992. *We Gotta Get Out of This Place: Popular Conservatism and Postmodern Culture.* New York: Routledge.

———. 1997a. *Bringing It All Back Home: Essays in Cultural Studies.* Durham, N.C.: Duke University Press.

———. 1997b. *Dancing in Spite of Myself: Essays in Popular Culture.* Durham, N.C.: Duke University Press.

———. 2005. *Caught in the Crossfire: Kids, Politics, and America's Future.* Boulder, Colo.: Paradigm Publishers.

Guattari, Félix. 1995a. *Chaosmosis: An Ethico-Aesthetic Paradigm.* Trans. Paul Bains and Julian Pefanis. Sydney: Power.

———. 1995b. *Chaosophy.* New York: Semiotext(e).

———. 1996. *The Guattari Reader.* Ed. Gary Genosko. London: Blackwell.

———. 2000. *The Three Ecologies.* London: Athlone.

Habermas, Jürgen. 1989. *The Structural Transformation of the Public Sphere: An Inquiry into a Category of Bourgeois Society.* Trans. Thomas Burger. Cambridge, Mass.: MIT Press.

Hacking, Ian. 1998. *Rewriting the Soul.* Princeton, N.J.: Princeton University Press.

Hage, Ghassan. 2003. *Against Paranoid Nationalism.* Sydney: Pluto.

Hall, Stuart. 1981. "Notes on Deconstructing 'the Popular.'" In *People's History and Socialist Theory,* ed. Ralph Samuel, 227–39. Boston: Routledge and Kegan Paul.

Hallward, Peter. 2006. *Out of This World: Deleuze and the Philosophy of Creation.* London: Verso.

Hamsson, Tom. 1976. *Living Through the Blitz.* London: Collins.

Hansen, Mark. 2000. *Embodying Technesis: Technology beyond Writing.* Ann Arbor: University of Michigan Press.

———. 2004a. *New Philosophy for New Media.* Cambridge, Mass.: MIT Press.

———. 2004b. "The Time of Affect, or Bearing Witness to Life." *Critical Inquiry* 30 (Spring): 584–626.

———. 2006. *Bodies in Code: Interfaces with Digital Media.* New York: Routledge.

Hardt, Michael, and Antonio Negri. 2000. *Empire.* London: Harvard University Press.

———. 2004. *Multitude: War and Democracy in the Age of Empire.* New York: Penguin Press.

Harman, Graham. 2005. *Guerilla Metaphysics: Phenomenology and the Carpentry of Things.* Chicago: Open Court.

———. 2007. *Heidegger Explained: From Phenomenon to Thing.* Chicago: Open Court.

Harper, D. 1994. "The Professional Construction of 'Paranoia' and the Discursive Use of Diagnostic Criteria." *British Journal of Medical Psychology* 67 (pt. 2): 131–43.

Harré, Rom. 1991. *Physical Being: A Theory for Corporeal Psychology.* London: Blackwell.

Harvey, David. 1989. *The Condition of Postmodernity: An Enquiry into the Origins of Cultural Change.* Oxford: Blackwell.

———. 2003. *The New Imperialism.* Oxford: Oxford University Press.

Hatfield, Elaine, John T. Cacioppo, and Richard L. Rapson. 1994. *Emotional Contagion: Studies in Emotion and Social Interaction.* Cambridge: Cambridge University Press.

Hayles, N. Katherine. 1999. *How We Became Posthuman: Virtual Bodies in Cybernetics, Literature, and Informatics.* Chicago: University of Chicago Press.

Heller-Roazen, Daniel. 2007. *The Inner Touch: Archaeology of a Sensation.* New York: Zone Books.

Hempel, Amy. 2005. *The Dog of Marriage (Stories).* New York: Scribner.

Herman, Ellen. 1995. *The Romance of American Psychology: Political Culture in the Age of Experts.* Berkeley: University of California Press.

Herman, Louis. 2002. "Vocal, Social and Self-Imitation by Bottlenose Dolphins." *Imitation in Animals and Artifacts,* ed. Kerstin Dautenhahn and Chrystopher Nehaniv, 63–106. Cambridge, Mass.: MIT Press.

Hesmondhalgh, David. 2007. "Television, Film, and Creative Labor." *Flow TV* 7. http://flowtv.org/ (accessed 10 March 2007).

Hewitt, Kenneth. 1994. "When the Great Planes Came and Made Ashes of Our City": Towards an Oral Geography of the Disasters of War." *Antipode* 26: 1–34.

Highmore, Ben. 2001. "Well-Upholstered." *Things* 14: 98–100.

Hochschild, Arlie R. 1983. *The Managed Heart: Commercialization of Human Feeling.* London: University of California Press.

Hocking, William. 1941. "The Nature of Morale." *American Journal of Sociology* 47(3): 302–20.

Hommel, Bernhard, Jochen Musseler, Gisa Aschersleben, and Wolfgang Prinz. 2001. "The Theory of Event Coding (TEC): A Framework for Perception and Action Planning." *Behavioural and Brain Sciences* 24: 849–937.

Honneth, Axel. 1995. *The Struggle for Recognition: The Moral Grammar of Social Conflicts*. Trans. Joel Anderson. Cambridge: Polity Press.

hooks, bell. 2000. *Feminist Theory: From Margin to Center*. London: Pluto Press.

Horkheimer, Max, and Theodor Adorno. 1972. *Dialectic of Enlightenment*. Trans. John Cumming. New York: Continuum.

Hume, David. 1975. *Enquiries Concerning Human Understanding and Concerning the Principles of Morals*. Oxford: Clarendon Press.

———. 1985. *A Treatise of Human Nature*. London: Penguin Books.

———. 2008. "Of the Standard of Taste" [1757]. In *Selected Essays*, ed. Stephen Copley and Andrew Edgar, 133–53. Oxford: Oxford University Press.

Humphrey, Nicholas. 2006. *Seeing Red: A Study in Consciousness*. Cambridge, Mass.: Harvard University Press.

Husserl, Edmund. 1989. *Ideas Pertaining to a Pure Phenomenology and to a Phenomenological Philosophy, Second Book*. Trans. Richard Rojcewicz and André Schuwer. Dordrecht: Kluwer Academic Publishers.

———. 2002. "The World of the Living Present and the Constitution of the Surrounding World That Is Outside the Flesh." In *Husserl at the Limits of Phenomenology*, ed. Leonard Lawlor and Bettina Bergo, 132–54. Evanston, Ill.: Northwestern University Press.

Huws, Ursula. 2003. *The Making of a Cybertariat: Virtual Work in a Real World*. London: Merlin Press.

Illouz, Eva. 2007. *Cold Intimacies: The Making of Emotional Capitalism*. Cambridge: Polity Press.

Isin, Engin. 2004. "The Neurotic Citizen." *Citizenship Studies* 8(3): 217–35.

Izard, Caroll E. 2007. "Basic Emotions, Natural Kinds, Emotion Schemas, and a New Paradigm." *Perspectives on Psychological Science* 2(3): 260–80.

Jamal, Ahmad. 1996. "Acculturation: The Symbolism of Ethnic Eating Among Contemporary British Consumers." *British Food Journal* 98(19): 12–26.

James, Susan. 1997. *Passion and Action: The Emotions in Seventeenth-Century Philosophy*. Oxford: Clarendon Press.

James, William. 1884. "What Is An Emotion?" *Mind* 9(34): 188–205.

———. 2003. *The Meaning of Truth*. New York: Dover.

Jameson, Fredric. 1991. *Postmodernism, or, the Cultural Logic of Late Capitalism*. London: Duke University Press.

Johnson, Barbara. 1986. "Apostrophe, Animation, and Abortion." *Diacritics* 16(1): 28–47.

———. 1998. "Muteness Envy." In *The Feminist Difference: Literature, Psychoanalysis, Race, and Gender*, 129–54. Cambridge, Mass.: Harvard University Press.

———. 2002. "Bringing Out D. A. Miller." *Narrative* (10)1: 3–8.

Johnson, Charles. 1994. "Exchange Value." In *The Sorcerer's Apprentice: Tales and Conjurations*, 25–40. New York: Plume.

Johnson, Spencer. 1998. *Who Moved My Cheese?* London: Vermilion.

Johnston, John. 1998. *Information Multiplicity: American Fiction in the Age of Media Saturation*. Baltimore, Md.: Johns Hopkins University Press.

Jones, Edgar, Robin Woolvin, Bill Durodié, and Simon Wessely. 2006. "Public Panic and

Morale: Second World War Civilian Responses Re-Examined in the Light of the Current Anti-Terrorist Campaign." *Journal of Risk Research* 9(1): 57–73.

Kaplan, Gisela. 2007. "Mimesis, Mimicry, Mind, and Music: Song Practice and Function in Humans and Birds, with Special Reference to the Australian Magpie." Paper presented at *Art of the Animal Symposium*, Gold Coast, Queensland, November.

Kellner, Douglas. 2003. "Toward a Critical Theory of Education." *Democracy and Nature* 9(1): 51–64.

Kennett, Lee. 1982. *A History of Strategic Bombing*. New York: Charles Scribner's Sons.

Kenny, Anthony. 1993. *Aristotle on the Perfect Life*. Oxford: Clarendon Press.

King, Stephen. 2000. *On Writing: A Memoir of the Craft*. London: Hodder and Stoughton.

Klingmann, Anna. 2007. *Brandscapes: Architecture in the Experience Economy*. Cambridge, Mass.: MIT Press.

Knowlton, Brian. 2007. "Bush Insists Al Qaeda in Iraq Threatens U.S." *New York Times*. July 24: A1.

Kohler, Evelyne, Christian Keysers, M. Alessandra Umilta, Leonardo Fogassi, Vittorio Gallese, and Giacomo Rizzolatti. 2002. "Hearing Sounds, Understanding Actions: Action Representation in Mirror Neurons." *Science* 29: 846–48.

Kojeve, Alexandre. 1969. *Introduction to the Reading of Hegel: Lectures on the Phenomenology of Spirit*. Trans. James H. Nichols. New York: Basic Books.

Koolhaas, Rem. 2001. *Projects for Prada: Part 1*. Milan: Fondazione Prada.

Kracauer, Siegfried. 1998. *The Salaried Masses: Duty and Distraction in Weimar Germany* [1930]. Trans. Quintin Hoare. London: Verso.

LaCapra, Dominick. 2000. *History and Reading: Tocqueville, Foucault, French Studies*. Melbourne: Melbourne University Press.

——. 2001. *Writing History, Writing Trauma*. Baltimore, Md.: Johns Hopkins University Press.

Laclau, Ernesto, and Chantal Mouffe. 1985. *Hegemony and Socialist Strategy: Towards a Radical Democratic Politics*. London: Verso.

Lakoff, George, and Mark Johnson. 1999. *Philosophy in the Flesh: The Embodied Mind and Its Challenge to Western Thought*. New York: Basic Books.

Landis, James. 1941. "Morale and Civilian Defense." *American Journal of Sociology* 47(3): 331–39.

Lapoujade, David. 2000. "From Transcendental Empiricism to Worker Nomadism: William James." *Pli* 9: 190–99.

Lash, Scott, and Celia Lury. 2007. *Global Cultural Industry: The Mediation of Things*. Cambridge: Polity Press.

Latour, Bruno. 2004. "How to Talk about the Body? The Normative Dimension of Science Studies." *Body and Society* 2(3): 205–29.

——. 2007. "A Plea for Earthly Sciences." Keynote lecture for the annual meeting of the British Sociological Association, East London, April.

Lauretis, Teresa de. 1994. *The Practice of Love: Lesbian Sexuality and Perverse Desire*. Bloomington and Indianapolis: Indiana University Press.

Law, John. 1994. *Organizing Modernity*. Oxford: Blackwell.

——. 2004. *After Method: Mess in Social Science Research*. London and New York: Routledge.

Lawrence, T. E. 1926. *Seven Pillars of Wisdom: A Triumph*. Harmondsworth: Penguin.

——. 1955. *The Mint*. Harmondsworth: Penguin.

Lazzarato, Maurizio. 2004. "From Capital-Labour to Capital-Life." *Ephemera* 4: 187–208.

Legg, Stephen. 2005. "Foucault's Population Geographies: Classifications, Biopolitics, and Governmental Spaces." *Population, Space, and Place* 11(3): 137–56.

Leslie, Esther. 2005. *Synthetic Worlds: Nature, Art, and the Chemical Industry*. London: Reaktion.

Levi, Primo. 1975. *The Periodic Table*. Trans. Raymond Rosenthal. New York: Schocken.

——. 1979. *"If This Is a Man" and "The Truce."* Trans. Stuart Woolf. London: Abacus.

——. 2001. *The Voice of Memory: Interviews, 1961–1987*. Ed. Marco Belpoliti and Robert Gordon. Cambridge: Polity Press.

Lewis-Williams, David. 2004. *The Mind in the Cave: Consciousness and the Origins of Art*. London: Thames and Hudson.

Lim, Jason. 2007. "Queer Critique and the Politics of Affect." In *Geographies of Sexualities: Theory, Practices, and Politics*, ed. Kath Browne, Jason Lim, and Gavin Brown, 53–67. London: Ashgate.

Lindeman, Eduard. 1941. "Recreation and Morale." *American Journal of Sociology* 47(3): 394–405.

Lindqvist, Sven. 2002. *A History of Bombing*. Trans. Linda Haverty Rugg. London: Granta.

Lippmann, Walter. 2007. *Public Opinion* [1922]. Charleston: BiblioBazaar.

Liu, Alan. 2004. *The Laws of Cool: The Culture of Information*. Chicago: University of Chicago Press.

Locke, John. 1997. *An Essay Concerning Human Understanding*. London: Penguin Books.

Lorde, Audre. 1984. *Sister Outsider: Essays and Speeches*. Trumansburg, New York: The Crossing Press.

Macey, Richard. 2007. "Too Overcome by Allure to Sniff the Truth." *Sydney Morning Herald*, Aug. 25.

MacFarquhar, Larissa. 2005. "Present Waking Life: Becoming John Ashbery." *New Yorker*, November 7: 86–97.

Maley, William. 2004. "Refugees." In *The Howard Years*, ed. Robert Manne, 144–66. Melbourne: Black Inc.

Manning, Erin. 2006. "Prosthetics Making Sense: Dancing the Technogenetic Body." *Fibreculture* 9. http://journal.fibreculture.org/ (accessed 3 November, 2007).

Marcus, Greil. 1986. "Critical Response." *Critical Studies in Mass Communication* 3(1): 77–81.

Margulis, Lynn, and Dorion Sagan. 1986. *Microcosmos: Four Billion Years of Evolution from our Microbial Ancestors*. New York: Summit Books.

Marks, John. 2000. "Foucault, Franks, Gauls: Il faut défendre la société; The 1976 Lectures at the Collège de France." *Theory, Culture, and Society* 17(5): 127–47.

Marks, Laura U. 2002. *Touch: Sensuous Theory and Multisensory Media*. Minnesota: University of Minnesota Press.

Marr, David, and Marian Wilkinson. 2003. *Dark Victory*. Sydney: Allen and Unwin.

Martin, Jeannie. 2000. "Shame and Violence." Paper presented at "Synthetics," the annual conference of the Cultural Studies Association of Australasia, University of Western Sydney, Australia, December.

Marx, Karl. 1974. *Economic and Philosophical Manuscripts*. Moscow: Progress Publishers.

Massumi, Brian. 1992. *A User's Guide to Capitalism and Schizophrenia: Deviations from Deleuze and Guattari*. Cambridge, Mass.: MIT Press.

——. 1993. "Everywhere You Want to Be: Introduction to Fear." In *Politics of Everyday Fear*, 3–38. Minneapolis: University of Minnesota Press.

——. 1995. "The Autonomy of Affect." *Cultural Critique* 31: 83–109.

——. 1998. "Requiem for Our Prospective Dead: Towards a Participatory Critique of Capitalist Power." In *Deleuze and Guattari: New Mappings in Politics, Philosophy, and Culture*, ed. Eleanor Kaufman and Kevin Jon Heller, 40–63. Minneapolis: University of Minnesota Press.

——. 2002. *Parables for the Virtual: Movement, Affect, Sensation*. Durham, N.C.: Duke University Press.

——. 2003. "The Archive of Experience." In *Information Is Alive: Art and Theory on Archiving and Retrieving Data*, ed. Joke Brouwer and Arjen Mulder, 142–51. Rotterdam: V2_Publishing/NAI Publishers.

——. 2005a. "The Future Birth of the Affective Fact." *Conference Proceedings: Genealogies of Biopolitics* 2. http://browse.reticular.info/text/collected/massumi.pdf (accessed 30 April 30 2006).

——. 2005b. "Fear (The Spectrum Said)." *Positions* 13(1): 31–48.

Massumi, Brian, and Mary Zournazi. 2002. "Navigating Movements." In *Hope: New Philosophies for Change*, ed. Mary Zournazi, 210–43. Melbourne: Pluto.

Maturana, Humberto, and Francisco Varela. 1980. *Autopoiesis and Cognition*. Boston: Reidel.

Mauss, Marcel. 1972. *A General Theory of Magic*. Trans. Robert Brain. New York: W. W. Norton and Company.

——. 2006. *Techniques, Technology, and Civilisation*. New York: Berghahn Books.

Mbembe, Achille. 2003. "Necropolitics." *Public Culture* 15: 11–40.

McCloskey, Deirdre N. 2006. *The Bourgeois Virtues: Ethics for an Age of Commerce*. Chicago: University of Chicago Press.

McCormack, Derek. 2005. "Diagramming Practice and Performance." *Environment and Planning D* 23: 119–47.

McCracken, Grant. 1996. *Big Hair: A Journey into the Transformation of Self*. Woodstock, N.Y.: Overlook Press.

McKercher, Catherine, and Vincent Mosco. 2007. *Knowledge Workers in the Information Society*. Lanham, Md.: Lexington Books.

McLaine, Ian. 1979. *Ministry of Morale: Home Front Morale and the Ministry of Information in World War II*. London: Allen and Unwin.

McLaren, Peter. 1989. *Life in Schools: An Introduction to Critical Pedagogy in the Foundations of Education*. New York: Longman.

McMahon, Darrin M. 2006. *Happiness: A History*. New York: Atlantic Monthly Press.

McNeill, David. 1992. *Hand and Mind: What Gestures Reveal about Thought*. Chicago: Chicago University Press.

McRobbie, Angela. 2004. "Post-Feminism and Popular Culture." *Feminist Media Studies* 4(3): 255–64.

McWilliam, Erica. 1996. "Admitting Impediments: Or Things to Do with Bodies in the Classroom." *Cambridge Journal of Education* 26(3): 367–78.

Meltzoff, Andrew N., and M. Keith Moore. 1995. "Infants' Understanding of People and Things: From Body Imitation to Folk Psychology." In *The Body and the Self*, ed. José Luis Bermudez, Anthony J. Marcel, and Naomi Eilan, 43–70. Cambridge, Mass.: MIT Press.

Merleau-Ponty, Maurice. 1974. *Phenomenology, Language and Sociology: Selected Essays of Maurice Merleau-Ponty*. London: Heinemann Educational.

———. 1999. *The Phenomenology of Perception*. Trans. C. Smith. London: Routledge.

Michaels, Eric. 1997. *Unbecoming*. Durham, N.C.: Duke University Press.

Mill, John Stuart. 1906. *Utilitarianism*. Chicago: University of Chicago Press.

Miller, Mark Crispin. 2002. *The Bush Dyslexicon: Observations on a National Disorder*. New York: Norton.

Miller, William Ian. 1997. *The Anatomy of Disgust*. Cambridge, Mass.: Harvard University Press.

Mills, C. Wright. 1953. *White Collar: The American Middle Classes*. New York: Oxford University Press.

Milton, John. 1998. "On His Blindness." In *John Milton: The Complete Poems*, ed. John Leonard, 84. London: Penguin.

Mitchell, Juliet. 2001. *Mad Men and Medusas: Reclaiming Hysteria*. New York: Basic Books.

Mitropoulos, Angela, and Brett Neilson. 2006. "Exceptional Times, Non-governmental Spacings, and Impolitical Movements." *Vacarme* 34. http://www.vacarme.org/ (accessed 21 August 2006).

Monroe, Jo. 2005. *Star of India: The Spicy Adventures of Curry*. Chichester: John Wiley.

Montessori, Maria. 1966. *The Montessori Method*. New York: Schocken Books.

Moran, Joe. 2005. *Reading the Everyday*. London: Routledge.

Morris, Meaghan. 1998. *Too Soon, Too Late: History in Popular Culture*. Bloomington: Indiana University Press.

———. 2006. *Identity Anecdotes: Translation and Media Culture*. Thousand Oaks, Calif.: Sage Publications.

Mousa, Suleiman. 1966. *T. E. Lawrence: An Arab View*. Trans. Albert Butros. Oxford: Oxford University Press.

Nancy, Jean-Luc. 2006. "Church, State, Resistance." In *Political Theologies: Public Religions in a Post-Secular World*, ed. Hent De Vries and Lawrence Sullivan, 102–12. New York: Fordham University Press.

Nathanson, Donald L. 1992. *Shame and Pride: Affect, Sex, and the Birth of the Self*. New York: W. W. Norton and Company.

Nealon, Jeffrey. 2008. *Foucault beyond Foucault: Power and Its Intensifications since 1984*. Stanford, Calif.: Stanford University Press.

Negri, Antonio. 1991. *The Savage Anomaly: The Power of Spinoza's Metaphysics and Politics*. Trans. Michael Hardt. Minneapolis: University of Minnesota Press.

——. 1999a. *Insurgencies: Constituent Power and the Modern State*. Trans. Maurizia Boscagli. Minnesota: University of Minnesota Press.

——. 1999b. "Value and Affect." *Boundary 2* 26(2): 77–88.

Neilson, Brett, and Ned Rossiter. 2005. "From Precarity to Precariousness and Back Again: Labour, Life, and Unstable Networks." *Fibreculture* 5. http://journal.fibrecul ture.org/ (accessed 11 November 2007).

Newnes, Craig, Guy Holmes, and Cailzie Dunn. 1999. *This Is Madness: A Critical Look at Psychiatry and the Future of Mental Health Services*. Llangarron, U.K.: PCCS Books.

Ngai, Sianne. 2005. *Ugly Feelings*. Cambridge, Mass.: Harvard University Press.

——. 2006. "Competitiveness: From Sula to Tyra." *Women's Studies Quarterly* 34: 105–39.

Nicholsen, Shierry Weber. 1997. "Aesthetic Theory's Mimesis of Walter Benjamin." In *Exact Imagination, Late Work: On Adorno's Aesthetics*, 137–80. Cambridge, Mass.: MIT Press.

Nietzsche, Friedrich. 1968. *The Will to Power*. Trans. Walter Kaufman and R. J. Hollingdale. New York: Vintage.

Noble, Greg. 2004. "Accumulating Being." *International Journal of Cultural Studies* 7(2): 233–56.

Nunes, Mark. 2006. *Cyberspaces of Everyday Life*. Minneapolis: University of Minnesota Press.

Oakes, Guy. 1994. *The Imaginary War: Civil Defense and American Cold War Culture*. New York: Oxford University Press.

Obama, Barack. 2007. *The Audacity of Hope: Thoughts on Reclaiming the American Dream*. Melbourne: Text Publishing.

Office of Strategic Services Planning Group. 1943. "Doctrine Regarding Rumors." http://www.icdc.com/~paulwolf/oss/rumormanual2june1943.htm (accessed 3 May 2007).

Ojakangas, Mika. 2005. "Impossible Dialogue on Biopower: Agamben and Foucault." *Foucault Studies* 2: 5–28.

Ophir, Adi. 2007. "The Two-State Solution: Providence and Catastrophe." *Journal of Homeland Security and Emergency Management* 4(1): 1–44.

Orr, Jackie. 2006. *Panic Diaries: A Genealogy of Panic Disorder*. London: Duke University Press.

Orwell, George. 1952. *Homage to Catalonia*. Orlando, Fla.: Harcourt.

——. 1975. *The Road to Wigan Pier* [1937]. London: Penguin.

——. 1980. "Such, Such Were the Joys." In *Collected Essays, Journalism, and Letters: In Front of Your Nose, 1945–50*, 330–68. Harmondsworth: Penguin.

——. 2003. *Down and Out in Paris and London* [1933]. London: Penguin.

Ó'Tuathail, Gearóid. 2003. " 'Just out Looking for a Fight': American Affect and the Invasion of Iraq." *Antipode* 35: 856–70.

Oyama, Susan. 2000. *The Ontogeny of Information: Developmental Systems and Evolution*. Durham, N.C.: Duke University Press.

Pape, Robert. 1996. *Bombing to Win: Air Power and Coercion in War*. Ithaca, N.Y.: Cornell University Press.

Parisi, Luciana. 2004. *Abstract Sex: Philosophy, Bio-Technology, and the Mutations of Desire*. London: Continuum.

Parisi, Luciana, and Steve Goodman. 2005. "The Affect of Nanoterror." *Culture Machine* 7. http://culturemachine.net/ accessed 30 April 2006).

Parisi, Luciana, and Tiziana Terranova. 2000. "Heat-Death: Emergence and Control in Genetic Engineering and Artificial Life." *Ctheory*. www.ctheory.net (accessed 30 April 2006).

Park, Robert. 1941. "Morale and the News." *American Journal of Sociology* 47(3): 360–77.

Parker, Ian, Eugenie Georgaca, David Harper, Terence McLaughlin, and Mark Stowell-Smith. 1995. *Deconstructing Psychopathology*. London: Sage.

Pastoureau, Michel. 2001. *Blue: The History of a Color*. Princeton, N.J.: Princeton University Press.

Pearson, Keith Ansell. 1999. *Germinal Life: The Difference and Repetition of Deleuze*. New York: Routledge.

Peirce, Charles S. 1998a. "The Categories Defended." In *The Essential Peirce*. Vol. 2., *Selected Philosophical Writings, 1893–1913*, ed. Peirce Edition Project, 160–78. Indianapolis: Indiana University Press.

——. 1998b. "Excerpts from Letters to Lady Welby." In *The Essential Peirce*. Vol. 2., *Selected Philosophical Writings, 1893–1913*, ed. Peirce Edition Project, 477–91. Indianapolis: Indiana University Press.

——. 1998c. "Of Reasoning in General." In *The Essential Peirce*. Vol. 2., *Selected Philosophical Writings, 1893–1913*, ed. Peirce Edition Project, 11–26. Indianapolis: Indiana University Press.

——. 1998d. "What Is A Sign?" In *The Essential Peirce*, Vol. 2, *Selected Philosophical Writings, 1893–1913*, ed. Peirce Edition Project, 4–10. Bloomington: Indiana University Press.

Pepperberg, Irene M. 1990. "Cognition in an African Grey Parrot." *Journal of Comparative Psychology* 104(1): 41–52.

Phelps, Elizabeth A. 2005. "Emotion and Cognition: Insights from Studies of the Human Amygdala." *Annual Review of Psychology* 57: 27–53.

Piaget, Jean. 1997. *The Language and Thought of the Child*. London: Routledge.

Plath, Sylvia. 2001. *The Bell Jar*. London: Faber and Faber.

"Plus de panique!" 2005. *La Presse* (Montreal), May 17: A22.

Postrel, Virginia. 2003. *The Substance of Style: How the Rise of Aesthetic Value Is Remaking Commerce, Culture, and Consciousness*. New York: Harper Collins.

——. 2005. "A Golden World." In *Glamour: Fashion, Industrial Design, Architecture*, ed. Joseph Rosa, Phil Patton, Virginia Postrel, and Valerie Steele, 24–35. New Haven, Conn.: Yale University Press.

Potolosky, Matthew. 2006. *Mimesis*. Routledge: New York and London.

Potter, Jonathan. 1996. *Representing Reality: Discourse, Rhetoric, and Social Construction*. London and Thousand Oaks, Calif.: Sage.

"President Bush Holds a News Conference: Transcript." 2007. *Washington Post*, August 9.

Prigogine, Ilya, and Isabelle Stengers. 1984. *Order Out of Chaos: Man's New Dialogue With Nature*. New York: Bantam Books.

Pringle, Rosemary. 1988. *Secretaries Talk: Sexuality, Power, and Work*. Sydney: Allen and Unwin.

Probyn, Elspeth. 2004. "Teaching Bodies: Affects in the Classroom." *Body and Society* 10(4): 21–43.

———. 2005. *Blush: Faces of Shame*. Minneapolis: University of Minnesota Press.

Proust, Marcel. 1992. *Remembrance of Things Past*, Vol. 3. New York: Vintage Books.

Puar, Jasbir. 2007. *Terrorist Assemblages: Homonationalism in Queer Times*. Durham, N.C.: Duke University Press.

Rancière, Jacques. 2004. *The Politics of Aesthetics: The Distribution of the Sensible*. Trans. Gabriel Rockhill. London and New York: Continuum.

Reay, Diane. 2005. "Beyond Consciousness? The Psychic Landscape of Social Class." *Sociology* 39: 911–28.

Redding, Paul. 1999. *The Logic of Affect*. Melbourne: Melbourne University Press.

Reed, Edward S. 1995. "Becoming a Self." In *The Self in Infancy: Theory and Research*, ed. Philippe Rochat, 431–48. Amsterdam: Elsevier.

Ricco, John Paul. 2002. *The Logic of the Lure*. Chicago: University of Chicago Press.

Rizzolatti, Giacomo. 1994. "Nonconscious Motor Images." *Behavioral and Brain Science* 17: 220.

Rizzolatti, Giacomo, and Michael A. Arbib. 1998. "Language within Our Grasp." *Trends in Neuroscience* 21: 188–94.

Roach, Joseph. 2007. *It*. Ann Arbor: University of Michigan Press.

Robin, Ron. 2001. *The Making of the Cold War Enemy: Culture and Politics in the Military-Industrial Complex*. Princeton, N.J.: Princeton University Press.

Roethke, Theodore. 1976. "I Knew a Woman." *The Penguin Book of Love Poetry*. New York: Penguin Press, 181.

"Romanian Orphanages." 2006. *ITV News*, September 21 (airdate).

Ross, Andrew. 2004. *No Collar: The Humane Workplace and Its Hidden Costs*. New York: Basic Books.

———. 2006. *Fast Boat to China: Corporate Flight and the Consequences of Free Trade; Lessons from Shanghai*. New York: Pantheon.

———. 2009. *Nice Work If You Can Get It: Life and Labor in Precarious Times*. New York: New York University Press.

Ross, Daniel. 2004. *Violent Democracy*. Cambridge: Cambridge University Press.

Rossiter, Ned. 2007. "YourSpace Is Mytime, or, What Is the Lurking Dog Going to Do— Leave a Comment?" Paper presented at New Cultural Networks: You Google My Second Space, Theater van't Woord, Openbare Bibliotheek Amsterdam, Stifo@sandberg Institute of Design, Amsterdam, Nov. 2. http://www.re-public.gr/en/ (accessed 11 November 2007).

Ryman, Geoff. 1992. *Was*. New York: Penguin.

Sadler, John Z. 2005. *Values and Psychiatric Diagnosis*. Oxford: Oxford University Press.

Scarry, Elaine. 1985. *The Body in Pain: The Making and Unmaking of the World*. Oxford: Oxford University Press.

———. 1997. "Imagining Flowers: Perceptual Mimesis (Particularly Delphinium)." *Representations* 57: 90–115.

Schlunke, Katrina. 2006. "Ecologue." *Cultural Studies Review* 12(1): 202–6.

Schmitt, Eric, and Richard W. Stevenson. 2004. "Admitting Intelligence Flaws, Bush Stands by Need for War." *New York Times,* July 10: A9.

Sedgwick, Eve Kosofsky. 1998. "A Dialogue on Love." *Critical Inquiry* 24(2): 611–31.

———. 2003. *Touching Feeling: Affect, Performativity, Pedagogy.* Durham, N.C.: Duke University Press.

———. 2006. "Teaching/Depression." *The Scholar and the Feminist Online* 4(2). http://www.barnard.columbia.edu/sfonline/heilbrun/sedgwick_01.htm (accessed Feb. 25, 2008).

———. 2007. "Melanie Klein and the Difference Affect Makes." *South Atlantic Quarterly* 106(3): 625–42.

Sedgwick, Eve Kosofsky, and Adam Frank. 1995a. "Shame in the Cybernetic Fold: Reading Silvan Tomkins." In *Shame and Its Sisters: A Silvan Tomkins Reader,* ed. Eve Kosofsky Sedgwick and Adam Frank, 1–28. Durham, N.C.: Duke University Press.

———, eds. 1995b. *Shame and Its Sisters: A Silvan Tomkins Reader.* Durham, N.C.: Duke University Press.

Sedgwick, Peter. 1982. *Psycho Politics: Laing, Foucault, Goffman, Szasz, and the Future of Mass Psychiatry.* New York: Harper and Row.

Seigworth, Gregory. 2003. "Fashioning a Stave, or, Singing Life." In *Animations of Deleuze and Guattari,* ed. Jennifer Daryl Slack, 75–105. New York: Peter Lang Publishing.

———. 2007a. "Cultural Studies and Gilles Deleuze." In *New Cultural Studies: Adventures in Theory,* ed. Gary Hall and Clare Birchall, 107–27. Edinburgh: Edinburgh University Press.

———. 2007b. "Little Affect: Hallward's Deleuze." *Culture Machine.* http://culturemachine.net/ (accessed 10 October 2007).

Semprún, Jorge. 1984. *What a Beautiful Sunday!* London: Sphere Books.

Sennett, Richard. 1998. *The Corrosion of Character: The Personal Consequences of Work in the New Capitalism.* New York: W. W. Norton.

Serres, Michel. 1982. "The Origin of Language: Biology, Information Theory, and Thermodynamics." In *Hermes: Literature, Science, Philosophy,* ed. Harari, Josue V. and David Bell, 71–83. Baltimore, Md.: Johns Hopkins University.

Shannon, Claude. 1948. "A Mathematical Theory of Communication." *Bell System Technical Journal* 27 (July & October): 379–423 and 623–56.

Shaviro, Steven. 2007. "Pulses of Emotion: Whitehead's 'Critique of Pure Feeling.'" *The Pinocchio Theory.* http://www.shaviro.com/ (accessed 1 July 2007).

Sherry, Michael. 1987. *The Rise of American Air Power: The Creation of Armageddon.* New Haven, Conn.: Yale University Press.

Shouse, Eric. 2005. "Feeling, Emotion, Affect." *M/C Journal* 8(6). http://journal.media-culture.org.au/ (accessed 13 August 2007).

Simmel, Georg. 1968. "Sociological Aesthetics" [1896]. In *The Conflict in Modern Culture and Other Essays,* 68–80. Trans. K. Peter Etzkorn. New York: Teachers College Press.

Simondon, Gilbert. 1992. "The Genesis of the Individual." In *Incorporations,* ed. Jonathan Crary and Sanford Kwinter, 297–319. New York: Zone Books.

Simpson, Christopher. 1994. *Science of Coercion: Communication Research and Psychological Warfare 1945–1960*. New York: Oxford University Press.

Skeggs, Beverley. 2004. *Class, Self, Culture*. London: Routledge.

Sloterdijk, Peter. 2007. "What Happened in the Twentieth Century? En Route to a Critique of Extremist Reason." *Cultural Politics* 3: 327–55.

Smail, David John. 2001a. "On Not Being Able to Eff the Ineffable." In *Spirituality and Psychotherapy*, ed. S. King-Spooner and C. Newnes, 47–51. Ross-on-Wye, U.K.: PCCS Books.

———. 2001b. *The Nature of Un-Happiness*. London: Robinson Publishing.

———. 2005. *Power, Interest, and Psychology: Elements of Social Materialist Understanding of Distress*. Ross-on-Wye, U.K.: PCCS Books.

Smith, Adam. 2000. *The Theory of Moral Sentiments*. New York: Prometheus Books.

Sofer, Andrew. 2003. *The Stage Life of Props*. Ann Arbor: University of Michigan Press.

Sorgente di vita. 2001. Television program. Italy. Jan. 25.

Soucy, Louise Maude Rioux. 2005. "Le virus de la prochaine pandémie de grippe n'existe pas encore." *Le Devoir*, October 19: A1.

Spinoza, Benedict. 1952. "Ethics." In *Descartes/Spinoza*, 349–463. Chicago: Encyclopedia Britannica.

———. 1959. *Ethics; On the Correction of Understanding*. Trans. Andrew Boyle. London: Everyman's Library.

———. 1994. "The Ethics." In *A Spinoza Reader: The Ethics and Other Works*, ed. and trans. Edwin Curley, 85–265. Princeton, N.J.: Princeton University Press.

Stafford, Barbara Maria. 2007. *Echo Objects: The Cognitive Work of Images*. Chicago: University of Chicago Press.

Stengers, Isabelle. 2007. "Diderot's Egg: Divorcing Materialism from Eliminativism." *Radical Philosophy* 144: 7–15.

Stern, Daniel N. 1985. *The Interpersonal World of the Infant*. New York: Basic Books.

———. 1993. "The Role of Feelings for an Interpersonal Self." In *The Perceived Self: Ecological and Interpersonal Sources of Self-Knowledge*, ed. Ulric Neisser, 205–15. Cambridge: Cambridge University Press.

———. 2004. *The Present Moment in Psychotherapy and Everyday Life*. New York: W. W. Norton and Company.

Stewart, Kathleen. 2007. *Ordinary Affects*. Durham, N.C.: Duke University Press.

Stiegler, Bernard. 1998. *Technics and Time: The Fault of Epimetheus*. Trans. Richard Beardsworth and George Collins. Stanford, Calif.: Stanford University Press.

Stoler, Ann. 2004. "Affective States." In *A Companion to the Anthropology of Politics*, ed. David Nugent and Joan Vincent, 4–20. New York: Blackwell.

Sullivan, Harry. 1941. "Psychiatric Aspects of Morale." *American Journal of Sociology* 47(3): 277–301.

Szasz, Thomas Stephen. 1974. *The Myth of Mental Illness: Foundations of a Theory of Personal Conduct*. Rev. ed. London: Harper and Row.

Taussig, Michael. 1993. *Mimesis and Alterity: A Particular History of the Senses*. New York and London: Routledge.

Taylor, Mark C. 2001. *The Moment of Complexity: Emerging Network Culture*. Chicago: University of Chicago Press.

Terada, Rei. 2001. *Feeling in Theory: Emotion after the "Death of the Subject."* Cambridge, Mass.: Harvard University Press.

Terranova, Tiziana. 2004. *Network Culture: Politics for the Information Age.* London: Pluto.

Thacker, Eugene. 2004. *Biomedia.* Minneapolis: University of Minnesota Press.

———. 2005a. "Nomos, Nosos, and Bios." *Culture Machine* 7. http://culturemachine.net/ (accessed 30 April, 2006).

———. 2005b. *The Global Genome: Biotechnology, Politics, and Culture.* Cambridge, Mass.: MIT Press.

Thrailkill, Jane F. 2006. "Emotive Realism." *JNT: Journal of Narrative Theory* 36: 365–88.

———. 2007. *Affecting Fictions: Mind, Body, and Emotion in American Literary Realism.* Cambridge, Mass.: Harvard University Press.

Thrift, Nigel. 2004. "Intensities of Feeling: Towards a Spatial Politics of Affect." *Geografiska Annaler* 86: 57–78.

———. 2005. *Knowing Capitalism.* London: Sage.

———. 2006. "Re-Inventing Invention: New Tendencies in Capitalist Commodification." *Economy and Society* 35(2): 279–306.

———. 2008a. "Talent Worlds." Paper presented at the Cultural Political Economy Workshop, University of Ottawa, June 16.

———. 2008b. "Re-Animating the Place of Thought." In *Community, Economic Creativity, and Organization*, ed. A. Amin and J. Roberts, 90–119. Oxford: Oxford University Press.

———. Forthcoming. "Halos: Finding Space in the World for New Political Forms." In *The Politics of Stuff*, ed. B. Braun and S. J. Whatmore. Minneapolis: University of Minnesota Press.

Tomkins, Silvan. 1962. *Affect, Imagery, and Consciousness: The Positive Affects.* New York: Springer Publishing Company.

———. 1992. *Affect, Imagery, Consciousness.* Vol 4. New York: Springer.

Tomkins, Silvan S., and Carroll E. Izard. 1966. *Affect, Cognition, and Personality: Empirical Studies.* London: Tavistock Press.

Toscano, Alberto. 2007. " 'European Nihilism' and Beyond: Commentary by Alberto Toscano." In *The Century*, by Alain Badiou, trans. Alberto Toscano, 179–201. London: Polity Press.

Trentmann, Frank. 2007. "Before 'Fair Trade': Empire, Free Trade, and the Moral Economies of Food in the Modern World." *Environment and Planning D: Society and Space* 25: 1079–1102.

Trevarthen, Colwyn. 1999/2000. "Musicality and the Intrinsic Motive Pulse: Evidence from Human Psychobiology and Infant Communication." In "Rhythms, Musical Narrative, and the Origins of Human Communication," special issue, *Musicae Scientae*: 157–213.

———. 2002. "Can a Robot Hear Music? Can a Robot Dance? Can a Robot Tell What It Knows or Intends to Do? Can it Feel Pride or Shame in Company? Questions of the Nature of Human Vitality." In *2002 Proceedings of the Second International Workshop in Epigenetic Robots: Modelling Cognitive Development in Robotic Systems*, ed. C. G. Prince et al., 79–86. Lund, Sweden: Lund University Press.

Tucker, Ian M. 2006. "Deterritorialising Mental Health: Unfolding Service User Experience." Unpublished Ph.D. diss. Loughborough University, U.K.

Turkle, Sherry. 2005. *The Second Self: Computers and the Human Spirit*. Cambridge, Mass.: MIT Press.

Turner, Graeme. 2004. *Understanding Celebrity*. London: Sage.

Ukai, Satoshi. 2001. "The Future of an Affect: The Historicity of Shame." *Traces* 1: 3–36.

Ulio, James. 1941. "Military Morale." *American Journal of Sociology* 47(3): 321–30.

Ullman, Ellen. 1996. "Come In, CQ: The Body on the Wire." In *Wired Women: Gender and New Realities in Cyberspace*, ed. Lynn Cherny and Elizabeth Reba Weise, 3–23. Seattle: Seal Press.

Ullman, Harlan, and James Wade. 1996. *Shock and Awe: Achieving Rapid Dominance*. Washington, D.C.: National Defense University.

United States Strategic Bombing Survey. 1947a. *Effects of Bombing on German Morale*. 2 vols. European Survey Report #64B Morale Division. Washington, D.C.

———. 1947b. *The Effects of Strategic Bombing on Japanese Morale*. Pacific Survey Report #14 Morale Division. Washington, D.C.

Van Baaren, Rick B., Terry G. Horgan, Tanya L. Chartrand, and Marit Dijkmans. 2004. "The Forest, the Trees, and the Chameleon: Context Dependence and Mimicry." *Journal of Personality and Social Psychology* 86(3): 453–59.

Van Creveld, Martin. 1991. *Technology and War: From 2000 B.C. to the Present*. Toronto: Maxwell Macmillan.

Van der Veer, René, and Jaan Valsiner. 1991. *Understanding Vygotsky: A Quest for Synthesis*. Oxford: Blackwell.

Varela, Francisco. 1999. "The Specious Present: A Neurophenomenology of Time Consciousness." In *Naturalizing Phenomenology*, ed. Jean Petiot, Francisco Varela, Bernard Pachoud, and Jean-Michel Roy, 266–312. Stanford, Calif.: Stanford University Press.

Varela, Francisco, Evan T. Thompson, and Eleanor Rosch. 1993. *The Embodied Mind: Cognitive Science and Human Experience*. Cambridge, Mass.: MIT Press.

Veenhoven, Ruut. 1984. *Conditions of Happiness*. Dordrecht: R. Rieidal Publishing.

Vick, Malcolm. 1996. "Fixing the Body: Prescriptions for Pedagogy 1850–1950." In *Pedagogy, Technology, and the Body*, ed. Erica McWilliam and Peter G. Taylor, 113–26. New York: Peter Lang.

Virilio, Paul. 2005. *City of Panic*. Trans. Julie Rose. London: Berg.

Virilio, Paul, and Sylvere Lotringer. 1997. *Pure War*. New York: Semiotext(e).

Virno, Paul. 2004. *A Grammar of the Multitude: For an Analysis of Contemporary Forms of Life*. Trans. Isabella Bertoletti, James Cascaito, and Andrea Casson. New York: Semiotext(e).

Virtanen, Akseli. 2004. "General Economy: The Entrance of Multitude into Production." *Ephemera* 4(3): 225.

Visram, Rozina. 2002. *Asians in Britain: 400 Years of History*. London: Pluto Press.

Vygotsky, Lev. 1986. *Thought and Language*. Ed. Alex Kozulin. Cambridge, Mass.: MIT Press.

——. 1987. "The Problem and the Method of Investigation." In *The Collected Works of L. S. Vygotsky*, ed. Robert W. Rieber and Aaron S. Carton, 1: 43–52. New York: Plenum Press.

Walkerdine, Valerie. 1984. "Developmental Psychology and the Child-Centred Pedagogy: The Insertion of Piaget into Early Education." In *Changing the Subject: Psychology, Social Regulation, and Subjectivity*, ed. Jacques Henriques, Wendy Hollway, Cathy Urwin, Couze Venn, and Valerie Walkerdine, 148–98. London: Methuen.

Watkins, Megan. 2005. "The Erasure of Habit: Tracing the Pedagogic Body." *Discourse* 26(2): 167–81.

——. 2006. "Pedagogic Affect/Effect: Embodying the Desire to Learn." *Pedagogies* 1(4): 269–82.

——. 2007. "Thwarting Desire: Discursive Constraint and Pedagogic Practice." *International Journal of Qualitative Studies in Education* 20(3): 301–18.

Weber, Samuel. 2004. *Theatricality as Medium*. New York: Fordham University Press.

——. 2005. *Targets of Opportunity: On the Militarization of Thinking*. New York: Fordham University Press.

Weissenstein, Michael. 2005. "Officials: NYC Terror Plot Uncorroborated." *Star-Ledger* (Newark, N.J.), Oct. 9: 6.

Whitehead, Alfred North. 1933. *Adventures of Ideas*. New York: Free Press.

——. 1979. *Process and Reality*. New York: Free Press.

Whyte, William H. 1963. *The Organization Man* [1936]. Harmondsworth, Middlesex, U.K.: Penguin Books.

Wiener, Norbert. 1950. *The Human Use of Human Beings*. Boston: Houghton Mifflin.

Williams, Raymond. 1977. *Marxism and Literature*. Oxford and New York: Oxford University Press.

——. 1979. *Politics and Letters: Interviews with New Left Review*. London: New Left Books.

——. 1980. *Problems in Materialism and Culture*. London and New York: Schocken Books.

Wilson, Jason. 2006. "Rough Chuckles: Mourning the Public Sphere in Online Comics." Paper delivered at the Association of Internet Researchers Annual Conference 7.0: Internet Convergences. Brisbane, September.

Winnicott, Donald W. 1965. "The Theory of the Parent-Infant Relationship." In *The Maturational Processes and the Facilitating Environment*, ed. Donald W. Winnicott, 37–55. New York: International Universities Press.

——. 1978. *The Child, the Family, and the Outside World*. Harmondsworth: Penguin Books.

——. 2006. *The Family and Individual Development*. London: Routledge.

Wolf, Nancy S., Mary E. Gales, Estelle Shane, and Morton Shane. 2001. "The Developmental Trajectory from Amodal Perception to Empathy and Communication: The Role of Mirror Neurons in This Process." *Psychoanalytic Inquiry* 21: 94–112.

Wolin, Sheldon. 2008. *Democracy Incorporated: Managed Democracy and the Specter of Inverted Totalitarianism*. Princeton, N.J.: Princeton University Press.

Wood, Michael. 2005. *Literature and the Taste of Knowledge*. Cambridge: Cambridge University Press.

Woodward, Bob. 2002. *Bush at War*. New York: Simon and Schuster.

Woodward, Kathleen. 1996. "Global Cooling and Academic Warming: Long-Term Shifts in Emotional Weather." *American Literary History* 8(4): 759–99.

Woolf, Virginia. 1957. *A Room of One's Own*. New York: Harcourt, Brace, and Jovanovich.

Yar, Majid. 2001. "Recognition and the Politics of Human(e) Desire." *Theory, Culture, and Society* 18(2–3): 57–76.

Yoshimi, Shunya. 2006. "Information." *Theory, Culture, and Society* 23(2–3): 271–88.

Žižek, Slavoj. 2004. "Passion: Regular or Decaf?" *In These Times* 27. http://www.inthese times.com/ (accessed 25 February 2008).

Žižek, Slavoj, Eric L. Santner, and Kenneth Reinhard. 2006. *The Neighbor: Three Inquiries in Political Theology*. Chicago: University of Chicago Press.

Zournazi, Mary, ed. 2002. *Hope: New Philosophies for Change*. Melbourne: Pluto Press.

——. 2003. "Navigating Movements: An Interview with Brian Massumi." In *21C Magazine* 2. http://www.21cmagazine.com/ (accessed 25 February 2008).

SARA AHMED is a professor of race and cultural studies at Goldsmiths College, University of London. She works at the intersection between feminist, queer, and critical race theory. Her previous books include *Differences That Matter: Feminist Theory and Postmodernism* (1998), *Strange Encounters: Embodied Others in Post-Coloniality* (2000), *The Cultural Politics of Emotion* (2004), *Queer Phenomenology: Orientations, Objects, Others* (2006), and *The Promise of Happiness* (2010). She is working on her next book, *Doing Diversity: Racism and Educated Subjects.*

BEN ANDERSON is a lecturer in human geography in the Department of Geography at Durham University (U.K.). His research falls into three areas: ethnographic research on the circulation of boredom and hope in contemporary Western everyday life; work on the emergence of affect as an object of governance in urban policy, science and technology policy, and military policy; and work that thinks through utopianism as an affective ethos of engagement. He is currently writing a book entitled *Spaces of Affect and Emotion* that synthesizes this work into an explicitly spatial theory of affect and emotion.

LAUREN BERLANT is the George M. Pullman Professor of English and the director of the Lesbian and Gay Studies Project at the Center for Gender Studies at the University of Chicago. Developing a concept of affective publics since *The Anatomy of National Fantasy: Hawthorne,*

Utopia, and Everyday Life (1991), she has completed the national sentimentality trilogy, with *The Queen of America Goes to Washington City: Essays on Sex and Citizenship* (1997), and *The Female Complaint: The Unfinished Business of Sentimentality in American Culture* (2008). She is also the editor of a number of emotional books, such as *Intimacy* (2000), *Compassion* (2004), and, with Laura Letinsky, *Venus Inferred* (2001). Her next project, *Cruel Optimism*, looks at varieties of contemporary political depression.

LONE BERTELSEN lectures in the School of Sociology and Anthropology at the University of New South Wales, Sydney. She is currently working on a project that studies the impact of what has been called the productive unconscious on modes of belonging. Her most recent article, "Matrixial Refrains," was published in *Theory, Culture, and Society*. She has written on affective photo-theory and a number of photo-based artworks.

STEVEN D. BROWN is a senior lecturer in psychology in the Department of Human Sciences at Loughborough University and a visiting professor in psychology and critical theory at the Universiteit voor Humanistiek in Utrecht, the Netherlands. He is the co-author of two recent books: *Psychology without Foundations: History, Philosophy, and Psychosocial Theory* with Paul Stenner (2009), and *The Social Psychology of Experience: Studies in Remembering and Forgetting* with David Middleton (2005). He has published widely in the areas of psychology, science and technology studies, and organizational and critical management studies.

PATRICIA T. CLOUGH is a professor of sociology, the coordinator of the Women's Studies Certificate Program, and the director of the Center for Research on Women and Society at the Graduate Center, City University of New York. Her work on critical studies of bodies, gender, sexualities, media cultures, and technoscience appears in her books *Feminist Thought: Power, Desire, and Academic Discourse* (1994), *The End(s) of Ethnography: From Realism to Social Criticism* (1998), and *Autoaffection: Unconscious Thought in the Age of Teletechnology* (2000).

ANNA GIBBS is an associate professor in the School of Communication Arts at the University of Western Sydney who was clinically trained in psychodynamic psychotherapy. Her previous research draws together affect theory, infant research, and feminist theories of the body in an investigation of mimetic communication in the social field. She is currently working with Virginia Nightingale on a project funded by the Australian Research Council entitled "The Power of the Image: Affect, Audience and Disturbing Imagery."

MELISSA GREGG is on faculty in the Department of Gender and Cultural Studies at the University of Sydney. She is the author of *Cultural Studies' Affective Voices* (2006), and the coeditor of "Counter-Heroics and Counter-Professionalism in Cultural Studies" in *Continuum* (2006). Her current projects include *Broadcast Yourself: Presence, Intimacy, and Community Online* (with Catherine Driscoll), and *Working From Home*, a study of the impact of new media technologies on gender and labor politics.

LAWRENCE GROSSBERG is the Morris Davis Distinguished Professor of Communications and Cultural Studies and the director of the University Program in Cultural Studies at the University of North Carolina, Chapel Hill. He is known internationally as one of the leading figures in cultural studies. His books include *It's a Sin: Essays on Postmodernism, Politics, and Culture* (1988), *We Gotta Get Out of This Place: Popular Conservatism and Postmodern Culture* (1992), *Dancing in Spite of Myself: Essays in Popular Culture* (1997), *Bringing It All Back Home: Essays in Cultural Studies* (1997), and *MediaMaking* (1998). He is the co-editor of several books, including *Cultural Studies* (1991), *Sound and Vision* (1993), and *The Audience and Its Landscapes* (1996), as well as the journal *Cultural Studies*. He is the author most recently of *Caught in the Crossfire: Kids, Politics, and America's Future* (2005).

BEN HIGHMORE is a reader in media and cultural studies at the University of Sussex. He is the author of *Everyday Life and Cultural Theory* (2002), *Cityscapes: Cultural Readings in the Material and Symbolic City* (2005), and *Michel de Certeau: Analysing Culture* (2006). He also edited *The Everyday Life Reader* (2002) and is the reviews editor of *New Formations*.

BRIAN MASSUMI is a professor in the Department of Communication Studies at the University of Montreal. His recent publications include *Parables for the Virtual: Movement, Affect, Sensation* (2002) and *A Shock to Thought: Expression after Deleuze and Guattari* (2002).

ANDREW MURPHIE is a senior lecturer in the School of Media, Film, and Theatre at the University of New South Wales. He has published on the work of Gilles Deleuze and Félix Guattari, cultural theory, virtual media, network ecologies, and popular music. He is the co-author with John Potts of *Culture and Technology* (2003) and the editor of the *Fibreculture Journal* (http://journal.fibreculture.org/). His current research focuses on the cultural politics of models of cognition, perception, and life; media ecologies; electronic music; and performance technologies.

ELSPETH PROBYN is a professor of gender and cultural studies at the University of Sydney. Her work focuses on questions of identity, sexuality, and bodies. She has published several books in these areas, including *Sexing the Self* (1993), *Outside Belongings* (1996), *Carnal Appetites: FoodSexIdentities* (2000), and *Sexy Bodies*, co-edited with Elizabeth Grosz (1995). Her latest book, *Blush: Faces of Shame* (2005), focuses on shame as a positive force in society. With Catharine Lumby, she is writing a book on girls' feelings.

GREGORY J. SEIGWORTH is a professor in communication and theater at Millersville University of Pennsylvania. He has co-edited two issues of the journal *Cultural Studies* on the work of Deleuze and Guattari (2000) and, more recently, a double issue (2004) on philosophies of everyday life. Seigworth has published widely, most recently contributing chapters to two books: *Gilles Deleuze: Key Concepts* (2005) and *New Cultural Studies* (2007).

KATHLEEN STEWART is a professor in the Department of Anthropology at the University of Texas, Austin, and is also the director of the Americo Paredes Center for Cultural Studies. She writes on political imaginaries and structures of desire in the United States. Kathleen is the author of *A Space on the Side of the Road: Cultural Poetics in an "Other" America* (Princeton, 1996) and *Ordinary Affects* (Duke, 2007).

NIGEL THRIFT is a vice chancellor of the University of Warwick. He is one of the world's leading social scientists and scholars of human geography. Thrift has been awarded many prizes and commendations recognizing his research and was elected fellow of the British Academy in 2003.

IAN TUCKER teaches at Northampton University in the areas of mental health, conceptual issues, qualitative social psychology, and research methods. His research interests lie broadly in the area of social psychology, with particular interest in psychology operating across disciplinary boundaries. Key areas of interest include psychosocial aspects of mental health, chronic illness, affect, and theoretical psychology more broadly. Tucker's research predominantly operates in the area of qualitative methods, with particular interest in discursive approaches that enable the analysis of the relation between discursive and material practices in the production of experience.

MEGAN WATKINS is a lecturer in literacy and pedagogy in the School of Education at the University of Western Sydney. She is the co-author of *Genre, Text, Grammar: Technologies for Teaching and Assessing Writing* (2005). Her research interests are in the areas of pedagogy, affect, desire, and embodiment. She has published scholarly articles in the areas of pedagogy, affect, and the role of the body in learning.

Page numbers in italics indicate illustrations.

excess of affect: affective labor and, 165–67, 184n4; affect theories and, 5, 9, 17, 162–63; autonomy and, 162, 164, 167, 172; becoming and, 162–63, 179–81; biopolitics and, 165, 222–23; biopower relations and, 162, 168, 172, 184n3; bodily capacity and, 161, 164, 165, 174, 177; capitalism and, 164–65, 183; control and, 162, 163, 165–66, 168, 171, 178, 183; cultural theory and, 17, 161–65, 182–84, 184n2, 186; cybernetics and, 173, 183; emotions and, 186–88, 191–92, 200, 202, 205n17; forces and, 162, 167–68, 173–74, 185n9; gender roles and, 163; hope and, 164, 166, 182; identity and, 155, 156; immeasurablity and, 162, 182; indetermination and, 163, 164, 176, 182–83; information channels and, 170, 178–83; modulation and, 161–62, 165, 168–69, 180, 182–83; morale and, 163–64, 169–83, 184–85n8, 185n10; movement and, 162, 167–68, 173–74, 177, 178; object of power relations and, 163, 168, 177, 182; the other and, 155, 156; passion and, 166, 168–69, 170; political ideology and, 164–69; population and, 165, 172–73, 178, 184n3; power relations and, 161–69, 178–79, 181–84; shock and, 181; structure and, 172, 178–79; "total war" and, 163, 169–75, 177–79, 181–83; transitions and, 162; virtualization of morale and, 162, 166, 177–78, 183; vitalism and, 162, 166, 169, 170, 183

experience/experiences: everyday life and, 7, 15–16; happiness and, 31–33, 35, 37–38, 40, 48–50; humanism and, 232–33; ineffable affect and, 230–33, 235, 237–40, 242, 245–47; mental health service users and, 230–33, 235, 242, 249n3; of nature, 123; optimism and, 94, 98, 111–16; threat as, 64–66; transformative, 111–16; writing shame and, 81–89

extimacy (public intimacy), 16, 290–91, 294–95, 304

family: and happiness, 38, 42–45, 47–49

far-from-equilibrium physics, 7–8

feeling/feelings: bad, 30, 31, 38–39, 43, 49–50; contagion of, 8, 36, 49; conversion of, 38, 43, 49; cultural studies and, 335; definition of, 140; emotions and, 8, 77, 148; good, 30, 34, 37–38, 39, 46; happiness as, 29, 33, 50–51; intentionality and, 31; mimesis and, 196–97, 204n13; movement and, 77; objects and correspondence with, 32, 37–38, 40; social aesthetics and, 120, 124, 130–32, 136n7; structure of, 7, 9, 21, 310, 313, 317–18, 322–23, 327, 330; threat and, 55, 63–64, 66, 69n14; writing shame and, 72, 77

feminism, 30, 38–39, 50, 136n4, 267n2, 316

feminist kill-joys, 30, 38–39, 50

force/forces: affect as, 1–3, 5; conscious experience and, 1, 4; excess of affect and, 162, 167–68, 173–74, 185n9; pedagogic process and, 269–70, 273–74, 278–80, 282–84; pre-individual, 207, 209, 219, 221, 235, 239; territories and, 139; threat and, 63, 65; workplace and, 263–64; worlding refrains and, 343, 346, 349; writing shame and, 78, 87

Foucault, Michel: on biopolitical racism, 223; on disciplinary power, 165; on environmentality of government, 68–69n12; on machinic process, 314, 315, 318; on pleasure, 231–32; on police, 179, 185n9; on political economy, 323; on population and the "public," 165, 184n3; on power relations, 165; on primary datum, 177; on subject as disappearing, 322; on words/objects relationship, 74–75

Frank, Adam, 5, 22, 74

Franzen, Jonathan, 125

Frasier (television show), 125

Freedom: and happiness, 42, 45–47

Freud, Sigmund, 2–3, 51n1, 122–23, 275, 311

future/futurity: affect theories and, 4, 9,

micropolitical events, 138, 139. *See also* political economy

Mill, John Stuart, 51n2

mimesis: agency and, 196–97, 201; becoming and, 16, 194, 204n11; behavior and, 194, 197–99, 202, 204n16; belonging and, 191, 203n5; brain and, 190, 198, 202; capacities and, 187–90, 201–3, 204n16; cognitive science and, 188–90, 196–98, 200, 204n13; conscious experience and, 200, 206, 209, 212–13; contagion and, 36, 186, 190, 191–92, 203n6, 203n7; description of, 186–88, 202; de-territorialization and, 194; embodiment and, 190, 196, 201; evolution and, 190, 194; feeling and, 196–97, 204n13; gesture and, 192, 197, 199, 202, 204n16; habit and, 187, 200; human biology and, 188, 190, 207; humanism tension with nonhumanism and, 15–16, 187, 203; humanities and, 187, 189–90; identity and, 195, 196; image and, 187, 191–92; imitation and, 186–90, 195–96, 202–3, 203n4, 204n12, 205nn21–22; innate theory and, 187–88, 195–96, 200–201, 204n12, 204n14; language and, 198–202, 204n15, 205n21; memory and, 187, 196, 200, 201, 209; mimetic communication and, 186–89, 191, 199–200, 202, 205n17; movement and, 186–88, 192–93, 195, 197–99, 203, 204n11, 204nn15–16; nature vs. nurture and, 190, 203n2; the other and, 195, 196; relationality and, 13, 186, 197–98, 202; representation and, 186, 191, 193, 203; rhythm and, 187, 195, 197–99, 204n15; semiosis and, 192, 193; senses and, 193, 198, 200–202, 204n9, 205n21; subjectivity and oscillation in, 15–16, 187, 203; sympathy and, 186–87, 193, 197–98; synchrony and, 186, 187, 197–98; temporality and, 190, 192, 201; vitalism and, 193; writing and, 198, 201, 203

mimetic communication, 186–89, 191, 199–200, 202, 205n17

mimicry, 188–91, 193–96, 202, 203nn3–5, 204n10

mind: body and, 23, 80–81, 86, 279, 317; somatic management and, 233, 235, 237, 242–49

modernity: future of, 318–19

modulation: affect theories and, 2, 6; excess of affect and, 161–62, 165, 168–69, 180, 182–83; power relations and, 16, 62

morale: life itself and, 176, 177, 182, 183; psychology and, 171, 173, 176; virtualization and, 162, 166, 177–78, 183, 320; war and, 163–64, 169–83, 184n8, 185n10

morals/ethics, 12–13, 105, 266–67, 307–8. *See also* ethico-aesthetic

more-than-human, 13, 16

Morris, Meaghan, 19, 328, 336

motion (movement). *See* movement (motion)

Mousa, Suleiman, 79–80, 81

movement (motion): affective turn and, 219–20; affect theories and, 8; biomediated body and, 211–13, 217, 219, 224n4; ethico-aesthetic and, 140, 146, 147, 149; excess of affect and, 162, 167–68, 173–74, 177, 178; feelings and, 77; mattering maps and, 21, 309, 316; mimesis and, 186, 192–93, 195, 197–99, 203, 204n11, 204n16; as proprioception, 77, 174, 193, 196, 224n5; statis vs., 4, 77, 234–36. *See also* rhythm/rhythms; senses/synesthesia

Murphie, Andrew, 15, 22. *See also* ethico-aesthetic

music, 19–20, 310, 311, 330–31, 335, 337–38

Nathanson, Donald L., 278

nature, 123, 190, 203n2

Negri, Antonio, 7, 164–68, 184n4

nervous system, 8, 146, 147, 149–50, 151

networks, 120, 147, 165, 182, 187, 196, 253, 257

neuro-cognitive sciences, 7–8

neurology/neuroscience, 6, 165, 188, 191, 204n9, 279, 285n6

Library of Congress Cataloging-in-Publication Data

The affect theory reader / edited by Melissa Gregg
and Gregory J. Seigworth.
p. cm.
Includes bibliographical references and index.
ISBN 978-0-8223-4758-3 (cloth : alk. paper)
ISBN 978-0-8223-4776-7 (pbk. : alk. paper)
1. Affect (Psychology)
2. Culture.
I. Gregg, Melissa, 1978–
II. Seigworth, Gregory J., 1961–
BF175.5.A35A344 2010
152.4—dc22
2010022500